Remembered Lives

Remembered Lives

The Work of Ritual, Storytelling, and Growing Older

Barbara Myerhoff

with Deena Metzger, Jay Ruby, and Virginia Tufte

Edited and with an Introduction by Marc Kaminsky

Foreword by Barbara Kirshenblatt-Gimblett

Ann Arbor

THE UNIVERSITY OF MICHIGAN PRESS

1995   1994   1993   1992   4   3   2   1

Library of Congress Cataloging-in-Publication Data

Myerhoff, Barbara G.
    Remembered lives : the work of ritual, storytelling, and growing older /
Barbara Myerhoff ; with Deena Metzger, Jay Ruby, and Virginia Tufte ;
edited and with an introduction by Marc Kaminsky ; foreword by Barbara
Kirshenblatt-Gimblett.
        p.   cm.
    Includes bibliographical references and index.
    ISBN 0-472-10317-2 (alk. paper). — ISBN 0-472-08177-2 (paper :
alk. paper)
    1. Jewish aged—United States—Social conditions. 2. Jewish aged—United
States—Social life and customs. 2. Social work with the aged—California—
Los Angeles. 4. Jewish aged—California—Los Angeles—Biography.
5. Venice (Los Angeles, Calif.) I. Kaminsky, Marc, 1943-   . II. Title.
HQ1064.U5M86   1992
305.26'089'924—dc20   92-12466
                                                                   CIP

for Deena Metzger

Acknowledgments

Grateful acknowledgment is made to the editors of the publications in which the majority of these essays first appeared:

"Aging and the Aged in Other Cultures: An Anthropological Perspective," in *Contemporary Gerontology: Issues and Concepts,* ed. James E. Birren (Los Angeles: University of Southern California Press, 1970), 545–81. This paper was originally prepared for and presented to the Summer Institute, Andrus Gerontology Center, University of Southern California, 1968. The same version was later published in *The Anthropology of Health,* ed. Eleanor E. Bauwens (St. Louis: The C. V. Mosby Co., 1978).

"We Don't Wrap Herring in a Printed Page: Fusion, Fictions, and Continuity in Secular Ritual," in *Secular Ritual: Forms and Meanings,* ed. Sally Falk Moore and Barbara G. Myerhoff (Assen: Royal Van Gorcum Press, 1977), 199–224.

"A Death in Due Time: Conviction, Order, and Continuity in Ritual Drama," unpublished manuscript, Myerhoff Archives, University of Southern California, 1–46. This paper was presented at the annual meeting of the American Anthropological Association, December, 1975. A later version of the essay, in which the conceptual framework was revised, was published under the title, "A Symbol Perfected in Death: Continuity and Ritual in the Life and Death of an Elderly Jew," in *Life's Career: Cross-Cultural Studies in Growing Old,* ed. Barbara G. Myerhoff and Andrei Simic (New York: Sage Publications, 1978). A third version, in which minor modifications were made in the theoretical discussion, appeared as "A Death in Due Time: Construction of Self and Culture in Ritual Drama," in *Rite, Drama, Festival, Spectacle,* ed. T. J. MacAloon (Philadelphia: Institute for the Study of Human Issues, 1984).

"Bobbes and Zeydes: Old and New Roles for Elderly Jews," in *Women in Ritual and Symbolic Roles,* eds. Judith Hoch-Smith and Anita Springs (New York: Plenum, 1978), 207–41.

"Experience at the Threshold: The Interplay of Aging and Ritual," excerpt from an essay entitled "Rites and Signs of Ripening: The Intertwining of Ritual, Time, and Growing Older," in *Age and Anthropological Theory,* eds. David I. Kertzer and Jennie Keith (Ithaca: Cornell University Press, 1984), 305–30.

"Life History among the Elderly: Performance, Visibility, and Re-membering," in *Life Course: Integrative Theories and Exemplary Populations,* ed. Kurt Back (Boulder, Colorado: Westview Press, for the American Association for the Advancement of Science, 1980), 133–53. The essay was republished in *A Crack in the Mirror: Reflexive Perspectives in Anthropology,* ed. Jay Ruby (Philadelphia: University of Pennsylvania Press, 1982).

"Life History as Integration: Personal Myth and Aging," by Barbara G. Myerhoff and Virginia Tufte, unpublished manuscript, Myerhoff Archives, University of Southern California, 1–11. This paper was presented at the 10th International Congress of Gerontology, Jerusalem, June, 1975. A subsequent version of this essay appeared as "Life History as Integration: An Essay on an Experiential Model," in *The Gerontologist* December 1975.

"'Life Not Death in Venice': Its Second Life," in *The Anthropology of Experience,* eds. Victor Turner and Edward M. Bruner (Urbana and Chicago: University of Illinois Press, 1986), 261–87.

"Surviving Stories: Reflections on *Number Our Days,*" in *Between Two Worlds: Ethnographic Essays on American Jewry,* ed. Jack Kugelmass (Ithaca: Cornell University Press, 1988), 265–94. This essay, which Barbara Myerhoff left unfinished at the time of her death, was revised and completed by Marc Kaminsky. Excerpts from the essay were published under the same title in *Tikkun* (vol. 2, no. 5, November/December, 1987), 19–25.

"A Crack in the Mirror: Reflexive Perspectives in Anthropology," by Barbara Myerhoff and Jay Ruby, originally appeared as the "Introduction" to *A Crack in the Mirror: Reflexive Perspectives in Anthropology,* ed. Jay Ruby (Philadelphia: University of Pennsylvania Press, 1982), 1–35.

"The Journal as Activity and Genre," by Barbara Myerhoff and Deena Metzger, in *Semiotica* 30 (1/2, 1980), 97–114. An early version of this paper was presented at the annual meeting of the American Anthropological Association, December, 1977. In a revised form, this version was published as "Dear Diary" in *Chrysalis* 7 (Winter, 1979), 39–49.

Foreword

Barbara Kirshenblatt-Gimblett

Barbara Myerhoff died January 7, 1985, one month before her fiftieth birthday. Her life was taken by cancer, after seven months of battling the disease. Her death ended a brilliant career at its peak. "Give her the fruit of her hands; And let her works praise her at the gates" (Proverbs 31). These words, chosen by Barbara herself for the dedication to *Number Our Days,* are a fitting epigraph for this homage to her.

Victor Turner, who wrote the foreword to *Number Our Days* (1978), said of Barbara that she was thrice-born. Her first life began in Cleveland, Ohio, where she grew up in an American Jewish milieu that was liberal and middle class. In her dissertation research and first book, she did what anthropologists are trained to do—she entered a culture remote from her own, that of the Huichol Indians of northern Mexico. In the last dozen years of her life, she returned to American Jewish culture, this time as a Jewish anthropologist living in Los Angeles. She embraced each of her lives with *leyb un lebn,* with body and soul, identifying deeply with those she studied and interweaving her lives with those of her subjects.

Barbara's training began at the University of California, Los Angeles, where in 1958 she received her bachelor's degree in sociology. Her master's work in human development at the University of Chicago culminated in 1963 in her thesis, "Father-Daughter Incest among Delinquent Adolescent Girls." In 1968 she was awarded the doctorate in anthropology with distinction at the University of California, Los Angeles. Her dissertation was published as *Peyote Hunt: The Sacred Journey of the Huichol Indians* in 1974 and was nominated for a National Book Award the following year.

Through the 1960s in Los Angeles, Barbara worked as a social worker with the elderly and as a research associate on projects dealing with youth problems ranging from juvenile delinquency and gangs to school success. By 1968, the year she finished her dissertation on the Huichol, Barbara was clearly formulating her ideas about the study of aging. The paper she delivered that summer for the Andrus Gerontology Center at the University of Southern California assessed anthropological approaches to the subject. Integrating her academic training and her social work experience, Barbara was laying the foundation for the two major projects on the Jewish elderly of Los Angeles that would occupy her for the rest of her life. The first focused on the Israel Levin Senior Adult Center in Venice and the second on the Jewish neighborhood of Fairfax.

When encouraged during the early 1970s to undertake a major research project on ethnicity and aging, Barbara thought immediately of Chicanos, a logical outgrowth of her previous work in Mexico. After all, anthropologists typically study someone else, not themselves. Only after the communities she approached kept asking her why she was interested in them and not in her own people did she turn to the Jews of Venice, much to her own amazement. She was to recall years later, "I sat on the benches outside the [Israel Levin Senior Adult] Center and thought about how strange it was to be back in the neighborhood where sixteen years before I had lived and for a time had been a social worker with elderly citizens on public relief. . . . I had made no conscious decision to explore my roots or clarify the meanings of my origins." As the Venice project progressed, Barbara kept asking herself, "Was it anthropology or a personal quest?"

In trying to understand why the Venice work had been so compelling to her, Barbara wrote, "However much I would learn from that [my work with the Huichol] was limited by the fact that I would never really be a Huichol Indian. But I would be a little old Jewish lady one day; thus it was essential for me to learn what the condition was like, in all its particulars. . . . I consider myself very fortunate in having had, through this work, an opportunity to anticipate, rehearse, and contemplate my own future. This had given me a temporal integration to my life that seems to me an essential ingredient in the work of maturing." Barbara never lived to be the little old Jewish lady she imagined as her fate, but in her characteristic anthropological fashion, she identified imaginatively with what it would be like, and in this way, we might say that anthropology allowed her to know what destiny would deny her.

In retrospect, it was almost as if Barbara had begun numbering her days with the Venice work. The epigraph to the first chapter of *Number Our Days,* an adaptation from psalms 144 and 90, reads:

Man is like breath,
His days are as a fleeting shadow.

In the morning he flourishes and grows up like grass
In the evening he is cut down and withers.

So teach us to number our days,
That we may get a heart of wisdom.

First she completed the film *Number Our Days,* which won an Academy Award as best documentary short subject in 1976. Then she finished the book, which appeared in 1978 and was selected as one of the ten best social science books by the *New York Times Book Review* a year later. Both the film and the book won other prizes as well.

The Venice experience had whetted Barbara's appetite. When she visited New York, I took her to Jewish neighborhoods in Brooklyn. When I visited Los Angeles, she took me to Venice. We compared notes— Fairfax, Boro Park, Poland, America, her childhood in Cleveland, mine in Toronto. . . . I had met Barbara just as she was finishing the book. She had turned to me as a specialist in Jewish ethnography and asked if I would read the manuscript. I saw immediately that she had produced a landmark volume in the anthropological study of American Jewish life.

It was even more astonishing to witness the process by which she had used the tools of her chosen discipline to transmit to herself (as well as to her readers) cultural knowledge that had passed her by in the course of growing up. Indeed, the very inventiveness that she attributed to her research subjects was equally true of herself. Despite the metaphors of inevitability conjured up when Barbara identified the elderly Jews of Venice with her "roots" and "origins," she had chosen—not inherited— them. She had made them her fictive kin and adopted their old age as a model for the old age she would never have. Barbara did not dig up her roots or unearth her origins so much as use her ethnographic tool kit to "invent" her culture of choice under the tutelage of masters, though her European-born grandmother had prepared her to discover richness in a world close at hand. Barbara recalled, as a very young child, moving into her grandmother's house after her father left the family. During the winter, when the kitchen window steamed up, her grandmother placed a penny against the glass, creating a peephole, and talked to her about the world they could see through the tiny opening.

American anthropologists have been slow to study Jewish culture in a sustained fashion. The reasons are worthy of study in their own right. They have also been reluctant, with some exceptions, to study American culture until relatively recently—since World War II. For these topics to command serious attention, they need to be engaged with theoretical imagination and discursive experimentation. Writing anthropologically about cultures at hand dramatizes the artifice of scholarly distance and challenges the ethnographer to make the ordinary interesting—what's more, those about whom one writes are likely to read what one publishes, particularly in the case of American Jews. Barbara met the challenge brilliantly.

Victor Turner, a close friend and collaborator, wrote in the foreword of *Number Our Days,* "Although this book celebrates the elderly and an ancient tradition, it is also in the vanguard of anthropological theory. With it anthropology has come of age: its extremes have touched. Barriers between self and other, head and heart, conscious and unconscious, history and autobiography, have been thrown down, and new ways have been found to express the vital interdependence of these and other mighty opposites." This is the hallmark of Barbara's work—it was in her intensely human and compassionate grasp of the lives of those around her that she most fully took hold of her own life. It was in this embrace that she also did her richest anthropological thinking and most eloquent writing.

As a student of ritual, Barbara understood the theatricality of culture at its most extravagant. But she was also attuned to the performative in everyday life, so much so that, in addition to writing about her subjects, she presented them in festivals and exhibitions, on film and in the theater—*Number Our Days* became a play at the Mark Taper Forum in Los Angeles. Barbara collaborated with artists, poets, and filmmakers —among them Deena Metzger, Naomi Newman, Lynne Littman—not only in the production of films and theater, but also in her teaching, where she was as experimental with her students as with her readers. Richard Schechner, founder and director of the Performance Group, brought Barbara to New York University in 1979, where she participated in his seminar "Performance and Anthropology." Together with Victor Turner, they forged a pioneering nexus between these two areas. Working on the principle that performing was a way of knowing, Barbara returned to NYU's Department of Performance Studies several years later to teach a memorable workshop with Arthur Strimling in which students gathered life histories and performed them. Marc Kaminsky, who has so ably prepared this volume, brought her to the Hunter/Brookdale Center on Aging to offer ritual and storytelling workshops with Strimling. Her workshops in New York City became legendary.

The Venice work completed, Barbara cast about for the next project. During her speech at the dedication of the new Freda Mohr building in Fairfax, Los Angeles, on December 12, 1982, she said,

> When I finished the Venice study, which became the movie, book, and play known as *Number Our Days,* I was worried about what I would do next. How would I find a project to match that one: it would have to have meaning to the people I was studying, they would have to participate and benefit from it in direct ways. I wanted it to be among Jews, nearby not far away; I wanted it to include the elderly, though not be confined to them. And I had to be a part of the people, so that I could produce a study that was not merely a scientific report but something with my own emotions as well as mind at work, something that would involve my own identity, and the Jewish identity of those I would work with.

The result was the last project she would undertake, a study of the neighborhood of Fairfax, a once thriving Jewish community that had declined and was making a strong comeback, as Soviet Jews and Lubavitcher Hasidim moved into the area. Barbara was to become part of the people she was studying in ways she could never have anticipated; two years into the project, she found herself battling the disease that was to take her life. The Lubavitcher Hasidim living in Fairfax embraced the challenge of trying to save Barbara's life through her interest in their faith.

In a manner that was so essentially her own, Barbara's anthropological research was simultaneously a battle for life itself. She let the Lubavitcher community rally around her. They had her visit the *mikve* (ritual bath), where in a state of purity she could make a wish. They changed her name so the angel of death would not be able to find her. They made her undergo a *get,* a Jewish divorce, to detach her soul from her former husband and return it to her. They helped her write a letter to the *rebe* for a miracle cure.

Facing the failures of medical science and the insatiable desire for knowledge of the people she was studying, Barbara came to know her subjects as they tried to save her. All these events Barbara recorded on film, perhaps the most reflexive medium of all, particularly in her hands. Barbara had tried repeatedly and without success to get Lynne Littman to make this film—Barbara had originally intended the film to deal with the diverse Jewish community of Fairfax (Lubavitcher Hasidism, Russians, and gays), but yielding to Lubavitcher protests about the mixture of subjects, she shifted the focus to them. After Barbara became sick, she prevailed on Lynne again. This time Lynne agreed, but only on condition that Barbara, and her relationship to the Hasidim, become the subject of the film.

There is a marvelous scene in the Fairfax film, *In Her Own Time,* where Barbara is fitted out with a *sheytl,* a wig, by a Hasidic woman. Barbara was worried that she would lose her hair during chemotherapy, a fear that proved unfounded. What she lost were her "Jewish curls," as she put it. As each wig is tried on, Barbara chats intimately with the saleswoman about what it is like to be an Orthodox Jewish woman, about the relations between men and women, about eroticism. As they tried to help her, the Jews of Fairfax became even more open to her profound desire to understand them from both a personal and an anthropological perspective, for Barbara tried and succeeded in integrating the two, nowhere more poignantly than in her last work.

Barbara's work inspired others because she addressed profoundly human questions—questions of survival, dignity, meaning, faith, aging, dying. She was bold and experimental. Her generosity and enthusiasm were boundless, her energy a beacon. In her short life, cut off in the morning of her mature years, she produced books and articles ranging over a stunning array of subjects—the family, juvenile delinquency, religion, shamanism, ritual, symbol and politics, ideology, women's values, life history, gender and ethnicity, and aging. She touched the lives of everyone who knew her, those she studied and those she taught.

A student of whom she was specially proud, Riv-Ellen Prell, remembered Barbara most appropriately with the words of Maimonides: "When one's teacher dies, the student rends his/her garments until the heart is exposed—and the tear may never be stitched again."

Author's Acknowledgments

Some of the research on which "We Don't Wrap Herring in a Printed Page" is based took place between 1972 and 1973. It was funded by a National Science Foundation Grant G1-34953X administered through the Andrus Gerontology Center of the University of Southern California, Social and Cultural Contexts of Aging Project, Los Angeles, California. All proper names of individuals and organizations are fictitious.

The fieldwork on which "A Death in Due Time" is based was funded by the National Science Foundation RANN Grant APR-75-21178 and the 1907 Foundation of the United Parcel Service, administered through the Ethnicity and Aging Project at the Andrus Gerontology Center of the University of Southern California. All names in the paper have been changed. Unfortunately, this makes it impossible to publicly acknowledge my gratitude to many of the people whose assistance made this paper possible. In particular, the family of the deceased, the Center director and president, the social worker, and the rabbi, all of whom were interviewed, were exceedingly helpful.

Much of the theoretical approach to ritual presented and applied here was elaborated with Professor Sally F. Moore over discussions lasting several years and culminating in a Wenner-Gren Conference on Secular Ritual (Burg Wartenstein, 1974). I find it no longer possible to say what is her part and what is mine. These ideas now appear as the "Introduction" in *Secular Ritual: Forms and Meanings,* Royal Van Gorcum Press, 1977.

The research on which "Bobbes and Zeydes" is based took place between 1972 and 1975. Information reported here is drawn in part from the Social and Cultural Contexts of Aging Project (V. L. Bengston, principal investigator; Barbara Myerhoff, project director) at the Andrus Gerontology Center of the University of Southern California. This program was supported by grants from the National Science Foundation (NSF)'s RANN program (APR-75-21178) and by the 1907 Foundation of the United Parcel Service. Conclusions are those of the author and do not necessarily reflect the views of NSF or the 1907 Foundation. All proper names of individuals and organizations are fictitious.

Part of the funding for the research on which "Life History among the Elderly" is based was provided by the National Science Foundation, through the Andrus

Gerontology Center of the University of Southern California, in connection with a study of "Ethnicity and Aging." All names of individuals and organizations have been changed.

Special thanks are due to Victor and Edith Turner, Richard Schechner, and Alexander Alland, whose seminar on "Performance and Anthropology" at the Graduate Department of Drama, School of the Arts, New York University in June, 1979, provided information and inspiration for many of the ideas discussed here. The 1977 Wenner-Gren Foundation conference convened by the author and Barbara Babcock on "Cultural Frames and Reflections: Ritual, Drama and Spectacle" was a critical event in developing some of my interpretations of reflexivity. Gelya Frank provided stimulation and generously shared references and ideas. Naturally, only I am responsible for the views given here.

The research on which "Life History as Integration" was based was funded by Grant G1-34953X under the Exploratory Research and Problem Assessment component of the National Science Foundation's Research Applied to National Needs Program.

Grateful acknowledgment is made to Morris Rosen, director of the Israel Levin Senior Adult Center, Venice, California, in which Life History classes for senior citizens were conducted (February to June, 1973), and to Elizabeth Thompson who assisted in running many of the classes.

The research on which the paper "'Life Not Death in Venice'" is based was part of a larger study entitled "Social Contexts of Aging," funded by the National Science Foundation and administered through the Andrus Gerontology Center of the University of Southern California. I would like to acknowledge the people who made the cultural festival entitled "Life Not Death in Venice" possible and to thank them for their generosity in helping to produce the festival and for assisting me in gathering the written and visual materials I needed to do this preliminary analysis. At the University of Southern California, Center for Visual Anthropology: Alexander Moore and Denise Lawrence; College of Continuing Education: Barbara Perrow; Department of Anthropology: Sherrie Wagner and Vikram Jayanti. Partial funding for portions of the festival was provided by the Ford Foundation and the California Council for the Humanities.

In "Surviving Stories," the exhibition titled "Life Not Death in Venice" was produced and coordinated by Vikram Jayanti in conjunction with the Center for Visual Anthropology, Department of Anthropology, University of Southern California, and by Alexander Moore and Timothy Asch, department chair and Center director, respectively.

I am particularly grateful to Marc Kaminsky for his leadership in exploring the area of survivor stories. The conference he convened on survivors' narratives at the Brookdale Center on Aging of Hunter College in 1983 was the occasion for my examining this genre more closely.

"A Crack in the Mirror" grew in part out of a day-long symposium organized by the author and Jay Ruby for the American Anthropological Association meetings in 1978 entitled "Portrayal of Self, Profession, and Culture: Reflexive Perspectives in Anthropology." The symposium consisted of the following participants and papers:

Stephen Lansing (University of Southern California), "An Island in the Liminal Zone"; Paul Rabinow (University of California, Berkeley), "Observer and Observed: New Forms of Anthropological Presentation"; Dennis Tedlock (University of Massachusetts), "Between Text and Interpretation: Toward a Dialogical Anthropology"; John Szwed (University of Pennsylvania), "Ethnography—A Meditation"; Denise O'Brien (Temple University), "Images of Women in the South Seas"; Carol Ann Parssinen (Institute for the Study of Human Issues), "Social Explorers and Social Scientists: The Dark Continent of Victorian Ethnography"; Barbara Babcock (University of Arizona), "The Dangers of 'Delight-making' and the Difficulty of Describing It"; Victor Turner (University of Virginia), "Performative and Reflexive Anthropology"; Jay Ruby (Temple University), "Ethnography as Trompe L'Oeil: Film and Anthropology"; Ira Abrams (University of Southern California), "A Reflexive View of Anthropology Through Its Film"; Richard Chalfen (Temple University), "Ethnofilm and Docudrama: Constructing and Interpreting Ambiguous Realities"; Eric Michaels (University of Texas), "Looking at Us Looking at the Yanomami Looking at Us"; Dan Rose (University of Pennsylvania), discussant.

—Barbara Myerhoff

Editor's Acknowledgments

I am thankful to Barbara Myerhoff for the gift of her colleagueship and friendship and am grateful to her for having asked me to edit her papers.

The Myerhoff Center at the YIVO Institute for Jewish Research offered the conditions of possibility and provided the support that enabled me to carry out this work.

To Deena Metzger, Barbara Myerhoff's lifelong friend, her literary executor, and codirector of the Myerhoff Center, I offer my thanks and gratitude. Her collaborative presence was indispensable in carrying through this task.

To Dr. Maury Leibovitz, President of the Myerhoff Center, I offer my thankfulness and gratitude. His commitment to Barbara Myerhoff's legacy and life-history work among the elderly as well as his generosity have been the foundation upon which the Center has been organized.

I extend my thanks and gratitude to Polly Howells who, as friend, colleague and co-chair of the Center's Committee on Research and Publication, has been crucial in sustaining the Center's work.

Diane Demeter has played an important role in the Center as a friend, board member, and co-chair of the Committee on Research and Publication. To her and to Steven Demeter I offer my thanks and gratitude.

I am grateful to Naomi Newman and Micah Taubman, who initiated the formation of the Center soon after Barbara Myerhoff's death; and to Harriet Rzetelny, Director of the Training and Workshop Program. Arthur Strimling directed the Living History Program between 1988 and 1990.

I acknowledge with thanks the contribution that Jerry Mark, Penninah Schram, and Steven Zeitlin have made to the Center through their dedicated colleagueship.

Bill McClellan and Tom Cole have been the friends with whom I have engaged in the long dialogue on cultural studies and gerontology that has constituted the good working conditions in which this project was completed. Their reading and criticism of the introductory essay through several revisions helped improve the text.

Two colleagues worked closely with me on editing Myerhoff's papers. Jack Kugelmass, then Associate Dean of the Max Weinreich Center at YIVO, was an invaluable anthropologist-informant, who answered my questions on textual problems related to the ethnography of the culture of Yiddishkeit. Audrey Levine, Research Associate at the Myerhoff Center, made an important contribution to the editing process not only by her dedication, through long hours of work, but also by her meticulous scrutiny of the essays. She was responsible for compiling the front matter and the bibliography.

The introduction was read and criticized by Sol Yurick and Stanley Aronowitz, whose comments were important to me in articulating my critique of Myerhoff's work. This text was produced betwixt and between and in dialogue with and across two different collegial communities: those of cultural studies and humanistic gerontology. I thank the members of the *Social Text* editorial board, particularly Sohnya Sayres, Bruce Robbins, and George Yudice, for their critical reading of the first section of the introduction. The gerontologists whose comments have informed my work on this book project include Andrew Achenbaum, George Getzel, and Robert Kastenbaum.

The YIVO Institute for Jewish Research, which provided an institutional home for the Myerhoff Center, has my thanks. The interventions of Barbara Kirshenblatt-Gimblett, Samuel Norich, and Adrienne Cooper, respectively Senior Researcher, Executive Director, and then Assistant Director, are deeply appreciated. The library, archival, and research staff deserve the high regard in which they are held by scholars: I acknowledge with gratitude the very great helpfulness and expertise of Jeffrey Shandler, Zachary Baker, Dina Abramowicz, and Marek Web.

I am grateful to the foundations that supported the Center's Research and Publication Program: the Emet Foundation, the Morris P. Leibovitz Foundation, the Lucius N. Littauer Foundation, the Morris J. and Betty Kaplun Foundation, the Pauline Yuells Markel Charitable Trust, and the Tides Foundation.

Pamela Ween Brumberg and William Frost, respectively Program Officer and President of the Lucius N. Littauer Foundation, warrant special acknowledgment for their understanding that scholarly labors often take longer than expected to see into print, and for their personal as well as financial support.

The support of Lawrence Newman, board member and Yiddish scholar, has likewise been personal as well as material, and is very much appreciated. Gratitude, too, to Leonard Fassler, whose gift helped establish the Research and Publication Program.

To Allen Bergson, Alice Fennessey, Harriet Rzetelny, Mark Weiss, Eric Werthman, and Carolyn Zablotny, I offer my thanks and gratitude for their involvement in the dailiness of my work at the Center.

Finally, and most immediately, the living through of this necessarily slow process was grounded in a house saturated with the *mentshlichkeit* of my wife and the ordinary miracle of my daughter's and son's discovery of language and life: for a daily life in contact with these transmitted and transmitting qualities, of which Myerhoff wrote in praise, I thank Maddy, Julia, and Daniel.

*   *   *

Editorial interventions were kept to a minimum. Obvious errors were corrected. Punctuation and mechanics were made consistent. The transliteration of Yiddish words was conventionalized, in accord with the YIVO system. The separate essays of a scholar necessarily contain many repeated elements, such as the presentation of the ethnographic background of the subjects or the conceptual framework to be implemented or "touchstone" quotations of authorities and informants. The question, in editing a volume of collected papers, is not whether to omit redundant passages, but from which text to cut which particular repetition. These infinitesimally small textual decisions were made on a case-by-case basis. The guiding principle was that, in determining the fate of a paragraph, a sentence, a phrase, or a word, mere "overuse" was not decisive; the separate essay had to be able to withstand the cut without palpable loss. In difficult instances, the decision was made to err on the side of excess.

—Marc Kaminsky

Contents

Introduction

Marc Kaminsky

> In all these texts we see a group of people creating themselves.
> —Barbara Myerhoff, "'Life Not Death in Venice': Its Second Life"

Toward the Third Voice

> ... an "ethno person," the third person who is born by virtue of the
> collusion between interlocutor and subject.
> —Barbara Myerhoff, "Surviving Stories: Reflections on *Number Our Days*"

> A life made up entirely from the imagination.
> —Shmuel, speaking of shtetl life, in *Number Our Days*

Remembered Lives: The Work of Ritual, Storytelling, and Growing Older
is a collection of the most important ethnographic essays that Barbara
Myerhoff wrote during the second phase of her career, between 1968
and her death in 1985, when she situated her work in the field of aging.
This volume seeks to make her essays readily available to the varied
audiences that she addressed. It also seeks to recuperate her contribution
from the stigma which it encountered due to her very success in reaching
a broad readership and, particularly, due to her mastery of popular
genres. Myerhoff's documentary film, *Number Our Days*, won an Academy Award in 1978. Her narrative ethnography of the same name was
enthusiastically received by a diverse general audience; it was accorded
canonical status across a range of disciplines (including gerontology,
Jewish studies, and folklore), and viewed by some of her colleagues as
a classic of urban anthropology and a pioneering model of "writing
culture." Nevertheless, the acclaim that her work received "abroad"
brought it under suspicion within her home discipline of anthropology,
where it was at once highly regarded and devalued. Insofar as Myerhoff's
reputation was depreciated by the impression that she was an anthropological popularizer, she was professionally framed by her fame.

The reasons that her work was underestimated by some anthropologists, even as it was revered by others, are complex, and have more to do with its strongly innovative character than its actual limitations. George Marcus, an anthropologist whose research interests in textuality and ideology overlap with Myerhoff's, has cogently accounted for the way she was seen by her colleagues in a statement that does honor to Myerhoff and to the range of problematic issues she posed and that offers us a glimpse of the "backstage" shoptalk in which professional reputations are negotiated. In a letter (1990) concerning the papers collected in this volume, Marcus writes:

> The essays [that she produced during] the second and most important part of her career . . . combined her interest in aged and aging in American society with a pioneering effort to change the manner of anthropological writing and, with it, the manner of anthropological research. Because her work communicated so effectively to a wide public, because she was a key figure in reviving during the 1970s a thoroughly humanistic anthropology, and because this phase of her work dealt with critical issues in American society rather than in some exotic context, she tended not to be taken as seriously as she should have been by many anthropologists. She was respected and appreciated, but her work might have been regarded as "light weight" or "media-oriented"—a Margaret Mead figure.

The task of this introduction is to "dispel this reaction" (Marcus' phrase) by demonstrating that Myerhoff's work, far from being "lightweight," warrants serious and searching attention. This long essay seeks to offer an appraisal and critique of Myerhoff's ethnographic papers in an effort to provide a description and evaluation of her contribution that is adequate to its actual significance and difficulty, which some readers have tended to overlook, mistaking the admirable accessibility of her writing as a sign of a lack of scholarly substance and depth. By engaging her ethnographic essays with the cultural theory of such major figures as Mikhail Bakhtin and Raymond Williams, it becomes possible to investigate the profound problems that Myerhoff poses in these texts, and to recuperate her work to the theoretical trends in anthropology and cultural studies that have informed scholarly research and debate over the past decade.

The analysis and evaluation offered in these pages is necessarily difficult and complex. I argue here that Myerhoff's important and enduring contribution is constituted by her case studies of the cultural creativity of a subordinated group. This is, in my view, a magnificent, substantial *oeuvre*. Nonetheless, close study of these texts also discloses their limitations, particularly their occlusion of the cultural history of the "elders" whom Myerhoff studied. The culture of these Yiddish-speaking immigrants was saturated, early and late, by the unionism and socialism that not only formed the mass movements of their youth, but also them—their worldview and the range of creative practices that Myerhoff describes and celebrates in terms of a Yiddishkeit bleached of its cultural politics. Myerhoff's writing is profoundly shaped by the conflict between her own (liberal, middle-class, social-scientific) view of the "elders" and their social world, and their different ("progressive," working-class, solidary, or partisan) view of themselves, their community, and the dominant society. This is at once an underlying conflict that pervades Myerhoff's writing and a "reflexively" formulated issue that partly constitutes Myerhoff's object of study. She is fascinated by the fights that the members of the Israel Levin Center wage with each other and, more importantly for her project, with the "outside" society, of which she is conscious of herself as a privileged member and representative (1980:25–28). She documents and affirms the strategies they use to assert their worth, gain attention, and contest their neglect and devaluation by a society that segregates and disdains them. Her case studies of secular ritual and other cultural performances describe these "collective acts of imagination" as the comeback of a subaltern group. In her strong work, then, Myerhoff explicitly takes ideological conflict as a dimension of the method and object of study that cannot be left out of the account. Her analyses of the Center members' rituals, personal narratives, and other cultural productions offer access to the social conflicts and ideological breaks that they symbolize, and her texts on "reflexivity" describe ethnographic research and writing as a problematic process in which the meaning-making practices of people of different cultures enter into contact and are used to produce social knowledge. The question of the social relationship between the "native" and the "anthropologist" has, since Myerhoff wrote, moved to the center of scholarly debate. And the important studies of ethnographic texts that have applied the discourse theories of Bakhtin, Foucault, Williams, Lyotard and other now-canonical thinkers have made the limitations and contradictions of Myerhoff's work visible:

these are produced by discursive strategies that evade or veil ideological conflicts that are intrinsic to the (participant-observer) method as well as the object of cultural study, both of which involve a dialogue with difference.

It has become necessary to begin the description and evaluation of Myerhoff's ethnographic essays "against" (the background of) *Number Our Days,* in whose long shadow they have appeared diminished, both to those who regard her famous book as mere popularization and to those who view it as a canonical work. For many of the latter, Myerhoff's papers on "the culture of aging and Yiddishkeit" were superseded by *Number Our Days,* which was widely adopted as a standard text in courses on aging and ethnicity, and praised for having worked through a genre of narrative ethnography that has been influential among ethnographic writers.[1] The essays, nonetheless, remain indispensable for three reasons.

---

1. No one is in a better position to speak of Myerhoff's influence on text production in anthropology than Jack Kugelmass, whose *Miracle of Intervale Avenue* was inspired by and modeled on *Number Our Days.* In a discussion of Myerhoff's impact on younger colleagues beginning in the late 1970s, Kugelmass says:

> The issue of self-reflexivity was emerging as a central issue in the field of anthropology. For most anthropologists, the problem centers [on] the obvious disparity between the scholar's own culture and that of the people whom he is investigating—usually non-western, non-industrial societies. For those of us studying Jews, most of whom are Jews as well, the relationship might seem less problematic—it seems as though we are simply studying ourselves—but it is, if anything, more complex. . . . Myerhoff pioneered this kind of ethnographic writing—not in the language of the scholarly elite, but in an accessible, personal narrative, as interesting as it is informative. . . . It rejects the notion that anthropology is a "hard" science, capable of finding objective, quantifiable, absolute truths. Instead anthropological studies are seen as individual, creative encounters with another cultural sensibility. (1989:10–11)

Kugelmass makes the essential point concerning the reception of Myerhoff's work within her own field: *Number Our Days,* taken in tandem with the critique of empiricism waged by the essays in the name of reflexivity, have helped clear a discursive space for "personal narrative." This is a major motif of the textualist movement; it is well analyzed by Mary Louise Pratt in "Fieldwork in Common Places" (1986). And it is an aspect of Myerhoff's work that has been, from the first, highly regarded and well understood. But "personal narrative/reflexivity" describes only those innovations that Myerhoff herself emphasized, and not the

First, there are profound differences in detail, orientation, and interpretation between the essayistic case studies and the chapters that Myerhoff subsequently worked up in writing *Number Our Days*. The chapters and the essays adhere to different literary conventions, belong to different genres. In the differences between genres, we can observe the text-in-the-making.

Second, the "novelistic" practice of *Number Our Days* problematized ethnographic writing for Myerhoff, and she turned to the essay to work on this issue. The essays that she produces after writing *Number Our Days* are saturated with this problematic, which she explores under the sign of reflexivity.

Finally, the essays interrelate a theoretical description and a narrative description of particular creative events: these texts are oriented toward demonstrating a way of thinking about social life. The chapters of *Number Our Days* that ostensibly present the same events emphasize the narrative, displaying wise, memorable, feisty characters, rather than the social thought that gave the representation its depth and complexity. The essays teach us how to gain analytic access to the symbol systems that others create; the chapters communicate how it feels to live in a world constructed and mediated by a particular set of symbols, with all the collective history and stored ways of being and thinking that these carry.

The notion of "the third voice" emerges, in retrospect, as one of the major formulations of Myerhoff's final years. Yet it appears nowhere in her published writings. And, to my knowledge, it was offered only once, and fleetingly, on a public occasion: at a panel discussion in 1983 on "Storytelling: Cultural Transmission and Symbolic Immortality."[2] There can be little doubt as to its importance to her: it was formulated as the answer to a burning question.

---

more profound and difficult discursive practices that she half-acknowledged, half-concealed under this formula. The major break with convention came with the introduction of novelistic (double-voiced) discourse in ethnographic texts that did not abandon their claim to documentary status and scientific authority. The present discussion is an attempt to demonstrate and explain what, in her writing, is finessed by textual subterfuges of great artistry. The use of novelistic discourse, in part, accounts for the esteem in which her work is held.

2. This panel discussion, which I organized in collaboration with Myerhoff, also included a presentation by Harry R. Moody and was held at the annual meeting of the Gerontological Society of America.

The question is: How does the ethnographer edit the informant's utterances? This is, finally, not one question, but several interrelated questions. And it is not, finally, a technical (and therefore limited) question, to be construed solely in terms of the textual relations between anthropologist and subject. It became, for Myerhoff, a burning question because the social relations between anthropologist and subject were linked to the kind of power the anthropologist assumed over the informant's word.

In *Number Our Days,* Myerhoff as author, as sole owner and proprietor of the ethnographic text she produces, answers this question as follows:

> As often as possible, I have included verbatim materials, heavily edited and selected, inevitably, but sufficient to allow the reader some direct participation. I have tried to allow many individuals to emerge in their fullness and distinctiveness rather than presenting a completely generalized picture of group life. . . . The format of this book is designed to meet several purposes. In addition to wanting to speak within it as a participant, and wishing to preserve particular individuals, I wanted to render the elders' speech. Many verbatim statements are included. (1980:30–31)

This is fascinating: the pull between monologic and dialogic principles is intense.[3] The result is a compromise: the informant's utterance, reduced to the status of raw empirical materials, is "heavily edited and selected, inevitably." The author as social scientist assumes a stance of authority which she does not feel compelled to articulate: she speaks in the name

---

3. In Bakhtin, dialogic discourse is a complex category, which describes the communicative process through which meanings are cocreated in social life and in art. His discourse theory offers a descriptive inventory of specific types of dialogic discourse, that is, discourse in which two semantic intentions come into contact. In the glossary of *The Dialogic Imagination,* Holquist offers the following explanation under the keyword "dialogue": In Bakhtin's theory, "a word, discourse, language or culture undergoes 'dialogization' when it becomes relativized, de-privileged, aware of competing definitions for the same things. Undialogized language is authorative or absolute" (Bakhtin 1981:427). Monologic discourse is undialogized language: it has a single, dominant semantic intention. Examples include official, pedagogic, or scholarly discourse. See also McClellan's discussion of monologic and dialogic discourse, which is quoted later in this essay.

of scientific knowledge which deploys the raw materials in the direction of elucidating a concept, and in the name of writerly craft, which eliminates surplus verbiage for the sake of textual efficiency. These values are implicit in the gesture of the adverb, "inevitably."

But there is a deeply felt dialogism at work, counteracting the pull of anthropological authority. Here, the verbatimness of the "elders' speech," no longer construed as raw material, is highly valued, and two different reasons are offered for this valuation. First, it is assumed that the fullness and distinctiveness of the individual can emerge only through his or her word, directly engaged. Second, it is assumed that only through dialogic relations can all parties concerned—writer, reader, and informant—participate in the text. Insofar as the writer is concerned with promoting this participatory interaction, she is interested in a dialogized text.

But the initial answer offered by *Number Our Days* not only finesses the problems with which Myerhoff had begun to struggle, it also mystifies the writing practice she developed in this book. The burden she was left with, then, was to develop a concept of ethnography–as–text that simultaneously described and legitimated her actual practice.

The notion of the third voice is an attempt to do just that. At the panel discussion on storytelling, she read the transcripts of a number of stories that she had collected from survivors, refuseniks, Hasidim, and others in the Fairfax neighborhood of Los Angeles, wondered aloud about what one is to do with all that material, and then commented that the "tales from Fairfax are to be written in the third voice, which is neither the voice of the informant nor the voice of the interviewer, but the voice of their collaboration."

This was a profound and momentous suggestion: it construes "writing culture" as Bakhtinian dialogic discourse. She did not know Bakhtin, and came to this formulation by other routes. This notion, offered as a writerly and critical working principle, was hardly worked through, yet it offers a glimpse of the direction that Myerhoff's writing probably would have taken, given her growing fascination with issues related to text production in ethnography.

In this notion, the immediate technical question (of editing an informant's utterance) is subsumed under a concept through which Myerhoff theorizes the interrelation between the text and a social process: the ongoing structured and informal dialogue between ethnographer and subject. This is, then, a genuinely complex notion. In discussing its significance, I want to take up the following points: the use of the third voice as a principle of editing texts, the link between text production and the informant interview, the specific form that the third voice takes in Myerhoff's writing, and the problem of the interrelation between textual and social relations in the transmission of culture.

The notion of the third voice proposes a dialogic principle for editing the utterance of informants. It authorizes a departure from the verbatim transcript, but it balances this license against a principle of constraint. The ethnographer's editorial intervention must adhere to the process of the interview: it must textualize communicative elements such as intonation and gesture that are as much a part of the utterance as the spoken word. And it can incorporate into the text additions, revisions, restructurings, and clarifications that adhere to and articulate the process and meaning of the informant's utterance. These criteria are intrinsic to Myerhoff's notion of the third voice.

Thus, it is possible for an ethnographic text to tell a theoretically sophisticated tale in the voice of a "naive" or native storyteller. A text of this type—and *Number Our Days* abounds in this hidden genre— dialogizes what the ethnographer knows and what the informant said. Here, however, the project of dialogic relations remains incomplete. A text fully constituted by dialogic discourse would give the informant evaluative access to what the ethnographer said. Only in Myerhoff's dialogues with Shmuel does this mutual refraction of the other's word occur; hence, the astonishing richness and power of these passages, which nonetheless do not accomplish a break with monological discourse: they serve as thesis-advancing argumentation.

The strength of the notion of the third voice is that it views the informant's information as utterance, not as inert data that is insensible to the categorical blade of the ethnographer's knowledge. That is, the "data" are generated in and through a lived process of face–to–face dialogue. This fact is finally what the notion of the third voice appeals to, by way of legitimating Myerhoff's "editorial" practices.

Framing the issue in terms of "editing" seeks to contain and minimize what is at stake here. Ethnographic text production, and not an element of it, is at issue. Myerhoff grounds the legitimacy of her writerly practice in the process of ethnographic research: in the dialogic character of the participant–observation method. Myerhoff profoundly grasped that the informant's utterances were constructed by the interview situation.

In Bakhtin, this realization is construed as the cocreation of the utterance by the speaker and the listener, and it is analyzed in terms of the principle that speech is oriented toward the listener. In Myerhoff's essayistic reflections on this question, the coproduction of the ethnographic dialogue is viewed differently. She interpreted it under a formalist, bipolar opposition between "the natural" and "the artificial." Commenting on the "permanent ethno-dialogue" that ethnographer-filmmaker Jean Rouche calls "shared anthropology," Myerhoff and Jay Ruby write ("A Crack in the Mirror," in this volume):

> Rouche does not go to the extreme of calling his native subject an ethno-person, but it would not be unreasonable to do so. The anthropologist and the subject of study together construct an interpretation of a cultural feature, an understanding of the interpreter, that would not have come into existence naturally. The study is an artifice and resembles nothing but itself, a collusion of two viewpoints meeting in a middle terrain, created by the artificial circumstances of the foreigner's visit and project.

This is a rhetorical attempt to transvalue "the artificial," by conflating it with scientific research and making it a category of "the experimental": set-apart conditions created in pursuit of scientific truth. Repudiated empiricism has lapsed back into the argument, subliminally, as a source of value. This critique, in fact, has never finally broken with empiricism. The real confusion is between the "laboratory conditions" set up by the pursuit of knowledge in the natural sciences, and the social conditions which are the "laboratory" of research in the human sciences "Artifice," in this passage, covers the different and contradictory senses of "the *experimental*" (as the method of the natural sciences) and "the *social*" in a single term. This can be readily demonstrated by replacing this mystifying abstraction with the senses it covers: "The study is an [*experiment*] and resembles nothing but itself, . . . created by the [*social*] circumstances of the foreigner's visit and project."

This passage is significantly reworked in Myerhoff's last essay, which was drafted contemporaneously with her panel presentation on the third voice. Here the conventional dichotomy of "the artificial" and "the natural"—a rhetorical move that views science under an aesthetic category—continues to organize the thought, but here this motif is developed and amplified differently. Referring to the heightened reflexive consciousness that ethnographic films can produce in their subjects, Myerhoff writes "the same process can be observed in interviewing" ("Surviving Stories," in this volume):

> When one takes a very long, careful life history of another person, complex exchanges occur between subject and object. Inventions and distortions emerge; neither party remains the same. A new creation is constituted when two points of view are engaged in examining one life. The new creation has its own integrity but should not be mistaken for the spontaneous, unframed life–as–lived person who existed before the interview began. This could be called an "ethno-person," the third person who is born by virtue of the collusion between the interlocutor and subject.

Here, "life" is construed as "the natural," not as a process that is socially constructed. This is then set off against the "inventions and distortions" that are implicitly legitimated as a concomitant of research in the interpretive human sciences. What is significant here is the emphasis on "a new creation" that has "its own integrity."

The argument, while resonating with artistic and psychological overtones—i.e., both parties are changed in unspecified ways—has moved decidedly to moral grounds. But Myerhoff confesses the duress under which she writes in an astounding moral oxymoron: "by virtue of collusion." Collusion is the telltale word in both statements and gives away Myerhoff's conflicted position between the norms of empiricism and the "new creation" she has produced and seeks to theorize.[4] In this word, a collaborative relation is charged with secret purpose, secret knowledge, and secret guilt. Collusion is a "secret agreement for fraudulent or treacherous purposes; a conspiracy"; collusive practices are "fraudulently contrived" (*Random House College Dictionary*). Myerhoff did not use the word without an awareness of its moral intonation; she was playing off the morally suspect character of the contrivance against the "virtue" and "integrity" of "the new creation." The brilliance of this passage lies in

---

4. It has not been possible for me to establish whether the word "collusion" originated with Myerhoff or with Ruby, but this incertitude as to origin does not invalidate my argument. The fact of co-authorship indicates that Myerhoff authorized the use of this term as hers, that it carried her semantic intention. Further, her subsequent, fully deliberate and highly playful use of it in "Surviving Stories" takes full responsibility for its paradoxical burden. Whether she originated the word or not, she claims it and uses it for her own purposes.

its double-voicedness: it sets two evaluations of the "new creation" side by side and does not blend them, but allows them antagonistically to confront each other. And yet this brilliance is used, finally, as a way of finessing the great problem of textuality that she was living and working through. What we get, rather than a direct engagement with the issues that were vexing not only her but had already emerged as a major debate in the human sciences, is an indirect confession.

Myerhoff's confession, her own "collusive" knowledge, was subsumed under the critique of empiricism. The indicting gesture made by these texts brings the ethnographic dialogue, construed as an instrument of empiricist research, under suspicion. But Myerhoff, characteristically, described and lived through the dialogue between anthropologist and informant in two distinct ways: under two different tropes or symbol systems. As an interview between social scientist and informant, it had an "artificial" character, separated from "natural" dialogues. But this face-to-face encounter between herself and an old person was also what might be called "a storytelling relationship." This term evokes a very different sort of meeting. It exceeds the boundaries and roles of social science research. It is represented and lived through with great (moral) intensity as a communication between the figures of the teller and the listener.

This second "face" of "ethno-dialogue," not as research interview but as a social relationship between a listener and a teller, is the aspect of Myerhoff's work that intersects with Bakhtin. The profound emphasis that Myerhoff gives to what, in a talk, she once called "the pathos of the absent listener" is encountered, in Bakhtin, as the suffering brought about by "nonrecognition" and the absence of a "watchful listener" (Bakhtin 1984a:288; Todorov 1984:110–11). In both, the attention of the listener is understood as a social necessity, ultimately continuous with maternal nurturance; it carries the same force as "mirroring" does in contemporary object relations theory: wholeness and self-knowledge are contingent upon it. (See "Life History among the Elderly," in this volume; "'Life Not Death in Venice,'" in this volume.)

The role of the listener was at the center of Myerhoff's practice as an ethnographer. There were moments, as I listened to her speak, when this appeared to me to be the still center of her restless thought—it isn't—by virtue of what she founded upon it: not only scientific knowledge, but "our" entire development, the wholeness and self-knowledge, that she conversationally described as "growing a soul." The listener not only gave the old people abundant supplies of fine attention, for which they were starving, but in the process was changed. Such listening was the gate through which the stranded and rootless anthropologist entered the cycle of generations, so that she could say (as Adrienne Rich triumphantly discovers at the end of a poem on immigrant grandparents), "I, too, live in history."

No concept in Myerhoff's work was more profoundly lived through, as a scientific practice and as an ethical stance, than that of the role of the listener. Here I must cast a glance at her life and mention two things: that Myerhoff had a genius for listening, and that this gift, which grew through her cultivation of it, was inseparable from her "hunger" to listen ("A Crack in the Mirror," in this volume). She experienced listening as something akin to soul-flight: a period of grace, when she was granted the gift of leaving her own life to travel in another's. She claimed for anthropology what Milosz claims for poetry (in "Ars Poetica?"):

> The purpose of poetry is to remind us
> how difficult it is to remain just one person,
> our house is open, there are no keys in the door,
> and invisible guests come and go at will.

Myerhoff's love of poetry is articulated in this passage: the poet who mattered most to her was Rilke, whose vigilant listening for the "angels" (of invisibility) was for her the image of a sacralization of a secular vocation. This spoke to the side of her aspiration that was moved, not by the production of scientific knowledge or by academic success, but by an experience she attained only in and through listening to the other: membership in a spiritual community that lifted her beyond the clock time in which she normally lived.

Myerhoff's gift as a listener had to do with communicating this sense of possible transcendence to others: for communicating the desire and inspiration with which she received the other's utterances. This listening had an extraordinarily powerful impact upon informants, students, colleagues, and friends. Deena Metzger, her lifelong friend, said that in the circle of Myerhoff's gaze, each person felt that he or she was "the most beloved." Immersed in this full and unusually intense attentiveness, received by a listener who offered herself as a "partner in security" (Grotowski's image of the ideal auditor before whom the actor can take all risks and go utterly naked); met, moreover, by someone whose steadiness of attention by turns offered a supple, accepting, lucid, brilliant auditor, Myerhoff's interlocutors felt free to think and feel through dimensions of their experience that they had not owned or connected before. She was often present at the saying-aloud for the first time of something long lived with, subliminally. The interview felt emancipatory. The gathered material registered the sense of discovery. What sometimes felt like wisdom literature resulted. This is nowhere more the case than in the late tales she collected in Fairfax.

Myerhoff, as an ethnographic writer, sought to do two different things with her experience of the storytelling relationship. She made the medium of the storytelling relationship an object of inquiry. In essays such as "Life History among the Elderly," she describes attention as a valuable but socially unrecognized form of work (usually performed by women, without compensation). In *Number Our Days,* she tells stories that exceed their status as exempla of anthropological concepts. One of the projects that she did not live to complete was titled *Tales from Fairfax.* Here, she sought to develop the storytelling side of her practice as an ethnographer. She wished to find a way of editing the tales so that everything she knew about them would be "invisibly" embedded in the tales, through the editing: the tales would be presented without the framing discourse of the interpreting anthropologist. Buber's *Tales of the Early Hasidic Masters* was an inspiration and a model of this sort of intervention. The notion of the third voice was formulated in her attempt to work through the problem of jettisoning explicit anthropological commentary.

The notion of the third voice is itself an instance of dialogic discourse: it answers back the internalized voice of empiricism, which challenges the moral and scientific legitimacy of Myerhoff's writing practice. In its contention with empiricism, the link that this notion makes between the writing and the listening, between text production and research interview, is axial. The highly ethical character and scientific respectability of the informant interview are thereby transferred to a writing practice that (for Myerhoff) is still untheorized and, therefore, questionable. The notion of the third voice is a seed of theory—and theory justifies as it explains—which, decoded and writ large, argues the following.

The (oral as well as the textualized) tale is at all points a social construct, produced in and through dialogic relations. The cocreation of the tale begins in the telling and carries through into the writing. Myerhoff is implicitly presenting a major idea that is made explicit in the cultural theory of Bakhtin and Raymond Williams: the notion of the third voice is founded upon a communication model of cultural creativity. In the communicative arena of the storytelling relationship, the listener overtly and covertly coproduces the teller's utterance. The gestures, intonations, and verbal interventions of the listener have a profound significance in shaping the teller's discourse, which is subtly modified from within by its orientation to the listener.

Myerhoff's notion of the third voice converges with Bakhtin's theory of discourse in that it carries over the relationship between teller and listener from "life" to writing. The process of communication at work in the formation of discourse is, in this view, no longer separated into "natural" and "artificial" categories. Discourse in speaking and discourse in writing are understood as a culturally formed social process. The categories of "the artificial" and "the natural" are themselves "artificial," constructed to separate what is a social process of communication through and through.

The crucial move made by the notion of the third voice is that it grounds the collaborative author's interventions in the process of communication between teller and listener. This notion construes the author as listener who continues, "on paper," a process that is initiated in face-to-face dialogue. Text and talk are inseparable. Positing the continuity of the role of the listener in the role of the ethnographic writer is, in the first instance, a biographical matter: the same person carries through these connected roles. But in the last instance, this link is a matter of discursive practice. Just as the listener/interviewer, in overt as well as uncontrollable and incalculable ways, shapes the dialogue, so the listener-as-author, engaged in the act of editing the transcript and writing the ethnographic text, now hears and sees the "meaning" of the utterance, and can intervene to help articulate this coproduced meaning more "clearly." Just as a concurring or clarifying word is inserted into the dialogue, so the writer-as-listener offers her suggestive or interpretative word into the cocreated discourse.

This brings us to Myerhoff's actual writing practice in *Number Our Days*. She "inevitably" shaped the transcript in ways that felt, in the writing, "natural" to her. This went beyond omitting and restructuring elements of the utterance. And it went beyond framing utterances in her strong interpretation of them. It meant subtle, nearly invisible acts of clarification and interpretation that were made by infiltrating the utterance and lodging her own distinct word within it, manipulating it from within. This writing practice, which is typical of novelistic discourse, was described by Bakhtin in the famous discourse typology that he presented in his book on Dostoevsky (1984a:181–269). In his cogent elucidation of Bakhtin's discourse typology, McClellan distinguishes double-voiced from single-voiced discourse as follows.

> In monologic discourse the author's relation to another's discourse is defined by these two essential characteristics: the boundaries of another's discourse are clearly marked but the objectified discourse is subjected to the direct dominance and control of authorial intention. This is not the case with . . . double-voiced or dialogic discourse.
>
> An essential characteristic of Bakhtin's definition of double-voiced discourse resides in the fact that such discourse, in addition to its orientation toward a referential object, is oriented as well toward another's utterance. In comparison, monologic or single-voiced discourse is oriented primarily towards its object of reference and contains a single dominating intention. On the other hand, double-voiced discourse has two semantic intentions, or two "voices" residing and conflicting in the utterance. The second intention, the authorial "voice" infiltrates the utterance from within redirecting but not obliterating the original intention. One way of doing this is to conventionalize the utterance creating a distance between the two voices. (1985:38–39)

In the Dostoevsky book, Bakhtin lays out a typology of various kinds of double-voiced discourse. The kind that corresponds to Myerhoff's notion of the third voice and her actual writing practice in *Number Our Days* is "narrator's narration."

Bakhtin distinguishes the narration of a narrator from authorial narration. The former is "a compositional substitute for the author's word." Pushkin's Belkin and Dostoevsky's Underground Man are offered as examples familiar to Russian readers; Chaucer's Wife of Bath, Dickens' Esther in *Bleak House* and "Joyce's voices" in *Ulysses* are familiar instances in English. Bakhtin defines narrator's narration as follows:

> someone else's verbal manner is utilized by the author as a point of view, as a position indispensable for him for carrying out the story. . . . But the narrator's discourse can never become purely

objectified, even when he himself is one of the characters and takes upon himself only part of the narration. His importance to the author, after all, lies not only in his individual and typical manner of thinking, experiencing, and speaking, but above all in his manner of seeing and portraying: in this lies his direct function as a narrator replacing the author. Therefore the author's attitude, as in stylization, penetrates inside the narrator's discourse, rendering it to a greater or lesser degree conventional. (1984a:190)

Shmuel's utterances, more than those of any other character-narrator in *Number Our Days,* are used by Myerhoff in this way, but narrator's narration is characteristic of the "elders' speech" throughout the book.

Discourse in *Number Our Days,* unlike discourse in the scholarly essays, is oriented toward three different social groups with which the author is affiliated and in conflict. These are: an educated middle-class audience, to whom Myerhoff speaks in a conversational style that easily mixes erudition and novelistic narrative; colleagues in the social sciences, who are (so to speak) positioned above this middle range of discourse, in a balcony reserved for the jury of her peers, to whom she gestures and before whom she feels accountable; and finally, the informants themselves, who are literate and whom she cannot entirely exclude from the company of her readers. These three different groups have different (and fluctuating) relations with the author as narrator ("Myerhoff") and as character (the "lady professor, Babrushka"). All this makes for the rhetorical complexity of this work, which combines monologic discourse with two kinds of double-voiced discourse: hidden polemic (both the author's and the elders'), which determines the form of key "definitional ceremonies,"[5] and narrator's narration.

---

5. Myerhoff worked up the concept of "definitional ceremonies" in two important case studies of the discursive forms used by "oppressed people" to wage political fights. These are: "For an educated man, he could learn a few things" (chapter 4 of *Number Our Days,* see especially pp. 140–50) and "'Life Not Death in Venice'" (in this volume, see especially 199–204). My paper, "Definitional Ceremonies: Depoliticizing and Reenchanting the Culture of Aging" (1992b) offers an analysis of these two cases studies and discusses the significance of this contribution. First, the concept of definitional ceremonies occupies a unique position in Myerhoff's work in that it is the sole theoretical description of culture that she formulated. Second, it is an important move in anthropological theory, in its effort to get beyond the schematic, bipolar thinking that marks social thought in the United States on the question of the relationship between

In the latter type of discourse, the author's narrative and evaluative intention is carried forward in the socially alien voice of a character. It is to be found wherever the author's focusing, reaccentuating, clarifying word takes up residence inside the character's utterance. Hannah's word for the tyrannical Center ritualmaker and president—"zealot"—is imported from Myerhoff's discourse (1980:85, 95). Moshe's descriptive term for a traveling group of gypsies or circus performances—"carnival"—emigrates also from Myerhoff's lexicon of privileged terms (1980:85, 83). When Heschel, in a moral tale that Myerhoff frequently quoted and republished, says that "you get a clarification" (1980:197); and when Shmuel, in the midst of the most tragic and awesome utterance in the book, conventionalizes and tags his memories of shtetl life with epistemological constructionalism, "A life made up entirely from the imagination," we hear Myerhoff's key words: the accent of the author's voice penetrates the character's utterance, saturating it with her knowledge, rendering it an example of her conceptual truth. Only as independent testimony do these little and big stories have value to her. They are offered in her book as evidence that demonstrates the validity of her interpretive moves and of her conceptual foundations.

It is impossible to know the extent to which Myerhoff engaged in the art of infiltrating the other's utterance, and depositing her authorial word

---

"the individual and society." Under this concept, Myerhoff offers a genuinely integrative theory that links life-review work and ritual theory. Third, it takes creativity as its object of study. This is a quality and a process that is exalted in American culture, but it has not usually been deemed a sufficiently serious topic of social science research. Fourth, in and through this concept, Myerhoff is able to represent and analyse the oppositional character of these elderly Jews' cultural productions, even as she occludes its social and cultural sources (in the workers' and Yiddishist movements and the popular socialism that played a decisive role in their formation). Too, in this paper I show the convergence between the cultural theory of Myerhoff and Bakhtin, whose work on discourse gives analytic access to the profound connections this concept makes between social position, cultural creativity, and mode of discourse. The unity of the concept of definitional ceremonies depends upon a genre-shaping intention, rather than any specific form of cultural performance. Myerhoff includes storytelling, public rituals, and ceremonies, meetings, murals, protest marches, and other enactments and displays under this category. The genre-shaping intention that these have in common is the intention to affirm the individual by grounding her personal identity and worth in the culture and social history of the group. In practice, this assertion of value is polemical and oppositional: it is made against the dominant social evaluation which denies the meaning and value of the group's

inside others' speech, so that it would speak her authorial truth without thereby erasing the others' viewpoint and social language. Was this "tampering with the evidence" or enlisting her writerly gifts to make legitimate interpretative moves, from within the utterance? That Myerhoff did not specify, in *Number Our Days,* what form her "editing" had taken may be read as a sign of her intimidation in the face of the power of empiricist norms. All of her subsequent work shows that she was moving toward acknowledging and legitimating the "liberties" and innovations of *Number Our Days.*

In summary, it is possible to specify the difference between *Number Our Days* and the ethnographic essays by the former's free and pervasive use of double-voiced discourse, particularly narrator's narration. As a veiled practice, this is unquestionably problematic, both scientifically and ideologically. Yet it arises out of the process of the "scientific imagination" that is engaged in anthropological field work and writing. As such, it can be argued that this writing practice is defensible as an act of interpretation: of entering the "experience-near" language of the informant and marking it with the "experience-distant" term that translates (conventionalizes) the unfamiliar speech for American middle-class reception (cf. Geertz 1983b:56–59.)

---

culture and social history. Hence, the intention is to contest the evaluative and interpretive social discourse of the dominant culture (ageism, sexism, anti-Semitism, devaluation of working-class and poor people). To do this, the assertion of value must directly or indirectly quote, cite, refer back to the dominant valuations, and directly or indirectly "answer back." In situations where "answering back" is too risky, the cultural performance must both lodge a complaint and persuade the auditors that the protesting word they are actually hearing is an innocuous or even flattering word. The concurrence of these two semantic intentions creates the type of double-voiced discourse that Bakhtin called hidden polemic. Myerhoff explicitly understands the Center members' discourse in this way. See, for example, her rhetorical analysis of the discursive means through which the elderly "inventors of tradition," in constructing the graduation-siyum ritual, "achieve the mundane function" of accusing those who neglect them:

> To address to their children and their better off fellow Jews the overt statement, "You are treating us badly" would embarrass and alienate them. By making their self-definition and protest indirect and ceremonial, the old people arouse guilt without having to state the humiliating facts of their condition. . . . For rituals allow people to maneuver, fight on their own terms, choose the times and shapes of their assertions. . . . (in this volume)

Myerhoff's authorial word enters the other's utterance from the lived subject position of the listener, that is, as if it were a gift of loving attention. This clarifying word seeks to translate the "greenhorn" voice of the Yiddish-speaking old person for the educated (and potentially condescending) auditor. In so doing, this mirroring word assimilates the elders' utterances to conventional discourse, rendering the speech more capable of commanding the respect of respectable persons, while it concurrently makes the truth that Myerhoff has discerned therein more recognizable to her educated, middle-class readers. This appropriation of the other's speech is a transformation of it that makes it "audible" to an audience that has classified this "broken English" as lower-class and ignorant. Myerhoff retains (and, in her acts of ventriloquism, exaggerates) Yiddish syntax, which, in its disturbance of the normal English syntactical patterns, creates a whiplash effect of immense (sardonic) emphasis. But she loads up these sidewinding sentences with educated diction. What she thereby "restores" to the old people's talk is the intelligence and self-knowledge that the Yiddish-English utterance, for a prejudiced or socially distant reader, would lack. This is done respectfully, tactfully, with great artistry and in profound allegiance with her subjects, whose "wisdom" she is promoting. Yet this lessening of the linguistic distance between the Yiddish-speaking old people and her middle-class audience, while it is a mark of Myerhoff's actual respect for the old people, is also a way of subordinating their difference and instituting a subjugating discourse that overrides theirs. The difference between the informants' and the dominant discourse—a linguistic zone that bears the audible traces of their politically engaged cultural history—is (ideologically) neutralized. At every point in Myerhoff's practice, we encounter the discursive effects of her position as liberal intermediary between antagonistic positions.

In the book, this contradiction is narrated as "the generation gap." Myerhoff avoids the banal term, but relies upon the conventional wisdom of the thought, as a crucial subplot in the making of the master narrative of the book. This is the narrative that turns informants, and especially very old informants, into the most recent addition to the great hall of nearly extinct tribes, the latest version of "the last of the Mohegans." It inserts the anthropologist into the process of cultural transmission as an essential, and salvific, protagonist. And it accounts for the practice of "salvage ethnology" (1980:150–51).[6] Shmuel, after hearing Myerhoff's

6. For a brilliant critique of "salvage ethnography," see James Clifford's "On

cunning and charming defense of this "work" (i.e., both the research and the book she is writing), responds: "It isn't science. It isn't history. It isn't art. You are cooking here a tsimmes from all these things you pick up. A carrot here, a prune there, in it goes" (1980:150–51). And this is something of a set up: it allows Myerhoff to make a brilliant defense of "salvage ethnology" that melds it, as a Geertzian blurred genre, with the old people's creation of culture through bricolage.

The textual authority of the ethnographer / editor is implicitly being legitimated by the narrative of salvage. In this narrative, the anthropologist is compelled to rescue precious cultural artifacts (practices, discourses, social wisdom) of a vanishing tribe that modernization has doomed. History, in Myerhoff's book, is personified by the immigrant's upwardly mobile children; the neglect of an uncaring society is primarily represented as the distance and indifference of the elders' children. This latter claim, crucial for Myerhoff's position in *Number Our Days,* is simplified and exaggerated. It leaves out of account the historical process that has produced the contemporary isolation of old people. This complex process is constituted by a division of labor that has standardized age-segmentation throughout the life-cycle and increased the segregation between "life stages" (Rosenmayr 1982:19–20), and by the transfer of functions connected with caring for the elderly from the family to the welfare state. The "incompleteness," the "ambiguity and failure" of this transfer (Hareven 1982:3–4) has produced political controversy at the level of policy, "gaps in service" within an everyday life dependent on welfare agencies, and it has been lived through as generational conflict. Because of her "imaginative identification" with the old people's disappointed—often shocked—expectation of being directly cared for by their children in old age, Myerhoff totalized her depiction of the difficult and often conflicted involvement of the second generation with their parents and with the culture of Yiddish.

In her project of salvage, Myerhoff (an assimilated Jew with no knowledge of Yiddish) assumes the role of cultural next-of-kin which, by extension, gives her property rights over the informant's words. She can dispose of them in what she believes to be the best interests of the treasure

---

Ethnographic Allegory." Clifford reads "allegories of salvage" as versions of "ethnographic pastoral," a genre whose rhetorical and ideological underpinnings he exposes through a reading model based largely upon Raymond Williams' *The Country and the City.*

entrusted to her keeping. She is called upon to transmit Yiddishkeit to succeeding generations because the actual children of these elders have discarded the precious legacy that was, but no longer is, theirs.

The topic of the panel discussion at which Myerhoff proposed the notion of the third voice turns out to have been more than a pretext and an occasion: "cultural transmission and symbolic immortality" are the lived historical context that, for Myerhoff, compel the ethnographer to learn to speak and write in the third voice. The elders, whom history and their children's neglect have robbed of successors, need the redemptive salvager of culture as their (female) Kaddish and as the sole responsible guardian and keeper of their legacy. In this master narrative, the textual relations between author/editor and informant are moralized in terms of a specific set of social relations: the property rights acquired by the true heir and successor. Here, the text is a warehouse of words in which everything is left in, even the items that the anthropologist can make nothing of; these "bits and pieces" are salvaged for future interpretation (1980:150–51). This image of the text as collection of cultural bric-a-brac has little in common with the counterimage of an efficient, heavily edited and selected text, except this: both internally legitimate the ethnographer's authorial control over the empirical materials contained therein, and both construe the elders' speech as raw material to be processed by the ethnographer. Both of the text's opposing self-representations legitimate the author's authority.

The essays that Myerhoff wrote after the mid-1970s are haunted by the "transgressions" and discoveries of *Number Our Days*. The work on reflexivity, in which ethnographic writing is taken up as a problem, can only be fully grasped when it is read "against" *Number Our Days*. The essays seek to work through (describe and legitimate) the exhilarating, but secret innovation of narrator's narration. The most dynamic aspect of the essays on reflexivity constitute a veiled confession of a hidden practice. In key passages on "exaggeration" (1980:66, 111; "Surviving Stories," in this volume); and in the bad faith written into the word "collusion," which is used in these texts as a telling alternative to "collaboration," Myerhoff is moving through confession toward a working through of the principle of dialogic discourse that she enunciated, once and briefly, in the notion of the third voice.

Three of the ethnographic essays included in this volume were subsequently reworked as chapters in *Number Our Days*. They are: "We

Don't Wrap Herring in a Printed Page," "A Death in Due Time," and "Bobbes and Zeydes." These were rewritten, respectively, as chapter 3 ("We don't wrap herring in a printed page"), chapter 6 ("Teach us to number our days") and chapter 7 ("Jewish comes up in you from the roots"). A quick perusal of the comparable texts shows how similar they are: nearly 50 percent of the essays were carried over into the chapters. Closer study reveals their profound differences. There are differences in the narratives they present and in the interpretations they offer; differences of orientation and purpose that are registered in the language they use, the status and presentation of theory, and the principles of text construction through which they are constituted.

In these matching essays and chapters, Myerhoff produced what few anthropologists have given us: completed texts describing the "same" cultural performances in different genres. This is rare, almost unheard of; it admits us, in quite remarkable ways, backstage. These corresponding texts amply reward extensive analysis; they have a great deal to teach us about how different genres construct and construe social reality.

In his foreword to *Number Our Days,* Victor Turner has stated what is, perhaps, the most conspicuous difference between the chapters and the essays: "The anthropological perspective is omnipresent but not intrusive, always made to serve the purpose of presenting specific people and events" (1980:xi). In the chapters, concepts are footlights, hidden themselves, in which brilliantly illuminated people communicate to each other and to the reader, through the events they create and the crises they enact, their experience of the culture they live. The chapters, as novelistic narratives, capture "the structure of feeling" (Williams 1977) of the culture of Yiddishkeit with a pungency and vividness that the essays do not and cannot match. The essays, however, focus on the "anthropological perspective." Not only do they make the conceptual machinery visible, they also offer a more complex and adequate narrative and theoretical description of secular ritual. The footlights, so to speak, are wheeled onstage, alongside the actors, and become demonstrably part of the action, as in Brechtian presentational theatre.

This is the interrelation of theory and narrative that Geertz calls "thick description" (1973a). What in the chapters is blended into the "perspective" from which people and events are witnessed, emerges, in the essays, as distinct, specifically bodied-forth anthropological ideas: concepts laden with actuality, theory whose application the text richly demonstrates. This permits the reader to enter into the anthropologist's workshop, not as a passive consumer of culture, who "merely" enjoys the completed object of the ethnographer's work, but as a present or future colleague; the reader is invited into an active collaboration with the text, to learn and refine a way of seeing and thinking about social life. The ethnographic essays seek to present models of the scientific imagination at work: models of the creative use of theory. The essays connect the meaning-making practices of their subjects with an explicit demonstration of the meaning-making practices of contemporary social science, narrating cultural events in the light of key ideas, with the aim of handing these keys over to readers.

But the chapters do not simply popularize and "sideline" the ideas that hold center stage in the essays. The shift in genres demonstrably involves a shift in the way in which social life is represented and evaluated. Over and against the manifest theory of the author, genres carry within them their own "theory" of the object, which casts a shadow on the content.

This can be demonstrated by a rhetorical case study of two corresponding texts. In what follows, I will compare a crucial segment of the essay titled "We Don't Wrap Herring in a Printed Page" (in this volume) with the "same" portion of the chapter of the same name. This segment is the narrative of the "graduation-siyum" ritual. In both cases, this narrative constitutes the object of the discourse: it documents the empirical materials which ethnographic interpretation or authorial commentary elucidates.

The two ethnographic texts differ considerably in the form and content of this narrative. In the ethnographic essay, it appears in chronicle form: an inventory or numbered list of the various speeches, songs, and other elements of which the ritual is composed. The form emphasizes the scientific, documentary status of the information: it "quietly" asserts that here we have a sequence of raw facts, unadulterated by the deforming hands of interpretation.

The narrative strategy of the chapter of *Number Our Days* mixes the conventions of realism of several genres, of which the ethnographic essay and autobiography are the most important, but the "new journalism," with its emphasis on the subjectivity of the witness-reporter, is probably an influence. This mix produces a "novel-like" effect—descriptions of character rehearse novelistic conventions—that has as much in common with novelistic practice as with "cultivated" magazine articles whose mixture of reflection and reportage produces an "irresistible-to-read" novel-like effect.

The different forms—chronicle-style versus novelistic magazine-article style—are not a matter of the same wine in different bottles; there are significant differences in content. Two discrepancies represent differences that emerge as generic, that is, systematic:

In the essay, "Diplomas were distributed by the Rabbi" ("We Don't Wrap Herring in a Printed Page," in this volume); in the chapter, "Kominsky began to pass out the diplomas" (1980:90). In the essay, the President of the Temple read messages of congratulation that "resulted from class members pooling their contacts in Israel and elsewhere"; in the chapter, "Kominsky began what he regarded as the highlight of the ceremony. He read congratulatory messages from Israel. These had been gathered by his friends and family there" (1980:91). These differences of detail—of "fact"—point to the profoundly different conceptions of subject and agency that these narratives present. The ethnographic essay describes a collective subject and a collective action: the ritual is a "collective act of imagination," which is planned and implemented in a contentious social process involving "the Center director, several of the graduating students, and the teacher of the class, Kominsky". In the chapter, the planning and implementation that was the work of many hands is ascribed to one master hand; the collective subject virtually disappears in a narrative that aggrandizes the role of a self-aggrandizing individual. In its parts (i.e., the messages from Israel) and as a whole cultural product, the ritual is drained of sociality: effects attained by the group using all its social resources become the narrative property of a single extraordinary individual. "Kominsky had planned the ceremony with exceeding care. . . . He had worked his networks skillfully" (1980:88).

The issues I am raising here emerge in a particularly intriguing— some will find it shocking—way in an instance of disagreement between the two texts that appears to contradict the overall pattern of differences. In the essay, Kominsky concludes his "charge to the class" by saying:

> In my family, when Papa opened his book we were all quiet. Sha! Papa studies. Papa looks in a book. All the house respects it. When a book is dropped, it is kissed. A worn-out book is buried. We don't wrap herring in a printed page, not even if it's a newspaper.

In the chapter, this signature piece, from which the whole assemblage of discourses draws its name, is spoken by the president emeritus of the Center, Jacob, immediately after Kominsky finishes his "charge to the class." Here is Jacob's speech about holy literacy:

> What Kominsky told you is basically true. All of us were raised this way, even those of us who don't believe in God; we have religion because we have the Law. For us all books are religious. Study is religious. Each page and each letter on the page has its own special character, even the white spaces between the letters are holy. A little boy is honored when he carries his papa's prayer book to synagogue on the Sabbath. In the family, when Papa opened his book, all the house becomes quiet. 'Sha, Papa reads,' the mama says to the children, and all the house respect it when there is study inside. When a book is worn out we give it a burial. It's like a living thing. All writing has something of holiness. Even when it's only a newspaper, it shouldn't be used for anything but study. So it is in the marketplace also. Because we are Jews, we don't wrap herring in a printed page. (1980:92)

How are we to make sense of these authorial interventions? Aside from flagrantly exemplifying the "made-upness" (Myerhoff's term) of the ethnographic text, can we learn something about Myerhoff's method of text construction in the face of what appears to be textual "craziness"?

Even here, in this apparently contradictory instance, Myerhoff abides by the genre laws we saw governing the writing choices throughout the text. The principle of redistributing social roles in the ritual to favor the dominant individual is not violated here. In the book of which the chapter is part, Jacob is one of the two leading protagonists; like Shmuel, he reappears throughout the book, a symbolic figure and a mouthpiece, a culture hero and a wise old man: beloved by the group, and so honored by Myerhoff that she changes his last name from Kovitz in the essay titled "A Death in Due Time" to Koved—Hebrew for honor—in the book, making him a personification of the dignity which he personally projects. And we must remember that neither Kovitz nor Koved are the man's actual name; in the essay on the "graduation-siyum," this "patriarch" is called Mr. Abraham; all these names are fictive. Neither the essay nor the chapter is a transcript of the ritual. Thus, in the book, the beloved and universally esteemed Jacob Koved is given a place of honor in whatever discourse he appears, whether it is the author's text or the Center's ritual. In the scholarly article, whose form and content are not structured through the representation of the symbolic pair—Shmuel / Jacob, two strong versions of wisdom in old age—Jacob's speech ends up in Kominsky's mouth.

Jacob's speech? What we can't know is what was "really" said at the ritual, and who did or didn't say it. It is my conviction, based on linguistic markers, that the speech ascribed to Kominsky in the essay was spoken by Jacob; and that, in the book, Myerhoff restored the speech to Jacob, but only after infiltrating it and, using Jacob as a ventriloquist uses her dummy, added much or all the bits of cultural information contained in the opening commentary. What gives away their origin in authorial intention is their overarticulateness, their character of being spoken to cue-in and instruct an uninformed auditor. They voice Myerhoff's thesis in the mouth of a native speaker: "All of us were raised in this way, even those of us who don't believe in God. . . . For us all books are religious. Study is religious." This carries no one's accent more than Myerhoff's, bringing this old revolutionary socialist into the fold of contemporary middle-class Judaism, and pushing her thesis about the sacredness of secular practices.

An authentic original cannot be recuperated from the textual variants we have to work with. For adherents to empiricism, this discredits the entire enterprise of ethnographic narrative, of which *Number Our Days* is an admittedly extreme case in its novelization of its materials. But if, as Geertz has claimed, the task of the "scientific imagination" is to "bring us into contact with the lives of strangers," then this book, even though it can be shown to "tamper" with the data, fulfills its obligation. Unfortunately, Myerhoff herself, at the time of writing *Number Our Days,* was not assured enough of the validity of her own practice to have openly declared her method of text construction and to have written a legitimating and necessarily controversial explanation of her "experimental" practice. Her subsequent work, as indicated above, is directed toward working through the contradictions that afflicted her writing. It is a misfortune that she died at age fifty, at the height of her powers, when she had already discovered and begun to acknowledge the third voice, but before she could carry through the textualist project she had initiated.

The foregoing analysis of Myerhoff's writing across genres raises, in a particularly acute way, the problem of the status of evidence in ethnographic narrative. It is crucial to insist here that, in her practice, Myerhoff is more representative than she is unique. The enormous contribution of Clifford, Marcus, Fischer, and their colleagues has been to demonstrate the "made-upness" of the conventional ethnographic text, to dispel its claim of impartiality and its status as a representation of objective truth, and to show that its fashioning and refashioning of its empirical materials adhere to conventions that are at once constraints of genre and ideology.

In discerning consistent patterns of representation in the two texts, I have argued that the apparently arbitrary differences are meaningful, and that their meaning can be specified in relation to their form-and-content unity. We can say that the "same" speech has been refashioned in the different texts, or we can say each text fashions its speech to accord with its different interpretation of the ritual. Geertz, who has hardly forsaken the notion that there is a social reality that is indisputably *there,* beyond all our attempts to capture it in texts, nonetheless stresses that anthropological writings are fictive things; and, wordsmith that he is, reminds us that fiction is derived from *fictio,* the Latin for "something made, something fashioned." For Geertz, ethnographies are like novels in that both are acts of the literary imagination; both are constructions of actor-oriented descriptions. But finally, for Geertz, the line between science and art, although "undrawable," is not to be crossed, and Myerhoff evidently crosses it. For Geertz, the "fictive" character of ethnographic narratives is intrinsic to their character as interpretative discourses. The boundary between actors and events that are (ethnographically) represented as actually the case, and those that are represented as belonging to the Imaginary, is to be steadfastly maintained. In Myerhoff's texts the quality of "fictiveness" infiltrates the empirical materials. But this "fictionalizing" adheres to conventions of realism in the novel which, in turn, refract and communicate our culture.

In summary, the move to a writing that dramatizes the individual at the expense of the social process is embedded in the shift from the ethnographic essay to the novelistic chapter. A different convention of realism determines the form and content of the ethnographic essay: it is a realism arising out of a commitment to theory and to foregrounding theory, and it is a realism with respect to the complexity, the dialogic messiness, of the social process in and through which large-scale rituals (and other cultural performances) are created.

We have seen that what differentiates the two texts about the graduation-siyum ritual goes well beyond any aesthetic of "intensification." The differences of detail refract a profound generic and ideological motif: the problem of individual versus collective agency. The different versions present alternative views of the problem of creative agency, and each view adheres to a position that Myerhoff deeply held and authentically lived. In her writing, the "crisis of representation" in the human sciences can be located in this specific contradiction: between the privileged individual subject (both the ethnographer and the informant) of the novelistic narrative, and the collective subject of the ethnographic essays. This contradiction, carried through as separate genres for the individual and for the group, is finally grounded in a social process that divides daily life into private and public domains, and that in practice impoverishes the latter to enrich the former. Myerhoff, in her search for wholeness of self and community, produced a writing whose internal division profoundly refracts her own, as well as a general, conflict. Her contradiction on this matter is the personally lived expression of the "crisis in community" which is a common experience in our individualistic culture.

The Discourse of Marginality

The moral vision that Myerhoff's work communicates—it proposes a domain in which "the last shall come first," exercising what liberation theology calls "a preferential option for the poor"—is substantiated in and through two key figures of marginality: the "liminal being" and the "pariah." These tropes personify and conceptualize a densely populated and thickly described discursive position. Rhetorically, they conflate figures of speech, representations of persons and ideological images of social thought. Myerhoff does not specify the ideological "station in mid-air" (Virginia Woolf's phrase for the narrator's point of view) on which she stands and from which she speaks of her subjects. But these figures of thought and speech locate her position: they are signs of "the liberal imagination."

One of the functions of these tropes is to cope with the problem of the relation between the subordinated subject of the discourse and the privileged, professionally educated, middle-class "us" that includes the author and the reader. The figures of the liminal being and the pariah—intriguing, exotic, almost picturesque—lift the already-segregated old people out of our world, distancing them in the imagination. They project a generalized realm of values, no longer tied to the specific social and historical locations and the specific roles and practices—caste systems and rites of initiation—from which they have been appropriated, for use as metaphors in "our" moral and scientific discourse. In this abstracted realm, which technical social science terms validate, the distanced elders are brought back to us, they are brought so near to us as to be like us: marginalized people one and all.

This process of refiguration plays up the otherness of the cultural other for the sake of denying actual differences of class, worldview, and social position. This is not Myerhoff's intention. Her wish is to write and to provoke an intense encounter with the old men and women whom she approaches with the "surplus of love and vision" that, for Bakhtin, characterizes Dostoevsky's dialogical openness to his characters. The conversations between Myerhoff and Basha or Hannah, or between Myerhoff and Shmuel, in *Number Our Days,* are profoundly moving and engaging because of this quality. Yet this intention, as Myerhoff becomes increasingly aware in the process of writing *Number Our Days,* goes awry. When it does, she has yielded to an aestheticising impulse that turns people into types of "the wily old man, the truly frightening powerful old witch, the curmudgeon recluse in the hills" ("Experience at the Threshold," in this volume). By the mid–1970s, she has begun to live through what Marcus and Fischer, in their pioneering study of this issue, have called "the crisis of representation" in the human sciences (1986). Myerhoff, as I will discuss later in this essay, is one of the forerunners of the "ethnography-as-text" school (Di Leonardo 1989). In her discussions of textuality and reflexivity (see the final four essays in this volume), she formulated and grappled with questions that are at the center of the present debate on discourse in the human sciences. Within anthropology, two books—*Anthropology as Cultural Critique* (Marcus and Fischer 1986) and *Writing Culture* (Clifford and Marcus 1986)— have been decisive in formulating these issues, in demonstrating the value of literary theory for social thought, and in offering brilliant specific analyses of ethnographic texts.

In a passage that describes the ethnographic tradition and forebears from which Myerhoff traced her lineal descent, Marcus and Fischer offer what can be read as a genealogy of her discursive position:

British and American ethnographic enterprises attracted women, foreigners, Jews, and others who felt themselves marginal, but yet belonged to social systems in which they were privileged intel-lectuals, and to which they were finally committed. Thus in the

1920s and 1930s, the forms of cultural criticism that arose in anthropology were none too radical, in the Marxist or surrealist sense of the Continent. They were the critique of marginal scholars whose primary concern was not their own societies, but others. The twentieth-century tradition of cultural criticism in anthropology had its roots in this qualified marginality of its practitioners. Thus, anthropologists as cultural critics developed a liberal critique, similar to that being expressed in other social sciences; they expressed sympathy for the oppressed, the different, the marginals, as well as emphasizing the modern dissatisfactions with privileged middle-class life. It was a critique of conditions, but not of the system or the nature of the social order itself. (Marcus and Fischer 1986:130–131)

Myerhoff's position of "qualified marginality"—her sympathy with the oppressed and her dissatisfaction with the privileged middle-class life that she led—fueled the ardor with which she took up Victor Turner's concept of the "liminal figure."

Turner derived his notion of liminality from the second of the three phases into which Arnold Van Gennep divided rites of passage: separation of novices, a betwixt and between phase (*limen*), and reincorporation into society in a new status. The Greek word *limen* means margin or threshold. In appropriating Van Gennep's concept, Turner would have preferred to translate *limen* as marginal, but "the term 'marginal' has been preempted by various sociologists . . . for their own purposes—so we are left with 'liminal'" (1977:36). Linguistically and conceptually, then, the exotic term is related to the common meaning of marginality.

In Myerhoff, as in Turner, this general idea is loosed from the hard edges of social-structural meaning. It is dehistoricized, ennobled, transformed into an eternal and recurring creative human type. The idea of marginality is reformulated in the direction of a higher calling, a privileged position in which a necessary condition is freely chosen. The "marginals" acquire spiritual status. In a proposal to the reader whose subjunctive verb form registers the mood of playfulness and serious speculation she often seeks to evoke, Myerhoff writes, "Then we may speak of specialists in disorder: the ritual clowns, transvestites, shamans, poets, rebels, mystics and vagabonds who move perpetually at the borders of known categories and agreements" ("Experience at the Threshold," in this volume). Moving between Whitmanesque heroic catalogue and sociological thought, this writing wants to behold the misery of marginal lives with a redemptive gaze.

Ordinary old people, by virtue of their "proximity to death," may graduate into this categoryless category. If they are lifelong poets and socialists, along with being Jewish and poor and female, they are liminal figures par excellence. Or, as Myerhoff often writes of them, three- and fourfold pariahs, again aggregating and glossing the common afflictions of marginal life with a spectacular term. This figure of thought, which Hannah Arendt privileged in essays that were written during the Holocaust and republished in *The Jew as Pariah* (1978), metaphorically accounts for the suffering of people at the bottom as the result of blows administered by a whole social system. But the more salient aspect of Arendt's concept of the "Jew as pariah" is that this figure corresponds to Turner's idea of liminal beings.

Through "sheer force of imagination," the pariahs—poets, artists, and political dissidents—create "a hidden tradition" in which they conceive of "the concept of the pariah as a human type," the shlemihl and dreamer who, as a spiritual aristocrat devoted to the common folk, accomplishes a transvaluation of values (Arendt 1978:68). Standing between the high culture of Europe and the organized forms of Judaism, an outsider in both worlds, but renouncing neither his Jewishness nor the intellectual heritage of the Enlightenment, the Jew as pariah likewise corresponds to the "marginal" anthropologists of the 1920s and 1930s. This concept, whose significance for Myerhoff appears in the number of times she invokes this morally potent epithet, profoundly informs her evaluation of the elders. Her writing, like Arendt's, both formulates the Jewish pariah as a human type and celebrates the tradition that Arendt calls "hidden" and that Myerhoff calls "little." Arendt, after citing Sholom Aleichem and Franz Kafka among its exemplars, writes that

> it is the tradition of a minority of Jews who have not wanted to become upstarts, who preferred the status of "conscious pariah." All vaunted Jewish qualities—the "Jewish heart," humanity, humor, disinterested intelligence—are pariah qualities. All Jewish short-comings—tactlessness, political stupidity, inferiority complexes and money-grubbing—are characteristics of upstarts. (1978:66)

Myerhoff relishes the satirical force with which the elders amplify and illustrate these dicta; and, in dialogue with the most self-conscious of the pariah-elders, she finds she has entered a world of values that she has in common with them.

Myerhoff's decision to devote her work, after 1972, to the culture of Yiddishkeit, reflected altered conditions in the third world that have generally made fieldwork a more complex and politically aware enterprise. The Chicanos whom she wanted to study told her to go home and study her own people. "Fieldwork became yardwork," as she used to say. Or, in the language of her profession, she was one of the pioneers of a necessary "repatriation" of anthropology, which turned its participant-observing eyes away from Bushmen medicine men and other "primitive" people and trained them on the socialization of North American physicians and other person-making practices of advanced capitalist societies. In Myerhoff's writing, anthropology became something else again—connected with what the natives are doing when they perform rituals and tell stories that evoke ancestors that are not solely theirs, but hers—and ours.

That problematized "ours" is Jewish in a way that is thick with specificity, but that also concerns other populations that are urban, marginalized, voiceless in history, the pariah peoples, the minority groups. Myerhoff is drawn, early and late, to those who don't live in "our" neighborhood, those who are subordinated by race, gender, class and age; for these, living in "internal exile" in the United States or Mexico, she seeks the shelter of an uplifting narrative: a cultural description in which not only they, but "we" also, can be redeemingly housed. And so, metaphorically transvaluing outsiderhood, in tropes of marginality, she constructs her position over the social fault that, as a woman of conscience, she cannot evade.

Myerhoff stood between the ghetto and the university, between the immigrant and the affluent generations, between the lower and upper-middle classes, at the boundaries among categories, between sacred and secular realms. Talking her head off, translating terms, sermonizing; between writing artistic prose and building intricate tables of interpretation that diagram her analysis of the data, Myerhoff stood between the pulpit and the lectern, between the poet's worktable and the scholar's desk, feeling the lure of other possible vocations, and turning such imaginary moves to the advantage of her calling. She was a master ethnographic storyteller who was not finished with an experience until it had been "shot through with explanation" (Benjamin 1969:89), and she was an erudite trickster-scholar who combined long, "poetical" cadences with dry, all-but-hidden in-jokes, burying an allusion to Eliot's "Whispers of Immortality" where no one but Geertz and a number of other polymath colleagues would get it. Proceeding according to the principle that "truth is concrete" (which is the motto that Brecht hung over the worktable where he wrote poems in exile, and also the method that Geertz conceptualizes as "thick description"), Myerhoff generalized the results. Her concerns—moral and scientific—reached out to embrace all disdained people, but were never presented with greater effect than when her "complex seeing" (Brecht's phrase for the task of poetry) was fastened upon the details of the Center folk's speech and actions, and the cold eye that she cast on the old people did not melt into congruence with her warm eye, which loved the elders who received her as kin and successor.

The tropes of liminality and pariahdom turn marginality, in Myerhoff's texts, into a two-sided motif: they are images, respectively, of resistance and subjugation. Pariahdom is the less rhetorically developed of the tropes. As an image of a subordinated population, it enters Myerhoff's writing either directly from Weber, who uses the term "pariah people" to describe the ancient Jews, or from work that cites or extends Weber's concept, of which Arendt's essays are the most significant and best known.[7]

---

7. Myerhoff offers no source for her use of a term that she probably took as a convention of social thought at the time she was writing. Insofar as the concept of "the Jew as pariah" was circulating in scholarly discourse, it owed its currency to Weber and Arendt. Given the inclusiveness of Myerhoff's "background" reading (which wasn't necessarily directly quoted or cited in her texts), as well as the learning-and-teaching character of her collegial conversation, it is possible that, even if Myerhoff had not read Arendt's essays on this theme, she knew of them. ("We Refugees" [1943] and "The Jew as Pariah: A Hidden Tradition" [1944] appeared, respectively, in *The Menorah Journal* and *Jewish Social Studies* before becoming generally available in *The Jew as Pariah,* which was published in 1978; i.e., too late for this book to have informed the writing of *Number Our Days* and the earlier ethnographic essays on the graduation-siyum and the birthday-memorial.) On the other hand, there is no question that she knew of Weber's use of this term. For instance, the preface of a work that she does cite, Solomon Poll's *The Hasidic Community of Williamsburg: A Study of the Sociology of Religion,* begins as follows:

> In his essay on Judaism, Max Weber described the ancient Jews as a pariah people, meaning "they were a guest people who were ritually separated, formally or *de facto,* from their surroundings." He continues, saying that "all the essential traits of Jewry's attitude toward the environment can be deduced from this pariah existence—espe-

In the figure of "the Jew as pariah," Arendt appropriated this term (from Weber as well as from Bernard Lazare) to develop a critique of bourgeois, assimilationist, respectable Western Jewish life, a critique in which the oppositional folk humor of East European Jewish culture is a major form of resistance (Arendt 1978:55–95). In Arendt's hands, "pariah" has acquired a modern cultural history, an ideological stance, and a particular social character that have already saturated it with the values and intonations that the figure of the shtetl Jew/immigrant carry for Myerhoff. What is crucial here is that Arendt's extending use of this concept is continuous with one of the meanings that this term has for Weber, in *Ancient Judaism:* there, it indicates the ritual separation of the Jews from co-territorial peoples and the way of life in and through which assimilation and domination were resisted. Nonetheless, when it crosses over into Myerhoff's writing, this sense of the term is lost, and its richness and difficulty are thinned out. Myerhoff uses this term to invoke the immiserization and endurance of East European Jews, but not their cultural inventiveness in counteracting and resisting domination. This interrelated sense is withdrawn from the term and transferred to the account of the liminal being. The separation of the active and passive senses of Weber's and Arendt's term, of the creative opposition and the centuries of suffering, consign this figure of speech to underdevelopment, to its marginal status in the text: it is an all-but-invisible clue to the categorical containment of opposition, which is a source of contradiction in the liberal discourse of marginality.

In these texts, pariahdom adorns the prose as an intensifier, as a term of ultimacy: a centripetal word in which various forms of social domination are uttered at once, and finally. Its use appears to be moral: it is a rhetorical gesture of ultimate concern. In fact, it is a politicized micronarrative that permits Myerhoff to split off the social history of this group into good and bad parts. Life in "America," the New World, is framed as a success story. All the oppression these working-class immigrants experience is contained within a narrative of Oldness, confined to the Old Country and old age, and contained in the tale of pariahdom. Thus, "America," as a personified representation of Liberty's dispensation of a good life, remains unimplicated in the social processes

---

cially its voluntary ghetto, long anteceding compulsory internment, and the dualistic nature of its in-group and out-group morality." (1962:v)

(i.e., poverty, age-segregation, the urban ghetto) that actually marginalize the old people. Their social histories are made kosher for liberalism by being separated into a milk-and-honey version (the narrative of Americanization, with its more or less happy ending) and a meatier fable (the tale of pariahdom, which symbolically admits the actual difficulty of their daily lives). These contending narrative structures are not permitted to recognize or interrogate each other; their categorical separation constitutes a mystification of what this group actually lived through in the United States. The narrative of the "one-generation proletariat," which Howe shows to be a myth (1976:142–44), epitomizes the erasure of the decades-long, difficult process of acculturation, a process in which the bewilderment and struggle of the second generation was as damaging, albeit different, from their own.

Liminality has a very different orientation in feeling and thought, and it occupies a far more active and complex space in Myerhoff's writing. It was, for instance, a term that Myerhoff used in conversation and teaching when she wanted to say what she valued, what she believed in: it was one of her sacred words, espousing a way of being that she felt authentically was her own no less than that of the people whose lives she studied and told. The origin of this term in ritual process, which was (often enough) the topic under discussion, permitted a literalization of the metaphor from which pariahdom was semantically sealed off.

The concept of liminality pervades Myerhoff's description of persons, her evaluation of events and processes, and her (indirect) critique of the culture of capitalism. Under the sign of liminality, the marginalized figure is the social actor of dissident practices; various forms of rebellion and opposition were personified. Among the women in *Number Our Days,* Basha and, even more so, Hannah are endowed with a sharp-tongued liminality. The most magnificent portrait of the liminal figure that Myerhoff rendered is Shmuel the tailor. He is Jacob Koved's counterpart and double. Both were revolutionaries when young. In both, their lifelong socialism is fused with an artistic practice: they are Yiddish writers, dedicated to writing autobiographical meditations in poetry and prose. Yet one is a cultural critic, a perpetual gadfly to the group to which he is tied; the other is a culture hero, the virtuous representative man, who is at once an official as well as a moral leader. Both men belong to the same social type which the Jewish working-class produced in abundance: the "worker-intellectual." Myerhoff admires Jacob; he is the "professional elder" who exemplifies the range of practices that can teach us how to age well. But Shmuel commands her profound love and respect. He is her spiritual mentor, the wise old man who is ethnographically exalted under the sign of the ever-dissident, ever-creative liminal being.

The "structure of feeling" of *Number Our Days*—and this is the great achievement of the book—is produced by superimposing various dimensions and languages of marginality upon each other, which gives both the narrative and the theoretical description of the elders' communal life a many-layered depth and richness. Here, liminality and pariahdom encode the intersection between the anthropologist's and the elders' positions. Here, despite their differences in thought and feeling, these key tropes move in the same evaluative direction. They transvalue and reposition the outsider with respect to the dominant culture. The pariah is, by definition, the victim of a systemic social evil; the term recruits the reader, as a man or woman of good will, to feel sympathy for the loudmouthed, left-wing, testy, relapsed-greenhorn Jews whom it has transfigured. The concept of liminality is used to turn the conventional hierarchy of judging a person's worth upside down, putting the person-at-the-bottom on top.

This reversal of the "normal" way of evaluating people and things is one sign of Myerhoff's "carnival sense of life" (Bakhtin 1984a:124). In a famous discussion, Bakhtin formulates a unified conception of carnival that includes the following components: (1) the free and familiar contact of persons of various social ranks; (2) eccentricity, a new mode of relationship between individuals, the revelation and expression of latent sides of human nature in half-real, half-playacted forms; (3) mésalliances, the combination and union of opposites, of sacred and profane, high and low; (4) profanation, bringing things down to earth.

The primary carnivalistic act is the ritual mock crowning and decrowning of the carnival king: in this ritual process all four components of carnival are brought into play. The status hierarchies of everyday life dissolve; and, as common members of the same world, people of various social ranks come into familiar contact and together celebrate "the creative power of shift-and-renewal, the *joyful relativity* of all structure and order" (1984a:124). Bizarre, surprising aspects of human beings are displayed, paraded, exposed. Grotesque couplings, weddings of ill-sorted pairs, take place. All that is holy is ridiculed; blasphemy becomes permissible, desirable, transformative. Carnival "opens and sanctifies" the world turned inside-out and upside-down (Bakhtin 1984a:122–27).

Bakhtin's notion of carnival has, in recent years, traveled far and wide, in the humanities and social sciences. Its value, as theory, is recognizable in its power of offering "a dazzling glimpse of the obvious" (Arendt's phrase): it confirms itself as revelatory by retroactively making obvious a set of relations that may have been so entirely unthinkable that they did not emerge as a problem to be investigated. What becomes obvious, in the refracted Bakhtinian light of carnival, is the profound interrelation of a set of motifs, images, and issues that reappear in Myerhoff's writing, early and late, as separated categories. *Bakhtin's four components of carnival—free contact, eccentricity, mésalliances, and profanation—correspond in Myerhoff's texts, respectively, to communitas, liminality, paradox, and "fighting" or deflating commentary.* Myerhoff does not unify these carnivalesque elements in a master-concept, but they are all brought into play, and in relation to each other, through narratives that profoundly enter into the "carnival sense of the world" (Bakhtin 1984a:122). The pervasiveness of the "carnival spirit" in her writing is the source of the "miraculous and liberating effect" (Montale's phrase for the impact of the artistic image) that these texts have upon readers.

This problem—the character and status of carnival elements in Myerhoff's texts and, more generally, in ethnographic narratives; carnival elements not only as content, but as *form-giving* content of scholarly case studies—warrants thorough analysis. Here, I can do no more than suggest the extent to which Myerhoff appeals to readers in and through a carnivalization of ethnography, by offering instances of images of carnival in her writing, early and late. These would include: the essay that contrasts carnivalized social practices among hippies and Huichols (1975:33–67); the great scene of running from paradise in *Peyote Hunt,* after the names of all things have been reversed, and the pilgrims have become "like circus clowns" (1974:147–68); the carnivalized boardwalk in *Number Our Days,* with its bizarre and surprising procession of social types (1980:83–84); the old people's tales, including memories of shtetl life that superficially cite aspects of carnivalized social life and owe their origin as much to Myerhoff's authorial intention as to the actual reminiscences of the old people, i.e., "a carnival came to town" (1980:85); life histories laced with parodic motifs of the learning-years of little people, i.e., "He went right off to the Judenstrasse and met some very nice people. They started him out in life by teaching him to become a thief, but an honest thief" (1980:115); profound problem-posing dialogues, particularly with Shmuel: in one instance that is openly presented as an act of discovery and imagination, this takes the form of a "threshold dialogue," where a living truth-seeker converses with a dead ancestor figure (1980:228–31), the dialogue at the threshold being one of the classical forms of carnivalized literature (Bakhtin 1984a:129–60). The juxtaposition of death and renewal, which is at the heart of all carnival performances, is spectacularly demonstrated in the funeral procession / protest march that ends in the celebration of the one hundredth birthday of one of the Center members ("'Life Not Death in Venice': Its Second Life," in this volume).

These are memorable and vivid instances. Myerhoff's most profound description of the carnivalization of social life occurs in her narration and analysis of great disputations that threaten to unravel Center life and microevents that are buried in a slanted word or meaning. Here, her discovery that carnivalized talk is *the* process of social life among these old Yiddish-speaking Jews has a Bakhtinian depth and richness, and it opens up specific interpretations of astonishing freshness and complexity. She understands the dialogic life of the elders as Bakhtin understands—formulates—the dialogic relation between Dostoevsky and his characters: "As major heroes Dostoevsky portrays only those people in his work with whom the argument has not yet ended (for indeed it has not yet ended in the world)" (1984a:284). This emphasis is brilliantly carried in Myerhoff's descriptions of and commentaries on the disputatious, kibitzing, quarreling talk in which all persons and positions are questioned; this is the talk that must never come to an end or reach a final conclusion because "we fight to keep warm" (1980:184, 188) and because "Among Center people, all talk is an intrinsic good" (1980:125).

Carnivalistic argumentation, joined to a decrowning narrative, is exemplified in the description of the rise and subsequent downfall of the young-old Center president, Kominsky (1980:118–52). Another instance of carnivalized talk as Center-threatening macroevent is the hilarious, grim cursing match between Sadie and Anna, whom the Center members are not so modern as to deem entirely lacking in the potentially catastrophic power of the witch; Anna's curse is the plausible cause of Sadie's sickness. Myerhoff juxtaposes this unsayable superstition, which determines the coded form of the old people's debate, with the professional language of the psychologist who is brought in to help them and who keeps missing the point. Here, Myerhoff carnivalistically parodies and comically stages the language game of group therapy as she displays and investigates the power of word-magic. This text links dialogism and carnivalization in its form (which dramatizes the mésalliance of different types of social discourse) and in its content (which narrates the power of traditional folk belief in contemporary urban social life).

Of greater importance, for the understanding of the place of carnivalized talk in the culture of Yiddishkeit, is a motif that appears in *Number Our Days*, but has been thinned away from the ethnographic essays; this is the impious, critical, satiric, debasing commentary that profanes all Center events, no matter how lofty. Every effort at transcendence is unmasked, relentlessly (often by Shmuel). Each major cultural performance is interrupted and/or exposed by whispered repartees and answerings-back of those on the sidelines, quick and laconic critics who sardonically communicate to the anthropologist why and how she must not be "fooled" by this or that ridiculous or pretentious assertion. This continual profanation serves to set off and heighten those rare moments when even the critics are silenced, and (nearly) everyone in the hall is swept up by a noble and ennobling emotion, as in the "awe" that follows Jacob's apparent control over the moment of his death.

It is not possible to comprehend the full semantic force of the figure of liminality in Myerhoff's writing unless it is recognized that, in these texts, it has not lost its connection with carnivalized talk and other carnival elements with which it is brought into combination and contact. Thus, although Myerhoff sets it off as a privileged category, she always writes of it as a constituent feature of a larger process: the specific character that liminality has here arises from its inseparable linkage to the joyous and liberating process of carnival. Its origin in the novice's fearful passage between stable social statuses and categories is left behind. The solemn, terrifying, pedagogical aspect of the liminal position, and its centrality in a socializing process that reproduces the official relations of the culture, are erased or downplayed. In place of this we get the shocking, bizarre, often hilarious, critical acting-out (in all senses) of suppressed truths, positions, possibilities: a figure of speech in which the meanings of coming out of the closet and social-scientific speculation are equally available. The range of senses in which this term is actively used bespeaks Myerhoff's carnivalization of the technical term itself.

In Myerhoff's writing, the discourse of marginality acquires its specific (high-spirited) character and its broad appeal because of its immersion in the carnival traditions of the oppressed, through which the genius of folk humor enacted its ritualized subversions against the official worldview and the social order (Bakhtin 1984b:71–98). Myerhoff's ethnographic accounts of marginal people and their cultural practices construct marginality in terms of cultural resistance: these texts celebrate the holiday times when subordinated populations turn the social enclaves in which they are ghettoized into a spiritual refuge, where they symbolically overturn the injurious order of everyday life. In the figures of the liminal "specialist in disorder" and the kibitzing pariah, marginality is represented as a potentially joyous, endlessly vitalizing, carnivalized break with business-as-usual.

However, Myerhoff describes the break with the dominant culture in and through a narrative paradigm that seeks to assimilate it to hegemonic values: she retails a wholesale carnival sense of the world in terms of individual "success stories." This extraordinarily complicated and unintended dimension of her writing crosses over into the realm of the obvious, once certain categorical separations are broken open.

Earlier, I spoke of the position that the key tropes of marginality take up, with respect to the dominant system of evaluation: they turn the conventional ladder of success upside-down, and re-position the bottom-dog at the top. What never appears in these pages is the proposal—intrinsic to Jewish socialism—to throw down the ladder itself and break its rungs: none of the dissident voices in these texts questions the authority of the "success story" as a conformity-producing value system.

Myerhoff goes against conventional value judgments in representing "stupid" old women and working-class socialist old men as superior people: superior—and her personal narrative subdues the reader's skepticism—to her: a professor of anthropology. All our assumptions about educated mobility, and the relation of the professional middle-class to working-class immigrant culture, are challenged here. And yet, Myerhoff doesn't go so far as to interrogate the "success story" in terms of which she valorizes the disdained Center folk.

What I have here called "the success story" is an "assumed part" of the discourse in the ethnographic essays and *Number Our Days:* a narrative structure that Myerhoff uses with so little knowledge and control of its status in her writing that it is more accurate to say, in the manner of deconstructionism, that is uses her. And precisely because the "success story" that "comes naturally" to Myerhoff in the act of writing, converges with "our" assumptions about the nature of "the good," we miss its determining force: it is what Bakhtin, and Jameson after him, calls an "ideologeme" (Bakhtin/Medvedev 1985:17; Jameson 1981:86–88).

A perusal of Myerhoff's texts, and particularly "We Don't Wrap Herring in a Printed Page" (in this volume), will persuade the reader that she fetishizes the word "success." It is used with incantatory insistence, an enchanting term of legitimation for her. As an ideological structure, "success" colors the content and shapes the form of the cultural description of many and varied objects: everything from the presentation of the persuasive powers of ritual to the influential notion of "old age as a career"—one in which the fortunate few attain great wisdom and prestige—are emplotted as success stories.

This mix of the conventionalist narrative structure of success and the carnivalized re-allocation of places within the same old story indicates, with rhetorical specificity, the contradictory discursive and social location from which these texts represent marginality. This problem is lived through and written about under the sign of the "guilty privilege" which these texts want to confess (1980:26–28, 91–92; "Surviving Stories," in this volume), and to overcome, in moves that rhetorically bestow spiritually privileged status upon the elders. Every move Myerhoff makes to erase the distance and difference between herself and the old people further compounds the difficulty.

And the difficulty—the thing that she is not permitted to see—is this: that the author of these texts valorizes the old people from two opposing positions, that of Carnival and that of the Success Story. These two antagonistic forms of social evaluation each carry on a separated status-shift on behalf of the old people. Side by side, these cultural forms/ narrative structures raise up the old people to new heights, yet each system not only denies the other's activity in the text, but represses the intense ideological and rhetorical conflict between them. The reader is profoundly moved by the impassioned polemic on behalf of a "disadvantaged group," and, with Myerhoff, loses sight of the actual social process from which the contradictory positions came into the text. In the dispute between Carnival and the story of the Success Ladder, cultural resistance (of those who don't have equal access to climb up) seeks to destroy the evaluative legitimacy of those with the power (to perpetuate their ascendancy). Inscribed in the contending evaluative paradigms of these texts, is Myerhoff's—and many readers', including my own—actual contradictory social location in a class-divided society.

The Real Transmission of Fictive Traditions

The culture they had invented to meet their present circumstances in old age was bricolage in the best sense—an assortment of symbols, customs, memories, and rituals, blending in a highly ecumenical spirit; they used something from all layers of their history: Old World, Yiddish, Jewish, modern, American, Californian, secular, and sacred. They knew that improvisation and invention were essential, but like all people they needed to convince themselves that these solutions were proper, authentic, believable, and occasionally traditional. Their need for such persuasions, and for being visible, coincided with their naturally performative bent, resulting in a highly dramatic self-presentational culture that was extroverted and often touched with a frenzy of desperation.

—Barbara Myerhoff, "'Life Not Death in Venice': Its Second Life"

Ritual may do much more than mirror existing social arrangements and existing modes of thought. It can act to reorganize them or even help to create them.

—Barbara Myerhoff and Sally Falk Moore,
"Secular Ritual: Forms and Meanings"

The value of Barbara Myerhoff's contribution can be fully recognized and asserted only if it is made against the grain of our usual canonizing gestures. She was not generally acclaimed to be a "major" figure. Geertz, for instance, in an apparently off-handed inventory, includes her among Victor Turner's "followers" (1983a:28). This evaluation does, in fact, describe Myerhoff's position in relation to Turner and to Geertz himself. But it does something else that I want to challenge here. It invokes the notion of a hierarchical system or "great tradition" within which Myerhoff is consigned, with a somewhat bemused and gentlemanly condescension, to a subordinate and negligible rank: one of the many unnamed researchers whose contributions are aggregated to the "remarkable series of works" produced by a seminal master.

In challenging Geertz's evaluation of Myerhoff, I do not want to claim for her the status of "major" writer, but rather to transvalue the dominant categories of evaluation, in a description that recognizes the position and affirms the value of "minor" writers. There has been wide agreement among Myerhoff's colleagues that the contribution that she made to cultural studies is profound. I share this view, and in support of it I argue here that it is a contribution that could have been made only by a "minor" writer. Myerhoff took hold of mainstream discourse in the human sciences and moved it "toward a minor literature." I am taking this contestatory notion of the "minor" writer and the literature she produces from Deleuze and Guattari, who construct it in their reading of Kafka. On this view, the notion of "a minor literature" has to do with the writing produced by a member of a minority group in a major language (1986:16–17). Myerhoff qualifies as a "minor" writer, in Deleuze and Guattari's privileged sense of the term, in that she speaks of things that the dominant culture holds sacred—creativity, human development, community—from a contradictory position.

The notion that cultural creativity and knowledge production can best be understood as a narrative concerning a genius or an extraordinary individual still haunts social thought, and Myerhoff was hardly exempt from its appeal. But the importance of her work is inseparable from the ferocity and narrative splendor with which she contested this position and offered an alternative description and evaluation of the making of culture.

This alternative position is powerfully, albeit ambivalently, presented in Myerhoff's ethnographic essays, which investigate cultural creativity as a *social* process, but it is effectively denied in what is usually considered her major work, *Number Our Days*. In the latter text, cultural creativity is construed as the product of the extraordinary individual, who is—in the face of the book's avowed feminism—male. The essays, on the other hand, in their exhilarating and elegant analyses of collective acts of imagination, offer an implicit critique of what may be called the great man theory of cultural production. That Myerhoff does not make the critique explicit is a sign of the conflicted character of her writing. Her texts, it must never be forgotten, are vehement in their gestures of subordination and allegiance to Geertz and his views. Myerhoff as ethnographic scholar is reluctant to recognize what she knows, not with her writing hand, but on the other hand.

And what she knows, what she lived through in collaborative relationship with theater artists and others, is the value of "cultural democracy."[8] This term indicates the dynamic counter-position from which these

---

8. Among Myerhoff's closest friends and collaborators were politically engaged artists who were either members of, or affiliated with, the Alliance for Cultural Democracy. These included Deena Metzger, a playwright, poet, and activist who was Myerhoff's confidante, critic, and all-around dialogic partner; Naomi Newman, the founding director of A Traveling Jewish Theater, with which Myerhoff worked as a consultant; Arthur Strimling, an actor and director with whom Myerhoff cotaught workshops on ritual and storytelling at NYU and the Hunter/Brookdale Center on Aging; and Lynne Littman, who directed Myerhoff's two films, *Number Our Days* and *In Her Own Time*. Her close personal and professional relationship with scholars of performance studies, particularly Richard Schechner, who founded and directed the Performance Group, is obviously closely connected with this dimension of her work.

texts subvert their allegiance to propriety: to the stance of a value-free inquiry. It refers specifically to the program and practices of artists and scholars who have been professionally engaged in recuperating and culturally performing the "lost histories" of marginalized communities and groups. Myerhoff, as teacher, colleague, consultant, and collaborator, was actively aligned with this position. And traces of this alignment are evident in every aspect of her work. For instance, in requiring that her students go back to their informants, read them the life histories they have taken, and incorporate the informant's revisions and amplifications, Myerhoff is adapting, for classroom use, the principles of the movement for cultural democracy: that the people whose life-histories are told in a theater piece or other project of community documentation have an active hand in shaping the work, so that it reflects their point of view, and that the formed work be given back to the community from which it arose, so that they can use it—as Myerhoff put it in a late talk on storytelling—"to erase the oblivion" (see "Life History as Integration," in this volume).

Cultural democracy, as an orienting position, does no enter her writing directly and under its own (political) name. But it is a reservoir of lived, principled experience from which intensity enters the writing: it is a source of what readers have registered as Myerhoff's moral authority. Its valuations saturate and enliven her case studies of ritual and storytelling among the elderly: it is palpable, for instance, in the characteristic emphasis upon giving attention to community-making acts of cultural creativity of marginalized people. It becomes possible to hear the ideological source of Myerhoff's unvoiced position by comparing the key concerns and emphases of her essays with those that Raymond Williams puts forward in openly arguing for a democratic reception of cultural works:

> A culture, while it is being lived, is always in part unknown, in part unrealized. The making of a community is always an exploration, for consciousness cannot precede creation, and there is no formula for unknown experience. A good community, a living culture, will, because of this, not only make room for but actively encourage all and any who can contribute to the advance in consciousness which is the common need. Wherever we have started from, we need to listen to others who started from a different position. We need to consider every attachment, every value, with

our whole attention; for we do not know the future, we can never be sure of what may enrich it; we can only, now, listen to and consider whatever may be offered and take up what we can. (1983:334–35)

What Myerhoff has to teach us—and this goes beyond the purview of Geertz's canon-erecting division of cultural creativity into upper and lower classes—concerns *our* need to listen to others who have started from a different position and the *mutual* enrichment that follows from bestowing attention upon the cultural other.

Myerhoff's sympathy with what Walter Benjamin calls "the tradition of the oppressed" is evident in her "imaginative identification" (1980:19) with the old Yiddish-speaking Jews whom she studies, and in her desire to admit their distinct accent and alternative evaluation into her texts (1980:30–31). The barbed, sardonic Yiddish word of the old people, which owes as much to their lifelong socialism as it does to their Jew-ishness, is crucial in constituting the richness of Myerhoff's narratives, and goes beyond the utterances of informants to inflect the ethnographer's discourse. This relation of alignment, whose intonation ranges from respect to frustration to veneration, stands in opposition to the skepticism of the social scientist whose orientation marks her allegiance to the dominant culture and the ruling discourse of her profession.

Contradiction, as I have previously shown, characterizes and shapes Myerhoff's texts. Earlier, I have offered analyses of two major discursive strategies through which the antagonism of opposing positions is neu-tralized in her writing. Contradictory descriptions of creative agency are *split off and normalized within different genres.* Contradictory evalua-tions are effectively *blended into a seeming unity* through the construction of a "discourse of marginality" that melds the value systems of opposing narrative paradigms (the "success story" versus the carnivalized narra-tive). The use of "narrator's narration" is another means of discursively blending different voices and blurring their distinct evaluative intonations. In the first instance, the object of representation is the locus of creativity (the dominant and exceptionally gifted individual versus the collaborative interrelation of Center members in a creative social process). In this instance, the contradictory narrative and theoretical descriptions are not permitted to come directly into contact with each other. In the second instance, the object of representation is a socially devalued group: people who are old, poor, Jewish, mostly female, and working-class immigrants.

This devaluation is contested from two different ideological positions whose antagonism is embedded and buried in the same text. The Americanism of the "success story" and the limited dissidence of the carnivalized narrative, which valorizes "troublemaking" and cultural resistance, both "emit" positive qualities that adhere to the affirming image of the "elders" that Myerhoff constructs. In the writing, the contradictory sources of positive evaluations disappear in the portraits of "successful aging"—of struggling against and surmounting bodily ills and social afflictions—that "win" the reader's admiration.

The strategies of splitting off contradictory positions and conventionalizing them within separated genres and of blurring them into a seeming unity both depend upon and point toward a third strategy of neutralizing difference that is more extreme and, in the range of discursive mechanisms that it enlists in its service, more complex and difficult than the strategies previously analyzed. Here, the whole terrain of contradiction is brought under the textual regime of repression. In this instance, the object of representation is ideology itself. One sign of the repression that (inconsistently) reigns over this writing can be immediately offered in evidence. Although the Center members identified themselves as socialists, Communists or "progressives" throughout their lives, these terms and the signs of their continuing political engagement are almost entirely erased from the ethnographic essays. In *Number Our Days,* ideologically radical utterance and declarations of political affiliation are permitted to enter the text, but they are separated in brief, verbatim sections titled "Bobbe-Meyseh" (literally, "grandmothers' stories," a pejorative term in Yiddish, denoting the exaggerated and unenlightened lore of unlettered old wives) or framed by anthropological commentary that devalues, distances (in time as well as significance) and segregates this area of activity, which saturated all aspects of Yiddish immigrant culture.

Ideological differences between Myerhoff and the Center members are neutralized through the use of what I would describe as a number of (overlapping) "mechanisms of textual repression." These include: omission and/or the use of substitute terms that render the banned concepts unrecognizable; "bad abstraction," in which disavowed aspects of the object of study are split off, under a generalization that categorically writes off or masks these elements[9]; and, finally, the use of a large

---

9. "Bad abstraction" is used by Raymond Williams and others as a technical term in the analysis and evaluation of discourse. It describes forms of general-

narrative structure—which I would describe as "the allegory of Americanization"—that retails the wholesale myth of "the one-generation proletariat" in the telling of lives, and that systematically "disappears" the collective memory of the Center members' cultural politics from the ethnographic essays.

Repression, which seeks to eliminate the source of conflict, can at best effectively cover it up; it cannot, however, evacuate all signs of conflict: these take shape as contradictions that are textual effects of repression and carry out its aim of rendering the source of conflict invisible. The very signs of repression, then, make the critique that a repressive discursive strategy is at work here appear implausible. It is necessary to specify how the veil that contradiction throws over this writing serves to ward off the reader's potential doubt and scrutiny.

All of Myerhoff's ethnographic work emphatically transfigures low-status subjects by representing them as "elders," the repository of high-status knowledge, practices, and qualities. This contestation of the dominant social evaluation of the old people allies itself with the "face work" that motivates all their acts of cultural creativity. The power of Myerhoff's work lies in its discovery and analysis of this motive—the subaltern group's struggle for social dignity—as it takes shape in a variety of forms, including storytelling and autobiographical writing, secular ritual, muralmaking, "creating difficulties, making scenes," demonstrating, and fighting with each other as part of the process of democratic decision-making and role allocation in Center social life. The problem can be summed as follows: Even as this writing cites and valorizes the old people's cultural creativity, describing it in terms of cultural resistance, it represses the actual cultural history in and through which they became the people they are. What is repressed, first, is a highly politicized culture that belongs not only to their past, but that immediately pervades their daily lives and that decisively informs their practices in form and ideological content. What is also necessarily repressed is the author's (ideological) discomfort, if not antagonism, to the old people's worldview. Their gestures of opposition are described with memorable specificity, but their meanings are conventionalized through acts of interpretation

---

ization that mask processes, relationships, and structures that are intrinsic to the object of study. "Bad abstraction" separates and suppresses knowledge of key elements that constitute the object of study. It is often used, as in this instance, to depoliticize discourse in the human sciences.

that substitute existentialist, aesthetic, and religious terms for political utterances and activities, and that bring the actual social history of the group into conformity with the hegemonic narrative of Americanization.

What is at stake here, viewed in terms of the discursive (ideological) struggle that is repressed in these texts, is the erasure of the left-wing cultural politics of this group of Jewish working-class immigrants by the liberal, middle-class discourse through which Myerhoff aligns herself with the reader whom she is addressing. "'Life Not Death in Venice'" is a case study in the art of depoliticizing and reenchanting the culture of this group. Here, the concept of definitional ceremonies, which offers analytic access to the social process that determines cultural production, operates as a form of "bad abstraction." In formulating the concept of definitional ceremonies, Myerhoff explicitly distinguishes it from Turner's concept of social dramas *on political grounds*. Like poetry, definitional ceremonies make nothing happen, whereas social dramas settle disputes and realign social relationships. Social dramas are political processes and have political outcomes; definitional ceremonies may have political origins—they begin in a "crisis of invisibility" caused "by a more powerful outside society"—but they have no political consequence.

Here, the rhetorical power of these texts, and the spell cast by "the mechanisms of textual repression," can be plainly demonstrated. Myerhoff's narrative description of definitional ceremonies, which adheres more concretely to the Center members' actual practices, flatly contradicts her theoretical description—and yet this has escaped the attention of her readers. Almost immediately after disavowing the possibility that the old people's definitional ceremony can make any actual impact on "the outside society," she writes "that the elders succeeded in altering more than their own version of themselves," as a result of their ceremonial "protest march." City officials began to implement a previously unenforced ordinance, "providing a four-block section [on the boardwalk] where the old people could walk without fear of traffic. A limited but decisive victory" ("'Life Not Death in Venice,'" in this volume).

Nothing the Center members do is construed in terms of politics; everything they do is subtracted from the realm of politics and credited to the account of existential self-affirmation or spirituality or imaginative activity. A fully adequate account would seek to show the interrelation of all these transformational processes in the lives and practices of the Center members.

The Center members "organized a protest march" after one of them was "killed by invisibility," run over by a bicyclist who claims he did not see her. Myerhoff evokes a scene in which the street-theater techniques of the anti-war movement are melded with signs of the old people's participation in the workers' movement. They carry placards whose Jewish symbolism Myerhoff traces. Of equal importance here is their cultural history of activism, and especially their historical role on the picket lines: one of the major contributions of this generation to life in the United States is the struggle they waged to form effective unions, such as the ILGWU (International Ladies Garment Workers Union). Myerhoff rewrites the Center members' protest march—their term is used at the moment when the event is being organized, and then dropped—as a procession, a secular ritual. It is not one or the other, but both: what is crucial is the intertwining of religion and politics. The problem remains to see the intersection of the sphere of the spirit and of politics, and to move toward an adequate account of this difficult terrain of culture, where the resistance of subaltern peoples often takes shape. This is a problem of urgent general significance: witness the role of the Catholic Church in the Polish Solidarity Movement and in revolutionary struggles in Latin America, the role of the black church in the civil rights movement in the United States, and the forms of spiritual resistance that Gandhi developed in the struggle to decolonize India. Our understanding of the culture of the Center is enhanced when it is embedded in the long history of emancipatory struggles of peoples whose links with religious tradition remain strong. For these old working-class Jews, marching with placards was at once a familiar and a sacred activity. It was common among them—Myerhoff records this fact in *Number Our Days*—to tell their children that the one thing that must be said in remembrance of them by the rabbis at their funerals is that they never crossed a picket line in their lives.

Repressing the formative experience of their youths from their life-histories means that its inescapable re-emergence in daily life has to be explained away when it cannot be simply omitted. In the mural, to which Myerhoff offers an otherwise stunning semiotic exegesis, one of the panels shows five women marching in a line, carrying signs ("'Life Not Death in Venice,'" in this volume). Myerhoff's dehistoricizing interpretation of this image in the group's "collective self-portrait" appears unquestionable, since it is based on the testimony and draws on the authority of Myerhoff's informant, herself an East European Jew who, as the group's art teacher, organized the mural:

Mrs. Nutkiewicz remarks: "And this is, you know, the Liberation movement. It started to grow at this time. Here are the suffragist women with their signs, 'Strike,' 'Fight,' 'Eight Hours of Work,' 'Arbeiten,' all in Yiddish. You see, they are in long dresses, heels, the old-fashioned dress but they are modern people, fighting for the improvement of their working conditions. Because after the sweatshops came the unions. That was their doing. They fought for themselves, for freedom and social justice, but everyone benefited." The merging of strikers and suffragettes is an interesting note, suggesting the peoples' identification with common causes for which they must struggle in their pursuit of freedom and social justice. Trade unions and the fight for women's rights merge here. That primarily women are depicted in the protest march is not unusual when we consider that all the painters of the mural were women. Clearly, it is the privilege of artists everywhere to personalize and localize the great themes, embuing the Great Tradition with the specific forms and personnel that give the Little Tradition its vivacity.

The overall discussion at several points makes explicit the elders' free interpretation of history, shaping and idealizing it to the level of near myth.

This final interpretation displaces onto the elders the idealization that Myerhoff's writing implements. This explication of the panel carries a good thing—the constructionalist position that construes culture as a symbol-system, a product of the collective imagination—too far, and turns the actual history of the group into a laudable, quite understandable, self-affirming piece of fiction: a work of self-idealization, bricolage, a near-myth.

In the culture of Jewish socialism, feminism and unionism were inseparably linked: the women who participated in the formation of the Bund (the major socialist organization in Jewish life) had a developed feminist position and were the first feminists in Jewish social life. That primarily women are depicted here celebrates the role of women in the heroic phase of the labor movement. Inspired by Clara Lemlich—"I am a working girl. . . . I am tired of listening to speakers who talk in generalities. . . . I offer a resolution that a general strike be declared—now"—twenty thousand shirtwaist workers walked off their jobs. This "uprising" of teen-age "girls" and young women initiated the era of great strikes (1909 until the war years).

> In the immigrant world, the shirtwaist makers had created inde-scribable excitement: these were our daughters. The strike came to be called "the uprising of the twenty thousand," and the phrase should be taken as more than socialist or Jewish rhetoric, for indeed it was an uprising of *people who discovered on the picket lines their sense of dignity and self* [emphasis added]. New emotions swept the East Side, new perceptions of what immigrants could do, even girls until yesterday mute. "*Unzere vunderbare farbrente meydelkh,*" "our wonderful fervent girls," an old-timer called them. (Howe 1976:300)

The panel of women on a picket line represents a "peak experience" in the collective history of the group, and as such receives a place of honor in their collective self-representation. Mrs. Nutkiewicz, who came to the United States after the Holocaust, that is, more than three decades after the historical moment presented in the panel, belongs to a younger generation and another historical experience. The dehistoricizing inter-pretation begins in her remarks, which subsume the workers' movement under the category of the struggle for women's liberation. Myerhoff's interpretation goes on to credit the feminism of the Center members and to discredit their actual participation in the workers' movement. Howe's passage makes clear that this generation's historical acts produced effects of cultural and self-creation that are consistent with Myerhoff's linkage of resistance, creative social and imaginative processes, and the main-tenance of a sense of self-worth in the immigrant world. An historically accurate reading of this group's cultural productions initially complicates but finally strengthens the case these essays make for viewing the capacity for late-life creativity and for resolution of late-life identity conflicts as inseparable from membership in a group whose collective history is a continuing source of meaning and value. The contribution of ideology to well-being in old age is evident in Myerhoff's writing. It is therefore necessary to present and analyze the actual range of the lived meanings and values that constitute the Center members' worldview.

This critique, even as it describes what Jameson has called the "politi-cal unconscious" of Myerhoff's essay, demonstrates the validity of the central interpretation that Myerhoff makes here. In a brilliant deep-structural gloss of the mural and the procession, she delineates the commonalities between these two "texts," and argues that they owe their origin to the collective history that is symbolically represented in them. Thus, it advances Myerhoff's thesis to show that memories of the picket line shape the form and content of both the mural and the procession.

The erasure of the ideological formation of these elderly Jews, and the mass movements within which this took place, leads to a loss of richness in the account that these essays offer of key areas of inquiry, such as ethnic identity, the learning process of this group, and bricolage. One final instance must suffice to exemplify what is lost in repressing the ideologically unpalatable cultural history of the old people. In an apparently incontrovertible and innocuous interpretation, Myerhoff writes: "Some individuals had expressed their Judaism by joining Yiddish political and cultural groups" ("We Don't Wrap Herring in a Printed Page," in this volume). In the context of these essays, which present an overall pattern of omitting or mystifying the character of the group's politics, "Yiddish" is used as a term of concealment. And the character of Yiddish immigrant culture as a whole is occluded in this formulation. "Some individuals" rhetorically thins out the substantial segment of the immigrant community that participated in the socialist and workers' movements. The significance of these struggles among East European Jews exceeded the actual number of activists. The values of socialism and unionism saturated everyday life in modern Yiddish culture, and constituted a "mass sentiment" that was intertwined with the ideal of *mentshlichkeit* and that exerted considerable moral authority—an authority bestowed by culture—even on those who were not directly engaged in political or union struggles (Schappes 1978:12–14; Howe 1976:310–24).

The context of the interpretation in question is Myerhoff's analysis of the constituent elements of the group's graduation-siyum ritual. This analysis is implemented under two "axial symbols" or general categories: "Being-a-Jew" and "Learning." The range of social practices covered under the substitute terms of "Yiddish political and cultural groups" are compelled to submit to a higher and more effective order of repression under the rhetorical dispensation of "bad abstraction." Here, Myerhoff construes their cultural politics as an expressive vehicle of ethnic identity, which is conflated with their "Judaism," and at the same time categorically segregates this sphere of activity from "Learning." In practice, the whole sphere of Jewish immigrant politics and cultural politics was oriented away from rabbinic Judaism, and it constituted a site of learning which was itself one of the most remarkable cultural creations of working-class Jewish immigrants. The "Yiddish political and cultural groups" included the Bund and the Jewish unions, various Yiddishist organizations that melded the culture of the Bund and the unions (notably the Workman's Circle and the Yiddishist day-school movement), and a range of related activities that were lived through as a continuous social process of learning. To subsume this historically innovative sphere of practice under a category of identity tied to rabbinic traditionalism, and categorically to segregate it from learning, denies and misrepresents two of the most important collective achievements of Yiddish immigrant culture: the development of a secular concept of person in which the Judaism of the *halakha* (religious law) was transformed into the Jewishness of the *mentsh;* and the development of a social process of learning within and by the Jewish socialist and Jewish workers' movements, a process in which the traditional valuation and practice of talmudic study were melded (in Russia) with such practices as the illegal study circles and libraries that formed a generation of Bundist worker-intellectuals, including Myerhoff's Shmuel and Jacob.

Inseparably related within this workers' sphere of culture were the socialist Yiddish newspapers, which aimed at educating and organizing the masses, the so-called lecture system (often offered by socialist discussion clubs and study circles, or by unions), the 300 cafes on the Lower East Side, which served the same function for Jewish factory workers that the cafes on the Left Bank had for students, artists, and intellectuals: as a warm, well-lighted place for ideologically intense talk on art, life, and politics. Ronald Sanders has described these inseparable aspects of a common culture as an ad hoc university without walls (1969:67). In *Number Our Days,* Myerhoff offers extensive life histories of Jewish working-class elderly who construe this experience in terms of learning: "The union was my college" (1980:116). The popular culture of these Jews was a sphere of extraordinary cultural creativity, in which the project of changing the world was inseparably linked with the pursuit of knowledge. That this whole cultural sphere of worker-created institutions of learning is repressed from Myerhoff's (and most other well-known and highly regarded) texts, although it constitutes the social formation of the people whom she studies, indicates the degree to which middle-class ideology saturates discourse in the human sciences. With the (monumental) exception of Irving Howe, himself a socialist, the mainstream social histories of this group restrict the discussion of their education to what went on in the public schools and yeshivas. The majority of Jewish working-class immigrants attended neither.

What happens in this interpretation, then, is that the break with tradition is conflated with the "return" to tradition. The immense difficulty of the process that these people lived through is, at crucial points of articulation, denied. This process, over a lifetime, involved renegotiating the conflicts between contradictory values, ideologies, and traditions. In this struggle, their radicalism and their Jewishness were lifelong dialogic partners. (Myerhoff's elders were born in the 1880s and 1890s; they were adolescents and young adults during the period of socialism's maximum impact, as a political and moral force, upon East European Jews, both in the immigrant community in the United States and the communities of origin in Europe.) The Yiddishkeit they "returned to" in late life, as they increasingly reincorporated aspects of Jewish tradition into the fabric of daily life, was not the Judaism they left in their youths. The break with orthodoxy was decisive; but the unfinalizable contention between opposing principles worked a continuous transformation, itself informed by history, upon their secularism, their Jewishness, and their politics.

It is necessary to reclaim this whole contested cultural history in order to understand the process that Myerhoff studies as late-life bricolage. This process, through which fragments of various ideological discourses are resynthesized and renewed to meet present circumstances, is grounded in the defining gesture of their early years: the radical break with the religion, and the continuing affiliation with the culture, of observant parents and communities. However, as Max Weinreich, Heschel, Zborowski and Herzog, and others have emphasized, in the cultural household of Ashkenaz, religion and culture were not marked off into separate areas of activity, but constituted the living space of everyday life. "For the shtetl, Judaism was not a religion but a way of life" (Zborowski and Herzog 1962:216; see also Weinreich 1972:282, and Heschel 1972:67–86). In practice, then, it was never quite possible totally to discard the religious system while retaining the Jewish language(s) and culture. This cultural fact, no less than the history of the immigrants' (revolutionary and pogrom-ridden) times compelled them to be bricoleurs from their youths.

The culture of this group in their old age, like the culture of their youths, was worked up through a complex and changing mix of Moses and Marx, with bits and pieces of Americanism thrown in.[10] This was, specifically, the culture that was created in the late nineteenth and early twentieth centuries in Yiddish-speaking communities that were saturated with the practices and values of the Jewish Labor Bund and the (inter-related) workers' and Yiddishist movements. The description and critique of Myerhoff's work that I am offering here seeks to assert this broken connection: the cultural creativity of this group, which Myerhoff mag-nificently describes and celebrates, is linked with the various forms of cultural resistance and cultural politics that are specific to their history as Ashkenazic Jews *and* as working-class participants in the popular socialism and unionism of their youths. The long crisis of ideological struggle and fragmentation within the Jewish community was the "school" in which people of this group and period learned to be bri-coleurs. If they used the arts of bricolage to repair, heal or (for a brief time) make whole the coats, egos, life stories, belief systems, rituals, or forums of self-governance that they found tattered in old age, it was because bricolage had always been their metier: it was intrinsic to their personal and historical task. In negotiating the break between the piety of their parents and their own secular, acutely self-conscious and polit-ically-founded modernism, they forged their distinct form of hybrid Jew-ishness along with the culture of Jewish socialism. Here, the traditional folkways and voluntary associations (*khevros*), which socially enacted a profoundly internalized ideal of collective responsibility, were trans-formed by being melded with the socialist emphasis on mutual social responsibility. The history of this extraordinarily difficult making of a usable tradition of struggle—it remained active until the Six Day War—is inscribed in the memories of the generation that Myerhoff studied. The irony of her work is that, in the name of "preserving an endangered

---

10. I am indebted to David Shuldiner for this phrase and for his meticulous documentation and description of the Yiddish working-class culture that this phrase evokes. His dissertation, *Of Moses and Marx: Folk Ideology within the Jewish Labor Movement in the United States,* is based on informant interviews with elderly Yiddish radicals who were members of, or affiliated with, the Israel Levin Senior Center, where Myerhoff did her fieldwork on "the culture of aging and Yiddishkeit." Shuldiner's work focuses on the process through which aspects of Jewish life and socialism were intertwined to create a "folk ideology" that constituted the actual culture of this generation of Yiddish working-class immi-grants. His long quotations of these elderly radical Jews, and his project as a whole, constitute an act of homage to the tradition of Yiddishkeit in which he was raised.

tradition," she has actually consigned a crucial segment of it to the very oblivion that she invokes as a source of the immense pathos that her writing communicates.[11]

All the contradictions through which discourse analysis can demonstrate the hidden dialogic conflicts of Myerhoff's writing are inseparable from the work's profound generativity and its centrality in the literature on late-life creativity (Moody 1984:231–36; Moody and Cole 1986:247–73). These conflicts arise from the fullness of the author's contradictory commitments to the position of the marginalized elders and to the position of the liberal, middle-class reader whose professional discourse is given the last word. Within the conventions of ethnographic realism, this writing is tortured into self-contradiction by the cry of solidarity it feels compelled to silence, in the name of scientific rigor. The moments of exaltation—of *communitas*—enter the texts as if they had come from

---

11. Here, I want to take a suggestion made by my editors and colleagues (Colin Day, Andrew Achenbaum, and Thomas Cole) and discuss my relationship with Barbara Myerhoff. "The introduction," Tom Cole wrote, "is written in the third person, and its 'implied author' (to borrow Wayne Booth's phrase) doesn't bear any recognizable relationship to Myerhoff. But we know that the 'real author' must have an intense and complicated relationship to Myerhoff—living and dead. The issue seems unavoidable." It seems unavoidable, I think, because the difference between the biographical author and the authorial voice of the editor-critic is cast under suspicion by a contradiction that comes from elsewhere: the introductory essay offers an intense and complicated evaluation of Myerhoff's work, in which the severity of the critique stands side-by-side in unreconciled relationship with high praise. Does this mixed evaluation reflect aspects of the "real relationship" between two people who knew each other and worked closely together? This is the implicit question that my editors and colleagues are asking me to address, in their concern that, in the absence of any recognition of this issue and of a personal statement regarding it, readers may come up with (critical) narratives of their own, to explain just how the scholarly critique and the close personal friendship go or don't go together. My response to the textual problem is to acknowledge it as a real problem, and to epitomize the conflict that it points to by saying: that my loyalty and love of Barbara Myerhoff complicated, burdened, and (at times) opposed my actually permitting myself to communicate what I had discovered through the long study and analysis of her papers; that the values of the scholar came into conflict with the values of the friend, which made writing this introductory text a years' long labor; and that one of the ways in which I dealt with guilt toward my friend was to separate "the man that suffers from the mind that creates" (Eliot's phrase) more emphatically, in prose that told the writer's truth, in the language of scholarship, not because it is the language of disguise, but because it is the conceptual language that made the

elsewhere, from another aspiration toward another "structure of feeling" in another genre. Myerhoff's writing seeks to constitute, within the dominant culture of individualism, a credible collective subject inhabiting a spiritually nurturing community. And this is one of the characteristics that, for Deleuze and Guattari, define "a minor literature":

> It is literature that produces an active solidarity in spite of skepticism; and if the writer is in the margins or completely outside his or her fragile community, this situation allows the writer all the more the possibility to express another possible community and to forge the means for another consciousness and another sensibility; just as the dog of "Investigations" calls out in his solitude to *another science*. (1986:17)

---

analysis and communication of the critique possible. Then, too, what I lived through in getting at and gradually articulating my critique had no place in the introductory text.

A number of different things saw me through this process. First, my sense of obligation to Barbara Myerhoff, as well as to the people who had helped turn the dream of the Myerhoff Center into a reality (Maury Leibovitz, Deena Metzger, Polly Howells, Diane Demeter) required that, one way or another, the task be carried through to completion. Since I was compelled to finish it, I had to do so in a way that didn't violate my sense of integrity, my sense of what was true and real, that is, my sense of vocation as a writer. Without Deena Metzger's active and profound support, in the face of our different readings of Barbara Myerhoff's work, the "values-dilemma" would have been more difficult to bear and work through than it was. I struggled with how much to hold back, and how much to disclose: to communicate my findings felt transgressive to me.

In the first draft of the introduction, I consequently presented the core issue of "lost histories" in so cursory a manner, I buried it, and I repressed any discussion of the "textual mechanisms of repression." The absence of these discussions left the textual critique that appeared elsewhere floating in mid-air, ungrounded, all too readily dismissible. Such backings-off were done at the behest of "Barbara's ghost," a presence in the writer's study, who had to be negotiated with, early on. The final source of empowerment, that enabled me to carry through the writer's task over the objections of the friend, had to do with the nature of my relationship with "the culture of Yiddishkeit," which was and is both personal and professional. To answer adequately the explicit and implicit questions that were posed by my editors and colleagues, I must intertwine my description of my personal and professional relationship to Myerhoff with a description of my relationship to my Yiddish-speaking immigrant grandparents and to the Jewish elderly with whom I have worked for twenty years.

Myerhoff and I became close between 1982 and 1985, during what were to

Myerhoff's writing, with its celebration of feast days, has apparently nothing in common with Kafka's stories, which appropriate the language of scientific reports to document fast days. Yet the points of convergence between them are startling in their specificity and their explanatory power. Both loved Hasidic storytelling and collective cultural performances of Yiddishkeit. Kafka encountered his culture of origin in the Yiddish theater, and Myerhoff found hers in the dramaturgical form of secular rituals. This common interest, by itself, means little. What gives their work a common problematic is that they loved their common culture of origin from *an impassable distance*. Kafka makes this the site and the plot of his narratives: a distance whose impossibility his protagonists minutely survey, as they live through the misfortune of daring to cross it. In this distance, Kafka digs down (constructing burrows) or builds

be the last three years of her life. I was then director of the Institute on Humanities, Arts and Aging at the Hunter/Brookdale Center on Aging, and in this position I was able to arrange to bring her to the Institute for conferences, seminars, and consultations with the faculty and students, both college and graduate students from a range of disciplines as well as the older adults in the Institute's community workshops and "lifelong learning center." Myerhoff was an extraordinarily inspired and inspiring teacher and colleague. Her two residencies at the Brookdale Center on Aging were the high points of my years there. And she returned from the nonstop learning-and-teaching dialogues that she engaged in at Brookdale, and from the seminars in life-history work (cotaught with Arthur Strimling, an actor and theater director with whom we both were working and at whose house we had met), energized and at the same time exhausted. I have heard from a number of people how enriched she felt by her experiences at Brookdale, where she had the freedom to try out workshop ideas that had no place in the anthropology classes she taught back home (at the University of Southern California). For Barbara, being at Brookdale meant collaborating with Arthur Strimling, and working up innovative ways of teaching the process through which definitional ceremonies are collaboratively created. It meant teaching intergenerational—and extraordinarily diverse and interesting— groups, that is, it meant teaching in New York, where refugees from the Holocaust, graduate students in art history, filmmaking, and social work, Brookdale faculty and many others besides signed up for her seminars. It meant being in New York and getting a chance to talk with Isaac Bashevis Singer, Barbara Kirshenblatt-Gimblett, and a host of others, including me. The institutional terrain of a university-based gerontology center was the site of a relationship that went well beyond the projects that we initiated and carried out at Brookdale and within the milieu of humanistic gerontology.

This was due to the range of common interests we shared, and the (impassioned) character of our commitments to the things that we were committed to.

up (constructing the ruined Tower of Babel or the Great Wall of China); where he refuses to be stopped, where he cannot get beyond, he constructs ironies. In this distance, it is possible to locate Myerhoff's situation as a writer. She seeks to resurrect the conditions of membership in a spiritual community on the far side of belief.

Contact with the culture of Yiddish, in the productive life of both these assimilated Jews, serves a kindred function: it inaugurates the phase of their freest, most significant writing. In and through Yiddish, both personally experience a historical process—the breakup of tradition—as a generative anguish. Acculturated through their education into the dominant culture, they are shocked and inspired to discover in the figure of the "shtetl Jew" a living connection with a tradition they had learned to dismiss. Their erased Jewishness is transformed into a voice that can

---

These were, chiefly, poetry and the theater (I was one among many artist friends); anti-nuclear politics, which were of increasing concern to her in the early 1980s; and, finally, our common love of and involvement in the culture of Yiddishkeit. We had first met through our writing. While she was working in a senior center on the West Coast, I was working (as a social worker and writer) in senior centers with Yiddish-speaking old people on the East Coast. She had read *What's Inside You It Shines Out Of You,* my book on conducting writing and reminiscence groups with elderly Jews when it appeared (in 1974), and I, of course, read *Number Our Days* when it was published. For both of us, the sense of sharing a mutual project began in the reading of the other's work. When we met, we began a dialogue that carried with it the promise of a long life of shared endeavors. And, in fact, we immediately set to work, planning occasions and contexts in which the dialogue we cared about—about modern Yiddish culture, and creativity, and survivors' stories, and . . . —could be extended. The time we spent together was brief, hurried, and usually occurred between public events we had planned together. Many of our face-to-face conversations took place in cab rides to and from airports. I mention this because it symbolizes and emphasizes the circumstances of our friendship: fleeting, through heavy traffic. The point I wish to make here is this: Everything, including our personalities, favored the discovery and articulation of all that we shared, loved, and enjoyed in common, and discouraged the discovery and articulation of our differences. There was a strong sense, in our friendship, of being and talking with a friend who could "get" and support what the other was trying to do in her or his life and work.

Barbara Myerhoff was, and this is something that I have heard many of her friends comment on, a great courage-teacher and ally. She was, to me, a generous and loving friend, and a wise one, whose counsel I sought. I felt a profound sense of love and devotion to her. I do now. But this passionate relationship to Barbara Myerhoff was neutralized, to a great extent, during the time that I was

no longer speak the dominant language without a note of protest and of impossible yearning. Kafka and Myerhoff are by temperament fanatics who are too sober for the Hasidic ecstasy they long for; for them, after their encounter with Yiddishkeit, the breakdown of tradition becomes unbearable. Kafka's pseudo-ethnographies and Myerhoff's ethnographic tales are incommensurate sites of loss where the desire for enchantment contends with the sober gaze that disenchants everything it sees. The ghetto walls of the Eastern European Jews are transformed into "The Great Wall of China," and the Mural in the Israel Levin Senior Center is the wall before which Myerhoff stands and decodes by what trafficking in symbols a pariah people survived ("'Life Not Death in Venice': Its Second Life," in this volume).

These narratives, which concern carrying a visionary project across

---

actively writing and revising the introductory essay (between 1988 and 1991). After she died, my working life increasingly began to be devoted to tasks I had undertaken at her request, or that were concomitants of carrying out the responsibilities that she had wanted Deena Metzger and me to share. (These included, for example, arranging for the establishment of the Myerhoff Archive at the University of Southern California, with a microfilm copy of the key papers housed at YIVO.) We had discussed a number of possible book projects "on the culture of aging and Yiddishkeit" during the last six months of her life. Her primary concern was that I complete and prepare for publication two of the lectures that she had given at Brookdale and elsewhere on storytelling. She proposed that these be "joined" with some of my works-in-progress on storytelling. (After her death, I realized that her posthumous texts should be published separately; they will appear under the title *Late Talks and Tales,* with an introduction by Deena Metzger.) We also discussed doing a volume of her published essays. On what turned out to be the last weekend of her life, I flew to California to see her. She was too mortally ill to see me. I spent the time working in her study, compiling the table of contents and coming up with a proposed title for the volume of her ethnographic essays. Diane Wolkstein, one of seven women who were caring for her around the clock, brought this to the hospital to show her and Deena; Barbara liked the title and approved the general outline of this volume. *Remembered Lives: The Work of Ritual, Storytelling, and Growing Older* was the first book project I tackled in 1988, three years after her death, when the Myerhoff Center at YIVO was set up. During the time of our friendship and collaboration, I had read only one of her ethnographic essays ("A Symbol Perfected in Death," a version of the birthday-memorial of Jacob Koved, and not the version included here, which I found in manuscript in her study). In the three years following her death, in preparation for this and other book projects, I started to read through her essays and papers with a sense of growing distress, occasional shock, and increasing anger. That anger is registered in the pages of the introduction in the

great distances and over a period of generations, indicate the final point I want to make, in pursuing this unlikely comparison. Myerhoff emphasized (in her writing, teaching, and conversation) that the transmission of culture was the insufficiently explained social process for which she sought to account in her studies of ritual and storytelling. Inseparable from the various transmissive practices which she deconstructed was the process of making up the meanings that these performances communicated. The theory of ritual that she derived from Turner and Geertz linked the artifice of the form with the fictive character of the content. The work she does in this vein has a strong formalist bias. The (conventionalized) social history is offered, but in a separated "background" account, which does not enter into her theorization of the ritual event. Thus, the invented content of the ritual is viewed as produced by the form itself, which relies upon all kinds of rhetorical and dramaturgical devices.

---

specifying analysis which points to discrepancies between *Number Our Days* and the essays, as well as to the other contradictions that pervade her work, an analysis whose task is to reclaim the "lost histories" that are buried there. As I have suggested earlier, this text was written betwixt and between my love and loyalty to Barbara Myerhoff and the necessity created for me by my love and loyalty to my Yiddish-speaking immigrant grandparents, in whose cultural household I was raised.

My childhood was spent "under the roof of their Yiddishkeit" (Jeffrey Shandler's phrase). Much of my writing life has been devoted to describing my four grandparents and their way of life. Here I will offer only this: my paternal grandfather Yeshieh, a worker-intellectual of the same generation as Shmuel and Jacob, the "heroes" of *Number Our Days,* was (like Jacob) an organizer who worked with the Bund and fought in the revolution of 1905; like Shmuel, he was an autodidact with a scathing tongue (his weapon of choice against power), a Yiddish writer and culture critic. He was blacklisted for the role he played in organizing the leatherworker's union in the United States; he spent his life as a Yiddish writer and educator, one of the founding figures and lifelong activists in the Yiddishist day school movement, which was situated within the milieu of the workers' culture of learning that I describe (reclaim) in these pages. This miniaturized portrait suggests the *field of personal and social relationships* that have made the task of the "implied author" of these pages at once so difficult and so necessary to carry through. In a famous passage, Walter Benjamin wrote that "even the dead" are not safe from a conformism that is always about to overpower the tradition in which their memory is preserved and that the struggle over collective memory is a continuous one. In this text, I felt compelled to struggle against my dead friend, who had become one of the monumental keepers of "the Little Tradition of Yiddishkeit," in order to wrest "the tradition of the oppressed" that the generation of my grandparents kept alive out of the mass grave to which conventionalizing accounts of their culture consigns their works and days.

This emphasis, which offers profound insights into the construction of cultural performances, nonetheless occludes the social relations that are themselves determinants of the form and, as form, are immanent within the content. For instance, in a brilliant rhetorical analysis of the graduation-siyum ceremony, Myerhoff shows that this secular ritual has been devised to deliver an indictment against the old people's children and the community's "wealthier Jews," while at the same time to deny that this protest is in fact being made ("We Don't Wrap Herring in a Printed Page," in this volume; also see note 6). This is the type of double-voiced discourse that Mikhail Bakhtin calls hidden polemic. By applying Bakhtin's theory of discourse to the utterances of old people and the Center officials who represent them, it can be demonstrated that this act of verbal disguise is a "fiction" that shapes the content and the form *in relation to each other,* while at the same time refracting the social rela-

---

Through these warring ghosts in my study, I have personally lived the meanings and feelings (of love and anger) that are transformed, in the work of the essay, into patient scholarship. That I have personally lived the general meanings, which are of wide historical and cultural interest, certainly intensifies and complicates my long posthumous debate with Myerhoff. But the source of the debate itself is not in our personal relationship, but in the different positions from which we view (and have lived in and with) the culture of Yiddishkeit. This is a debate between a liberal social scientist and a socialist writer over "the dead"—over the "re-membering of their lives"—that concerns the living, from whose consciousness the culture of capitalism seeks to wipe out all traces of useable traditions of struggle. The elderly Yiddish-speaking immigrants whom Myerhoff studied created a vital oppositional culture on American soil, waged a long fight on behalf of improved working conditions in this country—the eight-hour day, Social Security, unemployment insurance, and other now-embattled benefits were utopian ideals, and appeared ridiculous, when this generation put them on the social agenda and at the same time transformed the workers' movement into a historical force that struggled for decades to attain these goals. In their old age, the members of the Israel Levin Senior Center, where Myerhoff did her field-work—a group of people whose life-histories are inseparable from the culture and history of the radical Jewish labor movement and Jewish socialism—perceived and valued themselves (in degrees and ways that varied considerably) in terms of these historical struggles, and in terms of a cultural politics whose political voice(s) Myerhoff silences in the ethnographic essays, but allows to enter the writing of *Number Our Days.*

The difference in position between Myerhoff and myself is itself grounded in our life histories: in the social locations in which our worldviews were formed. Myerhoff was raised in the suburbs of Cleveland, in a family oriented toward upward mobility via small business (for the men) and artistic pursuits (for the

tions between the old people and the powerful middle-class people whom they need and accuse (Myerhoff 1980:87–100; Bakhtin 1984a:204–37). They resort, as weak people often do, to irony, to veiled complaint, to guilt-provoking remarks: to the subtle manipulation of words that disguise their aggression, to a verbal resourcefulness of which these people are masters; they draw upon the genius of the language itself, a deposit of linguistic resources acquired by Yiddish in its long history of feeding powerful enemies a placating but toxic word.

Hidden polemic saturates Kafka's artistic prose as profoundly as it does the ritual utterances of the old people. The genre to which Kafka's tales belong—or rather, in which they hunger for belonging—may, insofar as they deliberately constitute "a minor literature," be described as Yiddish stories in the German; or, again, as Hasidic tales written—in Marthe Robert's acute epithet—by "an atheist who believed that God did not want him to write."

A kindred intention inspired Myerhoff. East European Jewish storytelling, oral and written, in many of its forms, saturates her texts: citations and traces of the early Hasidic masters, of the late modern masters

---

women). I grew up in a white ethnic neighborhood in the Bronx, attending a "folk shul" five afternoons a week, while my classmates at P.S. 28 played stickball on a block in "America," to which I commuted daily from the immigrant milieu of my parents' and grandparents' homes and the Yiddishist community of the "shul," which had been organized (by my own grandfather, among others) as a critical bulwark against the danger of assimilation. In this enclave, modern Yiddish culture separated and segregated me from the Americanism which Myerhoff assumes. I say this in order to go past it, and also in criticism of the ghettoization implied in my description of my childhood. What I want to emphasize here is that, while my critique of Myerhoff has roots in my personal experience, it does not depend for its validity on such authority as I can claim as a witness or native at one remove, but rather on the adequacy of the analysis I offer and the evidence that I present. My engagement with Myerhoff's work, while for me inseparable from personally lived meanings, is not "about" two people, but "about" social knowledge. It is in terms of the scholarly debate that I hope the introduction will be received, evaluated, and criticised. This text has been improved in and through the critical dialogue it has generated among gerontologists and colleagues in cultural studies. Recently, members of the *Social Text* editorial board offered criticism that enabled me to realize that "moments" of idealization of Myerhoff remain embedded in the essay, particularly in the high claims that I make for her concept of the third voice, which I too nearly equate with Bakhtin's concept of dialogic discourse. Other readers will discover other problems, and in their responses and criticisms the issues that I have raised here will—so I hope—be clarified and debated.

(notably Isaac Bashevis Singer and Elie Wiesel), of folk tales and the narrative lore of everyday life (appropriated through social histories and historical ethnographies such as *The Jewish Woman in America* and *Life Is with People*), and of the stories told to her by the Center members appear with increasing emphasis in her texts and are a source of the richness of texture of *Number Our Days,* in which the *nign* or "melodic line" of Yiddish speech becomes an object of cultural representation. By the early 1980s, in the *Tales from Fairfax* project, Myerhoff openly avowed her intention to create a text that would belong as much to the tradition of Jewish storytelling as to the ethnographic tradition of compiling collections of sacred lore. Insofar as this intention shaped Myerhoff's work, and the narrative content was inflected by the accent of solidary relations with the speakers and protagonists of the stories, so that the contradictory pulls in Myerhoff's position entered the writing, Myerhoff produced what can be described as Yiddish literature written in English (by an author who could not but longed to speak Yiddish).

Kafka's tales, with their messengers who never arrive and doorkeepers who admit no one and nothing, narrate highly elaborate transmissive practices whose truth-content is undecidable. Here, transmission is burdened with two impossible tasks: getting the message across time and space, and figuring out its meaning. Kafka's narratives bring two of the key terms of Myerhoff's inquiry—transmission and fiction—into an entirely problematic relation. This is a problem that Walter Benjamin took up in his correspondence with Gershom Scholem. In one of his letters on Kafka, he discusses the meaning of the breakdown of tradition, whose value is that it transforms transmitted truth into widely possessed wisdom. The loss of tradition is thus also the social loss of wisdom.

> Kafka was far from the first to face this situation. Many had accommodated themselves to it, adhering to truth or whatever they regarded as truth at any given time and, with a more or less heavy heart, foregoing its transmissibility. Kafka's real genius was that he tried something new: he sacrificed truth for the sake of clinging to the transmissibility. (quoted in Arendt 1969:41)

Myerhoff is the ethnographer of this novel project. Her writing describes the real transmission of invented traditions, and shows what is at stake in these collective acts of imagination: the creation of a deeply lived sense of membership in a common culture that includes, within an expansive and "eternal" sphere of solidary social relations, the familial and ancestral forebears of the group and the unborn generations. This high note of Durkheimian cohesion and Turnerian *communitas* is the transcendence in which Myerhoff's ethnographic narratives seek closure: "These moments of intensely shared experience have been called by Martin Buber *Zwischenmenschlichkeit*. They are often euphoric, religious experiences that, paradoxically, occur when the self stands outside the self—ecstasy" (Myerhoff 1984:325). "The chanting of the ancient prayers brought a rare hush into the hall. Tears of awe gleamed on some of the most skeptical faces present" (Myerhoff 1980:91). These are the high notes that, in Kafka's "Josephine the Singer, or the Mouse Folk," are nothing more than the "piping" of a "frail little voice"—a voice, however, whose "ceremonial performances" keep alive the "tradition of singing" of the mouse folk and gives them the strength to bear their precarious daily lives: "Here piping is set free from the fetters of daily life and it sets us free for a little while. We should certainly not want to do without these performances." This affirmation attains a certain fragile grandeur by withstanding the assault of the ironies of the passage within which it is embedded (Kafka 1952:319–20). What Kafka affirmed in and through irony, Myerhoff affirmed by embedding her celebratory descriptions of moments of ritual transcendence in narratives that do not lose sight of the assaultive realities of aging bodies, fighting among group members, and the adverse social conditions in which the Center folk continue "to display and dramatize themselves in many forms, informal and formal, planned and spontaneously: by storytelling, creating difficulties, making scenes. . . ."

Author/Content/Reader

The essays collected in *Remembered Lives: The Work of Ritual, Storytelling, and Growing Older* trace Barbara Myerhoff's discovery of her central subject: the narrative and theoretical description of forms of creativity in everyday life. This is at once evident and far from obvious. The essays support this formulation in their evident fascination with creativity as a vocation, in their detailed recording of collective acts of imagination, and in their celebration of the creative process under the Proustian sign of the "re-membering" of lives. For Myerhoff, acts of creation reaggregate the lost members of a life, both a person's prior selves as well as the lives of others who have gone into the making of her or his life story ("Life History among the Elderly," in this volume). Through "re-membering" the old people's rituals, storytelling and other cultural performances become forms for constituting a collective subject, a social individual in whom the ancestors live on, renewed. The lives of the old people, and the artifacts and performances they create, are embedded in an ethnographic allegory of resurrection. The "aura" of spirituality that enters Myerhoff's ethnographic descriptions, and the source of their intensity and power, is to be found in the primary narrative structure through which she represents and "thinks" creativity. Her ethnographic essays construct what may be called "narratives of the second life." The profound significance of this concept—as narrative structure and as intrinsic theory of creativity—can be suggested by evoking the importance of this secularizing idea in modern thought on social acts of creation.

Myerhoff's central mechanism of the creative act—the re-membering of lives—is a conflation of Proust's "involuntary memory" and Butler's life-review process.[12] Proust uses the Greek and Christian terms "reminiscence" and "resurrection" interchangeably (Shattuck 1974:138ff.). Butler's famous article on the life review, under the genre-clarifying optic of discourse analysis, declares its actual structure as a particular type of redemption narrative: it is a hellfire sermon at one remove, in which psychoanalytic theory catalogues the latest credible system of Dante's inferno:

> Another group of individuals who appear especially prone to some of the more severe manifestations and outcomes of the life review are those who have exercised the human capacity to consciously injure others. The individuals, in whom guilt is real, . . . do not imagine forgiveness and redemption. Still another group who appear especially vulnerable . . . may best be described as characterologically arrogant and prideful. (Butler 1963:272)

They are consigned to a despair whose most terrible aspect is that it appears eternal.

---

12. As Myerhoff acknowledges in an article titled "Re-membered Lives" (in *Parabola* V:1:77), the term itself is taken from Turner: "Victor Turner has used the term 'Re-membering,' bracketing it by the hyphen to distinguish it from ordinary recollection." Turner's arresting conceit is already saturated with the memory of Proust; in Myerhoff's writing, it is extended to receive Butler's psychoanalytic treatment of "involuntary memory" as the life-review process.

In an evocative meditation that takes the instance of Proust as formative, Eugenio Montale speculates upon "the second life of art." This
is the "second and larger life" of a piece of music, a fragment of poetry,
or an image first seen on a museum wall that suddenly enters "the life
of memory and everyday circulation . . . , its obscure pilgrimage through
the conscience and memory of men, its entire flowing back into the very
life from which art took its first nourishment" (Montale 1981:19).

A third great instance that I want to bring forward, as a touchstone
text, is Bakhtin's description of medieval carnival as "the second life of
the people, who for a time entered the utopian realm of community,
freedom, equality, and abundance" (Bakhtin 1984b:81, 57, 9). The non-
hierarchical, laughing, creative life of the carnival square, with its free
and familiar contact among social groups, carries a range of meanings
that overlap with *communitas*.

Myerhoff's texts saturate the category of creativity with redemptiveness
through the potent indirection of their narrative structure. The "depth"
of her texts is attributable both to the lucidity and brilliance of her
analysis, and to the transformation of key terms in and through this
(necessarily hidden) narrative structure. These texts metaphorically run
the theme of creativity through the various domains that are foregrounded
in the writings of Proust and Butler, Montale and Bakhtin: individual
(psychological and spiritual) development, art, and social life.

The essay titled "'Life Not Death in Venice': Its Second Life" reflexively
claims and explicates this "deep structure." The transformation of the
ethnographer's primary narrative structure into an object of inquiry
accounts for the extraordinary complexity and richness of this text. It
is, as a work of semiotic analysis and an investigation of intersecting
discursive practices, arguably the most impressive ethnographic essay
Myerhoff wrote.

Yet it is notable that even here, in a text that pushes *l'esprit de finesse*
(intuitive or imaginative thinking) beyond ambiguous boundaries and
compels it to settle down within elegant tables of equivalent meanings
constructed by *l'esprit de geometrie* (mathematical or scientific thinking);
here, where magnificence of detail is magnificently framed by corre-
spondences of theory, the axial term—"the second life"—is used in a
deliberately open, unsettled, ambiguous way, and so escapes from the
regime of monologizing interpretation. Blurred together under the trope
of "the second life" are three distinct senses: (1) daily life or lived experience; (2) the "creator's consciousness," the realm of reflexivity that

"doubles the mirrors"; (3) cultural artifacts or performances. The first sense is immediately given in Myerhoff's quotation from Pericles: "The whole earth is the sepulchre of famous and ordinary men, and their story is not graven in stone, but lives on woven into the stuff of other men's lives." The second sense is given in the epigraph from Dilthey: "The power of breadth of our own life, and the energy of reflection upon it is the foundation of the historical vision. It alone enables us to give second life to the bloodless shades of the past." Here, the resurrection of the dead occurs not in the lives of their successors, but in "the historical vision." The third sense is emphasized in the narrative description of the "parade" and the mural. The locus of the "second life" shifts from the daily life of social actors to a deepened state of consciousness to a representation that infuses the daily life with the heightened consciousness, but these moves are made without clarifying the distinct senses of the term or theorizing their interrelation. The unification that the essay constructs is attained as a result of elusiveness, of mystification. This conflation of senses, even as it dehistoricizes (allegorizes) the text, opens it to artesian depths of suggestiveness that are supplied by the hidden tale of resurrection.

The idea that Myerhoff's central subject is the ethnographic study of "forms of creativity in everyday life" is defensible as an adequate formulation only if it is problematized, so that it can receive the richness and complexity of Myerhoff's writing on creativity. This writing is the product of long and increasingly assured multidisciplinary researches, and the refraction of these researches through an allegorical narrative structure that metaphorically transposes their meanings. Secular findings appear to promise a (symbolic) afterlife. The findings themselves cannot be abstracted from the fact that Myerhoff's investigation of cultural creativity is carried through in the form of narratives of the second life. The particular character of extreme lucidity and mysterious depth evoked by this writing—its detailed depiction of social process and its elating promise of happiness—can only be accounted for in this way.

The construction of Myerhoff's central research subject as "forms of creativity in everyday life" renders the texts recognizable in an immediate way by defining their determining intention and by naming the theme that links apparently disparate motifs. But this formulation also raises an immediate problem. These essays do not orient themselves toward the reader under this issue. They are immersed in an interrogation of creativity, but they look elsewhere for the language under which to describe the research issues they engage. This lack of congruence between the actual research process that claims Myerhoff's attention, and the disciplinary formulations under which it is constructed, is a sign of Myerhoff's position. She seeks to constitute her formal research projects, and the papers that describe them, in terms of a discursive practice that is oriented toward her colleagues in anthropology.

Current issues of theoretical concern in the field—"aging and ethnicity," "symbol and ritual"—organize and legitimate her work. She was hardly alone in her engagement with the issue of the social and cultural work of the imagination. In studying how rituals go beyond representing social cohesion in order to show how they create it, interpretive anthropology dropped the Durkheimian mirror—this is the "crack in the mirror" that the title of one of these essays refers to—and lifted the Geertzian lamp. Yet the status of the term "creativity" has remained problematic in this discourse. It remains under suspicion, as if its wide appropriation for kitsch usage rendered it unusable for a science that at once seeks to explain the role of creativity in social life and to celebrate it (as modern art does) as a secular form of spirituality. In the essays that appear, for example, in Turner's and Bruner's *Anthropology of Experience,* "create" is a privileged verb, linked to "experience" and "performance"; it does not, however, acquire the rights and privileges that accrue to formal research issues, deemed anthropological subfields. It is, in practice, a substantial area of research without formally being recognized as such. Myerhoff's work seeks to claim this issue and to view it as a valid object of anthropological inquiry. There is, then, a polemic of legitimation going on in these essays. Myerhoff does not find her subject given to her in an unequivocal and empowering way by the discursive practice of her field. What she then does is make creativity the inseparable, necessary, and explicit issue that is at stake in the investigation of every formal issue she signs up for: under the categories of aging and Yiddishkeit, ritual and symbol, life-history, narrative and reflexivity, she naturalizes research on the creative process and creative form within the mainstream of cultural anthropology.

The notion that "forms of creativity in everyday life" is Myerhoff's central subject must be further problematized to include the following complicating and contradictory senses.

First, the difficulty of this term in Myerhoff's writing arises from the inseparability in these essays of the emphasis on "self-creation" (life-history work, reminiscence and life review, the life-course perspective) and cultural production: a linkage that Myerhoff conceptualizes and investigates under the concepts of "re-membered lives" and "definitional ceremonies."

Second, creativity is described as a social process that is embedded in ordinary life, but it is valued in these texts as an escape or refuge from ordinary life. The sphere of everyday life is hardly being valorized. Rather, creativity offers access to the larger life (of community, of the spirit) and to a higher reality. These texts offer the reader evocations of valuable experiences—of illumination and fellow-feeling with other human and nonhuman worlds—that are necessarily intermittent and difficult to attain in a secular culture. Such "peak experiences" and "moments of possible sublimity" are now commonly sought for and understood in terms of "the creative."

Raymond Williams has accounted for this common sense of the "creative," in contemporary life and social thought, in profound discussions that trace the history of the changing meanings of this term (1961:3–40; 1976:72–76). Before the Renaissance, the category of the creative was the special province of divinity. Creation referred not to the imitative or innovating products of humankind, but to the world that God made in *Genesis*. A religious worldview linked the related senses of "creator/creation/creature." In the long process of secularization, humanism proposed and transvalued "creativity," and it became the special (but not exclusive) province of "the artist." Yet the sense of a reality that is both superior and hidden (inaccessible to ordinary perception) was retained. Here, from the time of the Romantic movement on, imagination and the "kingdom of the spirit" are, always in complex ways, interrelated.

By tracing this history, Williams specifies the complex sense that the category of "the creative" carries in Myerhoff's writing. It is a meaning constructed over the historical abyss that separates traditional congregational communities, into which these elderly Jews were born, and modernization, which this group lived through in direct, fully self-conscious, ideologically elaborated, and personally anguishing ways. Williams writes:

> The belief in artistic creation as the medium of a superior reality seems most likely to be held in a period of transition from a primarily religious to a primarily humanist culture, for it embodies both ways of thinking: that there is a reality beyond human vision,

and yet that man has supreme creative powers. But, in such a transition, the latter claim will be made on general grounds, thus tending to challenge the artist's singularity. (1961:12)

This locates the "belief" that Myerhoff has in common with the old people whom she studies, and it positions this widely held conviction in a historical discourse that has its origins in the literature of the Renaissance and that enters the human sciences—notably, psychology and anthropology—through twentieth-century theories that privilege the symbol (Jung, Geertz). The creativity whose interpersonal transactions Myerhoff grounds in everyday life does not sacramentalize the ordinary; rather, it is the collaborative production of a set-apart realm, and the recuperation of a worldview that separates the sacred from the profane. Everyday life, in this writing, is a domain of adversity, suffering, endless loss, in polar opposition to the "miraculous, liberating effect" (Montale) of the creative event: art, in the late Romantic view, produces "an effect of liberation and of understanding the world" (Montale 1981:19). An opposing and equally classic statement of this question—Williams's essay "Culture is Ordinary"—offers a very different evaluation of everyday life, in that it is inseparable from and on the same plane with, the liberation and category-break attained through creative acts.

Myerhoff's extending and deepening study of creativity and creative forms in everyday life becomes increasingly inseparable from her writing about the ethnographic text, which is itself construed in Bakhtinian terms as a creative event, a realm of dialogic relations among author, content, and reader. As the relation between discourse in life and discourse in the human sciences becomes increasingly problematic for Myerhoff, they are increasingly brought under the sign of the creative: bricolage and "blurred genres" have immense value for her not simply because they describe a modernist practice (of collage/montage), but because they transfer to her use the thinking and the authority of Lévi-Strauss and Geertz, who invented these terms for anthropological discourse.

Once all the complications and contradictions specified above are allowed to break into and pull apart the phrase, "forms of creativity in everyday life" can be viewed as the high ground that Myerhoff, because anthropological theory did not simply hand it down or over to her, had to take.

In its four-part structure, this volume follows the course of Myerhoff's development from 1968 to her death in January, 1985. The categories under which her essays are herein presented—aging, ritual, storytelling, and reflexivity—maintain what (to use an archivist's term) may be called the "intrinsic order of the papers," in that they constitute a lived chronology of Myerhoff's ethnographic interests, and they are based on the disciplinary discourse through which Myerhoff constituted her formal object of study and legitimated her developing investigation of cultural creativity.[13]

Part 1, "The Anthropology of Aging," consists of a paper that Myerhoff prepared for and presented to the Summer Institute of the Andrus Gerontology Center in 1968, "Aging and the Aged in Other Cultures: An Anthropological Perspective." It is written at the threshold: after Myerhoff's work on the religion of the Huichols and before her entrance into the Israel Levin Senior Center to do research on "aging and ethnicity." In this paper, she takes stock of what cultural anthropology has to say about aging and old age and equips herself intellectually for the ethnographic project she is about to undertake. This text, then, is formative of Myerhoff's work during the second and major phase of her career. It announces key motifs that will be profoundly developed in the case studies on ritual and storytelling: the old man and woman as keepers and transmitters of the wisdom of their people; the absence of and need for rituals that delineate life-course transitions within the vast and uncharted country of age; the symbolization and institutionalization of time in the culture of capitalism, and the impact of efficiency-based, productivistic measures of time upon the elderly. These are among the issues that are raised vividly here as anthropological conceptions, and that are subsequently developed in and through ethnographic research and writing. This text, as her anthropological point of departure, permits us to see how Myerhoff deepened and extended the ideas she was given by the theoretical tradition within which she worked.

This paper not only marks a crossroads in Myerhoff's work, but it

---

13. The "Introduction" to *Secular Ritual* is the one essay with a strong claim to be included in a volume of Myerhoff's initiatory or summative papers which I decided to omit. Co-authored with Sally Falk Moore, this widely influential essay was, necessarily, a difficult case. I thought, finally, that this text could not be compelled to transcend its introductory occasion without mutilation. What was decisive for me was that the important conceptual framework developed by Myerhoff and Moore is brilliantly presented and implemented in "We Don't Wrap Herring in a Printed Page" and "A Death in Due Time."

is also formative of the entire field of multidisciplinary studies on the culture of aging. It is an evaluative review of the anthropological literature on aging that was itself spurred by, and contributed to, a period of immense generativity in research on aging, which is associated with the contributions of such figures as Robert Butler, Bernice Neugarten, Tamara Hareven, Matilda White Riley, and others in the humanities and human sciences. In the vast literature that is produced during the next decade, Myerhoff's work emerges as central. In this formative discussion Myerhoff formulates, with her characteristic lucidity and moral passion, the issues and emphases that become central in interdisciplinary studies of aging and old age.

In its key discussions of "culture-as-ideology" (i.e., a set of shared symbols) and of the cultural construction of the life-course, this paper laid out an agenda for work in the field, and set forth theoretical formulations that are at the center of anthropological research and social thought on aging today, as a recent state-of-the-art review of the literature makes evident (Keith and Kertzer 1984:19–61).

Nonetheless, the value of this apparently well-behaved, academic text is not obvious today; it appears tame and "early" beside the work that followed. Its significance, as a foundational text, is that it negotiates and conflates three breaks: that of the author's development, that of the object of study (the cultural construction of aging), and that of the historical moment. These three dimensions—the history of author's professional life, the history of cross-disciplinary gerontological research, and the history of the society-at-large—are profoundly interrelated in this text and demonstrably constitute its orientation. This essay was written immediately after the most dramatic upheavals of the radical year 1968: the student revolt and general strike in France, and the 1680 incidents of student protest that occurred between April and June in the United States and throughout the world (Katsiaficas 1987:44–45). Myerhoff was engaged by these developments and was writing anthropological studies of youth culture. In her first text on old age, the emphasis on "culture as ideology" is continuous with her writing on "the Woodstock Nation" and the utopian quest of the commune movement (Myerhoff 1975). Social critique of the culture of capitalism enters her work in the form of a problem-posing anthropology that challenges the dominant ideology. The essay on aging and old age openly avows its critical stance toward the value system of North American society. Here, we already see an anthropologically articulated critique of ageism, a term coined by Robert Butler in 1968 that had not yet entered into general usage and that Myerhoff did not then know. But the social knowledge that is inscribed in this term, as a concept and as a position, is made available to Myerhoff by her alignment with the social movements to fight racism and sexism in this society.[14]

Part 2, "The Work of Ritual," consists of three case studies of the rituals of the "Center folk," written in the mid-1970s, and a fourth paper that conflates and theorizes the work of the 1970s. This latter text, titled "Experience at the Threshold: The Interplay of Aging and Ritual," is an excerpt from a longer paper that Myerhoff prepared for and presented to a workshop of colleagues at the National Institute on Aging (NIA) in 1981 (Myerhoff 1984:305–30; Riley 1984:8; Kertzer and Keith 1984:13–15). This fact is important for two reasons. First, it situates the text as an institutional practice within collegial discourse. This is of immense significance in the production of all Myerhoff's work, which must always be viewed in dialogic relation to the hegemonic and contested

---

14. In this text, the interrelation of language, ideology, authorial intention and the historical moment is foregrounded in a particularly vivid way. Here, we can see how deeply racism, sexism, and ageism are embedded in conventional usage. Had the essay been written after Edward Said's *Orientalism,* Myerhoff would have spoken of "Asians," not "Orientals." Despite her sensitivity to racism, it is still possible for her to write: "In the United States, regardless of chronological age, a Negro male may be called 'boy,' signifying that part of the American value system that equates economic impotence with immaturity." That part of "the American value system" is racism, which determines the economic impotence in the first place. Myerhoff, of course, writes in criticism of "the American value system," a formula that dignifies the practices that she means to oppose. Her use of "Negro," like her use of the term "Orientals," obviously dates the essay. In this essay, too, she uses "humankind" and "mankind" as interchangeable terms; in her later work, in which feminism is formative—and the critique by feminists has taken deeper hold of "enlightened" discourse—this would have been unacceptable to her. Finally, ageist concepts of the life-cycle still adhere to her use of conventional expressions that had not yet been subjected to minute interrogation and critique. Myerhoff speaks of the entry into old age as "the transition to the end of life"; elsewhere, to make this transition is to "pass out of adulthood." The conflation of old age with death, and the unconscious double entendre that fuses old age with loss of consciousness, show the extent to which social ageism still infiltrates a text aimed at critiquing ageism. This indicates the degree to which meanings are changed only gradually, through prolonged scrutiny and contestation. The instances offered here place this text within an ongoing historical process and exemplify the method of cultural studies that Williams developed as "historical semantics."

conceptions in her discipline: conceptions that her work advances, parries, amplifies, resists, subverts, answers, questions, prods, personifies, celebrates, expounds, worries over, seeks to transmit to successor generations. Second, the location of the professional discourse that constitutes the collegiality of these texts was not at the margins, but at the center of knowledge production in the field of aging in the United States. Her work was carried out in relation to, and intersected with, institutional bases (NIA, the Andrus Center, Hunter/Brookdale Center on Aging and others) that were advancing multidisciplinary research on aging.

The élan, the immediacy and the assurance of Myerhoff's case studies on the old people's rituals could not have entered these essays without the extraordinary empowerment that came with collegiality in a field going through a phase of discovery and rapid growth. Myerhoff wrote with the knowledge, from the mid-1970s on, that her descriptions of the old people's ritualized reinvention of their tradition would immediately enter professional discourse and stimulate new research, new models of gerontological practice, and serve as vital texts in the education of future gerontologists and ethnographers. The clarity of her presentation of theory, her novelistic gift, and her multidisciplinary perspective, made her work especially valuable for use in college and graduate education across a range of disciplines, including folklore, Jewish studies, women's studies, social work, and sociology. Her writing has been studied in creative writing programs because of its (narrative) embodiment of concepts concerning autobiographical narrative.

The essayistic case studies on aging and ritual formed the basis of *Number Our Days* and, taken together with the work on storytelling and personal narrative, are Myerhoff's most enduring contribution to cultural studies. The oeuvre was significantly shaped by, and contributed to, the initiatory phase of feminist anthropology in the 1970s, the phase that Henrietta Moore, in her comprehensive *Feminism and Anthropology*, has called the "anthropology of women" (1988:1–11).

The "anthropology of women" took as its focal concern the problem of the representation of women, which it addressed in two ways: by offering a critique of the forms that male bias has taken in social thought, and by offering a description of women and women's activities from a feminist perspective, in other words, a perspective that questions the use of analytical frameworks that assume the naturalness of female subordination and male privilege. Myerhoff's essay on "Bobbes and Zeydes:

Old and New Roles for Elderly Jews," notably epitomizes this emphasis in her work. Here, striking shifts of intonation and brilliance of imagery are mobilized in the service of Myerhoff's criticism of conventional gender roles and the symbols through which these are constructed. Images of the high-spirited independence of the old women, and the devitalization of the old men, are used to create "comic" moments in the writing, as part of a critique that ranges in tone from the playfulness and humor that Myerhoff praises in her grandmother Sofie, to the scathing irony that she values in the old women of the Center. The critique is aimed less at the men, whose suffering in old age is presented, than at the dominant gender symbols and roles that have shaped their lives as well as conventional readerly expectations. The old women of the Center have themselves got beyond the traditional stereotypes and "no longer assum[e] that the men have anything particularly worthwhile to contribute merely because they are men" (in this volume). The men may be the Center's officials, but the women do the "real work" of governance as well as nurturance. Myerhoff shows that these women take advantage of the "negative freedom" that old age has afforded them, in a way that is comparable to the use of the "contingent" or unofficial roles which were available to the women of the shtetl—*balebostes* (female house-holders, women of substance) with an all-around competence at running things, women whose activities and responsibilities spanned the household, the marketplace, and the communal voluntary associations.

The power of this essay lies in its description and transvaluation of the sphere of "women's work"—the source of the women's power in old age. The men wither in retirement; the women, who continue to be needed and useful, "expand" with age: "Roles based on nurturant functions are durable and expandable" (in this volume). The "domestic" sphere, described with a freshness of feeling and vividness that evidently draw on the writer's own experience of "the unglamorous stuff—the mess of life itself," is conceptualized in terms of bricolage and the creation of a miniature world in which "self-direction" and mutual responsibility can co-exist, a social space that is not hierarchically subsumed to the "public" sphere of work. This essay, then, offers a critical evaluation of the "domestic"/"public" model of social thought, which has been conventional since the nineteenth century, and which is saturated with the bourgeois ideology of the home as the safe haven from the public domain in which men compete for money and status. Myerhoff's refusal of the cultural valuations that have been naturalized in the "domestic"/"public"

paradigm is the theoretical move that underpins her affirming representation of women's labors, a critical move that Ortner's initiatory essay,
"Is Female to Male as Nature Is to Culture?" (1974) opened up for
Myerhoff and other important feminist texts of this period. Myerhoff
shows, for one thing, that rigid imposition of the "domestic"/"public"
opposition distorts the cultural history of Jewish women, who moved
freely and skillfully across these categorically separated domains. More
importantly, she demonstrates the value and the values of the sphere of
"women's work" by showing that this "mundane sphere" necessitates the
development of skills, personal qualities, and relationships that enable
the women to adapt to old age better than the men do. The contrast
between these elderly Jewish women and men dramatically overturns the
traditional dominance of the males in everyday life, although the men
and women revert to their traditional roles during ritualized islands of
time, which are satisfying both to the women and the men. Apart from
the cultural reversions that their rituals produce, the women are "vigorous, resourceful, indomitable, often rude and brazen, antiauthoritarian, and submissive to no one." The men, without their "instrumental"
roles as workers and breadwinners or their "official" roles in Center
secular or religious ritual, are "worn out and demoralized."

In tracing the different fates that typically await the women and men
of this group in old age, Myerhoff's analysis goes well beyond the concerns of the "anthropology of women," and moves into the terrain of
the subsequent phase of feminist scholarship in anthropology, which was
constituted by the study of gender and gender relations. Here, Myerhoff
carries the symbolic analysis of gender and the sociological analysis of
role into the anthropology of aging, and thereby makes a distinctive and
pioneering contribution that demonstrates the gain in knowledge that is
produced by the intersection of feminism and anthropology: she shows
that aging, if it is to be adequately studied, must be understood as a
gendered process.

Part 3, "Re-membered Lives," consists of four papers that, with one
exception, were written after *Number Our Days*. I have included an
earlier paper, "Life History as Integration: Personal Myth and Aging"
(1975), although it is a slighter effort, because of its value for gerontological education and practice. Co-authored with Virginia Tufte, a
professor of English with whom Myerhoff cotaught a course on the life-
history technique, it was published (in a considerably modified version)
in *The Gerontologist*. The version here has not appeared in print: it was

found in typescript among Myerhoff's papers after her death. This is also the case with the version of "A Death in Due Time" that appears in this volume.[15] In both instances, the original writing had a power

---

15. As noted in the Acknowledgments, there are three essayistic versions of Jacob's birthday-memorial—the original version, "A Death in Due Time: Conviction, Order and Continuity in Ritual Drama" (1975); a substantially rewritten version, "A Symbol Perfected in Death: Continuity and Ritual in the Life and Death of an Elderly Jew" (1978); and a conglomerate text—"A Death in Due Time: Construction of Self and Culture in Ritual Drama" (1984)—that conflates the key interpretive discussion of the second version and a discussion of "Dramas of Existence, Arenas for Appearing," which repeats important motifs of the late essays on life history (cf. especially "Life History among the Elderly" and "Surviving Stories"). The significant differences, then, occur between the 1975 essay titled "A Death in Due Time" and "A Symbol Perfected in Death." The latter essay was written during the same period that Myerhoff wrote the chapter in *Number Our Days* on Jacob's life history and his birthday-memorial (chapter 6). The novelistic description of this event has infiltrated the later essay and brought about the shift in interpretation that is also to be observed in the differing ethnographic descriptions of the graduation-siyum, which I discussed earlier in this Introduction. Myerhoff's original essay on the birthday-memorial offers a profound description of cultural creativity as a social process. The revised version of 1978 drains the essay of its critique of fragmentation under the culture of capitalism; and, under the administration of a monumental conception of "continuity," suffocates the vulnerable profundity of the first version. This has to do with the connection the first essay makes between the possible "failure" of ritual and human mortality. "A Death in Due Time" foregrounds the "made-upness" of ritual by suggesting a correspondence between the ever-present danger of the "failure" of ritual—the possibility that it will cease to persuade its participants— and the threat of death in old age. This correspondence, developed by a narrative and theoretical description that stresses the spontaneous (incalculable) and collective dimensions of the actual event, accounts for the particular texture of this essay—it is a "darker" writing than the accounts that followed, which offer the consolations of the narrative of continuity. Many differences of detail arise from the key difference between a text that views creative agency as a social process and the later versions, which place the entire process under the control of a culture hero, Jacob, who, like his namesake, wrestles with the angel (of Death). In the later versions, the introduction of Ariés's concept of "tamed death" is an essential move in the construction of the extraordinary individual who governs the entire process. Thus in a key passage, Myerhoff writes: "The turning point occurred when Jacob tamed his death, transforming the ritual into a numinous, enormously sacred, powerful drama" (1978:196). The original version construes this "turning point" more complexly, that is, as a discontinuous, social process. The "birthday party" and the "memorial" that follows are not presented as a unified ritual, as if the entire sequence had been planned in advance and were

that was lost when they were rewritten for publication. In the manual-like piece on life-history, this power is brought into play by Myerhoff's characteristically active voice, which is recast into the passive voice of social-scientific expertise in the *Gerontologist* text.

In the course of writing *Number Our Days,* Myerhoff's essayistic production underwent a double transformation, which is forcefully presented in the papers on storytelling, "collective autobiography," and related cultural practices. She began *Number Our Days* with the intention of situating her lifelong interest in ritual on home ground and in the field of aging. Her discovery of the cultural creativity of her subjects entailed her discovery of storytelling as a major interest for research and writing. Narrative gradually eclipsed ritual as the issue which most deeply engaged her. And this was inseparable from her investigation of reflexivity. In these papers, personal narrative becomes *the* form of reflexivity for old people: life review, as Myerhoff construes it, turns philosophical and is that dialogue (if only with oneself) through which the examined life is lived.

Part 3 is the site of Myerhoff's most important interdisciplinary work. The life-history method of gathering information about a culture is transformed into an object of study. A longitudinal means of conducting process-oriented research is redeployed to introduce a life-course perspective into anthropological writing (Keith and Kertzer 1986:35–48; Bertaux 1982:127–50.) Myerhoff draws on literary studies of autobiographical narrative, psychological and gerontological studies of reminiscence and life review, and social-historical studies based on oral history, and combines these different disciplinary perspectives with ethnography's focus on culture. She produces a detailed and broad description of how older people use various forms of narrative to transmit culture, to bear witness, to work toward personal integration, to create a self to be

---

all under Jacob's control; rather, the *two* rituals retain their distinct character, and the transformation of the secular ritual into a religious one is accomplished "by a collectivity":

> In the case of Jacob's death, matters are complicated because two rituals must be considered: the intended birthday party, a designed, directed secular affair with non-religious, sacred nuances, transformed spontaneously by a collectivity into a non-planned, fully sacred religious memorial. (34)

These contrasting interpretations of the agency of transformation and the very different descriptions of the ritual event epitomize the differences between the two essays.

remembered by, to engage in cultural politics, to garner attention and thereby to feel revitalized, and simply to pass the time pleasurably.

Part 4, "Reflexive Genres," consists of two essays, co-authored in the late 1970s and early 1980s, which have as their point of departure the necessary interrelation of a particular type of content, reflexive knowledge, and a baggy but nonetheless definite literary form, personal narrative. The form-and-content unity of reflexivity and narrative now becomes the position from which Myerhoff, in dialogical collaboration with colleagues (Ruby and Metzger) who ask of their writing that it interfere with conventionalist assumptions, raises the issue of the author's subject position in the text. These essays stand at the threshold of a decade that has produced a remarkable body of critical writing on this problem. The significance of this co-authored work on reflexivity lies in the brilliance with which it invents and poses questions that are now at the center of scholarly debate on "writing culture."

The two essays on reflexive genres move the discussion out of the senior center and offer a description of contemporary culture and society at large, but the emphases of the essays differ. "A Crack in the Mirror," which takes the production of the ethnographic text as a problem and as a social practice, contextualizes its discussion in relation to popular culture (the new journalism, film, a wide range of contemporary music). The map of culture constructed by this essay—Ruby's contribution here was crucial—stresses fragmentation, pastiche, parody, and ironic self-referentiality in the arts and Kuhn-like paradigm breaks in the social sciences. "The Journal as Activity and Genre" situates its description of "journal work" in the women's movement and in the culture of psychotherapy, where journal writing is used to give voice to parts of the self that are disdained and banished in everyday life. These essays offer "no final truths, only hints": what they evoke, in their extraordinarily suggestive and wide-ranging review of cultural texts, positions, productions, situations, and social movements, has come to be widely conceptualized and debated as "the postmodern condition."[16] The very method of these

---

16. The debate among three magisterial, celebrated texts has sent intellectual shock waves, opened theoretical fault lines and left gaps, aporias, fissures, discontinuities across discursive terrains everywhere in the human sciences, the humanities, and the arts. The three initiatory texts that constitute the locus classicus of postmodern thought are Habermas' *Legitimation Crisis*, Lyotard's *The Postmodern Condition* and Jameson's essay, "Postmodernism, or the Cultural Logic of Late Capitalism." Lyotard's text, in its critique of Habermasian con-

writings, which are filled with miniaturizations, fragments, dislocations, sudden shifts of direction and personal narrative, bespeak postmodernism. They actively practice the reflexivity they profess.

It is through her feminism, and in collaboration with a feminist writer and activist (Metzger), that Myerhoff's writing intersects with postmodernism, to which feminist social thought has made indispensible contributions (Owens 1983; Fraser and Nicholson 1988). In the celebrated debate between "fragmentation" and "totality" (or "the master narrative"), Myerhoff's writings are usually militant in their insistence that life is unlivable—meaningless—without the order provided by narrative closure. This idea has, in her work on secular ritual, the status of a universal truth: it is the foundation upon which Geertzian symbolic anthropology rests. And it is implemented in Myerhoff's texts through the use of a number of different primary narrative structures. These narrative structures include, in addition to "the narrative of the second life," a number of others that I have discussed in the course of analyzing Myerhoff's work: the carnivalized tale of pariahdom, the allegorization of Americanism in terms of "success stories," as well as the narrative of

---

sensus, sets the debate in motion. In *The Postmodern Condition,* Lyotard writes: "Simplifying to the extreme, I define *postmodern* as incredulity to metanarratives." In the course of a worldly—i.e., socioeconomic—analysis of the impact of the hegemony of "the system"—i.e., multinational corporate capitalism—upon knowledge production and distribution, an account whose power is (in part) derived from the immediately recognizable description it presents of the conditions under which research is funded and science is taught, Lyotard disengages the two "master narratives" that (formerly) legitimated knowledge production in the sciences. These are the great legacies of the Enlightenment to the modern period: the narrative of the emancipation of humankind (through scientific progress, or the proletarian revolution that will inaugurate the good society, etc.) and the narrative of the unity of all knowledge. These metanarratives are no longer credible under the dispensation in which the most important force of production is science and technology; in other words, the criterion of "performativity"—of efficiency gained by maximizing output and minimizing input (including rampant cost-cutting measures in all directions)—has displaced the great "narratives of legitimation" of the modern period. The break-up of the grand narratives has discredited "totalizing" scientific (and artistic) discourses that postulate the existence of universal truth, universal reason, and a universal (collective) subject (i.e., the "Man" of the human sciences, the "proletariat" of classical Marxism). For a brilliant discussion of "the collection of practices that call themselves postmodern," and the implications of the abandonment of universals and the global hegemony of capitalist practices upon the spheres of culture

rites of passage. Through the use of such narrative paradigms, interpretation in ethnographic texts is demonstrably an allegorical practice
(Jameson 1981:58ff; Clifford 1986:98–121). Now the single strong
exception to Myerhoff's commitment to the master narrative is her analysis of "women's culture," and particularly the discussion of "the fragmentary nature of women's experience" in the text on journal-work
(Myerhoff and Metzger, in this volume). In this view, gender roles and
the gendered division of labor ground a characteristically female mode
of consciousness in social relations. But this "fragmenting" or interruption of attention, so evidently a cause of frustration and suffering, is
shown to have potential benefits. The conversion of a weak position
into a strong one is a move that empowers Myerhoff's writing on old
people and accounts for its wide reception. The key point in this text
on reflexivity is that, under adverse conditions, women are compelled

---

and politics, see Andrew Ross's Introduction to *Universal Abandon?*, as well as
the essays collected in this volume, particularly the Jameson and Cornel West
interviews, and the texts by Foster, Aronowitz, and Fraser and Nicholson. This
volume offers sustained and important reflections on the Habermas-Lyotard-
Jameson debate. The two essays on reflexivity under discussion here traverse the
terrain of postmodernism in their discussion of the inadequacy of prevailing
scientific and aesthetic (narrative) practices and canons, and specifically in the
following respects: (1) in positing an agonistic relation between "science" and
"narrative" (between the canons of objectivity legitimated by the rules of posi-
tivist/empiricist scientific research and narrative or customary knowledge); (2)
in their incredulity toward and critique of "realism," and more particularly "naive
realism"; and (3) in their valorization of representational practices (both in the
arts and human sciences) of fragmentation, of interrupting and interrogating the
text-in-the-making, of appropriation and incorporation of heterogenous materials, including personal narrative and citations of the tradition that must be
used self-consciously since it no longer underpins the new work. The two texts
on reflexivity take up a stance of incredulity toward and criticism of "naive
realism" and "the anti-narrative tradition within the canons of scientific communication" on behalf of recuperating and adequately representing the occluded
subjectivity and social experience of women, and of recuperating and adequately
representing the occluded research method of the anthropologist doing fieldwork.
Then, too, what may be called "the mood" or texture of Ruby's contribution to
"A Crack in the Mirror" intersects with postmodern culture: incredulity and
paradigm-breaking experimentation is not, in the popular music and culture
cited by Ruby, governed by a nostalgia for lost narratives. "Most people have
lost the nostalgia for the lost narrative," Lyotard writes—many people, perhaps,
but "most"?!—alluding to such high modernist masterworks as *Ulysses* and *The
Waste Land,* and other productions of the "mythic method" that present the

to develop a mobility and tenacity of consciousness that allows them to work through an issue by returning to it frequently for brief periods of time (1980:109–10). In a comparable discussion concerning the fracturing of women's attention, Virginia Woolf, in *A Room of One's Own*, stresses that it is for this reason that women have historically chosen to write in short forms (1929:80–81).

The moment of postmodernism in the two texts on reflexivity has to do with their acute recognition that the reigning aesthetic and scientific paradigms have become inadequate—they leave out, for instance, the experience of women and ethnographers doing fieldwork—and that, as a consequence of the destabilization of the canons of realism in narrative

---

image of the modern as ruined sublimity or sublime ruins. This "most" does not, by and large, include Myerhoff. The main tendency of her work, obviously, is an effort to recuperate what Eliot, describing *Ulysses,* called "the mythic method" on behalf of science; in other words, her project is to extend and legitimate the domain of narrative within science, and to recuperate and maintain the legitimacy of metanarratives that can unify the subject, the field of knowledge, and the cultural history that links modernity and traditional society. This (desperate) effort, viewed from the purview of Lyotard's analysis of the "crisis of narratives," turns ritual into a dramaturgical social-bond machine. The Myerhoff text projects the system's sole criterion—performance—onto ritual, turning it into a machine of cultural production whose input is scraps of contemporary and outworn belief-systems, and whose output is a mood of collective elevation and consensus. Secular ritual as a social-bond machine performs the same function that administrative procedures, manipulation-by-education, the nexus of knowledge-acquisition, "career opportunities" and "development" or advancement and material incentives serve under the system: it evacuates difference, legitimates things as they are, and produces consensus. This interpretation of the Myerhoff text on ritual does not fail to notice the veiled protest that the text registers and even valorizes; but this writing regards this symbolic protest as a means of coming to terms with the order of things. The ritual is, after all, only a ritual: a matter of mirror and smoke, not power. In this conventionalist text, then, the protest that is indirectly and symbolically staged in this type of cultural production is, at the point where it makes its strongest move, nothing more than a moment of disruption and disequilibrium that the strong narrative of the ritual will unify, in the service of re-stabilizing and increasing the overall performativity of the system. The most damaging critique that emerges from reading Myerhoff in the light of Lyotard is that, by depoliticizing the cultural history and cultural productions of a group that brought a powerful alternative agenda into play, in every sphere of activity—i.e., they sought knowledge not to advance individually but to advance as a class and to change society—this ethnography fails to provide the counter-evidence that this group offers of a people who have not adapted their individual aspirations to fit the needs of the system.

discourse and positivism/empiricism in scientific discourse, text production is a problematic that must inform text production (see note 16 for a fuller discussion). The value of these essays is that they offer strong arguments for laying this process bare, and they invent ways of making the process of their own production visible. Thus, they give access to the difficult problem of how ideology informs social science discourse. Again, this stands at the threshold of a remarkable decade of work on discourse, culture, ideology, and knowledge production in ethnography and the human sciences, a literature in which Aronowitz's *Science as Power* (1988) and the contributions of Paul Rabinow and George Marcus have been summative and important, and, within the field of aging, the work of Daniel Bertaux (1982) offers a strong alternative to conventionalist descriptions of aging.

"A Crack in the Mirror" is a critique of the repressive discursive regime of "scienticism," which in its "anti-narrative tradition" and no longer credible value-free stance banishes the author/narrator from the ethnographic text. The discursive problem of the subject position of the anthropologist is here construed in terms of reflexivity. This personalizes the problem and largely contains it within the terms of the individual. The critiques cited above, which are based on Foucauldian and post-Marxist theories of discourse, generalize this issue in terms of the problem of the relation between knowledge and power.

"The Journal as Activity and Genre" is also vitally concerned with text production and views the text both as a literary form (a matter of artifice, an embodiment of knowledge) and as a process. Here, Geertz's reading of ritual as social text is reversed, and the journalkeeper's text is interpreted as a practice that is "our" contemporary, secular equivalent of ritual process. Here, as in "'Life Not Death in Venice,'" the primary narrative structure of the initiate's three-phase "journey" governs the interpretation. The motif of locating the position of the banished author/narrator appears here as it does in "A Crack in the Mirror," but with this difference: here text production is described as a potential healing process, a quest for wholeness of being, for recuperating parts of the personality that are suppressed or damaged in social relations that subordinate women and induce alienation generally.

The strong move of these two essays is that they espouse a communication model of text production (and all other forms of cultural creativity). This is a crucial development in Myerhoff's thought. She was undertaking a profound re-evaluation and re-theorization of ritual and storytelling toward the end of her life, in which the notion of *communicating culture* was replacing the earlier formulation of *transmitting culture*. This major shift is incompletely theorized in the essays on reflexivity, but this writing is evidently moving at the boundary of "interdisciplinary studies" and in the direction of "cultural studies." In the latter model, a specifying analysis of social discourse is linked to a general analysis of the social and cultural formations within which the discourse is constructed. This is the task of "cultural theory," as Raymond Williams has theorized it in a body of writing that has emerged as seminal in cultural studies.

The limitations of Myerhoff's work on reflexivity can be specified in two ways. First, the informant in relation to whom the ethnographer coproduces cultural interpretation does not emerge here as a full dialogical partner, a speaking subject who offers different, distinct, and contesting interpretations. This is a major point that is made in all the strong critiques of ethnographic narrative as a discourse of subjection or domination. (See, for instance, Rabinow 1986, Crapanzano 1986, and Rosaldo 1986.) The issue of "the dialogic roots of ethnographic knowledge" and "multivocality" has been well treated by Marcus and Fischer (1986:67–73), whose work moves toward the steady discovery and articulation of the interrelation between formalist issues of text production and the social relations of knowledge production. With characteristic summative power, they interrelate the constructionalist emphasis on the motifs of creativity and reflexivity with the move toward construing the ethnographic subject as a fellow author of and in the text:

> The view of culture as a flexible construction of the creative faculties encourages ethnographers to expose their procedures of representation, make them self-conscious as writers, and ultimately suggests to them the possibility of including other authorial voices (those of the subjects) in the texts. (1986:125)

The other limitation here is the absence of what Bakhtin calls the "immanent reader," that is, the listener projected by the discourse, the (imaginary) auditor in relation to whom the author positions herself and orients her discourse. This problem is strikingly evident in Myerhoff's and Ruby's use of a communication model that has three key terms: producer/process/product. This is actually a model of transmission (a one-way sending which posits the other as passive consumer), and not of communication (a two-way dialogue in which the other in determinate ways co-produces the content in relation to the author/speaker). In the essays on reflexivity, the other and otherness is cited (Myerhoff and Metzger, in this volume; Myerhoff 1980:111; Myerhoff and Ruby, in this volume), but the other remains at the borders of text production, as the actual recipient of the transmitted content. The other as an active voice or concrete subject position within the text is not actually specified. Although these essays lack a fully developed theory of discourse, they are pioneering moves that seek to ground text production in lived social-cultural practices. The questions they raise, the vividness of the instances they describe, along with their experimental form, give them their pro-vocative and initiatory power.

The work of Barbara Myerhoff reached a broad and various public and had a profound impact upon scholars in her field(s) of specialization, the anthropology of aging, and in related multidisciplinary fields of study and practice. The reception of her work, across audiences that are nor-mally divided, raises several important issues.

Myerhoff's work seeks to cross disciplinary as well as cultural bound-aries while leaving the boundaries themselves more or less intact. She inserts dialogical doors between alien discourses, so that many profes-sional and social languages enter into her anthropological texts, and anthropological discourse saturates the talks and articles in which she conversationally addresses various audiences, such as theater artists, Jew-ish communal groups, therapists, and others in the holistic health move-ment. She was a master of keying her speaking voice to the audience that she was addressing. This was more than a technical matter, although it shows how consciously Myerhoff constructed the various voices in which she spoke. The problem it foregrounds, and that Myerhoff increas-ingly came to engage, has to do with the role of the secular intellectual.

Myerhoff's intention, the large project she sought to accomplish, can-not be understood unless her scholarly work is interrelated with the important work she did in "popular genres." Her two films; her multi-media folk art and folk life exhibitions and events ("Surviving Stories," in this volume); her "novelistic" ethnography *Number Our Days;* her talks at community centers, synagogues, artists' gatherings, fundraising events, professional symposia, and conferences throughout the country; her articles in magazines such as *Parabola* and the *Center Magazine;*

her radio interviews—these communications reached very diverse audiences. It was her intention to overcome the separation of the language of cultivated intelligence and the language of the general culture. This was the case not only in discourse that addressed "popular" audiences, but in her ethnographic essays as well. And it is this intention that constitutes her distinction and her achievement.

She sought not only to make a contribution that would advance knowledge in her field, but also to make an intervention that would change cultural and social practice generally. She sought, actively, to oppose ageism and to promote "*communitas* groups." Again, her contribution to knowledge is inseparable from this practical intention, and scholarly evaluation of her work must give due weight to Myerhoff's social project. She was, as many of our most innovative and contributing scholars have been, conscious of her role as a secular intellectual.

Edward Said has written of the profound difficulty of carrying through this modernist role in a society in which "opponents, constituencies, audiences and community" are segregated among different and highly specialized languages. Of the now-traditional task of the intellectual, Said writes,

> The secular intellectual works to show the absence of divine originality, and on the other side, the complex pressure of historical actuality. The conversion of the absence of religion into the presence of actuality is secular interpretation. (1983:146)

The absence of divine creativity in the human world and the complex actuality of history were, for Myerhoff, the issue that forms the urgency of her task as a secular intellectual. Her response, like that of many social thinkers, was to seek to recuperate the domain of the sacred. The intervention she proposes, in the field of aging, in and through performative artistic practices, and in transformed face-to-face dialogues, is the invention of rhetorical practices that foster the experience of communal solidarity and spiritual experience.

This creative social project is, from the purview of scholarly work, an object of suspicion and desire. My concern here is to emphasize that it is inseparable from the power of her strong work in anthropology. This is the case, despite the fact that she split off her "popular work" from her "academic work." The two emphases, in her most fully developed work in anthropology, were brought together. This bringing together of the scholarly and the popular voices and concerns can be specified by examining the question of the intended audience for the ethnographic essays.

The essays collected in this volume were written for other anthropologists, except for "Life History as Integration," which addressed a multidisciplinary social science audience of gerontologists. Every essay was linked to a specific academic occasion; some were conference papers, others were commissioned chapters in scholarly texts. Each essay immediately emerges from, and/or contributes to, face-to-face collegial discourse. The written text is embedded in the ongoing life of professional shoptalk, which these texts crystallize and catalyze. All of Myerhoff's writing, even the essays prepared solely to be read as chapters in academic texts, retain the intonation and diction of high-spirited conversation at the conference or workshop session. Writing papers for presentation at academic conferences shaped and inspired Myerhoff's mastery of the ethnographic essay. The conference paper as literary text requires brilliant and lively epitomes of a theoretical position, which compose a well-wrought frame within which one or more attention-arresting case studies are exhibited, performed. The vivacity of Myerhoff's writing arises from an authorial stance and craft that vigilantly attends to the listener and her need to be really spoken to, not at.

Who is this reader/listener? Obviously, Myerhoff's colleagues: her peers, dialogic partners, and collaborators. The actual auditors and recipients of these papers consisted of a specialized audience, yet her actual and lived relations of colleagueship were very wide-ranging. Her anthropological writing was profoundly informed by her long history of collegial and collaborative work with artists (playwrights, poets, theatre and film directors, actors, musicians, particularly politically engaged artists); practitioners and academics in the field of aging; folklorists; psychologists; humanities scholars in the fields of English literature and Jewish studies; as well as the Huichol shaman, the Hasidic rabbis, and the elderly worker-intellectuals who were her informant-teachers.

Myerhoff, in teaching life-history work, asked of her students that they go back to the old persons whom they had interviewed, read the life-history they had written to its subject, and incorporate the subject's corrections and responses into the final text. The life-history text had to speak of and to its subject. Myerhoff's ethnographic essays do not include the subject as reader/listener as an essential condition of text production. Yet this principle, which Myerhoff professed both as a teacher and as a consultant in community life-history projects, is not merely abandoned in her scholarly work. The principle of "returning the life-history work to the community from which it arose" is enacted by the intonation of profound respect with which she speaks of the cultural other to her social peers. At one remove, then, the subject of the discourse enters into the formation of the immanent listener of the discourse. While the informant is not the immediate auditor, she at least must be able to overhear the discourse without feeling demeaned by it. Myerhoff's writing vigilantly protects the "honor" of this listener-at-one-remove and takes her into account in describing her way of life.

The immanent reader of these texts may be described as an anthropologist with "soul": a peer with the sensitivity to take offense at any affront to the cultural other, and who has entered into social relations of commitment to and "imaginative identification" with the ethnographic subject, as well as into collegial relations with a range of interests and discourses that have been traditionally welcomed within the permeable disciplinary boundary of anthropology, the field that imports knowledge from all other social sciences, humanities and arts and acculturates them into its ever-shifting understanding of what it means to be engaged in the study of culture. Myerhoff's immanent reader is the colleague who is constituted by the key discourses that speak and get spoken about in the term culture. This is, as Raymond Williams has said, "one of the two or three most complicated words in the English language" (1976:76). It has "three broad active categories of usage" in contemporary general as well as scholarly discourse. Culture refers to a "general process of intellectual, spiritual and aesthetic development"; "a particular way of life, whether of a people, a period or a group"; "the works and practices of intellectual and especially artistic activity" (1976:80). Myerhoff's ethnographic essays address a reader to whom none of the three senses of culture is alien, a listener who is urgently engaged with culture as a way of life, a process of (spiritual, aesthetic, intellectual) development, and a creative practice. These concerns are formative both of Myerhoff's content and of her listener.

These texts, then, address the reader as an anthropologist who construes culture in the widest and most general sense. The author as secular intellectual is enriching and complicating professional discourse by raising, in a particularly narrativized and evocative way, a range of cultural questions that are of broad social interest. The object of study is constituted not only by the great formal issues that advance knowledge production in the field, but by urgent social questions that lie beyond anthropology and that anthropological knowledge can respond to, in shaping an intervention.

Not only professional colleagueship, but also common membership in American society ground the interrelation among the author, the reader, and the content of these papers. These texts project a reader/ listener who is not only a professional scholar engaged in the study of culture, but also a citizen who is also living through the general crisis of culture—the fragmentation, marginalization, and secularization—that afflicts the author. The content of these texts, construed from this common social location, can be summarized as follows.

In these texts, Myerhoff locates the source of the deep emotional ties that upwardly mobile professionals continue to feel in relation to ethnicity.

She critiques and opposes ageism and ageist notions of the life-cycle by offering a detailed collective portrait of late-life courage, resistance, and wisdom. Thus, although her texts literally describe the "old old," they foreground the characteristics that are associated with the "new elderly," a concept that Bernice Neugarten formulated in 1974. The constitution and reception of these texts is shaped by the historical moment that sees both the rise of political activism among the elderly, and the scholarly production of conceptions of old age that legitimate and foster this broad social movement.

She investigates and honors the forms that creativity takes in everyday life, in a practice-oriented inquiry that emphasizes the value of such cultural practices for marginalized populations. In particular, she seeks to show that creative cultural and spiritual practices enhance the well-being of old people.

She inquires into and specifies unconscious and conscious mechanisms of cultural transmission, in a specifying rhetorical analysis of ritual and other cultural performances.

She offers a great testament to the cultural construction of self derived from fragments in her description, across a range of genres, of the remembering of lives.

She contributes to the general theory of ritual through her extending concept of definitional ceremonies, by means of which she is able to document the ritualization of the life-review process.

She describes, in the segregated enclave of a "vanishing culture," tenacious, profound, collective efforts to invest social life with dignity and the epic virtues (wisdom, courage) and to infuse it with the "aura" of (continuity with) "the Great Tradition."

She takes up questions that are associated with failure—with the "pariah" qualities of old age, poverty, ethnicity, and femaleness—and retells them as success stories.

The subtext of this writing is a lament for the spiritual dryness and atomization of American middle-class life and a celebration of plausible, contrived Proustian moments of transcendence.

Myerhoff's essays, like the cultural practices they decode, speak to the unofficial as well as the official interests of her colleagues. They intend to bring news concerning something for which her readers became anthropologists and which we all desire: a world larger than the one we've got to live in. This, Alan Tate advises us, is what Yeats summoned the spirits for. And it is what Frederic Jameson means when he speaks of the "utopian vocation" of (imaginative) writers. Myerhoff belongs to the "hidden" tradition of Jewish pariah writing as much as to the tradition of liberal social critique in anthropology because of the extremity of her concern: for what Jameson (1981:236) has described as "the place of quality in an increasingly quantified world, the place of the archaic and feeling amid the desacralization of the market system, the place of sheer color and intensity within the grayness of the measurable extensions and geometrical abstraction" of the dominant culture and its institutional practices.

REFERENCES

Arendt, Hannah. 1969. "Introduction." In *Illuminations,* by Walter Benjamin, translated by Harry Zohn. New York: Schocken Books.
———. [1944] 1978. "The Jew as Pariah: A Hidden Tradition." In *The Jew as Pariah: Jewish Identity and Politics in the Modern Age,* edited by Ron H. Feldman. New York: Grove Press.
Aronowitz, Stanley. 1988. *Science as Power: Discourse and Ideology in Modern Society.* Minneapolis: University of Minnesota.
Bakhtin, Mikhail M. 1981. *The Dialogic Imagination: Four Essays by M. M. Bakhtin.* Edited by Michael Holquist, translated by Caryl Emerson and Michael Holquist. Austin: University of Texas Press.
———. 1984a. *Problems of Dostoevsky's Poetics.* Edited and translated by Caryl Emerson. Minneapolis: University of Minnesota Press.
———. 1984b. *Rabelais and His World.* Translated by Hélène Iswolsky. Bloomington: University of Indiana Press.
Bakhtin, M. M./P. N. Medvedev. [1928] 1985. *The Formal Method in Literary Scholarship:*

A Critical Introduction to Sociological Poetics. With a Foreword by Wlad Godzich, translated by Albert J. Wehrle. Cambridge, Mass.: Harvard University Press.

Baum, Charlotte, Paula Hyman, and Sonya Michel. 1975. *The Jewish Woman in America.* New York: New American Library.

Benjamin, Walter. 1969. *Illuminations.* Edited and with an Introduction by Hannah Arendt, translated by Harry Zohn. New York: Schocken Books.

Berman, Marshall. 1982. *All That Is Solid Melts into Air: The Experience of Modernity.* New York: Simon and Schuster.

Bertaux, Daniel. 1982. "The Life Course Approach as a Challenge to the Social Sciences." In *Aging and Life Course Transitions: An Interdisciplinary Perspective. See* Hareven and Adams 1982.

Bruner, Edward M. 1986. "Introduction: Experience and Its Expressions." In *The Anthropology of Experience,* edited by Victor W. Turner and Edward M. Bruner. Urbana and Chicago: The University of Illinois Press.

Buber, Martin. 1947. *Tales of the Hasidim: Early Masters.* Translated by Olga Marx. New York: Schocken Books.

Butler, Robert N. 1963. "The Life Review: An Interpretation of Reminiscence in the Aged." *Psychiatry* 26:65–76.

———. 1975. *Why Survive? Being Old in America.* New York: Harper and Row.

Clifford, James. 1986. "On Ethnographic Allegory." In *Writing Culture: The Poetics and Politics of Ethnography. See* Clifford and Marcus 1986.

Clifford, James, and George E. Marcus. 1986. *Writing Culture: The Poetics and Politics of Ethnography.* Berkeley: University of California Press.

Cole, Thomas R. 1986. "The 'Enlightened' View of Aging: Victorian Morality in a New Key." In *What Does It Mean to Grow Old? Reflections from the Humanities,* edited by Thomas R. Cole and Sally Gadow. Durham: Duke University Press.

Crapanzano, Victor. 1986. "Hermes' Dilemma: The Masking of Subversion in Ethnographic Description." In *Writing Culture: The Poetics and Politics of Ethnography. See* Clifford and Marcus 1986.

Davidowicz, Lucy S. 1960. *The Jewish Presence: Essays on Identity and History.* New York: Holt, Rinehart and Winston.

———. 1967. *The Golden Tradition: Jewish Life and Thought in Eastern Europe.* Boston: Beacon Press.

Deleuze, Gilles, and Felix Guattari. 1986. *Kafka: Toward a Minor Literature.* Foreword by Reda Bensmaia, translated by Dana Polan. Minneapolis: University of Minnesota Press.

Di Leonardo, Micaela. 1989. "Malinowski's Nephews." *Nation,* March 13, 1989:350–52.

Erikson, Erik H. [1950] 1963. *Childhood and Society.* 2d ed. New York: W. W. Norton and Company.

Foster, Hal, ed. 1983. *The Anti-Aesthetic: Essays on Postmodern Culture.* Port Townsend, Washington: Bay Press.

Fraser, Linda, and Linda Nicholson. 1988. "Social Criticism without Philosophy: An Encounter between Feminism and Postmodernism." In *Universal Abandon? The Politics of Postmodernism,* edited by Andrew Ross. Minneapolis: University of Minnesota Press.

Geertz, Clifford. 1973a. "Thick Description: Toward an Interpretive Theory of Culture." In *The Interpretation of Cultures.* New York: Basic Books.

———. 1973b. "Religion as a Cultural System." In *The Interpretation of Cultures*. New York: Basic Books.

———. 1983a. "Blurred Genres: The Refiguration of Social Thought." In *Local Knowledge: Further Essays in Interpretive Anthropology*. New York: Basic Books.

———. 1983b. "From the Native's Point of View: On the Nature of Anthropological Understanding." In *Local Knowledge: Further Essays in Interpretive Anthropology*. New York: Basic Books.

———. 1983c. "Found in Translation: On the Social History of the Moral Imagination." In *Local Knowledge: Further Essays in Interpretive Anthropology*. New York: Basic Books.

———. 1986. "Epilogue: Making Experience, Authoring Selves." In *The Anthropology of Experience*. *See* Turner and Bruner 1986.

Girardi, Guilio. 1988. "Marxism Confronts the Revolutionary Religious Experience." *Social Text* 19/20:119–52.

Gold, Michael. [1930] 1965. *Jews Without Money*. With an Afterword by Michael Harrington. New York: Avon Books.

Guillemard, Ann-Marie. 1982. "Old Age, Retirement, and the Social Class Structure: Toward an Analysis of the Structural Dynamics of the Latter Stage of Life." In *Aging and Life Course Transitions: An Interdisciplinary Perspective*. *See* Hareven and Adams 1982.

Habermas, Jürgen. 1975. *Legitimation Crisis*. Translated by Thomas McCartney. Boston: Beacon Press.

Hapgood, Hutchins. [1902] 1966. *The Spirit of the Ghetto: Studies of the Jewish Quarter of New York*. New York: Schocken Books.

Hareven, Tamara K. 1982. "The Life Course and Aging in Historical Perspective." In *Aging and Life Course Transitions: An Interdisciplinary Perspective*. *See* Hareven and Adams 1982.

Hareven, Tamara K., and Kathleen J. Adams. 1982. *Aging and Life Course Transitions: An Interdisciplinary Perspective*. New York: Guilford Press.

Heschel, Abraham Joshua. 1972. "The East European Era in Jewish History." In *Voices from the Yiddish: Essays, Memoirs, Diaries,* edited by Irving Howe and Eliezer Greenberg. Ann Arbor: The University of Michigan Press.

Howe, Irving. 1976. *World of Our Fathers*. New York: Simon and Schuster.

Jacoby, Russell. 1975. *Social Amnesia: A Critique of Contemporary Psychology from Adler to Laing*. Boston: Beacon Press.

Jameson, Frederic. 1981. *The Political Unconscious: Narrative as a Socially Symbolic Act*. Ithaca and London: Cornell University Press.

———. 1984. "Postmodernism, or the Cultural Logic of Late Capitalism." *New Left Review* 146:53–92.

Kafka, Franz. 1952. *The Selected Stories of Franz Kafka*. Translated by Willa and Edwin Muir, Introduction by Philip Rahv. New York: Modern Library.

Kaminsky, Marc. 1972. *What's Inside You It Shines Out of You*. New York: Horizon Press.

———. 1984a. "The Uses of Reminiscence." In *The Uses of Reminiscence,* edited by Marc Kaminsky. New York: Hayworth Press.

———. 1984b. "Transfiguring Life: Images of Continuity Hidden Among the Fragments." In *The Uses of Reminiscence*. New York: Hayworth Press.

94　　*Remembered Lives*

———. 1988. "All That Our Eyes Have Witnessed: Memories of a Living History Workshop in the South Bronx." In *Twenty-five Years of the Life Review: Theoretical and Practical Implications,* edited by Robert Disch. New York: Hayworth Press.

———. 1991. "Story of the Shoe Box: On the Meaning and Practice of Transmitting Stories." In *Handbook of Aging and the Humanities,* edited by Thomas Cole, Robert Kastenbaum, and David Van Tassel. New York: Springer.

———. 1992a. "Go Tell These Things How You Grew Up: Storytelling as Life Review and Social History." In *Going Home,* edited by Jack Kugelmass. *YIVO Annual 22.* New York: YIVO Institute for Jewish Research.

———. 1992b. "Definitional Ceremonies: Depoliticizing and Reenchanting the Culture of Aging." In *Voices and Contexts: Toward a Critical Gerontology* (working title), edited by Thomas Cole, Andrew Achenbaum, and Robert Kastenbaum. New York: Springer. Forthcoming.

Karp, Abraham J. 1976. *Golden Door to America: The Jewish Immigrant Experience.* New York: Viking Press.

Katsiaficas, George. 1987. *The Imagination of the New Left: A Global Analysis of 1968.* Boston: South End Press.

Kazin, Alfred. 1951. *A Walker in the City.* New York: Harcourt, Brace and World, Inc.

Keith, Jennie, and David I. Kertzer. 1984. "Introduction." In *Age and Anthropological Theory. See* Kertzer and Keith 1984.

Kertzer, David I., and Jennie Keith. 1984. "Preface." In *Age and Anthropological Theory,* edited by David I. Kertzer and Jennie Keith. Ithaca and London: Cornell University Press.

Kugelmass, Jack. 1986. *The Miracle of Intervale Avenue: The Story of a Jewish Congregation in the South Bronx.* New York: Schocken Books.

———. 1989. "Publications: *Between Two Worlds.*" In *YIVO News 174.* New York: YIVO Institute for Jewish Research.

Lasch, Christopher. 1978. *The Culture of Narcissism: American Life in an Age of Diminishing Expectations.* New York: Norton and Co.

Lyotard, Jean-Francois. 1984. *The Postmodern Condition: A Report on Knowledge.* Translated by Geoff Bennington and Brian Massumi, Foreword by Frederic Jameson. Minneapolis: University of Minnesota Press.

Marcus, George E. 1986. "Contemporary Problems of Ethnography in the Modern World System." In *Writing Culture: The Poetics and Politics of Ethnography. See* Clifford and Marcus 1986.

Marcus, George E., and Michael M. J. Fischer. 1986. *Anthropology as Cultural Critique: An Experimental Moment in the Human Sciences.* Chicago and London: The University of Chicago Press.

McClellan, William T. 1985. *Dialogic Discourse in the Clerk's Tale.* Ph.D. diss., English Department, City University of New York.

Menes, Abraham. 1972. "The East Side and the Jewish Labor Movement." In *Voices from the Yiddish: Essays, Memoirs, Diaries,* edited by Irving Howe and Eliezer Greenberg. Ann Arbor: The University of Michigan Press.

Milosz, Czeslaw. 1974. *Bells in Winter.* New York: Ecco Press.

Montale, Eugenio. [1949] 1981. "The Second Life of Art." *New York Review of Books,* April 16, 1981, 19–20.

Moody, Harry R. 1984. "A Bibliography on Reminiscence and Life Review." In *The Uses of Reminiscence,* edited by Marc Kaminsky. New York: Hayworth Press.

Moody, Harry R., and Thomas R. Cole. 1986. "Aging and Meaning: A Bibliographical Essay." In *What Does It Mean To Grow Old? Reflections from the Humanities.* Durham: Duke University Press.

Moore, Henrietta. 1988. *Feminism and Anthropology.* Minneapolis: University of Minnesota Press.

Moore, Sally Falk, and Barbara G. Myerhoff. 1977. "Introduction: Secular Ritual: Forms and Meanings." In *Secular Ritual,* edited by Sally Falk Moore and Barbara G. Myerhoff. Assen, Holland: Royal Van Gorcum Press.

Myerhoff, Barbara. 1974. *Peyote Hunt: The Sacred Journey of the Huichol Indians.* Ithaca and London: Cornell University Press.

———. 1975. "Organization and Ecstacy: Deliberate and Accidental Communitas among Huichol Indians and American Youth." In *Symbol and Politics in Communal Ideology,* edited by Sally Falk Moore and Barbara G. Myerhoff. Ithaca: Cornell University Press.

———. 1978. "A Symbol Perfected in Death: Continuity and Ritual in the Life and Death of an Elderly Jew." In *Life's Career—Aging: Cultural Variations on Growing Old,* edited by Barbara G. Myerhoff and Andrei Simić. Beverly Hills: Sage Publications.

———. 1980. *Number Our Days.* New York: Simon and Schuster.

———. 1984. "Rites and Signs of Ripening: The Intertwining of Ritual, Time and Growing Older." In *Age and Anthropological Theory. See* Kertzer and Keith 1984.

Neugarten, Bernice L. 1974. "Age Groups in American Society and the Rise of the Young-Old." *Annals of the American Academy of Political and Social Science* 415:187–98.

Ortner, Sherry. 1974. "Is Female to Male as Nature Is to Culture?" In *Women, Culture and Society,* edited by Michelle Rosaldo and Louise Lamphere. Stanford: Stanford University Press.

Östör, Ákos. 1984. "Chronology, Category, and Ritual." In *Age and Anthropological Theory. See* Kertzer and Keith 1984.

Owens, Craig. 1983. "The Discourse of Others: Feminists and Postmodernism." In *The Anti-Aesthetic: Essays on Postmodern Culture,* edited and with an Introduction by Hal Foster. Port Townsend, Washington: Bay Press.

Plotkin, Sarah. 1980. *Full-Time Active: The Oral History of Sarah Plotkin.* Edited by Arthur Tobier. New York: Community Documentation Workshop at St. Mark's Church-in-the-Bowery.

Poll, Solomon. 1969. *The Hasidic Community of Williamsburg: A Study in the Sociology of Religion.* New York: Schocken Books.

Pratt, Mary Louise. 1986. "Fieldwork in Common Places." In *Writing Culture: The Poetics and Politics of Ethnography. See* Clifford and Marcus 1986.

Rabinow, Paul. 1986. "Representations are Social Facts: Modernity and Post-Modernity in Anthropology." In *Writing Culture: The Poetics and Politics of Ethnography. See* Clifford and Marcus 1986.

Riley, Mathilda White. 1984. "Foreword." In *Age and Anthropological Theory. See* Kertzer and Keith 1984.

Rischin, Moses. 1962. *The Promised City: New York's Jews, 1870–1914.* Cambridge, Mass.: Harvard University Press.

Robert, Marthe. 1986. *As Lonely as Franz Kafka.* Translated by Ralph Manheim. New York: Schocken Books.

Rosaldo, Renato. 1986. "From the Door of His Tent: The Fieldworker and the Inquisitor." In *Writing Culture: The Poetics and Politics of Ethnography. See* Clifford and Marcus 1986.

Rosenmayr, Leopold. 1982. "Biography and Identity." In *Aging and Life Course Transitions: An Interdisciplinary Perspective. See* Hareven and Adams 1982.

Ross, Andrew, ed. 1988. *Universal Abandon? The Politics of Postmodernism.* Minneapolis: University of Minnesota Press.

Sachar, Morley Howard. 1977. *The Course of Modern Jewish History.* Updated and Expanded Edition. New York: Delta.

Said, Edward W. 1979. *Orientalism.* New York: Random House.

———. 1983. "Opponents, Audiences, Constituencies and Community." In *The Anti-Aesthetic: Essays on Postmodern Culture. See* Foster 1983.

Sanders, Ronald. 1969. *The Downtown Jews: Portraits of an Immigrant Generation.* New York and London: Harper and Row.

Schafer, Roy. 1980. "Narration in the Psychoanalytic Dialogue." In *On Narrative,* edited by W. J. T. Mitchell. Chicago and London: The University of Chicago Press.

Schappes, Morris U. [1977] 1978. *Irving Howe's "World of Our Fathers": A Critical Analysis.* A *Jewish Currents* Reprint. New York: Jewish Currents.

Scholem, Gershom G. 1961. *Major Trends in Jewish Mysticism.* New York: Schocken Books.

———. 1982. *Walter Benjamin: The Story of a Friendship.* London: Faber and Faber.

Schwartz, Anita. 1988. "The Secular Seder: Continuity and Change Among Left-Wing Jews." In *Between Two Worlds,* edited by Jack Kugelmass. Ithaca and London: Cornell University Press.

Shattuck, Roger. 1974. *Marcel Proust.* New York: Viking Press.

Shuldiner, David. 1984. *Of Moses and Marx: Folk Ideology within the Jewish Labor Movement in the United States.* Ph.D. diss., Department of Folklore, University of California, Los Angeles.

The Frankfurt Institute for Social Research. 1956. *Aspects of Sociology.* With a Preface by Max Horkheimer and Theodor W. Adorno. Boston: Beacon Press.

Todorov, Tzvetan. 1984. *Mikhail Bakhtin: The Dialogical Principle.* Translated by Wlad Godzich. Minneapolis: University of Minnesota Press.

Turner, Victor W. 1977. "Variations on a Theme of Liminality." In *Secular Ritual. See* Moore and Myerhoff 1977.

———. 1980. "Foreword." In *Number Our Days,* by Barbara Myerhoff. New York: Simon and Schuster.

———. 1986. "Dewey, Dilthey, and Drama." In *The Anthropology of Experience. See* Turner and Bruner 1986.

Turner, Victor W., and Edward M. Bruner, ed. 1986. *The Anthropology of Experience.* Urbana and Chicago: The University of Illinois Press.

Vološinov, V. N. [1927] 1976. "Discourse in Life and Discourse in Art (Concerning Sociological Poetics)." In *Freudianism: A Critical Sketch,* by V. N. Vološinov. Translated by I. R. Titunik, edited in collaboration with Neal H. Bruss. Bloomington: University of Indiana Press.

Weinreich, Max. 1972. "Internal Bilingualism in Askenaz." In *Voices from the Yiddish: Essays, Memoirs, Diaries,* edited by Irving Howe and Elizabeth Greenberg. Ann Arbor: The University of Michigan Press.

Williams, Raymond. 1961. *The Long Revolution*. New York: Columbia University Press.

———. 1971. *George Orwell*. New York: Columbia University Press.

———. 1973. *The Country and the City*. New York: Oxford University Press.

———. 1976. *Keywords: A Vocabulary of Culture and Society*. New York: Oxford University Press.

———. 1977. *Marxism and Literature*. Oxford: Oxford University Press.

———. 1979. *Politics and Letters: Interviews with New Left Review*. London: Verso.

———. [1958] 1983. *Culture and Society: 1780–1950*. New York: Columbia University Press.

———. 1986. "The Uses of Cultural Theory." *New Left Review* 158:19–31.

———. 1989. "Culture Is Ordinary." In *Resources of Hope: Culture, Democracy, Socialism*, edited by Robin Gable, with an Introduction by Robin Blackburn. London: Verso.

Woolf, Virginia. 1929. *A Room of One's Own*. New York and London: Harcourt Brace Jovanovich.

Wright, Erik Olin. 1979. "Intellectuals and the Class Structure of Capitalist Society." In *Between Labor and Capital*, edited by Pat Walter. Boston: South End Press.

Zborowski, Mark, and Elizabeth Herzog. 1962. *Life Is With People: The Culture of the Shtetl*. Introduction by Margaret Mead. New York: Schocken Books.

Part 1
The Anthropology of Aging

Aging and the Aged in Other Cultures: An Anthropological Perspective

It is unfortunate that the stereotype of anthropology as "the study of the exotic by eccentrics" is not entirely unfair, for while a very strong case can be made supporting the relevance of an anthropological approach to the subject of aging, the fact is that very few anthropologists have considered the matter systematically. Some possible reasons for this have been suggested by Margaret Clark: she wonders if negative attitudes toward the aged disincline American anthropologists to consider a subject that is vaguely repellent to them (Clark 1967:56):

> My own experience with Americans (including some anthropologists) is that there is among them a common view that old age, or even late maturity, is a horrible state; one shouldn't really think about it or look at it too closely—as though it were the head of Medusa. To contemplate later life is often seen as a morbid preoccupation—an unhealthy concern, somewhat akin to necrophilia. Since anthropologists are indeed creatures of their own culture, it may be that prevailing American attitudes toward aging are manifesting themselves in unconscious decisions by ethnographers to ignore this aspect of the life cycle.

This possibility is rather appalling since one of the professional goals of the anthropologist is to rid oneself of cultural blinders in studying one's own as well as other ways of life. The neglect of the role of the aged and the nature of aging is particularly surprising since anthropologists have given close attention to the life cycle as a general topic of interest up to but excluding old age. Clark suggests that this may be in part attributable to the Freudian bias that characterized so much early work in culture and personality studies and that provided that early life experiences were the most significant explanatory forces in understanding adult behavior. Many anthropologists recently have given lip service to the proposition that personality changes over time, and that the adult cannot be understood fully in terms of infancy and childhood; however, this recognition has not been accompanied by greater attention to adulthood and old age in actual field studies.

There are important exceptions to this charge. Simmons (1960) has concentrated on the aged in primitive and preindustrial societies, using the Human Relations Area Files to identify relationships between cultural traits and the status of the aged. Specific studies of the age principle and age grading in social organization exist; especially notable here are the works of Eisenstadt (1956) and LeVine (1963). Considerable attention has been devoted to the relationship between the aged and political organization in studies of gerontocratic societies. Kleemeler (1961) has also gathered descriptions of aging and leisure in many diverse cultures. But in all, there is no great or systematic body of work such as one might expect despite the fact that ethnographers have traditionally relied heavily upon reports from the aged in collecting their field data. The old people are the repositories of experience, memories, authority, and wisdom, and many an anthropologist gives few thoughts to the accumulated information to be gathered from his or her own grandmother while devoting the utmost attention and solemn respect to the garbled mutterings of the feeble, gnarled "ancient ones" in some exotic place.

The state of affairs is especially unfortunate since those cross-cultural studies of aging that do exist make abundantly clear the cultural determinants of aging; if any generalizations can be made, they point to the great variety of styles and forms of aging in different cultural settings. Here one is struck by diversity rather than uniformity, by variation rather than universality. The studies that are available suggest that social scientists must be as diligent in including the role of cultural factors in aging as they are in including them in studies of childrearing and childhood. Not all anthropologists may agree, but in the opinion of many the data point toward the malleability of the human organism and the significant role of nonbiological factors; in other words, culture appears to explain more of the peculiarities and idiosyncrasies of aging than do factors that are attributable to a "common humanity." In comparison with old age, infancy and childhood display striking patterning and regularity in part because of predictable and inevitable physiological events. Ethological studies of primates are impressive for their suggestions that the socialization process has certain fixed determinants and sequences that result from the interaction of chemical, biological, and endocrinological factors (Roe and Simpson 1958; Washburn 1961; Washburn and Jay 1968). The primate mother (including human) lactates when she hears an infant crying. A primate adult becomes agitated by the sight and sound of a helpless child in distress and must offer assistance to maintain his own well-being. There are the physiological givens whereby the dependence of the child and the nurturant response by the adult are articulated, thus assuring the immature members of the group a heightened chance for continued existence. One of the most significant characteristics of the very old is also helplessness, yet one does not encounter similar built-in protective devices to assure the aged assistance. As Simmons (1960) has pointed out, concern and care for the aged are strictly human. Such concern is entirely the result of cultural as opposed to biological considerations.

Aging and the aged, then, are not "givens" in any sense. Because of the striking variability concerning them, nearly every statement made about attitudes toward the elderly, treatment of them, and conceptualizations and expectations concerning them in any one culture can be contradicted by equally valid but differing evidence drawn from another culture. No easy generalizations are presently justified by the literature.

Why, this being the case, should a person in one culture be concerned with the aged elsewhere? Why are cross-cultural studies of the aged relevant? Can't one suppose in the face of this variability that the study of aging in other cultures will be gratuitous—perhaps interesting and, like history, part of the human record, but basically unessential to the principal concerns of understanding aging in our own culture? In other words, why should we take the trouble to employ an anthropological perspective in considering aging at all?

The answer to this question occurs on two levels. First, theoretically, social scientists continue to seek generalizations, regularities, and even lawful relationships among the phenomena they study. In lieu of a true laboratory in which isolated variables can be manipulated the social scientist turns to varying social situations that occur naturally in the world in the hope of understanding the relationships among the issues they are concerned with. Differing social conditions, for the most part, are their only "experiments." These differences must be sought across as well as within societies in order to make "culture-free" generalizations about aging wherever it occurs. The specific task of anthropology has been to consider its subject matter cross-culturally. Second, on the practical level, a cross-cultural perspective can help investigators recognize and possibly suspend their own cultural biases. The necessity for doing so is underlined by Clark's previously mentioned observation that perhaps it is the American negative attitude toward old age itself that has prevented anthropologists in this country from examining this period of life with the specificity and care it merits.

But there is another reason, perhaps most significant of all, why anthropology makes a unique contribution to this subject. Mention has been made of the fact that old age, unlike earlier phases in the life cycle, appears less governed by well-known biological determinants and therefore may be more responsive to cultural conditioning than other periods of life. There is abundant evidence that aging follows a variable course psychologically as well as physically.[1] Reliable predictions are available about the behavior and capacity of three-year-olds or even twenty-one-year-olds in all cultures, but predictions about the interests, skills, and developmental sequences of fifty-year-olds cannot be made with equal confidence. If one can generalize about this part of life at all, perhaps the safest statement would be that it is more variable than regular, within as well as across cultures. This irregularity is greatly compounded by the societal variables that we see operating in our own culture. Old age in this country is a time of life with very little structure and support. Some expectations exist for people at this time of life but these are not uniformly imposed and often not even clearly recognized. Old people in rural areas often can expect greater social participation than urban people of comparable age. Some age-homogeneous organizations are available for social support but membership is far from universal and in some places not even widespread. This means that investigation of aging must be quite comprehensive in its inclusion of explanatory variables—the biological, psychological, societal, and cultural dimensions must be taken into account since so far as we know none can be cited as exclusively or even primarily responsible for the course and form of aging. Anthropologists are properly responsible for sorting out some of the societal and most of the cultural influences in this process.

The cultural dimension of aging and the aged is of special concern

---

1. Although some biologists would argue that aging is the playing out of a "programmed" series of events, others see it as a more idiosyncratic, biologically variable event, particularly in comparison with the growth cycle.

here. First, something must be said regarding the way the term "culture" is being used in the context of this discussion. Even anthropologists, who regard the culture concept as perhaps the single unifying concern that ties together the various specializations within the field of anthropology, do not agree on its definition. Most would agree, however, that the concentration on culture—its nature and consequences—is one of the features that sets anthropology apart from the other social sciences (Kroeber and Kluckhohn 1963).

Perhaps the simplest and most general view of culture considers it the conglomerate of customs, traditions, and habits of a particular group sharing a way of life at the same time and place. Some anthropologists stress the material manifestations of this way of life; others trace its historical development. Some focus on patterned social relationships between groups and individuals while others concentrate on institutions, their functions and interrelationships. Equally valid is the orientation that regards culture as an adaptation to a given environment and duly considers technological and ecological factors as of primary interest.

There is yet another orientation toward culture that seems especially useful for those interested in aging, and that is the view of culture as primarily an ideological phenomenon—a set of shared understandings that characterize a particular group; this orientation can be called a *Weltanschauung,* or a group's "collective representations." In this view, humankind is fundamentally a symbol maker. A person can bear almost anything but a sense of meaninglessness and chaos. Culture provides the individual with a means for interpreting the world, one's fellows, and one's life. Clifford Geertz (1973:99) has defined culture as a set of symbols that establish basic and powerful moods and motivations that formulate a conception of the order of existence. These shared symbols constitute what a group of people agree to be "reality." Mankind is able to tolerate anything, Geertz suggests, except the failure of our symbols, for this amounts to a threat to our very powers of conception. When such a failure occurs we are more helpless than the beavers. He puts it this way:

The extreme generality, diffuseness, and variability of man's innate (i.e.: genetically programmed) response capacities means that without the assistance of cultural patterns he would be functionally incomplete, not merely a talented ape who had, like some under-privileged child, unfortunately been prevented from realizing his full potentialities, but a kind of formless monster with neither sense of direction nor power of self-control, a chaos of spasmodic impulses and vague emotions.

Even the most remote suggestion that one's symbols may fail arouses the most severe anxiety, so great is one's dependence on them. In this approach, culture provides humanity with meanings, and the greatest and most definitive feature of humanness itself is the need as well as the ability for conceptualization. Langer has said (1957:187), "Man can adapt himself somehow to anything his imagination can cope with; but he cannot deal with Chaos." Culture in the form of shared symbols provides mankind's most important assets—the ability to "grasp" the world, to agree on what is "really real." These are ultimate concepts, which endow one with the sense that the world is orderly and is what it is supposed to be. It is the human quest for lucidity and meaning that enables mankind to deal with great pain. Evil, loss, suffering, misfortune, and disappointments can be accepted as long as life is an explicable experience.

One of the most dramatic examples of this quest for lucidity is described by Lévi-Strauss (1963) in his analysis of a cure by a South American medicine man. The medicine man in this analysis gives the suffering person a vocabulary, a set of labels for comprehending illness. In this case the mere naming of the ailment proclaims that the sick person's previously unique, confused experience has been known before, felt by others, and has a term that makes sense of the symptoms. Thus the term serves as a codified response to the individual's suffering by the culture. The application of the label makes a previously idiosyncratic event, which isolated and terrified the patient, into a social experience, predictable and treatable. In other words, the sickness is symbolized, hence incorporated as part of social and shared experience that can be understood. Being understandable, it now can be endured. It might be said that the mere provision of a name for the illness—that is, the application of a collective symbol—constitutes the greatest part of the cure. This is a useful and dramatic illustration of the power of symbols that conveys some of our justification for regarding culture as a set of shared meanings or symbols, and, as has been mentioned, this approach to culture is especially helpful concerning the matters of aging and the aged.

One of the most significant features concerning aging in contemporary

American society is the very absence of shared meanings and collective representations for this period of life. There are in this culture many rather vague feelings, attitudes, habits, and expectations about aging, but these are not truly symbols for they are not widely shared with clear connotations, nor do they provide us with meanings. It is important to distinguish between our diffuse and usually negative stereotypes and preconceptions regarding the aged and a collective, specific interpretation of the meaning of being aged in American culture. The ambiguity and confusion surrounding the last phases of life for most Americans is tantamount to an absence of meanings by which to comprehend its significance. This very lack is a cultural phenomenon, for when other societies are considered, especially preliterate and preindustrial ones, the greater clarity of conceptualizations regarding old age is impressive. That is not to say that "they" have "solved" it and "we" have not; let us not fall prey to that occupational hazard common among anthropologists of romanticizing "the natives" and pointing out with lightly disguised delight how much better they are doing than we civilized folk. It does seem fair to say, however, that industrial, Western civilizations have dealt with aging less directly and satisfactorily than many simpler societies. The reasons for this are manifold; perhaps most important is the fact that the aged are genuinely less necessary as well as far more numerous here and now than in other times and places.

One of the major tasks of an anthropological view of aging is the examination of some of the ways other societies have conceptualized and treated their old people, some of the social and cultural variables that seem to contribute to these alternatives, and some of the conclusions that may be drawn from these examples that are of potential use to our own society in solving what is considered, appropriately, a social problem. In considering other cultures the reader must bear in mind that definitive answers or even recommendations for our own problems cannot be anticipated; however, we can hope to locate some of the important questions and some useful clues. No attempt can be made here to survey other cultures systematically. The following cases and issues have been selected on two grounds: First, for their potential relevance for understanding our own culture's problems and circumstances concerning the aged. (Throughout this discussion the implications of phenomena in other cultures for our own will be brought out wherever possible.) Second, material is used that illuminates three dimensions pertinent to aging and the aged in any society: (1) the ideological dimension, that is, some of the collective representations and value orientations relevant to aging; (2) some social organizational features that appear closely related to differing modes and styles of aging; and (3) some of the implications of social complexity for aging and the aged.

The Ideological Dimension

To begin with conceptions of the stages of life, and their corresponding roles, expectations, and attitudes, we must note that no fixed cross-cultural definition of old age is valid. In our own society we have precise chronological and legal as well as psychological and biological cut-off points for each stage of life. Some psychological and biological definitions of age with varying degrees of precision can be found in all cultures, but exact chronological and legal definitions are unique to Western literate society, with its written records and preoccupation with quantified units. In all societies "perceived age" and "attributed age" exist and are relevant; what varies is the precision of the definitions and the amount of discrepancy between the two.

One of the most useful lessons of anthropology concerning life stages is this: that there are no universal criteria for life stages, nor are there even universal divisions of a crude sort. Some societies have no conception of a period of old age per se. This is demonstrated in some of those groups that stress the continuity of membership in corporate kin groups where, for example, the clan is considered to include all living members, all the forebears who have ever existed, and all children yet unborn within a given descent line. This is not to say that roles are not distributed according to chronological age, but rather that a distinct, well-formulated set of experiences and attributes for particular age spans is not provided.

Such a state of affairs may seem surprising at first glance, for one might expect that no society can fail to recognize the potentialities of different ages, just as no society can fail to take account of sex differences in its division of labor. But at one time our own society did not recognize the period that it is presently most preoccupied with—childhood. Before the Renaissance the child was viewed as a miniature adult having no distinctive characteristics or needs associated with his age (Ariès 1962). This means that even such matters as childhood and old age, which we are inclined to think of as "givens" in nature that all societies must acknowledge—even these life phases prove to be cultural conceptions that may or may not be present in various societies at different times.

Thus while every society differentiates among some life stages defined by age, there is no fixed correspondence across societies as to what these ages are, how many there are, and what features characterize them.

It is useful, therefore, to distinguish between age span and age grade. The latter is usually thought of as a general "human type," a broad cultural definition of human potentialities and behaviors appropriate to an individual at a time of life. As such, *age grading* provides a basis for self-identification and societal role allocation. One of the essential functions served by age grades is the maintenance of continuity achieved by the interaction of different age grades or generations. While some societies lack conceptions of childhood and old age, it seems that all have an age grade of "adult," a full-fledged member of the society who has received the social heritage from the previous age grade and transmits it to the younger one.

In contrast, we may think of *age span* as a chronological rather than sociological time period; in other words, it is a period of time rather than a set of expectations. Another useful category is that of *age set,* a social category for which expectations are quite precise. An age set is actually a corporate body with a definite and limited membership defined on the basis of the age principle. Age-homogeneous groups may be coterminous with the entire social organization in some cultures, so that the age principle is the fundamental basis for allocation of all rights and responsibilities; more will be said about such arrangements later.

The ethnographic record is quite explicit in showing that age, like sex and descent, is a biological building block that is very freely used by culture. Each society, therefore, must be examined empirically, for there are no absolute, universally valid definitions of the meanings or even the existence of a given set of life stages. The "clo" Bushman is the individual who has three living children. An Eskimo male who can no longer hunt, and the female whose teeth are too worn to chew the frost off frozen furs, are old. The Irish peasant whose father still lives and controls the family farm is called "boy," and although he is thirty or forty years old, he is not permitted to marry, and thus cannot become an adult member of his group. In the United States, regardless of chronological age, a Negro male may be called "boy," signifying that part of the American value system that equates economic impotence with immaturity. Very few cultures define age in formal, chronological terms as we do when we retire people at age sixty-five, permit them to marry and smoke at age eighteen, drink and vote at age eighteen or twenty-one, and so forth. Most definitions of age are more functional and flexible than this, but then the American approach to time, a quantifiable and objective entity, plays a large part in explaining our attitude toward age as chronological.

Part of a culture's conceptualization of a stage of "old age" involves its notions of "over-age" or senescence and death. Senescence is widely recognized culturally as the time of maximum dependence and minimum social utility, a universally pathetic and hopeless period of the life cycle. It is a time remarkable in our own culture because our technological competence has transformed it into a social problem by preserving substantial numbers of such people. At no other time and place has this been true. In simpler societies these dying members may be regarded as anomalies who are too few to require special institutions or elaborate conceptualizations. They may be treated more or less well. Our brethren in preliterate societies cannot be heaped with praise on this matter. The dying are charity cases everywhere, and their fate is subject to hazards. They may be exposed, abandoned, suffered, cherished, succored, ignored, or eliminated. This may be done with honor, indifference, or callousness.

The reasons for these different treatments are not always clear. The terribly poor and primitive Yahgan of Tierra del Fuego have been known to carry their ancient members on their backs despite one of the most extreme climates, a desperately impoverished and nomadic life, and a miserable technology. Their neighbors, the Ona, who share a very similar way of life, subject their old people to exposure. Elderly Eskimos who can no longer contribute to their society may walk off alone never to be seen again or they may be given a departure ceremony at which they are honored, then ritually killed. Here, for example, is a description of such a ceremony and its meaning among the Greenland Eskimo (Freuchen 1961:194–95):

In some tribes, an old man wants his oldest son or favorite daughter to be the one to put the string around his neck and hoist him to his death. This was always done at the height of a party where good things were being eaten, where everyone—including the one who was about to die—felt happy and gay, and which would end with the angakok conjuring and dancing to chase out the evil spirits. At the end of his performance, he would give a special rope made of seal and walrus skin to the "executioner" who then placed it over the beam of the roof of the house and fastened it around the neck of the old man. Then the two rubbed noses, and the young man pulled the rope. Everybody in the house either helped or sat on the end of the rope so as to have the honor of bringing the old suffering one to the Happy Hunting Grounds where there would always be light and plenty of game of all kinds.

In general, only immediate necessity has caused simple people to abandon their aged parents. The abandonment is often lightened by the cultural provision for their honorable death and the hope of an attractive afterlife.

Inherent in a society's conceptions concerning the aged are its handling and understanding of death. Death, like aging, is striking because of the variety of emotions it arouses in the hearts of men. It may be regarded as a final state or a transition; it may be glorified or denied; it may arouse fear, envy, or indifference in those remaining behind. The dead may be incorporated as part of the ongoing society, vigilantly watching and influencing continuing human life; they may be supplicated, shunned, or deified. Lévi-Strauss (1964:258–59) has an interesting approach to the question of social attitudes toward death. He sees a fundamental opposition between nature and culture, and considers death as the arch-enemy of man's humanity.

> In fact and law alike, death is both *natural* and *anticultural*. That is to say that, whenever a native dies, an injury is done not only to those near to him, but to Society as a whole; and Nature, in consequence, is held to be in debt to Society.

When a man dies among the Bororo of South America that debt is extracted from Nature in the form of a collective hunt to kill a large and important animal in retribution for the human loss.

Where the dead are deeply involved in the lives of the living, one may encounter many forms of death and/or ancestor cults. Interpretations of the reasons for death cults and ancestor worship have been numerous and often contradictory. Freud (1913) regarded ancestor worship as expressing the omnipresent ambivalence between the living and the dead and the resentment toward authority. Frazer (1890) considered it the oldest and most primitive form of religion, based on an "innate" fear of corpses. Malinowski (1916) stressed hostility toward death in general, which is then extended to the dead. Hertz (1907) saw death cults as serving to maintain continuity of succession between the generations. He felt that death cults serve to deny the mortality of the human body by stressing the immortality of the social group. This is achieved through worship of the group's dead. And Fortes (1961) has suggested that ancestor worship is the social projection of filial ties, which are extrapolated and extended to the spiritual level.

Ethnographic evidence exists that can contradict any one of these interpretations. That death does not necessarily arouse emotions of fear, dread, and resentment is attested, for example, by this excerpt describing the attitudes of the Eskimos (Freuchen 1961:194):

> Fear of death is unknown to them, they know only love of life. The Eskimos are themselves unaware of the difficulty of their existence, they always enjoy life with an enviable intensity and they believe themselves to be the happiest people on earth living in the most beautiful country there is. When an old man sees the young men go out hunting and cannot himself go along, he is sorry. When he has to ask other people for skins for his clothing, when he cannot ever again be the one to invite the neighbors to eat his game, life is of no value to him. Rheumatism and other ills may plague him, and he wants to die. This has been done in different ways in different tribes, but everywhere it is held that if a man feels himself to be a nuisance, his love for his kin, coupled with the sorrow of not being able to take part in the things which are worthwhile impels him to die.

Regardless of cultural variations of feelings about death and treatment of the dead, death is never overlooked by the living. Lévi-Strauss (1964: 256) may be quoted again here:

> There is probably no such thing as a society which does not treat its dead with consideration. At a time when mankind as we know it had hardly come into being, Neanderthal Man already buried his dead in tombs made up of a few rough stones.

Some societies have a concept of retirement, as they do about old age, and others do not. Simmons (1960) noted that the aged find most valuable occupation in societies of sedentary cultivators. Here they are gradually phased out of the work force as they assume progressively less demanding tasks. In simpler societies sustained by collecting, hunting, and fishing, fewer opportunities for productive work exist for the aged. Here the old people may retire to the campfire and take on a specific status of "no longer able to work." The meaning of such a period varies from culture to culture: it may be a time of deserved rest and honor or it may be a period of sadness and loss of social esteem. Simmons (1960:74) wisely suggests:

> Opportunities to keep on working at essential but light tasks are obvious psychological and social assets in old age; but such labors which continue far into senescence may insure little more than bare subsistence, if that, and quite often become very burdensome. Complete release from enforced labor may sometimes prove more rewarding than repeated demotions into lower levels of drudgery. Compromise tasks, while lighter than previous work, often involve threats to prestige, as in the case of the dignified old warrior confined to "woman's work" in the house. The physical efforts in the late stages of one's dotage prove to be little more than toeholds on security.

No discussion of the ideological components of age and aging can afford to overlook the closely associated collective representations concerning time, change, and progress. The Western view of time is linear—it has a beginning, middle, and end. It does not flow in a subjective continuum but marches jerkily along in quantifiable units. It is objectified, as Whorf (1956) has pointed out, and conceived of as a series of things, like apples sitting on a shelf. As such it can be added, subtracted, divided, multiplied, gained, lost, saved, earned, squandered, garnered, and allocated. Western notions of the nature of time are illuminated and revealed by our Calvinistic ethic where, as Tawney (1926) and Weber (1930) have demonstrated so convincingly, these notions may be seen as inextricably involved with our habits and values concerning money, growth, and power. Indeed, our conception of time can be regarded as pivotal to the Puritan dogma, which provided the substratum for so much of the American value system. If time is understood as finite, then the close of life is an irredeemable tragedy, an irreversible loss.

Without the sense of the continuous nature of time provided by some cultures, humans face the end of life as an extermination that severs them from everything meaningful. For some, the Christian afterlife cushions the shock, but it may not carry enough appeal to compete with the more entrenched and deeper value on the future of *this* life. In her writings on American value orientations, Florence Kluckhohn (Kluckhohn and Strodtbeck 1961) points out that as a culture we cherish the future over the present, the capacity to alter our environment over the acceptance of it, the importance of *becoming* rather than of *being,* and achieving over accommodating. Old people are devalued as belonging to the past, and they are slipped into parenthetical slots in the social structure. If they are accorded any importance other than that of being tolerated or ignored, it is because of their remarkable accomplishments as individuals. As a group they are not esteemed by the culture. Ironically, it is often the individual's refusal to demonstrate or accept old age, the very demonstration that *flaunts* his status, which wins him respect and attention.

Just how ironic this is has been shown by Clark (1961), who illustrated some of the ways our dominant value orientations work against the aged in this society. She has compared two groups of elderly people; one defined as adaptive in value orientations and the other as maladaptive to the point of mental illness. The members of the adaptive group are concerned with consideration for others, are congenial and interested in preserving their physical and financial resources. They try to coexist with the inevitable, are oriented toward relaxation, and have been freed from desire to compete. In direct contrast, the mentally ill aged people are interested in status and achievement, are acquisitive rather than conservative of their resources, are aggressive, try to control their lives, are ambitious, competitive, and more oriented toward progress than continuity and toward the maintenance of a high level of aspiration. A set of values that emphasizes achievement, success, change, progress, individualism, and the future is a source of disappointment for the aged, for these are categorically unattainable to them. Time is their enemy. They are defeated from the beginning. The mentally ill aged, of course, are demonstrating a type of behavior and orientation that may make a younger person successful. In other words, they are victims of a sharp cultural dichotomy that defines one type of behavior as a requisite for success at one time of life and quite a different, almost opposite type of orientation as a requisite for success at a later phase of life. It is difficult to comprehend how old people manage to make this reversal at all. Some people are simply more flexible than others and can accommodate to the role reversals. Despite the sharp discontinuities between adolescence and adulthood, many of those who are successful as adolescents also become successful as adults. Many adults make the successful shift in values to become well-adjusted old people.

Transitions from one period of life to the next are not managed with equal smoothness in any society. In our own society, relatively speaking, childhood is handled well, adolescence badly, adulthood well, and aging badly—all in terms of social support, consistent roles and expectations, appropriate training, and provision for esteeming those who achieve status and skills.

Industrial, rapidly changing societies favor the young while the aged fare better in more static, sedentary environments. More will be said later concerning the kinds of societies in which the aged are most likely to feel secure and valued. As a final consideration of the relationship between aging, change, and conceptions of time, Simmons (1960:88) has offered a general principle that is quite useful:

In the long and steady strides of the social order, the aging get themselves fixed and favored in positions, power and performance. They have what we call seniority rights. But, when social conditions become unstable and the rate of change reaches a galloping pace, the aged are riding for an early fall, and the more youthful associates take their seats in the saddles. Change is the crux of the problem of aging as well as its challenge.

Where change is equated with "the good" and where time is a commodity, the aged have little opportunity. Their life situation categorically denies them what is most valued, what gave the life they knew its significance. It is poignant and paradoxical that the virtues characterizing the well-adjusted old people in Clark's (1967) study amounted to "not getting in anyone's way." These virtues lead to invisibility, anonymity, and all too often, insignificance. The value syndrome can be indicated by an adage for the achievement of "good" adjustment by all dependent populations—children, hospitalized people, inmates of all kinds: "Don't make waves."

Clark (1967) points out that one should examine cultures whose values for those in the prime of life correspond to the values manifested by her well-adjusted group. Peasant societies, for example, typically regard all the virtues of life as in short supply; this is Foster's (1965) "image of the limited good." Peasants characteristically regard the good things of life as finite, of limited quantities, and beyond their power to increase. Such a value system is diametrically opposed to the American value system that dictates competition, acquisition, and the exploitation of the environment.

Aged people are faced with limitations on time that they cannot alter; hence, Clark reasons, the old should find themselves more comfortable in societies such as that of peasant groups, which esteem acquiescence. Similarly, the values of some Mexican-Americans may incline that group to the meeting of difficulties by adjusting to them and accepting them as "fate." Perhaps the aged feel less stress in societies that have such values, but they are not necessarily more secure or more greatly esteemed there. They may not be required to make a drastic shift in values as they pass out of adulthood, but their problems are only partly psychological to begin with. Their social position may be just as precarious as it is in our society. These are actually empirical questions: Do Mexican-Americans adjust more readily to old age than their fellow Americans who share dominant core value orientations? Is the concept of "fatality" and is acquiescence an aid in making the transition to the end of life?

We might go on to examine the adjustment of people with other conceptualizations of time, most particularly Orientals, who stress continuity with the past and who esteem those who have existed for a long while. People whose culture provides ancestor cults, in which the aged are regarded as founders of the group and are accorded the reverence usually reserved for the deities, should also be examined for the treatment of the aged. So should those cultures that have a circular conception of time usually associated with a religious scheme that stresses reincarnation.

In all these different cultures one may assume that the aged have a better environment than that of our own society. Our prognosis for solving our ideological problems concerning the aged is poor, for our evaluation of the old is a product of our most cherished symbols—as Langer would say, part of our very *Weltanschauung*. Basic values change very slowly, and even if our society successfully solves the mechanical, bureaucratic, maintenance, administrative, and economic aspects of the problems of the aged, it will still face the biggest task: that of finding a reason for them to exist, and of according them the esteem they need to feel wanted and secure. So much else would have to change before our society values the aged, regardless of how well they are treated, that little optimism on this point seems justified.

Social Organizational Dimensions

The ways in which the aged, the dying, and the dead are placed in the social organizations of different cultures are no less variable than the ideas and conceptions concerning them. Nor are they truly separable, for ideas both reflect and shape the institutions provided for handling these categories. Perhaps one of the social characteristics most relevant to explaining different placement of and expectations for the aged is a society's system of reckoning kinship. It is useful to reduce the great variations in kinship systems to two major types: those organized on the basis of the lineal and those on the collateral principles. The former stresses social relations in a single line of descent over time. The latter emphasizes both lines of descent so as to include as relatives all those living at a given time.

Two kinds of kinship groupings arise as a result of emphasizing one of these principles over the other: the kindred is one grouping, and the lineage or clan is the other. The kindred, characteristic of our own society, includes all those people defined as relatives traced from a single individual's point of view—its point of reference is, by definition, egocentric. Thus no two individuals except full siblings have the same kindreds. For this reason kindreds are not discrete membership groups, balanced and equal as are clans and lineages, but are more like networks of overlapping ties.

The lineal principle, by contrast, usually traces descent through one parent and includes as members all those descendants from a given ancestor (male or female) for a given number of generations. In its most complete form of expression, the lineage members regard their oldest common ancestor as the founder of the group.[2]

The implications of these two different arrangements are far-reaching, and it is not accidental that kindreds are more often found in the rapidly changing, industrial, and Western societies that stress individuality, achievement, and mobility. (No causal relationship is suggested here, for as Tawney [1926] has pointed out, the familial and the economic characteristics of our society developed simultaneously and reciprocally.)

---

2. Following British usage, a clan is regarded as a group of lineages, including as members the living, dead, and yet unborn; a lineage is all those living members, usually covering a three-generation span.

Where the lineal principle is used to generate the most important societal groups, the older members of the society accumulate great authority and status. The authority automatically accruing to age in this arrangement is nicely illustrated by the existence of the ancestor cults already mentioned. Such cults are a conspicuous feature of African religious systems. Fortes (1965:122) states that, "Among the Tallensi of Ghana . . . [ancestor cult] so pervades their social life as to put them on a par with the Chinese and Romans in this respect."

Ancestor worship among some peoples is interlocked with the political system, so that the social, religious, and political organizations are fused and undifferentiated. Societies that have elaborate ancestor cults are found on many different levels of complexity, from the very simple to those comprising entire kingdoms and nations. The king of the Swazi kingdom of South Africa appeals to his own ancestors on behalf of the entire nation. On the local level, the head of the compound appeals to his ancestors on behalf of the residents of the compound (Kuper 1964). Among the East African Tallensi, sacrifices to the ancestor can be offered by a son only through his older living male relatives in the same line: his father, uncle, or older brothers. The son has no individual right of ritual access to his ancestors while his elders are still alive (Fortes 1945). Thus ancestor worship becomes an extension of the authority of the older generation. This is the case regardless of the ancestor's personal attributes. Fortes (1965:133) puts the matter like this:

> This was repeatedly brought home to me by Tallensi elders. A man may be a liar, or a wastrel, or an adulterer, or a quarrelsome neighbor, or a negligent kinsman; he may be a mean and bad tempered parent who has made his sons' life miserable; he may have been abroad for years and have contributed nothing to their upbringing. If he dies leaving a son he becomes an ancestor of equal standing with any other ancestor. To put it in the believer's words, he acquires the power to intervene in the life and affairs of his descendants in exactly the same way as any other ancestor.

The ancestors are the source of all misfortune and of all prosperity. Just as a son cannot directly approach his ancestors except through his father, neither can these ancestors intervene in the life of the son except through his father. Such an arrangement encourages the greatest filial respect and responsibility, since the man who neglects his duties to his forebears incurs the wrath of a large population, both those living and those dead. A good relationship with his father is the means by which a son may ensure the intercession of supernaturals who affect his well-being. Of course, the observance of filial duty, which is assured by this arrangement, has no necessary emotional correlates; individuals may detest their fathers. Indeed, ambivalence between the generations is often most pronounced in societies with ancestor cults. Nevertheless, the official status of senior citizens is guaranteed regardless of private emotions that may be expressed toward them.

Among the Swazi, who are patrilineal and patrilocal, the social structure is dramatized by the actual physical arrangement of the compound or household, one of the most important features of which is the "Great Hut." This hut is presided over by the headman's mother and contains the skulls of cattle sacrificed to his ancestors. It is specifically dedicated to the headman's senior paternal relatives, a category of kinsman to whom only the old man has direct access, and whose supernatural hegemony contributes greatly to his control over the members of the entire compound. Daughters-in-law, living in their husbands' compounds, have no access to the Great Hut. In addition, they must detour to avoid passing the front of the doorway, avert their eyes, and drop their voices when they approach it. These in-marrying women must return to their own parental homes to participate in religious observances. Their participation is through their brothers and fathers who sacrifice on their behalf. Thus age and sex interact to delegate authority to a single group, the older men. Lineally based societies, in addition to solving the problems of distribution of authority by invoking the age principle, have also solved the problem of intergenerational continuity. Among these societies we can expect to find the transitions between age spans most neatly provided for and clearly structured.[3]

But once more it must be emphasized that smoothness in handling

---

3. Eisenstadt (1956:53) has developed a very complex theory concerning the relationship between the generations, which suggests that in societies where social maturity and status are withheld by the older generation from the younger, age-homogeneous units are likely to be very important. "These [age-homogeneous] units have their origin in the tension between generations, and as their function is to find outlets for these tensions, they may function . . . as starting points for deviant groups." In these situations the group's specific functions may be rebellion against the older generation rather than the complementary interaction that might otherwise occur between them.

these matters does not imply any particular psychological state. Tensions between the generations may be just as acute and acrimonious as those encountered in our own society where treatment of the aged is less structured. This will be illustrated by the use of the age principle to which I now turn: age-graded societies, or, more precisely, societies where age spans are formed into corporate groups and used as primary social and political units.

These units, sometimes called age sets, may take the form of ritual groups, military regiments, age-homogeneous villages, corps of occupational specialists, and so forth. One of the most striking features associated with the use of the age principle as a basis of social organization is the flexibility of groups so formed. The resultant units easily fill a great variety of different functions. In general, all the men born within a certain number of consecutive years are admitted to one age set and the number of years varies from place to place. At the end of a given period, the set is closed and recruitment for a new one begins. The sets are usually named and a man goes all through life with the same age mates with whom he may have the closest ties and the most serious obligations.

A typical series of age sets is found among the Galla of Southwest Ethiopia, where there are six sets, each composed of eight-year spans, rotating in a forty-year cycle. The first set is comprised of children, not yet counted as full citizens, who fill the tasks of messengers for junior and senior warriors, while the second set is made up of adolescent boys who function as shepherds. The third and fourth sets are junior and senior warriors, while the fifth set is made up of public officials with responsibilities for the administration of the government. The last set is the leaders who regulate and provide for the ritual life of the people. The head of the most senior set functions as "president" of the entire group; the head of the senior military set is chief military commander, and so forth. Thus the age sets function as tribal police, parliament, warriors, administrative staff, and religious leaders. Socialization and intergenerational continuity are handled automatically by the age set system.

Another advantage of the system is that among dispersed people, age sets may function to achieve cross-tribal unity, since age set members are frequently recruited by stressing age and disregarding local residence. Thus a man from a given age set has age mates in the surrounding tribes, to whom he can turn for aid and hospitality when he is out of his own territory, and who provide him with support. Age mate solidarity may also function as a bulwark against entrenched authority in strongly age-oriented societies. An Australian aborigine who believes he is being wronged by the seniors of his horde may turn to his age mates for support against the elders and wrest his rights from the old men with the assistance of his peers, who are organized into cohesive and enduring groups. Among the Tiv, in fact, there are regular rebellions against the entrenched authorities, which are launched by groups of age mates who seize power and hold it until younger men wrest the leadership from them.

One of the most distinctive characteristics of societies that use the age principle to form age sets is that transitions through the life cycle take place, not gradually and imperceptibly as is the case for many of the transitions in our society, but in a series of jumps. Each of these jumps is characterized by (1) status change of the entire group rather than of individuals, and (2) ceremonies and rituals that accompany the passage into each new stage. The formal transfer from one grade to another is always an occasion of public significance to the entire community.

The major features of these age set systems in general can be summarized as follows: (1) the age principle is used as a means of establishing corporate groups; (2) formal transitions of these groups from one social status defined by age to another occurs; (3) they result in the exercise of authority by a senior group or council of elders whose authority is backed by the influence and sanctions of ancestors on whose good will the well-being of the entire group ultimately depends; and (4) where age sets are not used as the basis for forming local or residential groups the grades may be used to provide unity and cohesion over a wide range that cross-cuts locale and is synchronized with age groups among neighboring people. Age grades thus serve multiple and quite diverse functions: they may provide for quick mustering of armed warriors among peoples who are not highly centralized politically; they handle socialization and continuity between generations; they buttress traditional values and provide authority; they train occupational specialists and they serve as public welfare organizations by requiring support (financial and emotional) among age mates. Describing conservative Swazi households, Kuper (1964:51) shows how age grades sustain the status quo and may serve as a bulwark against change:

> When conflict breaks out in conservative homesteads between parent and child generations or between older and younger siblings,

it is not a conflict of ideologies but of personality. Sons may covet the power of the father but when he dies they hope to exercise over their own sons the authority they themselves once resented. Young people are anxious to possess the privileges of their seniors, not to abolish the privileges of seniority; young brides may rebel against the way particular inlaws abuse the rights of age, but they agree to the principle that age and sex are entitled to those rights. At the present time, the social structure which gives power to the older generation is challenged by the money economy, a new legal system, and schooling for a literate society.

Examples may be found in societies with age set systems in which relations between generations involve more stress than in our culture, and in which hostility toward the aged is as acute. Examples of societies may also be found where old people are accorded the greatest esteem and security. Smooth transitions from one stage of life to another and effective structuring of cross-generational continuity assured by age set systems have no necessary correlation with emotion or attitude. This state of affairs may be interpreted optimistically for our own society. Although we have not yet solved the problem of the place of the aged in the social structure, because the ethnographic evidence suggests that emotion and social status may vary independently, we hope eventually to untangle our mixed emotions toward our aged members and to accord them esteem and value, if not power, influence, and structural relevance.

Social Complexity, Technology, and Division of Labor

It is frequently remarked, and indeed has been a recurrent theme throughout this discussion, that literate, complex, Western, industrial societies penalize old age most heavily. It is the rapid change endemic to such societies, rather than the fact of complexity itself, that is probably responsible for this condition. Ethnographic data suggest that the simplest societies are not the best for the aged, since these societies are often (but certainly not always) found in harsh environments with very rude technological development. These foraging and hunting or fishing societies are often marginal in terms of subsistence and simply cannot afford to support any sizable body of people that can no longer support itself. Infanticide and something for which the term "geronticide" might be used occur in these cultures, although attitudes toward children and the aged may be those of the greatest affection and esteem. Accounts of Eskimo and Bushmen young people leaving their beloved parents behind to die are heart-wrenching precisely because of the absence of justifying values or rationalizations. Such behavior is a matter of stark necessity but is no less sharply lamented. Such a situation is the inverse of that in our society; we sustain our old people physically but abandon them psychologically and emotionally. Thus it may be said that for quite different reasons the situation of the aged in the simplest and the most complex societies, the richest and the poorest, is equally unsure.

Simmons (1960) has offered a very interesting hypothesis indicating that it is in the middle-range societies—rural, agrarian, peasant communities—that the aged are most useful and sometimes (again, not always) because of this, more secure. There are opportunities in these settings for the aged to perform many tasks requiring manipulative skill rather than heavy manual labor, and thus they are more able to hold their own. One might further speculate on the reasons for the security of the aged in agricultural societies: that is, the common value accorded to the ownership of land and the association of the land with time. Here, too, one finds lineage-based social organizations such as ancestor cults and clans in which land is often owned by the group (which is to say, owned by the ancestors and administered by the elders). Just such a configuration is found in Vietnam but is given little recognition by the intervening nonpeasant powers. There the attempt to relocate a family jeopardizes its affiliation, contact with, and protection by its ancestors.

But regardless of societal complexity, the division of labor awarded to the elderly has many similarities across cultures. Midwifery, entertainment, storytelling, beauty treatment, scarification, socialization, and ritual and religious specialization are often the business of the old men and women of the group. In preliterate societies, the acquisition and retention of knowledge and experience are directly related to living. Thus the old are the repositories of the wisdom accumulated and transmitted orally. This is one reason why anthropologists, in their work, must rely so heavily on aged informants. Age is often directly related to the amount of cultural knowledge accumulated. The point is illustrated by Thomas (1958:71–72) in her ethnography on the Bushmen. In this passage the author describes how the Bushmen have just caught a springbok and the anthropologists ask one of the men to dissect it in an effort to ascertain the extent of the group's knowledge of anatomy and systems of the body.

> Gai agreed to tell what he knew, so the springbok was dragged to a sandy spot and a small fire was built. All the people sat around to watch as Bill opened the belly of the springbok and rolled it onto its back. He pointed to the diaphragm and asked what it was. Gai told him the name.
>
> "What is it for?" Bill asked.
>
> "We eat it."
>
> "Is it for anything else?"
>
> "We don't know. We just eat it."
>
> . . . Gai became embarrassed . . . and Ukwane then said that he would explain instead, because he was an old man. . . . Gai could not speak of sex in front of women because it was both improper and dangerous and would weaken his power to hunt, but Ukwane was too old for hunting and besides was past the age when many of the tabus concerning sex applied to him. Old Bushmen understand everything better anyways, young Bushmen say.
>
> Ukwane knew a great deal. He named every major part, inside and out, of the animal, even naming the major veins and arteries that lead to and from the heart. . . . "I am an old man," he would say, "and I know that the diaphragm separates the heart and lungs from the stomach," or, "I am an old Ukwane and so I know that, when the heart is gone the animal cannot live . . ."

In many gerontocratic societies, such as the Arunta of Australia, the old men jealously guard their knowledge instead of sharing it. They often form secret societies that they use to increase their influence by withholding knowledge. The power they wield over younger members by keeping this knowledge from all but those of whom they approve gives them the assurance of group stability. The old are deeply entrenched in the status quo and use all their authority to inhibit change of any kind through the closely regulated transmission of the accumulated tribal wisdom and ideology. Naturally, literacy and with it the provision of equal access to knowledge by younger men rapidly undermine the authority of the elders.

It is not merely elderliness and the accumulation of knowledge that seem to explain the frequency with which one finds the aged (and the dead) in special ritual positions. Individuals who have passed a certain age often take on mystical attributes in the eyes of their group; they are the magicians and religious specialists—the shamans, witches, priests, medicine men, and sorcerers. Seemingly, they have withstood the attrition of life itself and are regarded as beyond and therefore immune to the spiritual hazards of mortality. They are almost spirits themselves and they begin to command the knowledge and influence of the dead over the living. Fear of the extremely old and the attributing to them of evil will are quite common; witches, even in Western lore, are usually old people.

The affinity of the aged for the dead and the spirit world is analyzed brilliantly by Eliade (1964). He suggests that these are the people viewed as most likely to be able to transcend time itself by returning magically to a lost paradise, a dream time that existed before men became mortals and lost touch with the gods, the dead, animals, the underworld, and the heavens. Old people bring back special knowledge of this primordial timeless condition and may share it with their people by relating and interpreting their dreams and visions. Special treatment accorded the dead is often extended to the aged who have almost reached this sacred state. Interestingly, the sacred state is shared by children as well as old people. Both categories of people are often viewed as mystical and are felt to be privy to the special powers of the innocent. The bond between grandparents and grandchildren among the Huichol Indians illustrates this concept of continuity between the recently born and the about-to-die. On their Sacred Peyote Hunt when these Indians symbolically and actually return to the land of their origins where the gods live (which the Ancient Ones left in becoming mortal) and when they arrive at this home of their ancestors, the old men are called and treated as little children.

Concluding Remarks

In looking over these observations for any generalizations of value to us in this culture, two points emerge as particularly relevant. First, there is no fixed or given manner of aging, or viewing or treating the aged and the dead. Our own society represents one alternative among a great variety. It is unique only in representing the extreme along a continuum, since this society is changing more rapidly than many. More important, it is unique in that there are more old people to understand and place in the social structure as usefully as possible. In actuality there are more old people among us to assimilate and accommodate, for at present it seems fair to say that the aged constitute a dislocated group—societal refugees—structurally alienated and unabsorbed. In dealing with the "problem of the aged" we are concerned with a number of equally urgent, closely related problems. Enhancing the meaning of leisure in an acquisitive society is one of these problems. It is a problem that must be solved for great numbers of people in our automated society, not merely for the aged. We must attempt to utilize the talents and experiences of the aged that are presently wasted. This situation also exists among other disprivileged populations—women, blacks, Chicanos, rural folk, and the unskilled. When the numbers of all these groups are tallied, it may appear that our country is distributing its privileges to and accepting the services of a group so small as to constitute an elite. Broadening this base is a challenge indeed and will carry us far toward our self-conception as a culture that values humanity for its own sake in all its many forms. For idealistic as well as practical reasons, it behooves us to turn our closest attention toward these populations, and solutions achieved for the aged should be able to be generalized far beyond this particular group. The anthropological survey conducted here suggests that if there is no single desirable solution, neither is failure foreordained; it is both frightening and reassuring to conclude that anything is possible.

Part 2
The Work of Ritual

We Don't Wrap Herring in a Printed Page: Fusion, Fictions, and Continuity in Secular Ritual

A Working Definition of Ritual

Ritual is full of contradictions and paradox. Most paradoxical of all, by selecting and shaping a fragment of social life, it defines a portion of reality. The very act of consciously defining reality calls to our attention that, indeed, reality is merely a social construct, a collusive drama, intrinsically conventional, an act of collective imagination.

Rituals are not only paradoxical intrinsically, they are built out of the paradoxes suggested by their symbols. They cope with paradox by mounting the mood of conviction and persuasion which fuses opposing elements referred to by their symbols, creating the belief that things are as they have been portrayed—proper, true, inevitable, natural. How this is accomplished is one of the most challenging of the analyst's tasks.[1]

A working definition of ritual may be suggested, each element of which points to its capacity to achieve one of its special tasks— persuasion. Ritual is an act or actions intentionally conducted by a group of people employing one or more symbols in a repetitive, formal, precise, highly stylized fashion. Action is indicated because rituals persuade the body first; behaviors precede emotions in the participants. Rituals are conspicuously physiological; witness their behavioral basis, the use of repetition and the involvement of the entire human sensorium through dramatic presentations employing costumes, masks, colors, textures, odors, foods, beverages, songs, dances, props, settings, and so forth. Critical, analytic thought, the attitude which would pierce the illusion

---

1. See especially Turner (1967, 1968, 1974) for a description of the processes by means of which contrary and paradoxical referents of ritual symbols are fused and reconciled.

of reality, is anathema to ritual. The fiction underlying ritual is twofold: first, that rituals are not made-up productions, and second, that the contradictions embraced by their symbols have been erased. The enemy of ritual is one who is incapable of or unwilling to voluntarily suspend disbelief—the spoilsport.

Because of its repetitiveness, formality, and rigid precision, rituals can take on dangerous matters. Victor Turner has made the felicitous comment that rituals are to symbols as is a metal container to a radioactive isotope, containing without snuffing out its content (1974). Rituals are stylized because they must be convincing. People must recognize what rituals are saying, and find their claims authentic, their styles familiar and aesthetically satisfying. Rituals can be distinguished from custom and mere habit by their utilization of symbols. They have significance far beyond the information transmitted. They may accomplish tasks, accompany routine and instrumental procedures, but they always go beyond them, endowing some larger meaning to activities they are associated with.

The most salient characteristic of ritual is its function as a frame. It is a deliberate and artificial demarcation. In ritual, a bit of behavior or interaction, an aspect of social life, a moment in time is selected, stopped, remarked upon. But this framing is a fiction. Artificial, its very artifice is denied and the claim is made that its meanings are discovered rather than made up. It claims that things "are as they seem," as presented. This applies to rituals large and small: the encounters and separations in ordinary human transactions are punctuated by ritual gestures or statements, announcing our agreement on what has occurred—we have met, been amiably disposed to one another, parted with regrets, and so forth. Something of note has occurred. Ritual gestures announce instrumental activities very often. As such they call the subject's attention to his undertaking. He is acting with awareness. He has taken the activity out of the ordinary flow of habit and routine, and performed the gesture to arouse in himself a particular attitude, demonstrating that his actions mean more than they seem.

It is this very feature of framing which coincides with Durkheim's (1915) conception of the sacred as the set-apart. But being set-apart is a matter not of kind but degree. Rituals are not either sacred or secular, rather in high rituals they are closer to the sacred end of the continuum, entirely extraordinary, communicating the *mysterium tremendum* and are often associated with supernatural or spiritual beings. Or, they are closer to the mundane end of the continuum, perfunctory genuflections to form, "good form," meaning good manners that acknowledge and punctuate social interactions, smoothing them, eliminating potential disruption, unpredictability and accident. Whether more or less set-apart, rituals are always rhetorical and didactic, inducing certain attitudes and convictions, blending wish and actuality until history and accident assume the shape of human intention.

The Nonce Ritual: Sequencing and Guiding Metaphor

The case at hand is an illustration of what might be called a nonce ritual, a common form in Western, urban, mobile societies. It is a complex ceremony parts of which are sacred and parts secular, parts unique improvisations (open) and parts stable, recurrent and fixed (closed). This arrangement is very characteristic of rituals among strangers and acquaintances gathered together on an *ad hoc* basis for the nonce, once only bringing with them diverse experience and personal histories.

Non-repeating or nonce rituals whose participants have only secondary ties to each other must overcome special handicaps in achieving their ceremonial goals. Blatantly made up and designed for specific occasions by one or more "masters-of-ceremony," nonce rituals must nevertheless convey a sense of rightness and inevitability. Nonce rituals are those awkward, self-conscious "first annual" events, laboring under their obvious contrivance, and the often touchingly transparent hopes and intentions of their participants. Such rituals do not have at hand those powerful, consensual, "self-evident" basic symbols that convey the rightness which endows with authenticity and conviction any circumstance where they occur. Lacking reservoirs of shared beliefs, deities, and histories, having none of the ready sources of emotional dynamism available to intimates, people in traditional societies, or stable circumstances, the masters-of-ceremonies in nonce rituals must use symbols which refer to the most basic common denominators of belief and experience—usually general, shallow and abstract, and little able to arouse deep emotion or profound conviction.

This presents a serious problem in a ritual. Without the emotional response provided by basic, deep symbols, how are rituals to move and persuade participants and witnesses? A common solution found in many rituals in secular situations involves sequencing—of two kinds, sacred/ secular, and open/closed. The first is an alternation of secular and sacred themes or symbols. Here, the secular elements—usually quite particular and unique—are juxtaposed with those regarded as unquestionable and permanent. By this juxtaposition, particulars are painted with the colors of the sacred, so to speak, borrowing the latter's sense of specialness and significance. Such sequencing is found everywhere—in political meetings which may be begun, closed and intermittently punctuated with references to deities. All the business in between, it is suggested, has the tacit approval of the gods. And rhetorical speeches often follow this pattern, weaving together National Destiny and the raising of funds for a particular candidate until the candidate somehow becomes a manifestation of that Destiny. Local affairs are considerably aggrandized by the process, and, conversely, remote abstract ideas are vitalized and specified. A fusion of sacred and secular can substitute in ritual for the work done in other circumstances by strong, collective symbols.

In addition, open/closed sequencing occurs in complex secular rituals. Rigidly fixed, recurrent, highly specific ritual acts, gestures—set forms such as toasts, poems, salutes, dances, songs, pledges and oaths—alternate with open spaces, which are used for improvisation and particularization; in secular rituals these are often given over to speeches. These openings provide opportunities for participants to establish their individual emotions, identities, motives and needs, and allow the ritual masters-of-ceremony to convey the specific, idiosyncratic messages which are unique to the occasion at hand. The fixed segments are highly predictable, allegedly unchanging, and are the traditionalizing ingredients in a complex ritual. The open segments are the particularizing opportunities, available for the purpose of the day, preceded and followed by closed sections.

The open or improvised sections may be short or protracted, may involve several people or one, may be rather conventional or truly new, but withal they must convey a sense of accuracy and authenticity. They must communicate to the participants and audience what is being done at any given moment. Clearly such communications are redundant in the established, familiar sections of rituals. But within the improvised sections, coordination between participants must occur in order for those involved to be certain that they are in the same play, so to speak. In cases of nonce rituals, it is especially important that communication and coordination be done well, lest emotional momentum flag, self-consciousness develop and the made-up quality of the occasion become conspicuous.

One way in which the improvisations are guided and coordinated in secular rituals is through the use of a mnemonic device in the form of a metaphor. The guiding metaphor in ritual serves to remind all concerned who they are, where they are, and what they are doing there. It is essential that the metaphor have ample and emotionally vital referents, sufficiently specific to be used as the basis of enactments. Metaphor cross-references domains of meaning to supply information from one well-known realm in understanding another, lesser known realm. It operates by analogy, and ultimately by blending the domains, to some extent. Reference to a guiding metaphor obviates the questions, "what do I do next?" for participants, and "what are they doing now?" for the audience. By naming the event, with a familiar name (i.e., "graduation"), audience and actors are quickly oriented within the less familiar sections of a nonce ritual. Ritual drama is a complex form requiring precision, flow and details. Ritual dramas must be fully staged, abounding in vocabulary and props to flesh them out, conceptually and sensually. The guiding metaphor provides these details as well as basic orientation.

The ritual event presented here, a nonce ritual, is characterized by the sequencing of sacred/secular, and open/closed elements, and by a clear and fruitful guiding metaphor, "Graduation-Siyum."[2] The ritual was a totally unique event, blending the sacred and secular, and successfully linking two entirely distinct realms of meaning and experience into a strong, convincing ritual drama. It was an occasion which transcended many contradictions, fused disparate elements, glossed conflicts, and provided a sense of individual and collective continuity in the course of mounting a bold and original fiction.

The Graduation-Siyum, Participants and Their History

A graduation is a common secular ritual in which a class of students marks a termination of a course of study, prescribed by and occurring within an educational institution. A *siyum* (Hebrew, "completion") is a traditional Ashkenazic ceremony marking the completion of a course of self-assigned study of a Jewish sacred text, usually a portion of the

---

2. In addition to the sequences mentioned in this ceremony, a series of alternations between sensory/presentational and discursive symbols occurs (cf. Langer 1957). Usually the discursive symbols appear in the open segments, but not always. This set of sequences is probably general to all kinds of rituals, whereas the other two are especially germane in secular rituals, for reasons mentioned.

Talmud. In the shtetls of Eastern Europe, the siyum was a simple affair which took place in the synagogue after the Saturday morning service; the individual who had completed his studies provided refreshments, received congratulations and announced his plans for another round of study, since "the Torah has no beginning and no end," and "a Jew studies all his life." As will be seen, graduation and siyum were drawn from utterly distinct domains of meaning and experience—cultural, religious and historical. Nevertheless, the graduation-siyum achieved a fusion among many conflicting ingredients; it was used once and once only, but for that occasion it was more than adequate as a guiding metaphor.

The Graduation-Siyum took place on a November Sunday afternoon in a small dilapidated hall which housed a Jewish senior citizens' center on the boardwalk at the beach in a California city. Assembled there were the graduates, thirty-one members of the Yiddish History Class, which had just completed a year of study, and an audience of about a hundred and fifty. The graduating students, all women save eight men, were in their eighties and nineties. All were Eastern European Jewish immigrants, all had grown up in shtetls. The Senior Citizens' Center, sponsored and supported by a large city-wide organization, was made up of a very stable membership with a common history and culture. It was a highly visible and well-bounded community with a distinctive life-style, some thirty years in the making. Three decades before, it was founded by newly retired Jews from East Coast urban centers of America, who were drawn to the climate and the Yiddishkeit which flourished there. As recently as the late 1950s there were an estimated 10,000 such people in the area. Losses due to death and urban renewal had shrunk the present population to approximately 4,000.

A collective portrait can summarize the history of the people partici-pating in the Graduation-Siyum, and with varying goodness of fit, the same outlines characterize the majority of the Center members. Shtetl life has been well documented, and here I shall limit my comments to those features most pertinent to the ritual at hand. Shtetls were tiny ethnic enclaves surrounded by hostile peasants; anti-Semitism was legal and traditional. Life was precarious and relentlessly poor. But the culture within was strong, rich and stable. The shtetls from which these people came were profoundly religious, conservative, ethnocentric and provin-cial, separated from Jewish and non-Jewish centers. They were late in receiving the full impact of the secular and religious movements which swept the rest of the Jewish world in the late nineteenth and early twentieth centuries, and ultimately drew shtetl youth away from their parents' traditional ways.

Shtetl folk were tradesmen, peddlers, petty artisans, craftsmen, and the like, legally forbidden to own land or grow crops. In this highly stratified community even the powerful and relatively affluent were impotent outside their limited world. A pogrom might wipe out a family or a whole village at any moment. In education, all shtetl people were literate, in contrast to the surrounding peasantry whom they disdained accordingly. Though legally forbidden to attend public secular schools or institutions of advanced learning, nevertheless, religious education was pursued with passion in the shtetl. Yiddish, the everyday language, was read and written by all; Hebrew, the sacred language, was read and written by all men and some women, though proficiency varied considerably.

These communities were self-regulating, jointly administered by the Rabbi and a social elite based on wealth and religious scholarship. There was little sustained interaction with the surrounding world of non-Jews except for peripheral exchanges in the marketplace or occasional intimate relationships with trusted servants. Cultural and social separatism were very thorough. A dual but conflicting social structure existed, one— internal, indigenous, sacred and politically impotent; the other—external, coercive, powerful and hostile. In these circumstances one would expect family and community ties to be exceedingly strong, and so they were.[3]

Age and sex, as always in such groups, were major determiners of role allocations, with women's participation in religious and educational realms sharply limited. Family stability and harmony were highly valued and occasionally attained. Life was hard but folkways were treasured— in Redfield's sense (1953) it was a sacred society, in its peoples' feeling of the complete rightness of its way of life, their unquestioned fusion of place, tradition and primary group, and their total identity with community.

In many ways the shtetl was similar to one of the small, traditional, well-integrated, stable pre-literate groups that anthropologists usually study, with two major exceptions: their link to a religious Great Tradition

---

3. Zborowski and Herzog (1962), Heschel (1972), Dawidowicz (1967), Levitats (1981), Dubnow (1916–20), Samuel (1943), Roskies and Roskies (1975), Howe (1976) and Shulman (1974). Sholom Aleichem, Mendele Moher Sefarim, I. L. Peretz and I. B. Singer, great writers of Yiddish fiction, also provide valuable ethnographic information about shtetl life.

through literacy, and a sense of unity as a people through time and space with a common destiny and sacred history.

This way of life was ended definitively by Hitler's physical destruction of the shtetl, but before the Holocaust many thousands of young people had left their homes in a search for a new life. Soon everyone had a relative in America who could help him or her come over and get started. They came in masses, fleeing poverty, anti-Semitism and often the restrictive orthodoxy of their parents and community.

Most of the people involved in this study came to America in their late or middle teens, and soon became petty merchants, retailers, wage workers, artisans and peddlers. None had more than a year or two of secular or religious education behind them. They struggled with poverty and loneliness in America. All who could manage to do so went to night school to learn English. They married people like themselves and with determination dedicated themselves to their children's future. So successful were they in assuring an education for their children that they constituted what has been called a one-generation proletariat. Their children were lawyers, doctors, professors, scientists, artists, businessmen and entrepreneurs. And they were "real Americans." They disdained Yiddish, abandoned religious orthodoxy, firmly turned away from the culture of their parents. Herberg (1955) points out that theirs was an age of militant secularism "since a clean break with religion seemed the best and surest way of becoming an American."

In many ways the immigrants were highly successful. Their children were secure, respected, accomplished people. The parents had, by middle age, acquired the possibility of a respectable and secure retirement, and they had flocked to the beaches of California.

For the past decade the beach neighborhood in which they now live has been becoming increasingly marginal. Housing costs are rising, and muggings and violent crimes keep the elderly off the streets after dark. Other retired Jews like themselves are not moving into the neighborhood. There are almost no other younger Jews in the immediate area; the nearest large temple is several miles away. Their little community is distinctive and set apart—a closed enclave.

Thus the people described here constitute a highly stable, cohesive, relatively small group, whose members share a common cultural and religious historical background. They are alike in education, work history, income, age, language, and family status. Despite their long and intense relationships with each other and despite their well-developed community life, they are lonely, quite cut off from their families and from other and younger Jews. Most live in tiny rundown rented rooms and economically are well below the national poverty level. They are unwilling to accept any assistance in the form of "charity" and maintain a dignified, genteel facade of independence, while in actuality they are under more stress every day, due to the growing loss of physical and sometimes mental powers, exacerbated by the torments of living on a small, fixed income in times of soaring inflation.

Ritual Elements of the Graduation-Siyum

The Yiddish History Class is the elite of the Center membership, those most involved in all its activities and most committed to the highest goal of the entire membership, the study of Jewish life in general and Yiddishkeit in particular. The program for the Graduation-Siyum was designed by the Center director, several of the graduating students, and the teacher of the class, Kominsky, a dynamic younger man of sixty-eight possessed of great energy and charisma. For the ceremony he had two clear purposes in mind: to bring the students back to the religion they had abandoned as teenagers in America, and to bring them to the attention of those who were neglecting them—their children and wealthier Jewish organizations in the city.

The little hall was filled with folding chairs for the Graduation-Siyum; the students sat together facing the audience. At one end of the room, a platform served as a stage, flanked by flags of Israel and America and decked with flowers. The walls were adorned with the seniors' art work, and photographs and drawings of important Jews, especially Zionists and Yiddishists.

The audience consisted of other members of the Center, friends, representatives of the Jewish Alliance, the philanthropic organization which funds and sponsors the Center, and officials from Temple Beth Shalom, a well-to-do synagogue a few miles away which had "adopted" the Center the previous year in an effort to assume some responsibility for its unmet needs. Also attending were the director of the city senior citizens' programs, and approximately fifteen individuals who were kin and progeny of the graduating members, twelve from the family of the Center's president. As important to the ceremony were those who did not attend:

members (as opposed to officials) of any of the organizations mentioned above, and any significant number of the family of the seniors.

Gathered on the platform were the representatives from the formal organizations, the Center director, and the teacher, Kominsky. Though those to whom the event was ostensibly addressed were absent, the hall was packed with well-wishers in a festive mood. Flowers of blue and white—the national colors of Israel and the Jewish flag—adorned tables, and the graduating elders wore their finest clothes beneath blue and white satin banners crossed from shoulder to waist. For the next three hours, the program proceeded as follows:[4]

1. The Pledge of Allegiance to the American flag was recited. (secular/closed)
2. Kominsky introduced the students and officials to the audience, and made some general remarks concerning the significance of the occasion. He then explained,
    First we are Americans, then we are Jews. According to the Talmud, the law of the country precedes the law of the Jews. That is why we are beginning with the national anthem. (open/secular)
3. The ninety-two-year-old, greatly esteemed Center president read a Yiddish poem he had written about his childhood in the shtetl. (closed/sacred)
4. Class valedictorian delivered a short speech in English, the major theme of which was a eulogy to America, the land of freedom and democracy. (open/secular)
5. A twenty-year-old Hebrew student of Kominsky's read a poem by the poet laureate of Israel. (closed/sacred)
6. Greetings and congratulations were read by the Alliance president from "Jewish civic and community leaders" throughout the city. There were some messages from national Jewish organizations commending the class members for their accomplishments and citing them as exemplary Jews and senior citizens. (open/secular)

---

4. Sacred and secular are not always clearly separate. All references to Judaism are somewhat sacred; more clearly sacred are references to Yiddishkeit, life in the shtetl, Jewish Law and scholarship and Jewish historical and collective identity. Bases for these classifications are discussed in more detail later.

7. The "Commencement Address" was delivered by the Rabbi of Temple Beth Shalom lauding the students, stressing the connection between Judaism and scholarship, and the good fortune presented to retired Jews by the opportunity to finish their lives in study and learning. (open/secular and sacred)

8. Diplomas were distributed by the Rabbi. These were in Hebrew, printed forms actually intended for children graduating from Hebrew schools and temple confirmations. As such, they carried messages referring to "Hope for the future," "Passing on the religious heritage to the young who will improve the world," and "Creating a brighter tomorrow." The diplomas bore the date 5733, following the ancient Jewish calendar. Inscribed on them were the names of the senior citizens in Yiddish, ending in the diminutive. Leahle, Rechele, Schloymele, and so forth. These were shtetl names for children known to each other, but not generally used in everyday affairs. (open/secular and sacred)

9. The Rabbi's young daughter and her friend entertained the group with Israeli folksongs. (closed/sacred)

10. The president of the temple's Men's Club read messages from organizations and individuals all over the world, congratulating the senior citizens. These had resulted from class members pooling their contacts in Israel and elsewhere, requesting their friends to find "dignitaries" to send telegrams and cards to the graduates. The project was facilitated by the Center's reputation as a reliable and generous supporter of Israel. One message came in the form of a tape recording made of young Orthodox Jews praying and reciting their lessons in a religious school immediately adjacent to the Western Wall in Jerusalem; this wall is a remnant of the Second Temple of biblical times. (open/secular and sacred)

11. Kominsky read "The Charge to the Class." Here he discussed his students' exemplary conduct, told the audience how despite their poor health and bad weather, they came eagerly and well-prepared to each class session. Limited means notwithstanding, they had their own libraries. Despite their lack of formal religious training in childhood and rejection of religiosity in youth, despite an adulthood devoted to becoming Americans and earning a living which left no time for study, now, as older people,

they were learning the Hebrew alphabet and beginning to be able to read the sacred texts. He closed his remarks by explaining the importance of the Law and Learning to the Jews in general and to his family in particular, closing by saying,

> In my family, when Papa opened his book we were all quiet. Sha! Papa studies. Papa looks in a book. All the house respects it. When a book is dropped, it is kissed. A worn-out book is buried. We don't wrap herring in a printed page, not even if it's a newspaper. (open/sacred)

12. Kominsky led the students in the "Class Song," a shtetl folksong in Yiddish describing the warm room in which the hearth glows as the Rabbi teaches his little children the Hebrew alphabet. (closed/sacred)

13. The Center director made his address, which included the following comments:

> You are our parents and we honor you today. You are the people who gave the world, by your efforts, the finest doctors, scientists, professors, philosophers, artists and musicians that have ever been seen. Your children have given you *nakhes* (pride and pleasure), and now it is the time for you, the parents, to give your children *nakhes*.

Then, addressing the audience,

> How proud you must be of your parents and grandparents today. You can rejoice over them; it is your turn. All their lives, without recognition, they worked for others, raising children, sending money to Israel, and now it is time for you to express your appreciation.

> Their lives have meaning and they are a model to us. Look at Mr. Abraham.[5] He has written a book, and produced four devoted, successful sons. He writes poetry every day. From him we learn what life can be. He is always learning. He is a "filosof" (philosopher). Learning is lifelong. We Jews are the People of the Book. Study is the highest activity for any phase of life. Old and young,

---

5. The Center's "patriarch," Mr. Abraham, is called Jacob Kovitz in "A Death in Due Time" (in this volume). In *Number Our Days,* he is renamed Jacob Koved. (See "Teach us to number our days," in this volume).—Ed.

every Jew is supposed to study a little bit each day. Learning is what makes us stay young forever, so a real Jew is ageless. (open/secular and sacred)

14. Hatikvah, the national anthem of Israel, was sung. (closed/sacred)

15. A group of teenagers, the class of the Temple Beth Shalom, served cookies and punch to the graduates and the audience. (open/secular)

16. An important but unplanned event occurred next—the provision and service by several class members of brandy, herring, and honey cakes. This was done rather furtively, so that no one could be sure who was responsible, for Kominsky had been adamant that on this one occasion the senior citizens should be the receivers of applause, praise, food and service; today, at least, they should not provide for or serve those younger than themselves. (open/sacred) A blessing was said in Hebrew before eating. (closed/sacred)

17. Another unexpected event took place; one of the class members took to the stage to present "Reb Kominsky," "our chaver" (Hebrew: comrade)[6] a "filosof" with a certificate indicating that the class had gathered contributions from among its members to enter their teacher's name in "The Golden Book," where a record is kept of donors of $100 or more in funds for Israel. (open/sacred)

18. The ceremony was officially closed with the singing of the American national anthem. (closed/secular)

Axiomatic Symbols in the Ritual: Being-a-Jew and Learning

Rituals when they succeed do so in large part through the power of their axiomatic symbols. In this case, two such symbols operate, unifying and condensing a vast array of referents; these symbols are Being-a-Jew

---

6. In Hebrew and Yiddish, *chaver* means "comrade, friend, mister." In this context, it might be translated as "colleague." *Chaver* is at once a conventional title of respect, prefixed to the last name, and a mark of common membership, therefore a word saturated with the warmth of belonging to the same social group. It carries the same emphasis as the title "brother" in Black Baptist churches.—Ed.

and Learning.[7] Being-a-Jew is a particularly complex, dense symbol, referring to four distinct forms of Jewish experience: the Great Tradition of scholarship, the Little Tradition of Yiddishkeit, The Jews as One People (Klal Isroel), and American Temple Judaism.

Loosely following Redfield (1953), the "Great Tradition" is used to refer to the abstract, eternal, impersonal verities in which a culture participates. Local institutions expressive of the Great Tradition may exist but are controlled by literati remote from the community. And indeed, the great centers of learning, the great scholars, and the great historical events were spatially and temporally removed from the experience of the shtetl. The Great Tradition of Judaism is learned, exalted, specialized, pure and perpetual. Awesome and somewhat forbidding to these ordinary people, it is quite distinguishable from the meaning of Judaism as folk religion, the Little Tradition, in this case Yiddishkeit. This form of Judaism for them was a matter of everyday life and mundane concerns, but no less authentically Jewish because more homely. This is the Judaism which guided everyday decisions, the interpretation of events, the folkways, local histories, styles, and customs. It is Judaism in the form of the Little Tradition which makes a Jew from Berditchev nearly unrecognizable to one from Morocco or Berlin; the folk traditions separate Jews from different locales, and the Great Tradition provides the overarching connections between them. The Great Tradition, manifested especially in the use of Hebrew, prayer, study, and an awareness of sacred history allows Jews to experience most powerfully a sense of peoplehood; though they are spatially dispersed and culturally heterogeneous, nevertheless they are a unified group, "One People," Klal Isroel.

Among these people the Great Tradition was and is incompletely woven into everyday life. It might be said that it covers their local forms of Judaism like a fine bedspread on a straw pallet. In fact, very few of those participating in the Graduation-Siyum were deeply learned people. The Great Tradition of Jewish scholarship was venerated by them but not part of their direct experience. A reading knowledge of Hebrew among the men, enough to get through the Psalms, knowledge of some prayers and a little Jewish history, was all that time had allowed them.

---

7. A third major symbol appeared in the ceremony, patriotism and Americanism, including modernity and freedom in its referents. It is not treated as an axiomatic symbol of the depth of Being-a-Jew and Learning because compared to these it appeared only in the elders' middle years, whereas the other two have been passionate concerns throughout their lives.

None of the women knew Hebrew and only two had had a year or two devoted to Jewish study.

Local traditions are matters of daily life, occurring first and foremost in the familial setting, in association with the child's earliest experiences in the safety of the home, in the routines of ordinary affairs. They have a kind of sacrality, despite their mundane nature, which comes from being so completely embedded in every feature of a culture. Judaism as Little Tradition was learned pre-verbally, intertwined with nurturance and survival, occurring in the form of the small, physical and sensory events and experiences which correspond to Turner's (1969) orectic or physiological pole of dominant symbols, "relating to desire, appetite and feeling." Local tradition is largely unconscious and unconsidered, a profoundly familiar mix of household odors and habits, gestures, sounds, tastes, and sentiments which set down the deepest roots in the individual.

In the Graduation-Siyum, the Great Tradition of Judaism was brought in by means of a mediating symbol, representing another expression of Judaism-Israel. Israel was always and is still a very personal matter to these people, regarded by them almost as a child, precious and precarious, needing their help, making mistakes but deserving complete faith and devotion, forgiveness and indulgence. For them, Israel contains and refers to the Great Tradition theme, for it is a historical place of sacred origins and the place where the sacred language and history flourishes and is preserved. At the same time it elicits profound responses which are more immediate and less lofty. Their identification with the Holy Land goes back to their childhood and has constituted one of the most continuing, passionate concerns throughout their lives. Israel is for them the Millennium, representing spiritual salvation, but in addition, it is a worldly, historical salvation, the ingathering of the Jews as a people, the real and symbolic homeland for their depleted families. Here is the site of the total Jewish community, Klal Isroel. Through Israel, identification with the broadest reaches of group membership is achieved. It links these people to a larger destiny, beyond Yiddishkeit; as such it is part of the Great Tradition, but less awesome and unattainable than its scholarly expression. For though they hold scholarship in the highest regard, the elders know full well that they are not and will never be deeply educated people. But for the maintenance and support of Israel, even the most ignorant and humble are needed and welcome. As a mediating symbol, Israel coalesces the highest and most fundamental forms of Being-a-Jew for the senior citizens.

American Temple Judaism offered its own special meanings and conflicts which had to be incorporated into the ritual. For most of the
graduates, since adolescence, Being-a-Jew had become associated with
being old-fashioned and un-American. In this country for the first time
Jewish identity became optional to some extent. It was a somewhat
bewildering condition, sometimes a little embarrassing—a social imped-
iment. Being-a-Jew in America as young adults was never satisfactorily
resolved by most of these people. Judaism in this country lacked the
firm roots and social supports of the shtetl, and the Great Tradition
part of Judaism had never really constituted a compelling, immediate
way of life for them. What, then, did it mean Being-a-Jew in America
during their middle years? On this there was more variation among them
than the other meanings of Being-a-Jew. Some individuals had expressed
their Judaism by joining Yiddish political or cultural groups. A few joined
small orthodox temples. Most had no time for these activities, and Being-
a-Jew became blurred and uneasy. The distinctly American institutions
referred to in the Graduation-Siyum were the modern, less orthodox
temples and schools. In these institutions the elders had never participated
directly. The features in the ritual ceremony associated with the temple
were viewed with some indifference by the graduates. They constituted
a kind of ritual cargo that the seniors had to include so as not to be
overtly rude. Men's clubs, confirmation classes, sisterhoods, English
prayers led by beardless, bareheaded rabbis were not part of Judaism
as they had known it. These were forms without emotional resonance.

A symbol of a different kind is also active in this ritual, Learning.
Like Being-a-Jew, it is an axiomatic good, an end in itself, but it is also
a means, a strategy for appropriate social and spiritual action.[8] As a
symbol and strategy it has been relevant throughout the many phases
and changes in these elders' lives. It is one of the strong, unifying concerns
of their personal histories. In the shtetl, Learning determined a family's
social as well as religious standing. Learning benefited community and
the individual, and was a certain source of upward social mobility.

Later in America, in their middle years it was Learning, as symbol
and strategy, which served these people and their children so well. Now,
Learning was for secular, instrumental and more individualistic purposes
but it retained its aura of sacrality. The seniors could not achieve it for

---

8. This corresponds to what Ortner (1974) calls a "key scenario," a method
for attaining a valued cultural goal.

themselves but they could and did provide higher education for their children.

Now, in old age, Learning assumed a somewhat different form while remaining a major concern. At this point, it had become the means of expressing the successful culmination of a life. Jews, they say, need never stop Learning, and old age provides the leisure they never had before for its pursuit. "We are the People of the Book," they often said, and as such more fortunate than other retired people. Pursuit of Learning is regarded as a blessing, defiant of time. In this stage of life, Learning included secular and sacred meanings, an activity intrinsically and extrinsically valuable. The content of the Graduation-Siyum repeatedly employed the symbol, Learning, in the speeches, songs, and poems, lauding a man by referring to him as a "filosof," reverence demonstrated for the teacher of the Yiddish history class, signified in many ways, including the use of the respectful term "Reb," and honoring him by entering his name in the Golden Book. And of course the very form of the ceremony, commemorating completion of studies, is based on this axiomatic symbol.

Both axiomatic symbols, it must be said, are touched with irony and ambivalence. One of the major postulates of "Being-a-Jew" is that "We are one People, Klal Isroel." It is generally agreed, certainly by these people, that the ultimate expression of Being-a-Jew is not praying but taking responsibility for other Jews. "Among Jews one is never lost," goes the proverb. But it is no secret that these senior citizens are being neglected by the wider Jewish community as well as their own progeny. This realization is close to the surface and a very delicate matter. No less painful is the uneasy recognition that the solidarity among the members of the Center is strained and fragile, for many reasons. The people help one of their members in distress but are reluctant to share each other's joys. In the end, they are fellow Jews but not family. Internal discord breaks out with great intensity and frequency and on ritual events such as this one, the harmonious atmosphere is understood to be temporary. Being-a-Jew makes them One People but the sense of Peoplehood is strongest when external threats are grave, and correspondingly weak in times of relative external peace.

Ambivalence toward Learning is also distinct, but subtler. Though Learning was the key to the success of the people's children, it was also the path by means of which their progeny escaped from them and their traditions. All children leave their parents behind, but the speed and completeness of the break between the generations here is extreme. Their American-born children were exceptionally well equipped to make their way up and out of the ghetto, and their parents were genuinely proud of their accomplishments. But at the same time, there is sadness and bitterness as well as pride in the elders' talk about their children. Hannah's daughter told her, "Mamale, you are sweet but so stupid." "And," Hannah agreed, "I know it's true. After all this time in America, I still can't spell." Learning was the strategy for assimilation and success in America, but as it became an escape route for the children it was also an irony, and a source of great hurt for the old people.

Functions of the Ritual: Fusions, Fictions, and Continuity

The Graduation-Siyum served several functions: it was an occasion in which the axiomatic symbols, Being-a-Jew and Learning, were activated and used to fuse disparate domains of experience, to dramatize a fictive version of themselves made in the form of assertions and denials, and to provide a sense of individual and collective continuity. It was an elaborate staging of a great fiction, an official, if momentary, collective interpretation of the participants' past and present lives. Being-a-Jew, and Learning, as symbols, provided form and substance which were used to build the ritual, the symbolic sources sustaining the metaphor which guided the ceremony—the Graduation-Siyum.

The Fusion of Domains: Graduation and Siyum

The Graduation-Siyum was a fusion of two disparate domains, and in this, it was a fiction. Some of the features of both domains were selected and used, and others overlooked, in order to present a definition of self, by participants, for themselves and the world. The coherence and conviction of the ritual were achieved despite its fictive nature. On close look it becomes evident that the guiding metaphor is connecting and fusing extremely different domains of meaning. Indeed, graduation and siyum stand in an analogous, not homologous relation to each other, as is seen in table 1.

Outside of the context of a ritual drama, persuasively mounted, it is hard to imagine that such a connection between domains would be credible, but in fact the differences between them were not in the least troublesome on the afternoon of the ceremony. Both were essential sources of form and emotion. The guiding metaphor, it can be seen, is very useful in coordinating assorted cultural materials, resulting in a ritual which addresses diverse populations with differing perspectives, beliefs and experiences. The audience, in this case, comprehended and had directly experienced graduation ceremonies. It may be assumed that this domain constituted the most meaningful dimension of the ritual for

TABLE 1. Graduation and Siyum   Contrasts Domains Connected by the Guiding Metaphor

Traditional Graduation ("commencement")	Traditional Siyum ("completion")
1 secular content	sacred content
2 associated with adulthood	associated with childhood
3 English language	Hebrew language
4 occurred in America	occurred in Eastern Europe
5 public school setting	synagogue setting
6 rite of passage marking lineal progress and clear transitions through fixed stages	repeating rite marking cyclical movement, without transitions or stages
7 benefits the individual	benefits the community, all Jews, and mankind
8 direct means of achieving worldly success	may lead to worldly success indirectly; primarily leads to understanding for its own sake
9 materials selected by and learning paced by the institution	materials selected by and learning paced by the individual
10 learning occurs in a group with secondary relations between members; group usually disperses after ceremony	learning occurs in a group with primary relations; group endures after ceremony
11 group is age homogeneous; sexually heterogeneous	group is age heterogeneous; sexually homogeneous—only men undertake the course of study and participate in a traditional siyum
12 ceremony marks beginning of adulthood; growing social and biological capacities and prospects; associated with hopes for the future	ceremony is ostensibly age-free, actually here associated with waning social and biological capacities and prospects; associated with a restricted future
13 ceremony is not part of the direct experience of the seniors; it is their children's experience, and the experience of the audience	ceremony is part of the direct experience of the senior men; it is not a direct experience for the senior women; not for their children or the audience

them. For the seniors, the greater emotional response was clearly provoked by references to the childhood associations. The graduation domain provided most of the formal ingredients in the ritual (Charge to the Class, Valedictorian, and so forth), while the siyum domain was the source of the deep emotional significance at least for the participants. Altogether, the event was generally accepted as authentic and traditional by audience and participants, though no one had ever witnessed such a unique creation before.[9]

Fictions: Claims and Denials

Rituals not only fuse disparate elements but they also make assertions, claims that are at the same time denials of unacceptable realities. In part the ritual dramatized an interpretation of the consequences of coming to America. In this drastic move, the elders had exchanged many cherished features of life in the Old World for a new life. As always, a trade-off was involved, and America had brought them gains and losses. They had gained religious freedom but lost their sacred traditions; they had gained physical safety and security for themselves and their children but had lost their natal families and communities; they had gained the educational and economic accomplishments of their children but ultimately this led to the isolation and loneliness of their old age. Sonya summarized matters this way:

> Well, of course, life in America isn't what it was in the Old Country. There, we loved our parents, we took care of them. Now, look at us . . . On the other hand, this is a wonderful country. Look at my children. My daughter is a teacher, my son is a doctor. In Glowno my mother couldn't keep shoes on our feet. You know what that means to a parent? So, if I'm a nobody here, who cares? Who

---

9. While considerable freedom is available in the use of a guiding metaphor, traditions require the inclusion of certain critical elements. Thus the seniors debated at length as to whether a real graduation could take place without a procession. They did not feel they could manage a slow, stately walk down the aisle. Fortunately, Manya remembered attending a graduation in which students stood in place when their names were called. Thus, they too could do this and it would be proper. And without a formal discussion, several had agreed that traditional shtetl food—herring, honeycakes and brandy—were essential for a genuine siyum.

needs an old lady like me anyway? I'm happy. I did all I could and I didn't do so bad.

The ceremony, while making claims and denials, also stressed gains over losses. Here is a summary of principal assertions.

TABLE 2.   Claims and Denials

1   *One People*
Claim being dramatized and asserted:
We Jews are One People through time and space, sharing a single identity and destiny.

Denial of the reality that:
Jews are diverse in nearly every way, from belief to life-style, sometimes more different than alike.

2   *Common Fate*
Claim
As One People, we Jews share each others' destiny—all are part of each other, a community.

Denial
The seniors are neglected by family and neighboring well-to-do Jews; they are needy and isolated.

3   *Judaism is Forever*
Claim
Judaism is timeless; it will endure. Though America is a secular state, Jews here will not be assimilated and disappear.

Denial
Judaism practiced by young Americans is so different and so diffuse as to be nearly unrecognizable to the seniors. The most important aspect of Judaism for them, Yiddishkeit, will die out with their generation, almost certainly.

4   *Lifelong Study*
Claim
We Jews practice lifelong study. This is appropriate for old people as well as young; though old age means many losses, we are fortunate since we can always pursue our studies and thus always live a meaningful life.

Denial
Study is extremely difficult for these older people. They have severe handicaps in the form of short concentration spans, poor eyesight, poor hearing, memory lapses, difficulties in sitting for long or holding a pen, impatience with each other in discussions.

5   *Meaning and Use of Learning*
Claim
We have always loved learning. We have been trained to study and understand. We need never cease growing. We are becoming educated even now.

Denial
They study what is, in actuality, very thin fare. Lacking formal preparation, their attitude is one of awe and respect before almost all printed matter. The act and attitude of studying is more important than the substance.

TABLE 2—*Continued*

6 *Successful Lives*

Claim

We have realized our dearest goals in life; it has all been worthwhile. Our children are educated, wealthy, and they respect us. We know they are too important to have time for us, but we don't expect that. Who could ask for more than we have? We know children must live their own lives. After all, we left our parents when we needed to.

Denial

Family ties are the only connections that are counted as completely trustworthy and valuable. It is terribly painful for them to be so cut off from children and family. They feel isolated and useless, and wonder, "Is this what our parents felt like when we left them? Did they deserve such treatment? Do we deserve such treatment?"

In addition to the fusion of separate domains of experience and the demonstration of a set of fictions, there is also a more mundane function being achieved in this ritual drama—an accusation is being made against those who neglect them. To address to their children and their better off fellow Jews the overt statement "You are treating us badly" would embarrass and alienate them. By making their self-definition and protest indirect and ceremonial, the old people arouse guilt without having to state openly the humiliating facts of their condition. Their self-esteem is built upon their conception of themselves as independent, even supporters of others. The statement of need in any form, especially to those they need most, is unthinkable. And the very point of the ritual is that it need not be thought. Fortunately, in ritual, fictions can be presented which disguise truths, save face, and convince all concerned that matters are in order. For rituals allow people to maneuver, fight on their own terms, choose the times, places, conditions and shapes of their assertions, as Burke (1957) says of proverbs. Such maneuvering may result in action, encounter and change, or may end in poetry, ". . . where instead of being moved anywhere we are accommodated in many subtle ways to our condition in all its contrarieties and complexities" (Fernandez 1971:53). Here, in the Graduation-Siyum the old Jews can present themselves as people of significance and dignity while they are shaming those who deserted them, and at the same time bolster and define their own sense of worth. In this ritual they exercise that basic human prerogative, the right to indicate who they are to the world, to interpret themselves to themselves instead of allowing the world, accident, history and reality, if you will, to provide an interpretation for them. Here eloquently demonstrated is mankind's undying insistence on stating not only that life has meaning but also specifying precisely what that meaning is.

Continuity—Individual and Collective

Rituals provide continuity of two distinct but related kinds, the individual's sense of unity as a person (individual-biographical continuity), and the sense of being "One People" on the part of the whole group (collective-historical continuity). Despite great changes and disruptions, the individual must be convinced of his/her continuity; thus, must be able to re-experience parts of the past in the present, and of course, the most charged and essential segments of this retrieval come from the remote past, the events of childhood. Continuity is, in this case, especially critical, due to a combination of factors: the extreme age of the ritual participants, their proximity to death, and the drastic rupture with the past caused by emigration. Reviewing one's life and reminiscing, much practiced by the very old, are expressions of the concern for integration, efforts to experience oneself as the same individual through time. As elderly and as Jews, their striving for a sense of integration and continuity, unity and oneness, were parallel, powerful concerns, addressed in this ritual.

The sense of being One People is especially important to Jews, a collectivity dispersed all over the world for centuries.[10] The group, to think of itself as One People, must connect with those of their kind who have gone before and those who are yet to come. The difference between "us then" and "us now" is enormous. This sense of unity, of identity, with one's past and future, "We have been here and we will continue, despite so many changes," is a very important function frequently managed by ritual. It has long been characteristic for Jews to achieve a sense of oneness by means of ritual. The question "What makes us a people?" is never far from the lips of the thoughtful Jew, ancient or modern. Not race, geography, mother tongue or way of life unite them. Above all, it is the commitment to the study of the sacred books. Several times weekly, Jews come together to read synchronized portions of the Law all over the world. The ceremony described here signified the unity and perpetuity of Jews as a People at several important points: in its inclusions of messages from widely dispersed Jews, in the presence of representatives from nearby Jewish organizations, and by the participation of the young people who signified the survival of Judaism in the future. The most numinous symbol of the history of the Jews was the tape of students

---

10. Cf. R.-E. Prell-Foldes, 1973, for discussion of this point.

praying beside the Western Wall, which is the *axis mundi* of the Jewish world. Its inclusion in the program did much to sanctify the entire ceremony.

The Graduation-Siyum established individual and collective continuity by using at least three distinct cultural-historical layers as the sources of symbols and specific ritual details. First, it drew heavily upon the participants' childhood experiences in the East European shtetl; the emotions, meanings and particulars associated with this cultural level were drawn upon for the siyum domain in the guiding metaphor. A second cultural level was provided by the graduation domain of the guiding metaphor, referring to the experiences of America, adulthood and, to some extent, old age. Yet a third layer was incorporated, referring to Judaism in all its forms, a consistent theme running through all the historical phases of the lives of the people.

All these layers supplied cultural materials, employed in the ritual in a highly eclectic fashion. The Graduation-Siyum usually drew on people's associations rather than their direct and historical experiences. Most had not been to Israel, had not belonged to an American temple or attended an American school (though many went to night school for a time, none graduated ceremonially), most had not participated in a siyum. Nevertheless, they assembled bits and pieces from their common past and present lives, memories and fantasies, gathering thus sufficient ritual and symbolic elements to make their own statements about the meaning of these occasions. Secular rituals, like myths, thus appear to be susceptible of construction with whatever diverse and heterogeneous materials are at hand. Lévi-Strauss (1966) used the word *bricolage* to describe this process in myth and mythic thought. Though their ritual was made of fragments, assembled willy-nilly, they were adequate, allowing the people to write their own history, fight on their own terms, frame and interpret events that never actually happened to them but were no less vital and real because of that. By calling upon all these layers, sources of their axiomatic symbols, personal and collective continuity, the sense of oneness, as Jews and as individuals, were dramatized and experienced. One of the means by which continuity is experienced is through the use of axiomatic symbols, those storehouses of meaning and emotions that carry over shades of all their referents to each particular situation in which they appear.

The three cultural layers drawn upon to develop the Graduation-Siyum bear an interesting relation to each other. On one hand they constitute a series of sharp shifts over the life span, discontinuities which must be knitted together for the people to experience a sense of coherence and integration when reflecting upon their histories. On the other hand, there are some strong continuities, especially between the worlds of childhood and old age. The total picture is complex, but in general it can be said that the ritual event emphasized, subtly and often unintentionally, the continuities in social and cultural phases of their lives and glossed the discontinuities. The existence of the continuities made the work of the axiomatic symbols much easier, since they had references which obtained throughout the life cycle. Table 3 summarizes and compares these continuities and discontinuities across the seniors' lives. The summary was compounded of individual life histories and represents a kind of collective profile, emphasizing features most mentioned by the senior citizens themselves.

The table clearly reveals the materials out of which the present subculture was built, freely, unsystematically, using materials at hand to meet present needs. No doubt it would not have come into being, at least in this elaborate form, if the seniors had remained embedded in a context of family and community. Their very isolation gave them much of their freedom and originality; they improvised and invented, unhampered by restraints of tradition and social disapproval, with only themselves to please. For the first time since coming to America, they were able to fully indulge their old love of Yiddish and Yiddishkeit, without fear of ridicule from their sophisticated children. The beloved *mamaloshen,* the language which their children rejected in order to be modern, which the old people gave up as a marker of their status as greenhorn immigrants, could come into its own once more.

Living again in a small, integrated community, which emphasizes Learning, where Yiddishkeit flourishes, where individual freedom and autonomy are exercised in isolation from mainstream society, all of these are familiar—replications of earlier phases of life, revitalized and useful now in old age. Poverty, impotence, physical insecurity and social marginality reiterate shtetl existence. Such continuity is adaptive despite its painful contents. People who have always known that life was hard, and fate unreliable if not downright treacherous, are not surprised to encounter these hazards again. They know how to cope with them and they are not discouraged.

Most continuities are between childhood and old age; between childhood and adulthood, discontinuities are more evident. Above all, the

TABLE 3.   Continuities and Discontinuities in Life Circumstances

	Childhood/ Adolescence	Middle Age	Old Age
1 Locale	Eastern Europe	America	America
2 Community	*Gemeinschaft of small settlements and villages	Gesellschaft: urban centers and suburbs	*Gemeinschaft of an urban ghetto
3 Family	extended, patriarchal, stable, cohesive	nuclear, more egalitarian, less stable and cohesive	shallow and narrow; infrequent contacts with family members
4 Generational continuity	*rejection of their parental traditions; geographical and social separation between generations due to immigration	strained relations with children as assimilation occurs; social separation grows, geographical proximity	*virtually severed relations between generations; strong geographical and social separation between generations
5 Religion and Ideology	*Zionism; growing agnosticism; Yiddishkeit; "Learning" a major form of religious expression; pronounced identity as Jews	*Zionism; agnosticism; Yiddishkeit; "Learning" as a religious expression is superseded by "learning" for assimilation and social success; less pronounced identity as Jews	*Zionism; less pronounced agnosticism, more preference for traditional religious forms; "Learning" a major form of religious expression; pronounced identity as Jews
6 Language	*Yiddish; some Hebrew for men; Slavic languages for some	English gradually acquired and replaces Yiddish to some extent	*Yiddish assumes more importance; some study of Hebrew; all fluent in English
7 Age, sex distinctions	sharp division between sexes; males dominant economically and ritually; seniority valued	age and sex roles blurred; women become important economically; seniors largely absent; juniors dominant socially	age and sex roles no longer relevant; females dominant; males largely absent; younger generations absent
8 Autonomy and nurturance	nurtured by family and community; dependent on others	nurturant of own children, independent	some nurturance by others (health and economic matters); some nurturing of others (Israel); partially dependent on others

TABLE 3—*Continued*

	Childhood/ Adolescence	Middle Age	Old Age
9 Economic circumstances	*poverty; little or no social mobility; insecurity	relative affluence; security and much social mobility	*poverty; no social mobility; pronounced insecurity
10 Relation to outside, dominant society	*physical danger; religious oppression; social and cultural separation, enforced externally and self-imposed	no physical danger; very little religious oppression; moderate and diminishing social and cultural separation, more enforced than self-imposed	*physical danger; no religious oppression; moderate social separation; pronounced cultural separation, some external enforcement but primarily self-imposed

*indicates distinct continuity

dissolution of the family as they knew it stands out. The centrality of a stable family group was essential to a *Weltanschauung* which held that though all Jews were one, non-family Jews were only to be trusted more than the gentiles. The breakdown of the natal community, the segmented social relations in the American urban centers, the rapid social change, and social and geographical mobility constituted a profound contrast with the stable rhythms of the past. Not less important as a discontinuity was their sense of hope and potency, characteristic of the American middle period when new, undreamed of possibilities seemed to open at every turn. These senior citizens went from a small, stable folkworld, familiar and predictable, guided by a tight consensus of family, rabbi and community, in one sudden movement to an entirely different world. This shift coincided with changes in the life cycle which lent the latter additional force, no doubt. Their biological dependence gave way to biological maturity, and this was paralleled by social autonomy which occurred within the expanding circumstances provided by immigration.

But in the end, it was the continuities between the world of childhood and the world of old age which provided the basis for their creation of an authentic and distinctive subculture, fragmented, contrived, often thin, constructed out of desperate need, nevertheless, to be counted as a major gain over and against losses in the history of their lives.

Conclusion: Success in Ritual

Did this ritual succeed in its purposes? This requires that we consider what constitutes success for ritual in general. I suggested earlier that above all rituals are dramas of persuasion. They are didactic, enacted pronouncements concerning the meaning of an occasion, and the nature and worth of the people involved in the occasion. In many ways rituals may be judged like any drama—they must be convincing. Not all the parties involved need to be equally convinced or equally moved. But the whole of it must be good enough to play. No one can stand up and boo. Not too many people can shift about in embarrassment, sigh or grimace. The appearance of attention is essential, and everyone is in it together—stage hands, master-of-ceremony, audience, players—all must collude so as not to spoil the show, or damage the illusion that the dramatic reality coincides with the "other, out-there reality."

Why should people collude as much as they do? As Goffman (1956) has demonstrated so well, most individuals sharing a social scene wish to preserve the surface appearances, to reassure themselves and others that "things are going well," "are as they appear to be." Courtesy is a norm always, and ritual is an instance of high courtesy. Unless they are downright bad, wanting all knowledge, art, and care, rituals are likely to be received with courtesy. The ritual participants and designers owe themselves and the audience sufficient competence to aid the pre-existing wish to support it. All involved are offended if the suspicion develops that most of those present are bored, confused or self-conscious. Craft may replace genuine emotional involvement without damaging the ritual; the reverse is not true. Ritual, in general, may be judged a success when it is not a conspicuous failure.

Was the Graduation-Siyum ritual convincing? It was. Not only was its success unhampered by the fact that those to whom it was ostensibly addressed were absent (the graduates' children and families), but it was more successful because they were absent. As a group, the proper audience was represented by a few individuals who were disposed to agree with the justice of the claims being made in the ritual. It is likely that the mood of self-confidence, even self-pride on the part of the graduates would have been impaired if the older people had to face their own children as they made their claims. Instead, the senior citizens were able to make their interpretations of themselves with subtlety and even without completely conscious intent, while they shamed those delinquent in their obligations to them, stated their own importance as people, and the basis of that importance. In their ritual, they emphasized their accomplishments while minimizing their losses.

Did the old people themselves believe in what they were doing? It must be assumed that they did. In ritual, not only is seeing believing, doing is believing. A fine example of this is provided by a Hasidic tale called "The Sabbath Feeling." Two rabbis decide to make a test to see if their Sabbath feelings are "genuine" by conducting a Sabbath meal on a weekday. After their services, they find they have the Sabbath feeling and are alarmed because it is a weekday. They bring this problem to a third, more learned rabbi. He tells them,

> If you put on sabbath clothes and sabbath caps, it is quite right that you had a feeling of sabbath holiness. Because sabbath clothes and sabbath caps have the power of drawing the light of sabbath holiness down to earth. So you need have no fears. (Buber 1947:241)

In the case of the Graduation-Siyum, the people involved were certainly better off having undertaken this venture than had they not bothered. The very actions, the mounting of a major, complex event of consequence— public, sustained, original—gave them intense pleasure and satisfaction. For the time, they were what they said they were, despite the most pressing contrary realities. They were a community, a people agreeing on their past and present lives, individuals learning and growing, ageless and indomitable.

A Death in Due Time:
Conviction, Order, and Continuity
in Ritual Drama

When the fig is plucked in due time it is good for the fig and good for the tree.

Mankind has ever chafed over its powerlessness in facing the end of life. Lacking assurance of immortality and insulted by the final triumph of nature over culture, humans develop religious concepts which explain that if not they, someone or something has power and a plan. Then death is not an obscene blow of blind chance. No religion fails to take up the problem, sometimes affirming human impotence thunderously:

> Know that everything is according to the reckoning and let not thy imagination betray thee into the hope that the grave will be a place of refuge for thee. For without thy consent wast thou created and born into the world, without any choice; thou art now living without volition, and will have to die without thy approval; so likewise without thy consent wilt thou have to render account before the supreme King, the Holy One, praised be He. (Goldin 1939:220)

Nevertheless, people yearn for a good death, timely and appropriate, suggesting some measure of participation, if not consent. Occasionally, a subtle collusion occurs where human and natural plans seem to coincide, revealing a mysterious agreement between mankind, nature, and the gods, and providing a sense of profound rightness and order that is the final objective of religion, indeed of all cultural designs. Belief and reality are merged at such times and death is more partner than foe. The questions of supremacy and power are rendered irrelevant and an experience of unity and harmony prevails.

This paper presents such an event, tracing its origins and following its consequences, over a period of several months.[1] The entire sequence is analyzed as a single event, a drama of several acts. It is a social drama in Victor Turner's (1974) sense, but it is more strikingly a cultural drama, illustrating how a group draws upon its rituals and symbols to face a crisis and find a resolution; it handles conflicts, not of opposing social relationships, but between uncertainty and predictability, powerlessness and choice. A final reconciliation is achieved when the community has selected among and modified its prevailing conceptualizations, using some traditional materials, improvising and innovating others, until it has made a myth of a historical episode and found messages of continuity, human potency and freedom amidst threats of individual and social obliteration.[2]

---

1. Methods used as the basis for this paper were the conventional anthropological techniques of participation-observation, interviews, tape recordings, group discussions, film and photographs. I was fortunate in that there were many records of the events of the day described. The entire sequence was filmed, and I photographed and taped it. Those present at the ceremony numbered about 200. My interpretation is based on protracted discussions before and after the event with about 50 of the people present.

2. In a later version of this essay, titled "A Death in Due Time: Construction of Self and Culture in Ritual Drama" (1984), Myerhoff here inserted the following discussion under the heading of "Death as a Cultural Drama":

Jacob Kovitz [Koved in *Number Our Days*] died in the middle of his ninety-fifth birthday . . .

> The case is remarkable for several reasons: it illustrates the use of ritual to present a collective interpretation of "reality," and it demonstrates the capacity of ritual to take account of unplanned developments and alter itself in midstream into a different event. Further, it illuminates how one man can make himself into a commentary upon his life, his history, and his community, mirroring his social world to itself and to himself at the same time. The case is an example of the transformation of a natural, biological event—death—into a cultural drama, shaped to human purpose until it becomes an affirmation rather than a negation of life.

> Though quite rare in our times, such deaths are not unprecedented. The French social historian Philippe Ariès refers to ritualized, ceremonial deaths as "tamed," and points out that in the Middle Ages, knights of the *chanson de geste* also tamed their deaths. Forewarned by spontaneous realization of imminent departure, the dying person prepared himself and his surroundings, often by organizing a ritual and presiding over it to the last. Death was a public presentation, often simple, including parents, children, friends, and neighbors.

The case is an especially useful one for the light it throws on some of the general characteristics and functions of ritual. Ritual has been defined variously, but there is a core of agreement as to its form and uses. It is prominent in all areas of uncertainty, anxiety, impotence and disorder. Ritual dramas are elaborately staged and use presentational more than discursive symbols, so that our senses are aroused and flood us with phenomenological proof of the symbolic reality which the ritual is portraying. By dramatizing abstract, invisible conceptions, it makes vivid and palpable our ideas and wishes, and as Geertz (1973:112) has observed, the lived-in order merges with the dreamed-of order. Through their insistence on precise, authentic and accurate forms, rituals suggest that their contents are beyond question—authoritative and axiomatic.

Tamed deaths were not necessarily emotional. Death was both familiar and near, evoking no great fear or awe. Solzhenitsyn, too, as Ariès notes, talks about such deaths among peasants. "They didn't puff themselves up or fight against it and brag that they weren't going to die—they took death calmly. . . . And they departed easily, as if they were just moving into a new house." Death was not romanticized or banished. It remained within the household and domestic circle, the dying person at the center of events, "determining the ritual as he saw fit."

Later, as the concept of the individual emerges, distinct from the social and communal context, the moment of death came to be regarded as an opportunity in which one was most able to reach—and publicly present—a full awareness of self. Until the fifteenth century, the death ceremony was at least as important as the funeral in Western Europe. . . .

All the elements of a tamed death are present also in the case of Jacob's birthday party: his foreknowledge of death, its occurrence in a public ceremony, which he directed, his attitude of calm acceptance, his use of the occasion to express the meaning of his life, and the presence and participation of those with whom he was intimate.

Unlike the Eskimo or the medieval knight, Jacob constructed his death alone, without support of established ritual and without expectation of cooperation from his community. This was his own invention, and his only partner was *Malakh-hamoves,* the Angel of Death, who cooperated with him to produce a triumphant celebration that defied time, change, mortality, and existential isolation. Through this ritual, Jacob asserted that his community would continue, that his way of life would be preserved, that he was a coherent, integrated person throughout his personal history, and that something of him would remain alive after his physical end.—Ed.

Ritual inevitably carries a basic message of continuity and predict-ability. Even when dealing with change, new events are connected to preceding ones, incorporated into a stream of precedents so that they are recognized as growing out of tradition and experience. Ritual states enduring and underlying patterns, thus connects past, present and future, abrogating history and time. Ritual always links fellow participants but often goes beyond this to connect a group of celebrants to wider col-lectivities, even the ancestors and those yet unborn. Religious rituals go farther, connecting mankind to the forces of nature and purposes of the deities, reading the forms of macrocosm in the microcosm. And when rituals employ sacred symbols, they may link the celebrant to his/her very self through various stages of the life cycle, making individual history into a single phenomenological reality.

Ritual appears in dangerous circumstances and at the same time is itself a dangerous enterprise. It is a conspicuously artificial affair, by definition not of mundane life. Rituals always contain the possibility of failure. If they fail, we may glimpse their basic artifice, and from this apprehend the fiction and invention underlying all culture.

> Underlying all rituals is an ultimate danger, lurking beneath the smallest and largest of them, the more banal and the most ambitious—the possibility that we will encounter ourselves making up our conceptions of the world, society, our very selves. We may slip into that fatal perspective of recognizing culture as our con-struct, arbitrary, conventional, invented by mortals. (Moore and Myerhoff 1977:22)

Rituals then are seen as reflections not of the underlying, unchanging nature of the world but the products of our imagination. When we catch ourselves making up rituals, we may see all our most precious, basic understandings, the precepts we live by, as mere desperate wishes and dreams.

With ritual providing the safeguards of predictability, we dare ultimate enterprises. Because we know the outcome of a ritual beforehand, we find the courage within it to enact our symbols and what would otherwise be preposterous. In ritual, we incorporate the gods into our bodies, return to Paradise, and with high righteousness destroy our fellows.

What happens when a ritual is interrupted by an unplanned develop-ment, when it is not predictable, when accident rudely takes over and chaos menaces its orderly proceedings? What do we do if death appears out of order, in the middle of a ritual celebrating life? Such an occurrence may be read as the result of a mistake in ritual procedure, as a warning and message from the deities, or as a devastating sign of human impotence. But there is another possibility. The unexpected may be understood as a fulfillment of a different, loftier purpose, and a new, higher order may be found beneath the appearance of the original disruption. A ritual may be transformed in midstream to take account of reality and thereby fulfill its purposes. Then a new meaning and a new ritual emerge, made from older, extant symbols and rites. This occurred in the case to be described, where it might be said that culture had the last word after all.

Ethnographic Background

The death in question was unusually dramatic. Jacob Kovitz died in the middle of the public celebration of his 95th birthday. The ceremony was being held at a senior citizens' community center, the focal life of a small, stable, socially and culturally homogeneous group of elderly Jewish immigrants who originated in the shtetls of Eastern Europe. Now, alone and old, the earlier pressures to be assimilated Americans had abated. They were free to revive and elaborate a way of life which combined elements from their childhood beliefs and practices with modern, American features, suited to the needs of their present circumstances. These were harsh. Family members were distant or dead. Most of the group were poor, very old and frail, suffering from social and communal neglect, extreme loneliness, and isolation. As a people, they were marginal to the concerns of the larger society around them. Their social, political, physical and economic impotence were pronounced and except on a very local level, they were nearly invisible.

Added to these afflictions was their realization that the culture of their childhood would die with them. The Holocaust wiped out the shtetls and all their inhabitants. They clearly apprehended the impending complete extinction of themselves as persons and as carriers of a way of life. The group was entirely age-homogeneous, and except for ceremonial occasions, no real intergenerational continuity existed. Their own membership was being depleted constantly, and there was no one to replace them. Death and impotence were as real as the weather and as persistent.

Moreover, the social solidarity of the group was weakened by the people's ambivalence toward one another, due in part to enforced association and perhaps, too, to displaced anger. Their cultural traditions inclined them to a certain degree of distrust of non-kin, and despite the stability, homogeneity and distinctiveness of past experiences, circumstances and extensive time spent together, they had less than entirely amiable feelings for each other. Factions, disagreements, and long-standing grudges marred their assemblies, most of which took place in secular and sacred rituals within the Center and on benches outside it.

Ideologically, they were united by their common past above all. This was expressed as Yiddishkeit, referring to the local customs, language and beliefs that characterized their parental homes and early life in the shtetl. Very few were orthodox in religious practices. They had broken with strict religious Judaism before leaving the Old Country. A great many were agnostic, even atheistic and anti-religious. But all were passionately Jewish, venerating the historical, ethnic and cultural aspects of their heritage. Most had liberal and socialist political beliefs and had been active at one time or another in the Russian Revolution, various workers' movements, labor unions and similar activities. Since the Holocaust, all were Zionists, despite some ideological reservations concerning nationalism. For them Israel had become an extension of their family, and its perpetuation and welfare were identified as their own. This constellation of beliefs and experiences—the childhood history of the shtetl, Yiddish language and culture, secular and ethnic Judaism, and Zionism—were the sacred elements that united them.[3]

For a dozen years, birthdays had been celebrated by the members in their small dilapidated Center. These were collective occasions, grouping together all those born within the month—modest, simple affairs. Only Jacob Kovitz had regular birthday parties for him alone, and these parties were great fêtes. This reflected his unusual standing in the group. He was

---

3. Here I am distinguishing between "religious" and "sacred" and treating them as categories that may exist independently or be joined. Where ideas, objects, or practices are considered axiomatic, unquestionable, literally sacrosanct, they are "sacred," with or without the inclusion of the concept of the supernatural. Their sacredness derives from a profound and affective consensus as to their rightness; their authority comes from their embeddedness in many realms of tradition. Over against the sacred is the mundane, which is malleable and negotiable. When sacredness is attached to the supernatural, it is religious *and* sacred. When sacredness is detached from the religious, it refers to unquestionably good and right traditions, sanctified by usage and consensus.

a kind of patriarch, a formal and informal leader of the group. He had served as its president for several years, and even after leaving the community to live in a rest home, he returned frequently and had been named president emeritus. He was the oldest person in the group and the most generally venerated. No one else had managed to provide leadership without becoming entangled in factional disputes. He regarded himself and was generally regarded by others as an exemplar, for he had fulfilled the deepest wishes of most people and he embodied their loftiest ideals.

Jacob Kovitz enjoyed the devotion of his children, four successful, educated sons, who demonstrated their affection by frequently visiting the Center and participating in many celebrations there. At these times they treated the members with respect and kindness, and always they were generous, providing meals, entertainment, buses for trips and other unusual gratuities. Moreover, when the sons came they brought their wives, children and grandchildren, many of whom showed an interest in Judaism and Yiddishkeit. Family was one of the highest values among all the old people, and here was a family that all could wish for.

Jacob himself had been a worker. He had made and lost money but never lost his ideals and concerns for charity and his fellows. Without a formal education, he had become a poet and was considered a Yiddishist and a philosopher. He was not religious but he had religious knowledge and practiced the life of an ethical and traditional Jew. Jacob was a courageous and energetic man. After retirement he had become active in organizing senior citizens' centers and he drew the attention of the outside world for what his people regarded as the right reasons. All this he managed with an air of dignity and gentleness. Without dignity, no one was considered worthy of esteem by them. Without gentleness and generosity, he would have aroused sufficient envy to render him an ineffective leader. He was accepted by everyone in the group, a symbol and focus of its fragile solidarity.

Jacob also symbolized and modeled a good old age. He advised his followers on how to cope with their difficulties, and he demonstrated the possibility that old age was not necessarily a threat to decorum, pleasure, autonomy, and clarity of mind.

Following the usage suggested by Moore and Myerhoff (1977), the ritual of Jacob's party-memorial is described in three stages: 1) its creation, 2) its performance and 3) its outcome, sociologically and in terms of its efficacy.

The Creation of the Ceremony: Format, Ritual
Elements, Symbols

The explicit plan in the design of the ceremony specified a format with
several ritual elements that had characterized Jacob's five preceding birthday parties. These were (1) a *brocha,* here a traditional Hebrew blessing
of the wine; (2) a welcome and introduction of important people, including the entire extended Kovitz family, present and absent; (3) a festive
meal of kosher foods served on tables with tablecloths and flowers and
wine, paid for mostly by the family but requiring some donation by
members to avoid the impression of charity; (4) speeches by representatives from the Center, sponsoring Jewish organizations under which
the Center operates, and local and city groups, and by each of the Kovitz
sons; (5) entertainment, usually Yiddish folk songs played by a member
of the family; (6) a speech by Jacob; (7) a donation of a substantial sum
to the Center for its programs and for Israel by the family; (8) an
invitation to those present to make donations to Israel in honor of the
occasion; and (9) a birthday cake, songs, and candles.

The format had a feature often found in secular ritual dramas. Within
it fixed, sacred elements alternated with more open, secular aspects, as
if to lend authenticity, certainty, and propriety to the open, more optional
sections. In the open sections, modifications, particularizations, and
innovations occur, tying the fixed sections more firmly to the situational
details at hand, together providing a progression that seems both apt
and traditional. In this case, for example, the *brocha* is followed by the
meal, the meal by a toast, the toast by a speech, the speech by a song,
then the song by another speech, and so on. The *brocha,* songs, donations, and toasts are predictable; they are unvarying, ritual elements and
symbolic acts. The personnel, as representatives, are also symbolic, signifying the boundaries of the relevant collectivities and the social matrix
within which the event occurs, but the specific contents of their speeches
are less predictable, although they inevitably repeat certain themes.

In this case the repeated themes of the speeches touched on the character, accomplishments, and personal history of Jacob; the honor he
brought to his community and family; the honor the family brought to
their father and their culture; the importance and worth of the attending
Center members; the beauty of Yiddish life; the commonality of all those
individuals, organizations, and collectivities in attendance; the perpetuity
of the group and its way of life.

The style of the ceremony was another ritual element, familiar to all those who had attended previous parties, and familiar because it was drawn from a wider, general experience—that of many public festivities among strangers and mass media entertainment. It reached for a tone that was jovial, bland, mildly disrespectful, altogether familiar, and familial. It was set by a master-of-ceremonies (a son, Sam) who directed the incidents and the participants, cuing them as to the desired responses during the event, and telling them what was happening as the afternoon unfolded. Despite a seemingly innocuous and casual manner, the style was a precise one, reaching for a particular mood—enjoyment in moderation, and cooperation, unflagging within the regulated time frame. Things must always be kept moving along in ritual; if a lapse occurs, self-consciousness may enter, and the mood may be lost. This is especially important in secular rituals, which are attended by strangers or people from different traditions, to whom the symbols used may not be comprehensible. Ritual is a collusive drama, and all present must be in on it.

In this case specific direction was unusually important. The old people are notoriously difficult to direct. They enter reluctantly into someone else's plans for them; for cultural and psychological reasons, they resist authority and reassert their autonomy. For biological reasons they find it hard to be attentive for extended periods of time and cannot long delay gratification. Programs must be short, emotionally certain and specific, skillfully interspersing food and symbols. The people can be engaged by the calling of their names, by praise, and by identifying them with the guest of honor. But their importance must not be inflated overmuch, for they are quick to perceive this as deception and insult. Furthermore, the old people must not be too greatly aroused, for many have serious heart conditions. Perhaps it was the intense familiarity with their limits as an audience or perhaps it was the uncertainty that underlies all secular ceremonies that caused the designers to select as the master of ceremonies a directive leader, who frequently told the audience what was occurring, what would come next, and reminded them of what had occurred, reiterating the sequences, as if restatement in itself would augment the sense of tradition and timelessness that is sought in ritual.

The affair was called a birthday party, but in fact this was a metaphor. The son Sam said in his speech, "You know, Pa doesn't think a birthday is worth celebrating without raising money for a worthy Jewish cause." The event had a more ambitious purpose than merely celebrating a mark in an individual life. The birthday party metaphor was used because it symbolized the people's membership in a secular, modern society. But as only a birthday, it had little significance to them. None of them had ever celebrated their birthdays in this fashion. Indeed, it was the custom to remember the day of their birth by reckoning it on the closest Jewish holiday, submerging private within collective celebrations. More importantly, the event was a *simcha,* a *yontif,* a *mitzvah*—a blessing, a holiday, a good deed, an occasion for cultural celebration and an opportunity to perform good works in a form that expressed the members' identity with the widest reaches of community, Israel and needy Jews everywhere.

Its most important message was that of perpetuation of the group beyond the life of individual members. This was signified in two ways, both of which were innovations and departures from Kovitz's usual birthdays. First, temporal continuity was signified by the presence of a group of college students, brought into the Center during the year by a young rabbi who sought to promote intergenerational ties. It was decided that the young people would serve the birthday meal to the elders as a gesture of respect. That a rabbi was there with them was incidental and unplanned, but turned out to be important. Second was Jacob's announcement that he was donating funds for his birthday parties to be held at the Center for the next five years, whether he was alive or not. Occasions were thus provided for people to assemble for what would probably be the rest of their lives, giving them some assurance that as individuals they would not outlive their culture and community.

Another of the repeated ritual elements was the personnel involved. Most of these have been identified, and reference here need be made only to two more. These were the director of the Center and its president. The director, Abe, was a second-generation assimilated American of Russian-Jewish parentage. A social worker, he had been with this group a dozen years and knew the people intimately, usually functioning as their guardian, protector, interpreter, and mediator. He, along with Jacob and his sons, developed the format for the ceremony and helped conduct it. The president, Moshe, was a man of eighty-two, with an Hasidic background.[4] He was a religious man with a considerable religious education, and a Yiddishist. It was to him that questions about Judaism

---

4. Hasids (Hasidim) were, and are, a deeply religious, semi-mystical group practicing a vitalized, fervent form of folk Judaism originating in Eastern Europe during the mid-eighteenth century.

and its customs were likely to be referred. After Jacob he was the most respected man in the group, and one of Jacob's closest friends.

Symbols carry implicit messages, distinguishable from the overt ingredients intended by the designers of a ritual; they are part of its creation but not clearly planned or controlled. When they are well chosen and understood, they do their work unnoticed. The following are the symbols within the planned ceremony. Others were spontaneously brought in when the ceremony was interrupted and they will be taken up later.

Many of the symbols employed have been mentioned. Every Yiddish word is a symbol, evoking a deep response. The man Jacob and his entire family were significant symbols, standing for success, fulfillment of Judaic ideals, and filial devotion. The dignitaries and the publics they represented, too, were among the symbols used. The birthday metaphor with cake, candles, and gifts was a symbol complex along with "M.C.," "Guest of Honor," and the tone of the program, which incorporated American, contemporary secular life. Also present were symbols for the widest extension of Judaic culture and its adherents, in the form of references to Israel and *mitzvas* or charity and good works. The attendance of small children and young people symbolized the continuity and perpetuity of Judaism. The traditional foods symbolized and evoked the members' childhood experiences as Jews; they were the least ideological and possibly most powerfully emotional of all the symbolic elements that appeared in the ritual.

Antecedents of the Ritual

Everyone at the Center knew that Jacob had been sick. For three months he had been hospitalized, in intensive care, and at his request had been removed by his son Sam to his home so that he could be "properly taken care of out of the unhealthy atmosphere of a hospital." Before, Jacob had always resisted living with his children, and people interpreted this change in attitude as indicative of his determination to come to his birthday party. The old people were aware that Jacob had resolved to have the party take place whether he was able to attend or not. People were impressed, first, because Jacob had the autonomy and courage to assert his opinions over the recommendations of his doctors—evidently he was still in charge of himself and his destiny—and second, because Jacob's children were so devoted as to take him in and care for him. But most of all they were struck by his determination to celebrate his birthday among them. They were honored and awed by this and closely followed the daily developments that preceded the celebration: details concerning Jacob's health, the menu for the party, the entertainment—all were known and discussed at length beforehand.

As the day grew close, much talk concerned the significance of the specific date. It was noted that the celebration was being held on Jacob's actual birthday. The party was always held on a Sunday, and as the date and day coincided only every seven years, surely that they did so on this particular year was no accident. Again, they noticed that the month of March was intrinsically important in the Hebrew calendar, a month of three major holidays. And someone claimed that it was the month in which Moses was born and died. He died on his birthday, they noted.[5]

A week before the event, it was reported that Jacob had died. Many who were in touch with him denied it, but the rumor persisted. Two days before the party, a young woman social worker, a close friend of Jacob's, told the college group that she had dreamed Jacob died immediately after giving his speech. And she told the people that Jacob's sons were advising him against coming to the party but that he would not be dissuaded. Nothing would keep him away.

The atmosphere was charged and excited before the party had even begun. Abe, the director, was worried about the old people's health and the effects on them of too much excitement. There were those who insisted that on the birthday they would be told Jacob had died. Jacob's friend Manya said, "He'll come all right, but he is coming to his own funeral."

And what were Jacob's thoughts and designs at this point? It is possible to glimpse his intentions from his taped interviews with a son and a granddaughter. In these, common elements emerge: he is not afraid of death but he is tormented by confusion and disorientation when "things seem upside ways," and "not the way you think is real." Terrible thoughts and daydreams beset him, but he explains that he fights them off with his characteristic strength, remarking, "I have always been a fighter. That's how I lived, even as a youngster. I'd ask your opinion and yours, then go home and think things over and come to my own decision." He describes his battles against senility and his determination to maintain coherence by writing, talking, and thinking. He concludes,

---

5. In fact, Moses died on the seventh of Adar. He did, however, die on his birthday.

I was very depressed in the hospital. Then I wrote a poem. Did
you see it? A nice poem. So I'm still living and I have something
to do. I got more clearheaded. I controlled myself.

Jacob had always controlled himself and shaped his life, and he was
not about to give that up. Evidently he hoped he might die the same
way. "I'll never change" were his last words on the tape.

It was difficult for Jacob to hold on until the party and to write his
speech, which seemed to be the focus of his desire to attend. Its contents
were noteworthy in two respects: first, his donation and provision for
five more parties; and second, his statement that whereas on all his
previous birthdays he had important messages to deliver, on this one he
had nothing significant to say. Why, then, the desperate struggle to make
this statement? The message, it seems, was that he could and would
deliver it himself, that he was still designing his life and would do so
to the end. The preparations for and the manner of the speech's delivery
conveyed and paralleled its message.

The Performance of the Ritual

The day of the party was fair and celebrants came streaming toward
the Center out of their rented rooms and boardinghouses down the small
streets and alleys, several hours too early. That the day was set apart
was clear from their appearance. The women came with white gloves,
carrying perfectly preserved purses from other decades, and wearing
jewelry, unmistakable gifts from their children—golden medallions bearing grandchildren's names, "Tree of Life" necklaces studded with real
pearls; Stars of David; gold pendants in the form of the word *Chai,*
Hebrew for life and luck. All were announcements of connections and
remembrance. Glowing halos from umbrellas and bright hats colored
the ladies' expectant faces. Men wore tidy suits polished with use over
well-starched collar-frayed shirts.

The Center halls, too, were festively decorated and people were formally seated. At the head table was the Kovitz family and around it the
dignitaries. Jacob, it was learned, was behind the curtain of the little
stage, receiving oxygen, and so the ceremony was delayed for about half
an hour. At last he came out to applause and took his seat. Music called
the assembly to order and people were greeted with *shalom,* Hebrew for
peace. The guest of honor was presented, then introductions followed,

with references to the Kovitz family as *mishpoche* ("kin"), the term finally being used for the entire assembly. By implication, all present were an extended family. Each member of the Kovitz family was named, even those who were absent, including titles and degrees, generation by generation. The assembly was greeted on behalf of "Pa, his children, his children's children, and even from their children." The religious *brocha* in Hebrew was followed by the traditional secular Jewish toast *Le' Chayim*. Sam set out the order of events in detail, including a specification of when Jacob's gift would be made, when dessert would be served (with speeches), when the cake would be eaten (after speeches), and so forth. The announcement of procedures was intended to achieve coordination and invite participation. The audience was appreciative and active. People applauded for the degrees and regrets from family members unable to attend, and recognized the implicit messages of continuity of tradition, respect from younger generations, and family devotion that had been conveyed in the first few moments.

The meal went smoothly and without any public events, though privately Jacob told the president, Moshe, that he wished people would hurry and eat because "*Malakh-hamoves* [the Angel of Death, God's messenger] is near and hasn't given me much time."

As dessert was about to be served, Sam, acting as master of ceremonies, took the microphone and began his speech, in which he recounted some biographical details of Jacob's life and certain cherished characteristics. He emphasized his father's idealism and social activism in the Old Country and in America, and spoke at some length about the courtship and marriage of his parents. Though his mother had died twenty-four years ago, she remained a strong influence in keeping the family together, he said.

During Sam's speech, Jacob was taken backstage to receive oxygen. People were restive and worried, but Sam assured them that Jacob would soon return and the program continue. Eventually Jacob took his seat, leaning over to tell one of the young people in English, and Moshe in Yiddish, that he had little time and wished they would hurry to his part of the program, for now, he said, "*Ikh reingle sikh mitn Malakh-hamoves.*" "I am wrestling the Angel of Death."

The program was interrupted briefly when all those in charge recognized Jacob's difficulty in breathing and gave him oxygen at his seat. A pause of about ten minutes ensued. The thread of the ritual lapsed entirely while people watched Jacob being given oxygen. Moshe and

Abe were worried about the impact of this sight on the old people. The previous year someone had died among them and they had been panic-stricken. But now all were rather quiet. They talked to each other softly in Yiddish. At last Sam took the microphone again and spoke extempore about his father's recent life, filling the time and maintaining the ritual mood until it became clear that Jacob was recovering. Sam told the group that maybe his wife's chicken soup—proper chicken soup prepared from scratch with the love of a *yiddishe mame*—had helped sustain Jacob. This was received with enthusiastic applause. Most of those in the audience were women and their identity was much bound up with the role of the nurturant, uniquely devoted Jewish mother. In fact, the earlier mention of the importance and remembrance of the Kovitz mother had been received by many women as a personal tribute. They also appreciated the appropriateness of a daughter-in-law showing this care for a parent, something none of them had experienced. Sam went on to explain that since leaving the hospital Jacob had "embarked on a new career, despite his age." He was teaching his son Yiddish and had agreed to stay around until Sam had mastered it completely. "Since I am a slow learner, I think he'll be with us for quite a while." This too was full of symbolic significance. The suggestion of new projects being available to the old and of the passing on of the knowledge of Yiddish to children were important messages.

Sam went on, extending his time at the microphone as he waited for a sign that Jacob was able to give his speech. By now Sam was improvising on the original format for the ritual. He made his announcement of the gift of money, half to the Center for cultural programs, half to Israel, reminding the audience that Jacob did not believe a birthday party was worth celebrating unless it involved raising funds for deserving Jewish causes.

Still Jacob was not ready, so the microphone was turned over to Abe, who improvised on some of the same themes, again and again, touching important symbolic chords. He, like Sam, referred to Jacob as a stubborn man and to Jews as a stiff-necked people, tenacious and determined. He reassured the assembly that they were important people and would be remembered, that outsiders came to their Center to share their *simcha* and appreciate their unique way of life. They, he said, like Jacob, would be studied by scientists one day, for a better understanding of the indivisibility of mental and physical health, to see how people could live to be very old by using their traditions as a basis for a good and useful life. He finished by emphasizing Jacob's most revered qualities: his devotion to his people, his learning and literacy, and his courage and dignity. He was an example to them all. "And," he went on, "you, too, you are all examples."

At last the sign was given that Jacob was ready. Abe announced the revised sequence of events: Jacob's speech in Yiddish, then in English, then the dignitaries' speeches, then the cake. Jacob remained seated but began his speech vigorously, in good, clear Yiddish.[6] After a few sentences he faltered, slowed, and finished word by word. Here are selections from his speech in translation:

> Dear friends: Every other year I have had something significant to say, some meaningful message when we came together for this *yontif*. But this year I don't have an important message. I don't have the strength. . . . It is very hard for me to accept the idea that I am played out. . . . Nature has a good way of expressing herself when bringing humanity to the end of its years, but when it touches you personally it is hard to comprehend. . . . I do have a wish for today. . . . It is that my last five years, until I am 100, my birthday will be celebrated here with you . . . whether I am here or not. It will be an opportunity for the members of my beloved Center to be together for a *simcha* and at the same time raise money for our beleaguered Israel.

The message was powerful in its stated and unstated concepts, made

---

6. All these people are completely multilingual and use different languages for different purposes, with some consistency. For example, political and secular matters are often discussed in English; Hebrew is used to make learned, final points in settling debates; Russian and Polish appear in songs, poems, reminiscences, in arguments and bargaining. Yiddish, the *mame loshen,* punctuates all the areas, but appears most regularly in times of intense emotion. It is also used most in conversations about food, children, cursing, and gossiping. For some, Yiddish has connotations of inferiority since it was associated with female activities, domestic and familial matters (in the shtetl, few were educated in Hebrew and so Yiddish dominated the household). It was the language of exiles living in oppression and, later, of greenhorns. For others, the Yiddishists in particular, it is a bona fide language to be treated with respect and used publicly. Careful pronunciation, proper syntax, and avoidance of Anglicized words are considered signs of respect for Yiddishkeit. On the whole, Jacob was always careful in his Yiddish, and this was seen as an indication of his pride in his heritage.

even more so by the dramatic circumstances in which it was delivered. Jacob's passion to be heard and to complete his purpose was perhaps the strongest communication. He was demonstrating what he had said in the earlier interviews, namely, that he sustained himself as an autonomous, lucid person, using thinking, speaking, and writing as his shields against self-dissolution and senility.

Jacob finished and sat down amid great applause. His and the audience's relief were apparent. He sat quietly in his place at the table, folded his hands, and rested his chin on his chest. A moment after Sam began to read his father's speech in English, Jacob's head fell back, wordlessly, and his mouth fell open. Oxygen was administered within the surrounding circle of his sons as Abe took the microphone and asked for calm and quiet. After a few moments, his sons lifted Jacob, still seated in his chair, and carried him behind the curtain, accompanied by Moshe, Abe, and the rabbi.

Soon Abe returned and reassured the hushed assembly that a rescue unit had been called, that everything possible was being done, and that Jacob wanted people to finish their dessert:

Be assured that he knew the peril of coming today. All we can do is pray. He's in the hands of God. His sons are with him. He most of all wanted to be here. Remember his dignity and yours and let him be an example. You must eat your dessert. You must, we must all, continue. We go on living. Now your dessert will be served.

People complied and ate quietly. Regularly Abe came to the front to reassure them, with special firmness when the fire department siren was heard outside. He explained at length all the steps that were being taken to save Jacob, and concluded,

He's very delicate. Your cooperation is very beautiful. Jacob wants us to continue. You heard his speech. We all have a date to keep. Out of love and respect for Jacob we will be meeting here for the next five years on his birthday. We will be here, you will be here, whether to celebrate with him or commemorate him. They are taking Jacob away now. The hospital will telephone us and we will tell you how he is doing.

People complied and continued eating. There were many who quietly spoke their certainty that Jacob was dead and had died in their midst. The conviction was strongest among those few who noticed that when the rabbi and Moshe left Jacob behind the curtain, they went to the bathroom before returning to their seats. Perhaps it was only hygiene, they said, but it was also known that religious Jews are enjoined to wash their hands after contact with the dead. Hence the gesture was read as portentous. One of the religious men moved his lips quietly, not praying but uttering, "*Ehad, ehad, ehad,*" Hebrew for "one." This is to be the last word heard or, if possible, said at the exact moment of death.[7]

The room was alive with hushed remarks:

He's gone. That was how he wanted it. He said what he had to say and finished.

It was a beautiful life, a beautiful death.

There's a saying, when the fig is plucked in due time it's good for the fig and good for the tree.

Did you see how they carried him out? Like Elijah, he died in his chair. Like a bridegroom.

He died like a *tzaddik.*[8]

Moses also died on his birthday, in the month of Nisan.[9]

---

7. *Ehad* is the final word of the phrase, "The Lord is One," which according to some authorities signifies that the soul unites with Deity as the word "one" is said (Goldin 1939:109).

8. A *tzaddik* in Hasidic tradition is a saintly man of great devotion, often possessing mystical powers. It is noted that important Hasids sometimes died in their chairs, and it is said that they often anticipated the dates of their death. There is also a suggestive body of custom surrounding the symbolism of the chair, which figures importantly in at least two Jewish male rites of passage. In Hasidic weddings it is customary for the bridegroom to be carried aloft in his chair. And an empty chair is reserved for the prophet Elijah at circumcisions; this is to signify that any Jewish boy may turn out to be the Messiah, since Elijah must be present at the Messiah's birth.

9. As noted above, Moses died on the seventh of Adar, on his birthday; he was allowed to "complete the years of the righteous exactly from day to day and month to month, as it is said, the number of thy days I will fulfill" (Talmud Bavli Kaddushin 38A). Hence the tradition in folklore that the righteous are born and die on the same day. Elijah did not die in his chair, however. He is believed to have "been taken up by a whirlwind into Heaven," passing out of this world without dying. His "passage" was not a normal death in any event, and this is probably why his death was brought up in this discussion. These points were clarified in personal communication by Rabbi Chaim Seidler-Feller of Los Angeles.

Order was restored as the dignitaries were introduced. Again the ritual themes reappeared in the speeches: Jacob's work among senior citizens, the honor of his family, his exemplary character, and so forth. A letter to Jacob from the mayor was read and a plaque honoring him proferred by a councilman. Then a plant was given to his family on behalf of an organization, and this seemed to be a signal that gifts were possible and appropriate. One of the assembled elderly, an artist, took one of his pictures off the wall and presented it to the family. A woman gave the family a poem she had written honoring Jacob, and another brought up the flowers from her table. The momentum of the ritual lapsed completely in the face of these spontaneous gestures. People were repeatedly urged by Abe to take their seats. The artist, Heschel, asked what would be done about the birthday cake now that Jacob was gone, and was rebuked for being gluttonous. With great difficulty Abe regained control of the people, reminding them sternly that the ceremony had not been concluded. There remained one dignitary who had not yet spoken, Abe pointed out, and this was insulting to the group he represented.

Abe was improvising here, no longer able to utilize the guidelines of the birthday metaphor. The ceremony threatened to break apart. In actuality, Abe was worried about letting people go home without knowing Jacob's fate. It would be difficult for him to handle their anxieties in the next few days if they were left in suspense. No one wanted to leave. The circumstances clearly called for some closure, some provision of order. The last dignitary began to talk and Abe wondered what to do next. Then the phone rang and everyone was still. The speaker persisted, but no one listened. Abe came forward and announced what everyone already knew.

God in his wisdom has taken Jacob away from us, in His mystery He has taken him. So you must understand that God permitted Jacob to live ninety-five years and to have one of his most beautiful moments here this afternoon. You heard his last words. We will charter a bus and go together to his funeral. He gave you his last breath. I will ask the rabbi to lead us in a prayer as we stand in solemn tribute to Jacob.

People stood. About a dozen men drew *yarmulkes* out of their pockets and covered their heads. The rabbi spoke:

We have had the honor of watching a circle come to its fullness and close as we rejoiced together. We have shared Jacob's wisdom and warmth, and though the ways of God are mysterious, there is meaning in what happened today. I was with Jacob backstage and tried to administer external heart massage. In those few moments with him behind the curtain, I felt his strength. There was an electricity about him but it was peaceful and I was filled with awe. When the firemen burst in, it felt wrong because they were big and forceful and Jacob was gentle and resolute. He was still directing his life, and he directed his death. He shared his wisdom, his life with us and now it is our privilege to pay him homage. Send your prayers with Jacob on his final journey. Send his sparks up and help open the gates for him with your thoughts. We will say Kaddish. "*Yitgadal veyitakadash shmeh rabba . . .* [Sanctified and magnificent be Thy Great Name]."[10]

The ritual was now unmistakably over but no one left the hall. People shuffled forward toward the stage, talking quietly in Yiddish. Many crossed the room to embrace friends, and strangers and enemies embraced as well. Among these old people physical contact is usually very restrained, yet now they eagerly sought each other's arms. Several wept softly. As is dictated by Jewish custom, no one approached the family, but only nodded to them as they left.

There were many such spontaneous expressions of traditional Jewish mourning customs, performed individually, with the collective effect of transforming the celebration into a commemoration. Batya reached down and pulled out the hem of her dress, honoring the custom of rending one's garments on news of a death. Someone had draped her scarf over the mirror in the ladies' room, as tradition requires. Heschel poured his glass of tea into a saucer. Then Abe took the birthday cake to the kitchen, and said, "We will freeze it. We will serve it at Jacob's memorial when we read from his book. He wouldn't want us to throw it away. He will be with us still. You see, people, Jacob holds us together even after his death."

---

10. In Jewish mysticism, represented in the Kabbalah, a person's soul or spirit is transformed into sparks after death. "Kaddish" is a prayer sanctifying God's name, recited many times in Jewish liturgy; it is known also as the Mourner's Prayer and recited at the side of a grave.

Finally, the Center had emptied. People clustered together on the benches outside to continue talking and reviewing the events of the afternoon. Before long, all were in agreement that Jacob had certainly died among them. The call to the rescue squad had been a formality, they agreed. Said Moshe,

> You see, it is the Jewish way to die in your community. In the old days, it was an honor to wash the body of the dead. No one went away and died with strangers in a hospital. The finest people dressed the corpse and no one left him alone for a minute. So Jacob died like a good Yid. Not everybody is so lucky.

Over and over, people discussed the goodness of Jacob's death and its appropriateness. Many insisted that they had known beforehand he would die that day. "So why else do you think I had my *yarmulke* with me at a birthday party?" asked Beryl. Sam commented, "After a scholarly meeting it is customary to thank the man. Jacob was a scholar and we thanked him by accompanying him to Heaven. It's good to have many people around at such a time. It shows them on the other side that a man is respected where he came from." Bessie's words were "He left us a lot. Now the final chapter is written. Nu? What more is there to say. The book is closed. When a good man dies, his soul becomes a word in God's book." It was a good death, it was agreed. Jacob was a lucky man. "*Zu mir gezugt*—it should happen to me" was heard from the lips of many as they left.

Outcome: Sociological Consequences

Two formal rituals followed. The funeral was attended by most of the group (which, as promised, went in a chartered bus), and a *shloshim* or thirty-day memorial was held at the Center, when the birthday cake was indeed served, but without candles.

At the funeral, the young rabbi reiterated his earlier statement concerning the electricity he had felt emitting from Jacob just before he died, described how Jacob used his remaining strength to make a final affirmation of all he stood for, and revealed that, at the last moment of his life, Jacob—surrounded by all the people he loved—believed in God.[11]

---

11. Others disagreed with this and were certain that Jacob died an agnostic. They did not confront the rabbi on the matter, however; said Heschel, "If it makes the rabbi happy, let him believe it."

In his eulogy, Jacob's son Sam said, "In our traditions there are three crowns—the crown of royalty, the crown of priesthood, and the crown of learning. But a fourth, the crown of a good name, exceeds them all." Spontaneously, at the graveside, without benefit of direction from funeral officials, many old men and women came forward to throw a shovel of earth on the grave, sometimes themselves tottering from the effort. Each one carefully laid down the shovel after finishing, according to the old custom. Then they backed away, forming two rows, to allow the Angel of Death to pass through. They knew from old usage what was appropriate, what movements and gestures suited the occasion, with a certainty that is rarely seen now in their lives. Moshe, one of the last to leave, pulled up some grass and tossed it over his shoulder. This is done, he explained later, to show that we remember we are dust, but also that we may be reborn, for it is written: "May they blossom out of the city like the grass of the earth."

A month later, the *shloshim* was held. In it a final and official interpretation of Jacob's death was forged and shared. He was a saint by then. He must be honored, and several disputes were avoided that day by people reminding one another of Jacob's spirit of appreciation and acceptance of all of them and his wish for peace within the Center. The cake was eaten with gusto as people told and retold the story of Jacob's death.

Funeral and *shloshim* were the formal and public dimension of the outcome of Jacob's death. Informal, private opinions and interpretations are also part of the outcome. These were revealed in subsequent individual discussions, informal interviews, casual group conversations, and a formalized group discussion on the subject. On these private, casual occasions people said things they had not, and probably would not, express in public, particularly about matters that they knew might be regarded as old-fashioned, un-American, or superstitious. In confidence, several people expressed wonder at and some satisfaction in what they regarded as the divine participation in the event. One lady said with a chuckle, "You know, if the Lord God, Himself, would bother about us and would come around to one of our affairs, well, it makes you feel maybe you are somebody after all." Said Bessie,

You know, I wouldn't of believed if I didn't see with mine eyes. Myself, I don't really believe in God. I don't think Jacob did neither. If a man talks about the Angel of Death when he's dying that don't necessarily mean anything. Everybody talks about the Angel of Death. It's like a saying, you know what I mean? But you gotta admit that it was not a regular day. So about what really went on, I'm not saying it was God working there, but who can tell? You could never be sure.

Publicly the subject was discussed at great length. A debate is a cherished, traditional form of sociability among these people. And this was certainly a proper topic for a *pilpul*.[12] A kind of *pilpul* was held with a group in the Center that had been participating in regular discussions. One theme considered by them in detail was the young social worker's dream, in which she anticipated the time and manner of Jacob's death.[13] Dreams, they agreed, must be carefully evaluated, for they may be sent by God or the demons, and as such are not to be taken as prophecy on face value. After much discussion one of the learned men in the group said that perhaps the young woman should have fasted on the day after the dream. This assures that the previous night's dreams will not come true. Sam quoted Psalm 39, in which King David prayed to God to know the measure of his days. The request was denied because God decreed that no man shall know the hour of his death. Could it be that God granted Jacob what he had denied Kind David? Why had the girl had the dream? She knew nothing of these matters. Why had it not come to one of them, who understood the significance of dreams? After an hour or so of disagreement only two points were clear. First, that the news of the dream had received widespread circulation before the birthday party; and second, that it added to people's readiness to participate in a commemoration instead of a party. It made what happened more mysterious and more acceptable at the same time. Did it convince anyone that God had had a hand in things? Some said yes and some no. Perhaps the most general view was that expressed by Moshe, who on leaving said, "Well, I wouldn't say yes but on the other had I wouldn't say no."

Another aspect of the ritual's outcome was the impact of the day on

---

12. Literally, *pilpul* means "pepper" and refers to the custom of lively scholarly argument about religious texts.

13. Dreams were very significant among shtetl folk, being elaborately discussed and much used in pursuit of symbolic meanings and ritual usage. Indeed, four members of the group owned and used dream books, which they had brought with them from the Old Country.

various outsiders. The attending dignitaries were included in the moment of *communitas* that followed Jacob's death, and were duly impressed. Before leaving, one of the Gentile politicians told the people around her, "I have always heard a lot about Jewish life and family closeness. What I have seen here today makes me understand why the Jews have survived as a people." This praise from an official, a stranger and a Christian, to a group that has always regarded Christians with distrust and often deep fear, was a source of great satisfaction, a small triumph over a historical enemy, and an unplanned but not unimportant consequence of the ritual.

The events of the day were reported widely, in local newspapers and soon in papers all over the country. Members of the audience were given opportunities to tell their version of what happened when children and friends called or wrote to ask them, "Were you there that day . . . ?" The impact on the Center members of the dispersion of the news to an outside world, ordinarily far beyond their reach, was to give them a temporary visibility and authority that increased their importance, expanded their social horizons, and accelerated their communication with the world around them. These, along with their heightened sense of significance, were the apparent sociological consequences of the ritual.

Outcome: The Efficacy of the Ritual

How shall the success of a ritual be estimated? How is one to decide if it has done its work? These are among the most complex and troublesome questions to be faced in dealing with this topic. It is not impossible to examine efficacy in terms of the explicit intentions of the performers. But it is necessary to go beyond this and inquire, too, about its unintended effects and the implicit, unconscious messages it carries. Then, one may ask, for whom did it work? For there may be many publics involved. In religious rituals even the deities and the unseen forces are addressed and, it is hoped, moved by the performance. The official plan for a ritual does not tell us about this. Many levels of response may be specified, for this is not given by the formal organization of a ritual. Sometimes audiences or witnesses are more engaged by watching a ritual than are its central subjects and participants. When we inquire about conviction, it is necessary to ask also about the degree and kind of conviction involved, since a range of belief is possible, from objection and anger if the ritual is incorrectly performed, through indifference and boredom, to approval and enjoyment, and finally total and ecstatic conviction. The long-range as well as immediate effects of the event must be taken into account, since rituals have consequences that reach past the moment when they occur; their outcome is usually to be known only in due time. It is impossible to take up all these questions. The fieldworker never has such complete information. And the symbols dealt with in ritual are by definition inexhaustible in their final range of referents. Subjects cannot verbalize the totality of their apprehensions in these areas because so much of their response is unconscious. Inevitably there are blanks in our inquiry, and ultimately the fieldworker interested in such questions takes responsibility for inference in explanation, going beyond the observed behavior and "hard" data; to do otherwise would mean losing all hope of understanding the issues that make ritual interesting in the first place. In discussing ritual, an analysis of outcome is always an interpretation and an incomplete one.

All rituals are efficacious to some degree merely by their taking place. They are not purposive and instrumental, but expressive, communicative, and rhetorical acts. Their stated purpose must be regarded not as an illustration of a piece of life but as an analogy. No primitive society is so unempirical as to expect to cause rain by dancing a rain dance. Not even Suzanne Langer's cat is that naive. A rain dance is, in Burke's felicitous phrase, a dance with the rain, the dancing of an attitude. The attitude is the one described earlier—collectively attending, dramatizing, making palpable unseen forces, setting apart the flow of everyday life by framing a segment of it, stopping time and change by presenting a permanent truth or pattern. If the spirits hear and it rains, so much the better, but the success of the ritual does not depend on the rain. If a patient at a curing ceremony recovers, good, but he or she need not do so for the ritual to have successfully done its work. A ritual fails when it is seen through, not properly attended, or experienced as arbitrary invention. Then people may be indifferent enough not to hide their lack of conviction; their failure or refusal to appear to suspend disbelief is apparent and the ritual is not even efficacious as a communication.

In the case of Jacob's death, matters are complicated because two rituals must be considered: the intended birthday party, a designed, directed secular affair with nonreligious sacred nuances, transformed spontaneously by a collectivity into a nonplanned, fully sacred religious memorial.

The birthday party, as far as it went, was a success. It is hard to imagine how it could have failed to make its point and achieve its purposes, which were entirely social. It was convincing to all concerned and received by the audience with appreciation and cooperation. It demonstrated social connections and implied perpetuity of a collectivity beyond the limited life span of its central figure. It honored the man Jacob and his friends, values, and traditions. It reached beyond its immediate audience to include and allow for identification with a wider, invisible Jewish community. The goals of the birthday party were relatively modest and not unusual for secular ceremonies of this sort. The turning point occurred when Jacob died; the message and impact of the day's ceremonies took on a new dimension, and the sacred ritual replaced the social, more secular one.

In dying when he did, Jacob was giving his last breath to his group, and this was understood as a demonstration of his regard for them. His apparent ability to choose to do what is ordinarily beyond human control hinted at some divine collaboration. The collective and spontaneous reversion to traditional religious death rituals was hardly surprising. Death customs are always elaborate and usually constitute one of the most tenacious and familiar areas of religious knowledge. According to some authorities, saying Kaddish makes one still a Jew no matter what else of the heritage one has relinquished.[14] The saying of Kaddish makes palpable the community of Jews. According to the rabbi at the party-memorial, the Kaddish always includes not only the particular death at hand but all a person's dead beloved and all the Jews who have ever lived and died.[15] Mourners coalesce into an *edah,* a community, connected beyond time and space to an invisible group, stretching to the outermost reaches of being a people, *Kol Isroel*—the ancestors, those unborn—and most powerfully, one's own direct, personal experiences of loss and death.

For religious and nonreligious alike that day the Kaddish enlarged and generalized the significance of Jacob's death. At the same time, the Kaddish particularized his death by equating it with each person's historical, subjective private griefs, thus completing the exchange between the collective and the private poles of experience to which axiomatic

14. Joseph Zoshin, "The Fraternity of Mourners," in J. Riemer, ed., *Jewish Reflections on Death* (New York, 1974).

15. The rabbi was in attendance fortuitously that day, in his capacity as leader of the young people. Without him the Kaddish would not have been said. His unplanned presence was subsequently interpreted by many as another sign that the memorial was meant to take place when it did.

symbols refer. When this exchange occurs, symbols are not mere pointers or referents to things beyond themselves. A transformation takes place: "Symbols and object seem to fuse and are experienced as a perfectly undifferentiated whole."[16] Such transformations cannot be planned or achieved by will, because emotions and imagination, as D. G. James observes, operate more like fountains than machines.[17] Transformation carries participants beyond words and word-bound thought, calling into play imagination, emotion, and insight and, as Suzanne Langer says, "altering our conceptions at a single stroke." Then participants conceive the invisible referents of their symbols and may glimpse the underlying, unchanging patterns of human and cosmic life, in a triumph of understanding and belief. Few rituals reach such heights of intensity and conviction. When this occurs, all those involved are momentarily drawn together in a basically religious, sometimes near ecstatic mood of gratitude and wonder. That Jacob's death was a genuine transformational moment was attested to by a profound sense of *communitas* and fulfillment that people appeared to have experienced with the recitation of the Kaddish.

We are interested in the unintended, implicit messages conveyed by ritual as well as the planned ones. Therefore, in this case it must be asked, What were the consequences of the set of items that suggested uncanny, inexplicable factors—Jacob's references to the presence of the Angel of Death, his seeming ability to choose the moment of his death, and the prophecy of his death in the form of a dream? The questions are particularly important because ritual is supposed to deliver a message about predictability and order, and here were intrusions beyond human control and therefore disorderly and unpredictable.

Paradoxically, these very elements of the uncanny, mysterious, and unpredictable made the ritual more persuasive and more convincing rather than less so. All these surprises were clothed in a traditional idiom, and while perplexing were not unfamiliar. There were well-used accounts for such matters; there were precedents for prophetic dreams, the presence of the Angel of Death, the deaths of the *tzaddikim,* and of Moses. Conceptions existed for handling them, and if most people involved did not deeply believe in the dogma, they were not unwilling

16. Suzanne K. Langer, *Philosophy in a New Key* (Cambridge, Massachusetts, 1957).

17. D. G. James, *Scepticism and Poetry* (London, 1937).

to consider the possibility that explanations previously offered, though long unused, might have some validity after all.

Renewed belief in God at the end of life is hardly rare, and indeed it might even be that people were more reassured than frightened at the turn of events of the day. When a man dies, as Evans-Pritchard reminds us, a moral question is always posed: not merely, Why does man die? But why this man and why now? In our secular society, we are often left without an answer, and these celebrants, like most whose religion has decayed or been jettisoned, were ordinarily alone with these questions, dealing with ultimate concerns, feebly and individually. The result of Jacob's death, however, was the revival of the idea, or at least the hope and suspicion, that sometimes people die meaningfully; occasionally purpose and propriety are evident. Death in most cases may be the ultimate manifestation of disorder and accident but here it seemed apt and fulfilling. More often than not death flies in the face of human conception, reminding us of our helplessness and ignorance. It finds the wrong people at the wrong time. It mocks our sense of justice. But here it did the opposite and made such obvious sense that it came as a manifestation of order. It helped fulfill the purposes of ritual, establishing and stating form drawn forth from flux and confusion.

Remarkably enough, in this ritual the distinction between artifice and nature was also overcome. The ritual, though unplanned, was not susceptible to the danger of being recognized as human invention. Ironically, because no one was clearly entirely in control—neither Jacob nor the designers and directors—and because it unfolded naturally, the ritual was received as a revelation rather than as a construction. It did not suffer the usual risks of ritual, displaying the conventional and attributed rather than intrinsic nature of our conceptions. Had there been no intimations of the supernatural, the death would probably have been frightening, because it would have exaggerated mortal powers beyond the credibility of the people participating. The hints of mystery suggested powers beyond Jacob's control, making a religious experience of one that otherwise might have been simply bizarre. Despite the interruption of the party and the resultant radical change of course, the celebration that occurred had that very sense of inevitability and predictability of outcome which is the goal of all human efforts in designing and staging a ritual.

Ritual and Time

Any discussion of ritual is ultimately a discussion of time. In the case of a ritual dealing with death and birth, the theme of time is thrown into high relief. Ritual alters ordinary time, emphasizing regularity, order, predictability and continuity. Ironically, it uses repetition to deny the empty, diffuse, trivial, endless, repetitiveness of human and social experience. It finds hints of eternity in recurrences, presented in rituals as re-enactments of timeless patterns, proper and inevitable. Chance is not necessarily denied in ritual, but may be incorporated into a larger framework, where its mutability is reduced in scale and contained within a grander, tidier totality. By inserting traditional elements into the present, the past is read as prefiguring the present, and by implication, the present foreshadows the future. Religious rituals are more sweeping than secular ones in this elongation of time, since sacred rituals aspire to be eternally true, where secular rituals usually refer only to remembered human history. When religious rituals are completely successful, history is transformed into myth, *illud tempus* of no time, no beginnings and no endings.

Ritual disrupts several distinct kinds of time. First, it interferes with the ordinary public broken-up sense of time, where hard, precise and measurable units are used to coordinate collective life. Here, time marches along with great regularity, regardless of human response, stimulation, emotion and mood. Public, quantitative time is quite unsuitable to the mood sought in ritual, which attempts precisely to sweep us away from this objective and rational, evaluative frame of mind. Ritual, like art, may disrupt this kind of time merely by interesting us sufficiently.

A second time sense pertinent to ritual is the subjective, individual perception of events. This is Bergson's duration, intuited flowing, paced according to personal significance. This time is quite irregular, both internally and among assembled individuals. Rituals reach for this time sense, appropriate to a mood of conviction. But then it is necessary in ritual to coordinate the participants so that their private temporal experiences are shared without being too tightly regulated. Synchronization of some sort is necessary, and when it is achieved its collective force is considerable. It is in part this simultaneity of individual time that gives such power to *communitas* states. When the integration of individual moments and responses occurs within the ritual context, a temporary collectivity is made of the participants.

Another kind of temporal interruption may occur in ritual, especially in rites of passage. This is the integration of the individual across the time span of the life cycle, so that a retrieval of a sense of personal integration is achieved. Fragments of experience associated with different phases of personal history are brought to life in ritual, bringing with them their original social and emotional contexts. These assembled fragments allow one to re-experience oneself as a child or youth, to feel again that earlier person as comprehensible, familiar, still present within. Coherence of the "I" is not inevitable, as Fernandez (1974) points out, and the chaos of individual experience, especially when the experience covers great periods of time and sharp disruptions in culture or society, can be acute. How can one identify with the feelings and perceptions of the child one was so long ago? How can one retrieve and recognize all the creatures one has ever been?

Because ritual works through the senses and largely without interference by the conscious mind, it has a singular capacity for bringing back earlier emotions, and allowing one to return to earlier states of being. The past returns with the ritual movements, gestures and recapitulations that link the individual to numinous, unaltered fragments of previous times. Perhaps more than any other thinker, Proust was fascinated with this process. He felt that the past could sometimes be recaptured in its original purity, without the modification of intervening events and without passing through the crucible of the conscious mind. When such re-experiences of past time come back, usually evoked through the senses, unaltered by the chemistry of thought, untouched by time, they carry with them their original, pristine associations and feelings. Mendilow (1952) refers to this experience of timelessness as

> hermetical magic, sealed outside of time, suspending the sense of duration, allowing all of life to be experienced in a single moment. . . . These are pin-points of great intensity, concentrations of universal awareness, antithetical to the diffuseness of life. (1952:137)

Such moments are beyond the experience of duration and flow. In them one may experience the essence of life, eternally valid, very close to the sacred *illud tempus* where history becomes myth.

The rituals that are the most resonant and basic are those associated with the earliest social experiences, inevitably experiences of nurturance and dependence—familial, domestic, often non-verbal, profoundly physiological. In our own world of plural cultures, we often speak of the first, familial experiences as one's ethnic origins, a label for the events associated with first foods, care, language, songs, tales and the like, carried forever by rituals and symbols. Ethnic materials are redolent with early, fundamental associations, and thus contain the possibility of carrying one back to earlier selves, overcoming time and change. Consider the statement made by one of the old men present that day at Jacob's birth-death ritual.

Whenever I say Kaddish, I chant and sway, and it comes back to me like always. I remember how it was when my father, may he rest in peace, would wrap me around in his big prayer shawl. All that warmth comes back to me like I was back in that shawl where nothing, nothing bad could happen.

The Kaddish prayer was probably the most important single ritual that occurred on the day of Jacob's death. It was the most potent emotionally, the most frequently and deeply experienced ritual event, the most ethnically rooted moment, sweeping together all the individuals present, connecting them with earlier parts of self, with Jacob the man, each other, with Jews who had lived and died before, and finally with the great heroes and holy figures of Jewish myth and history. The life of the single man, Jacob, was made into an archetypal event, a myth enacted by mortals whose mundane affairs were enlarged to become full of light and portent. Here is ritual achieving its final purpose, of altering our everyday understandings. Ultimately we are interested in ritual because it tells us something about the mythic condition, the human condition and our private selves at the same time. It may portray an archaic event, but it must be an event that we experience, and the characters, though different from us, must shed light on our own condition. Jacob is a symbol by the end of the day, and as such the pinpoint from which radiated the enlarged meanings of his life and death as well as the immediate ones, the grand and the minute, the remote and the particular—all simultaneously presented, and implying each other.

It might be said that the rituals surrounding Jacob's death altered time in still one more way—by giving the people present more time. Contained in the intimations of the immortal, which most people felt were so present all the day, is the possibility of immortality—perhaps oblivion after death was not a certainty after all.

The old people's long lives stretch far behind them and there is little time ahead. The time they have remaining is heavy and hard to fill. They are not known outside their own small, dying circle. They have no reason to expect their children to remember them more after death than they do in life. They bear besides the enormous burden of individual extinction the knowledge that their way of life is passing out of existence with them. Said one of Jacob's friends:

> It's hard enough to die. All right, we all have to die. But when I think about the streets of my little town, no one will come down the streets anymore. There is nothing left. Maybe even there aren't my parents' gravestones left. That good life, our good Yiddish life, our beautiful language, nobody to talk it any more. Whether there's a god or not, I don't know. What I do know is if there is a god, he's playing marbles with us.

Jacob's death couldn't change the hard realities. But if people lived only by realities there would be no rituals, no symbols, no myths. The power of rituals, myths and symbols is such that they can change the experience we have of the world and its worth. Jacob's death rites may be considered an extraordinarily successful example of ritual, changing the world at a single stroke, opening the experience of more connections, more perpetuation, making a little less certain the oblivion of a culture and collectivity than anyone had thought possible before the day began.

Bobbes and Zeydes: Old and New Roles for Elderly Jews

Introduction

When I received a grant in 1972 to study the cultural characteristics of an aged, ethnic group living in an urban setting, my first inclination was to examine Chicanos. I had previously worked in Mexico and the comparative basis thus provided would be useful. But the political climate was not hospitable, and American ethnic minorities were not welcoming outside investigators at that time. "Why don't you study your own people?" I was frequently asked. The idea never occurred to me, since anthropologists are conventionally trained to study remote, often simpler cultures, or, when they work in urban, complex settings, they do not usually do fieldwork within ethnic or subcultural groups to which they belong. Of course, there would be hazards in such a study, particularly that of overidentification with people about whom one was supposed to be objective and detached, but there might be advantages too. The idea was intriguing. And there was no alternative.

I would work among elderly Eastern European Jewish immigrants, then. I was raised by my Ukrainian grandmother, and luckily, I admired her greatly. Sofie Mann had always been old, it seemed to me as a child. She liked being old, liked her "drapes," as she called her wrinkles, liked being stout, and thought her long hair made her look dignified. She was a *bobbe,* a grandmother, and a *baleboste,* a matron or householder. Only *bobbes* could tell folk stories well and make proper traditional foods, she thought. Wisdom, humor, and certain slowly acquired skills were the natural rewards of aging for her. Sofie felt her innate qualities were standing her in good stead as she grew older. Her common sense, her great, comfortable strength, her good health, and her inner poise were sources of pride. Somewhere in her background, one of her Jewish forebears must have mated with a peasant, she said jokingly, and this accounted for her endurance. She was born in a cabbage field; "that's Jewish fruit," she said. Her mother delivered her in the field, wrapped her in her shawl, rested awhile, then finished the hoeing. "This was a good start," said Sofie. She was raised in a shtetl, within the Pale of Settlement of the Russian empire to which half of the world's Jewish population was confined in the nineteenth century. Desperately poor, regularly terrorized by outbreaks of anti-Semitism initiated by government officials and surrounding peasants, shtetl folk found life precarious.[1] Yet the worse things became externally, it seemed, the more the internal community ties deepened, and people drew sustenance and courage from each other, their religion, and their traditions, to a point. For many, life became unbearable with the reactionary regime of Czar Alexander II. The pogroms of 1881–1882, accompanied by severe economic and legal restrictions, soon began to drive out the more adventurous *shtetl* people. The great surge of Eastern European Jews swelled rapidly until by the turn of the century hundreds of thousands were leaving for the New World.

Sofie left her childhood home in the early 1880s, a young bride, married to a determined, taciturn man, Jacob, a stranger to her since it was the custom for Orthodox Jews to arrange their children's marriages. Without relatives or friends in the New World, without skills, education, or knowledge of English, they managed to survive, then succeed in their life goals. Jacob at first was a peddler, eventually owned a small grocery store. They had many children. Five lived to maturity; two received a college education. All the children had considerable musical training; all understood Yiddish when spoken to but replied in English. None learned Hebrew or received any religious education. It was a time, as one scholar has remarked, when assimilation into American life was thought to

---

1. This view can be characterized as the negative idealization of "shtetl life" as the site of absolute oppression. It is the monochromatic counterpart of the positive idealization of "shtetl life" as the site of communal spirituality and of intensely lived traditions. The first is refracted through the narrative of exodus to the land of plenty, of freedom and justice; the second is refracted through the nostalgia for rootedness. The negative ideal is a selective citation and intensification of history, and is as simplified a representation of actual social life as the obviously nostalgic myth of ancestral origins. The conditions of social life for Jews in Eastern Europe showed considerable variety, with respect to economic status and to relations with the authorities and the surrounding populations. —Ed.

require the jettisoning of all cultural baggage from the Old World, and religion was the first bundle to go.

During the American depression, Jacob and Sofie's house was filled with people. Their children worked and their grandchildren were cared for by Sofie. It was probably the happiest time of her life. She loved the full, noisy house. She found time during this period to go to night school to learn to read and write English. More educated than many of her childhood girlfriends, Sofie had been taught to read and write Yiddish. She learned to speak and read English herself but never mastered writing. She knew America and foresaw that one day her grandchildren would be moving away; she would have to write to them in English. The grandchildren enjoyed helping her with English; the children were less patient. They always wanted her to be modern and urged her to wear stylish clothes and cut her hair so she would not look like a "greenhorn."

As the years passed, Jacob grew even more silent and morose and less certain of himself. We had always thought of him as the absolute head of the house. On Sabbaths and holidays, he was referred to as the King. Only he knew Hebrew; only he could pray. Little by little, we grew to feel less afraid of his stern looks, more sorry for him, especially after he retired. He was physically around the house more but he was not a presence. He had nothing to do but pray, and he was not a deeply religious or learned man. He had no friends. He was not needed.

Sofie was doing what she had always done, taking care of people and the house. In contrast to Jacob, she expanded with time. She grew stouter, jollier, cried and laughed more, talked freely about her childhood. It was hard to account for the differences between them. But I remember feeling that Jacob, whose life was now confined to the house, watched us enviously, not knowing how to get "in" to the family. He hung about and read the paper as Sofie cleaned, cooked, sewed, knitted, sang, baked, visited sick neighbors, and taught the grandchildren her skills and stories. On Friday mornings she was fairly feverish with excitement, plucking the chickens and baking the braided Sabbath challah, dancing to "The Russian Hour" on the radio, whirling a laughing child or two across the kitchen floor covered with feathers, blood, and flour. She never sat down, and she thrived.

Now, thirty years later, I have seen a similar role reversal among the old people in the Center community, and whatever the problems of objectivity I have encountered, I wonder if, without the earlier experience of living with Sofie and Jacob, I would have noticed.

Before describing the present lives of these elderly folk, additional comments about their early, common shtetl culture are helpful in understanding their contemporary situation.

Male and Female Roles in the Shtetl

The dominant force in the shtetl was religion. The strongly patriarchal character of the religion was replicated in family and community organization with perfect consistency. Religion was the concern of everyone but was the specific responsibility and privilege of the men. Women were extremely important, absolutely essential, and highly regarded, but primarily as facilitators of the men's religious activities. The woman was to bear children and train them to carry on the faith. She was to provide a harmonious home, conducive to men's prayer and study. She had the task of carrying out the exacting dietary laws, according to the men's instructions and interpretations. Whenever possible, women worked outside the home, enabling their brothers, sons, and husbands to spend more time in religious study (Baum 1973). The woman provided the support system, the mundane base for the primary undertakings of the men.

In her own right, woman was nothing. Her prayers were not necessary except for her own pleasure. They did not benefit the community; therefore, it was a waste to educate women. But to the extent that a woman fulfilled her supportive role, she could achieve great esteem. Folklore extols a woman who sold her hair for money, which gave her husband economic freedom that permitted him to study. Another tale tells of a woman who sold her soul for her husband. (But this story may be apocryphal since there was debate as to whether women actually had souls [Zborowski and Herzog 1962:136].)

The shtetl woman fulfilled herself through others—children and men. She had to obey only three positive religious commandments. (She observed the same negative commandments as men.) Their substance illuminates the role of woman's nature and place. She must purify herself in a ritual bath after menstruation, so as not to pollute her husband and her community. She brings her household a taste of Paradise by lighting the Sabbath candles. She must burn a bit of dough when she bakes bread, "taking challah," which represents a sacrifice to God, made in the household oven ever since the destruction of the Temple. All these commandments pertain to her biology and her position of homemaker and keeper (Hyman 1973:67).

It would be a mistake to assume that this explanation exhausts the question of woman's life in the shtetl. In all societies, women and men transcend, change, distort, enlarge, and otherwise make habitable restrictive roles. But it would also be a mistake to overlook the consequences of the stereotypes provided for by roles. Roles specify the norms against which behaviors are measured, and self-evaluation often follows these norms more closely than actual conduct.

The social role of the woman in the shtetl—performing her household and religious duties in a quiet and self-effacing manner—was the ideal. It specified not only her duties but the manner in which they were to be performed, that is, the kind of person she was supposed to be. She was expected to be submissive, docile, decorous, retiring, modest, patient, and utterly devoted to her family, without ambitions or aspirations of her own. In fact, a separate sexual stereotype was available to women, generated not by design and not according to ideals. It grew out of the practical necessities of her work outside the home, primarily in the marketplace. This role, less overt and not formally extolled, was nevertheless accepted and admired. It was a *contingent* sexual role, arising in response to and maintained because of its situational appropriateness. What were the attributes of this role, the *baleboste* in the marketplace? First, the shtetl housewife was required by circumstance to be a pragmatist. She needed business acumen and great energy. She needed to know how to deal with government officials and peasants, and as a result often had a superior command over the vernacular languages—usually Russian and Polish—superior to that of her pious male relatives. She was the intermediary, more often than men, navigating the conflicting waters between home, shtetl, and the outside world. She had to manage the household, earn and budget money, regulate time, funds, and attention within the family, make the decisions, allocate the labor, organize and integrate family schedules and internal and external demands.

In addition to her activities in marketplace and household, the shtetl woman devoted herself with intensity to community work. She attended to the sick, shared home duties and child care with other needy women, collected money for brides without dowries, fed visitors and strangers, raised money for orphans, made clothes for Jewish refugees in Palestine, and worked on behalf of poor and needy Jews all over the world.

It was clear that the *baleboste* had to be purposive, robust, intrepid, and efficient. Jokes and stories about this stereotype abound, deriding her as fishwife, the shrew. No doubt some of these women were domineering, shrill, and implacable. But this was forgiven, since it was felt that woman's nature inclined her to great vigor and volatility. Naturally, she was seen as given to outbursts of emotion and was expected to be more expressive than her male counterpart. She was, after all, closer to natural forces, while men were regarded as more naturally spiritual. And because women were viewed as weak and imperfect, their complaints were acceptable. They were fortunate in having at hand explanations for their failures not available to men: after all, what could be expected from a poor, uneducated, sinful woman?

If there was a contingent role available to shtetl men, I have not come across it, in literature or ethnographic descriptions. It seems that men were more limited by the religious obligations that constituted the core of their sexually stereotyped role; and this is not surprising since their religious activities were of more public concern than the conduct of women. The ideal Jewish shtetl male, in physical type and demeanor, could not have been more different from his wife in her contingent role. He was expected to be dignified, soft-spoken, poised, reflective, and gentle; his hands were soft, his eyes weak, his brow furrowed, his skin pale—indicating the many hours devoted to spiritual questions and religious study. With an ideal and a contingent role available, women, it seems, had more options than men, more flexibility, more opportunity to express their individuality and adapt to circumstances. And it was the contingent female role, as we shall see, that years later provided some of the most adaptive features of these women's responses to old age, prefiguring their future accommodation, equipping them with the flexibility and pragmatism that ultimately serve them so well.

Sexual stereotypes aside, there were other consequences of the shtetl's radical separation of the responsibilities of men and women. The domination of the home and marketplace by women is certainly not unique to this society. Wherever it occurs, it offers to women the possibility of considerable accumulation of power and influence. When men withdraw from the mundane world and leave to the women those presumably lesser duties of "running things," they lose all but titular control. Ultimately, everyday decisions shape everyday life and these are made in terms of situational needs by women. The men make the important decisions: when the Messiah will come, what the Torah means, and what the attributes of God are. The wife decides how much money to spend on clothes, whether or not to pawn the family candlesticks to apprentice the son, when the daughter shall marry, and whether it is better to buy fish or chicken for the Sabbath meal. None of this alters the basically patriarchal form of the society, all would agree. This common development (called a cryptomatriarchy by one anthropologist) is often the butt of jokes, but the laughter is aroused by the embarrassment of instant recognition.

The world of the shtetl shaped the men and women of the Center community. Their childhoods there provided them with the basic materials on which they drew in formulating responses to the New World. They encountered some radical changes; among the most significant was the substitution of a different set of sacred duties assigned to men and women. In the New World, religion quickly gave way as the center of life. Work and money were the ultimately serious affairs and, as before, the most important concerns were assigned to men. As soon as possible, women were pulled out of the labor market, since in America a man did not want his wife to work. In America, immigrant women were soon confined to the home. They became more dependent on their husbands, more isolated from public life. In the absence of family, community, and economic activities, they contacted the outside world indirectly, through husbands and children. The *baleboste*'s qualities of strength and competence, energy and autonomy, were not to find adequate outlet during her middle years, and only in old age do these women rally and demonstrate once more some of the features associated with their roles in the shtetl.

Sex Roles among the Elderly Men and Women

The world of the senior citizens' Center is predominantly female, since the members are very old—nearly all in the middle 80s to middle 90s—and the women have outlived most of the men. Their community is small and territorially bounded, and, though coexisting with other ethnic groups, constitutes a culturally intense and distinctive enclave. The old people all live far from children and family and, due to their long-shared residence, have established primary ties with each other; relations among them are ambivalent but stable and intense.

All these people are on small, fixed incomes—pieced together from pensions, savings, children's contributions, occasionally welfare—and the great majority are considerably below the national standards for official poverty. Every part of their lives is lived with great care, so as to conserve waning resources in terms of health, strength, and money. Virtually all live in substandard housing, even those few with savings. The majority of the people in this group, perhaps 150, are widows living alone in a rented room or rooms, with meager cooking facilities or kitchen privileges. There are about a dozen couples, all of whom run their own households, and two of whom own their own homes. About 40 women and men live in boarding houses and the rest, perhaps 60, are single men living alone in rented rooms.

It would be reasonable to assume that men would dominate and lead the life of this group. Culture and belief, combined with scarcity of men, on logical grounds should give rise to male supremacy. The picture is not this simple, although everyone says that men, of course, are more important than women. Women with men, whether long-term spouses or newly acquired boyfriends, are regarded as enormously fortunate and viewed with envy and pain by the single women. Men exert a drawing power on the women. It is not unusual for a single woman to seek to insinuate herself with an amenable couple, forming a stable triad. Competition among women for men's favors and company is fierce, and many outbursts of jealousy occur, sometimes breaking up female friendships of long standing. The men are closely watched and fussed over. However, it cannot be said that they are leaders or even consistently significant in all the Center's activities.

In group discussions, men are not deferred to, and since they do not usually talk as loud or as much as women, they exert little influence on the flow of talk, though serious discussion was one of the exclusively male activities in the shtetl. It has become clear to the men and women, after years of association, that the men are no brighter, no better educated, no more perceptive than the women. Except for occasional pieces of specialized religious knowledge, or statements made by the two men who are rabbis' sons (wise, by definition), it is not assumed that the men have anything particularly worthwhile to contribute merely because they are men. Women are more outspoken and assertive in other verbal activities, abundantly producing essays, stories, poetry, and songs. Only one man—the president emeritus, Jacob Kovitz—writes regularly, this though literacy was a totally male endeavor and of the highest value among Old World Jews.

Center events that require physical endurance are likewise female-dominated. Only a couple of men attend the exercise class. Men come with women to dances but are usually left to themselves, since they tire more quickly than their female partners. Men are passed around somewhat, since every woman wants to have a male partner for at least one dance. But the woman often appears inhibited by her male partner, dances with him slowly, then becomes more animated after depositing him on one of the benches lining the hall, where he sits smiling, clapping to the music, nodding his head, tapping his feet, and waiting for the next woman to sweep him away for a dance. Meanwhile, with undiminished enjoyment, women alternate "being the man" in dances that call for a male partner.

In governance, where one would certainly predict male domination, the pattern is repeated. The real work is done by the women—the organizational tasks, keeping of records, arranging for speakers and programs, planning agendas, collecting fees and dues, and performing those maintenance and administrative jobs that amount to running things. Several men are officials—officers and board members. The president is always a man and the president emeritus and the Center director are men. But, with one exception, they are allied with or married to important women whose direction and influence are unmistakable. Another of the most important activities in the Center, charity in the form of raising funds and gathering food and used clothing for Israel, is entirely female-dominated.

Men are used symbolically by women for various purposes. It is a common sight to see a woman entering the hall, marching across it accompanied by her male companion, bearing herself proudly, almost with disdain, asserting publicly her superiority in being "attached," then leaving her male companion on the benches while she enters the fray, unwilling to be encumbered or slowed down. On leaving, she stops for the man and departs as she entered, on his arm, grandly, donning him as she might her gloves. The men often appear as passive tokens manipulated in the more significant interpersonal exchanges between women.

As a group, the men appear more worn-out and demoralized than the women. It is impossible to do more than speculate as to why this might be so. Perhaps the same biological factors that cause men to die sooner than women contribute to earlier debilitation. At any event, there seems to be a definite difference between the sexes in terms of energy level, and this probably reflects some complex combination of physiology and culture. One may speculate also about the part contributed by different social roles of men and women, and here I refer to the sexual stereotypes that informed these people's earliest experiences with the sexes: their parents. These old men appear to be enacting the part of the idealized shtetl male—dignified, remote, self-absorbed, given to thought more than action. The women emerge in terms of the contingent *baleboste* sexual stereotypes for shtetl women, that which I described as issuing from their circumstances as custodians of the mundane realm. For the women are vigorous, resourceful, indomitable, often rude and brazen, antiauthoritarian, outspoken, and submissive to no one. They exude a presence, a sharp-tongued dynamism expressive of their determination to get by and make do, regardless of harsh external realities. In their present lives, men and women are cut loose from all the usual ties and obligations—economic, kinship, and ritual. They have a certain negative freedom as a result of the social vacuum in which they now live, and it constitutes an opportunity to do things in their own way; for the women it is usually the first such chance in their lives. None of them would choose this detachment, but since it is an unalterable fact, they must deal with it; the men do so by resting and waiting; the women by shaping their lives, exerting themselves, and molding their world. Nevertheless, there are two specific circumstances in which Old World role stereotypes of men and women reappear. In these two situations, male and female roles are once again complementary and unequal, genuinely reciprocal, and expressive of mutual need and service. In the two situations that I shall now describe, the interaction between the sexes is short-lived but intense, in contrast to the shallower and less comfortable associations characteristic of their usual relations. It is not surprising that these two circumstances revolve around matters thoroughly basic: ritual and food.

Men and Women in Ritual: The Sabbath

Elderly women, without their own households, have no access to the most important religious duties enjoined upon them, the ritual bath (*mikve*), making the Sabbath challah, and lighting Sabbath candles (*bentshn likht*). Post-menopausal, they do not attend the ritual bath. They no longer bake, so do not prepare or sacrifice the Sabbath loaf. And having neither home nor family, they do not light the Sabbath candles; though it would be technically possible for them to do so alone in their rooms or boarding house, it is probably too painful a reminder of their isolation from family and community. The women's only access to the three positive religious commandments pertaining to them is provided by the Center, which each Friday conducts an *Oneg Shabes* ceremony to welcome the Sabbath.

The *Oneg Shabes* is the climax of the week's activities. It is always well attended. People bring guests, wear their best clothes, and come to it in high spirits. There are scoffers and cynics who claim it is not *Shabes* at all. It is held much too early in the day. But old people cannot be out in the streets of their deteriorating neighborhood after dark, so they cannot wait for twilight. Neither is there a Sabbath meal; for economic and mechanical reasons this is not possible at the Center. Thus the entire ceremony consists of what properly would be a ritual prologue to the meal. Nevertheless, the *Oneg Shabes* is unfailingly effective and genuinely sacred.

People assemble in the early afternoon. A table, covered with a white linen cloth by the women, is placed before the audience facing it. The important men are seated there, the Center director, the president, the president emeritus, a young rabbinical student assigned to the Center for this occasion, and two or three honored guests. The latter may include women, but they are outsiders, never members. For this event, the men at the table wear head coverings, usually richly decorated velvet *yarmulkes*. Before them on the table is the ritual equipment: wine, glasses, prayer book, candles, matches, and two covered twisted Sabbath challahs. The ceremony opens with a greeting from the director, who welcomes guests and makes announcements concerning the activities for the coming week. The president then takes over and leads the rest of the program. The content varies little. The rabbinical student makes a short speech in English and leads the people in Hebrew Sabbath songs. The president emeritus reads the Yiddish poems he has written during the week. Then Bessie or Pauline is invited to sing, tell a story or folktale, or recite a poem that she has prepared in advance, concerning some aspect of the meaning of the Sabbath, usually in the *shtetl*. Some reference to the shared past, the childhood world of Yiddishkeit, is always brought in. More songs follow, and then there is a speech or discourse by one of the guests. Frequently young people attend, bringing guitars and accordions, leading the members in Israeli folk songs and dances. This program lasts about two hours, and people frequently grow restive. In uncharacteristically loud and authoritative voices, the men at the table admonish the audience to be more restrained. "What's the matter with you? Is this any way to act on Sabbath?" shouts Jake and pounds on the table. But to little avail. The women continue to engage in side conversations with each other and burst out in response to that which interests them when they are supposed to be listening.

Their excitement builds and the ceremony seems to be degenerating into complete confusion just before the climax, which occurs at the very end. The president indicates that it is time to light the candles, that a woman will be asked to *bentsh likht,* bringing the holiness of the Sabbath into their midst. This was the highlight of the week for all the shtetl, an event more sacred than the high holidays, the foretaste of Paradise on earth, the source of meaning for everyday life. And it is the moment of supreme significance for the woman, when her mundane activities are bent toward bringing Paradise to the home. Literally and figuratively, her kitchen becomes a sacred place and her most trivial, repetitive tasks of maintenance and sustenance are sanctified. Appropriately, the Sabbath is female, the Bride who comes to the people of Israel, and it is the woman, now Queen of the home, who brings this blessing to her family. When she takes challah her ordinary oven serves as high altar, and she is a priestess offering a sacrifice. For all the old women at the Center, the earliest memories of childhood are bound up in *bentshn likht.* Everyone remembers watching her mother perform this blessed obligation. It is a moment of the deepest personal as well as religious significance.

The *Oneg Shabes* at the Center is predictable in every detail, except in the designation of the woman who shall light the candles. This is not established ahead of time. The tension before a woman is called, therefore, is acute and palpable. Who will be so honored this week? In the silence before one is named, there is a subtle fluttering of those women who know the prayers and wish to be called to the candles. They flutter their scarves quietly in their laps, wordlessly signaling their readiness. One is named. It is Sadie. She approaches the candles slowly, turns her back to the assembled group, and drapes her head. Barely audibly, she says the short Hebrew prayer, blessing "the Lord who has commanded us to kindle the Sabbath light." She lights the candles, bows her body forward over the flames, then circles her hands over them three times, drawing their holiness toward her face. She finishes this gesture by covering her eyes with her hands as she silently and privately prays to herself in Yiddish. Tears course through her fingers and she elongates the moment. When she removes her hands, she looks about with transformed visage, smiles at the assembled people, and bids them *Gut Shabes.* She circulates among the people, kissing her special friends, shaking hands, wishing everyone *shavua tov,* a good week, while the men at the table exhort her to be seated and allow the ritual to continue. Reluctantly she does so, but smilingly reaches to clasp the hands of her neighbors, who thank and compliment her. Her characteristically strong, assertive personal style is nowhere in evidence. She is gentle, subdued, nearly wordless, submitting reluctantly to the president's annoyance at her disruptive behavior. Uncharacteristically, she does not make a sharp retort to his admonitions that she sit down and be quiet.

The ritual resumes with difficulty, since the women feel the important part of it has been completed and the Sabbath has entered. The men feel the most important part, the blessing and drinking of the wine, has not yet taken place. At last, the president restores order, says the prayers, and passes the glass of wine to those at the table. Then he concludes by taking up the Sabbath challahs and, blessing them, tears off a piece and hands the bread to the men beside him, who do the same. Finally, the women in the audience receive a piece of the challah and serve paper cups of wine to the guests.

Always it is a good ritual. The Sabbath never fails to come, and while the afternoon lasts, the people treat each other with uncharacteristic generosity, respect, and even tenderness. The atheists and the Orthodox purists complain about one thing or another but come again the following week. The event is a hierophany that lasts but a couple of hours, for when they meet again the next morning, it has fled without a trace. Normality reasserts itself. Outside of the ritual setting, the men resume their usual quiet and repose. As they walk out, Sadie spots a friend whom she presses to come to the *Kahal* luncheon next week, to raise money for Israel. An argument begins among the women as to who will bring what dish. The men shuffle toward the benches and sit facing the ocean, quietly enjoying the lingering light of the afternoon.

Men, Women, and Food: The Kahal Luncheon

Food never exists in its own right. It comes in a context—social and cultural. It is always a matter of ritual and symbol, in some cases richer than others but never absent. Food among these people is heavy with significance, part ritual, historical, part as a result of being poor, old, and alone. The ritual meaning of Jewish food is a subject of enormous complexity. The people described here were all raised in kosher homes; none of them observes the dietary laws at present. Nevertheless, they have very strong ideas about Jewish food (clean, more nourishing) and *goyishe* food (without nutritive value and dirty). Over and under their overt, stated beliefs are their associations of Jewish food with the women who prepared and served it, their wives and mothers. Here the sexual division of labor was absolute and unchanging throughout their lifetime. When men and women came together, the women cooked and served, the men received and enjoyed. Both sexes shared a verbal and nonverbal vocabulary based on food, expressive and satisfying to giver and receiver alike.

As always in such matters, personal statements and interpersonal manipulations took place in terms of this vocabulary. At table, a woman bestowed or withheld good feelings, read her worth and standing from the man's reception or rejection of her offerings, manifested her various moods and talents. For men food was never neutral; it did not exist apart from a profoundly social and emotional setting. The folklore surrounding the *yidishe mame* and her preoccupation with food, urging children to eat, interpreting their refusal as a rejection of love, is abundant. Like much folklore, it is an overstatement of a partially accurate observation.

Boys were especially favored with food. One man put it this way: "My mother on Friday, when she made the challah, always made me a little loaf of my own. Just for me she would do that. She loved my sisters, naturally, but only I got my own special loaf."

Food had significance beyond the family. It was an expression of nurturance and responsibility for all who were in need, and anyone who came within the ambit of the Jewish householder in the shtetl was treated as one deserving of care. Food was the symbol of membership in the Jewish community, a gesture of household acceptance and hospitality, and in terms of the woman's role, it evoked her dominant function as a caretaker. Denial of this function was equivalent to denying her the major source of identity and self-esteem. Sadie explained that many older women would rather not live in their relatives' homes because they would not be able to cook for the family. And of course food was manipulated in these terms by husband and children, just as the *baleboste* manipulated them with food. Hannah remembered her mother this way:

My mother, you had to admire her. No matter how poor we were—and believe me we were poor—my mother had the samovar going and a little piece of herring hidden away. When someone came to our house she would never let them go away without taking a glass of tea and a little herring, maybe some bread. To this day, when I go to someone's house, if they don't at least offer me, I don't feel like I'm welcome.

Meals were the focus of daily and religious life. Each holiday had its special dishes and stylistic variations. Regional identities were given in terms of the variations, and the strong antagonism between Litvaks and Galitzianers, for example, was stated in terms of the propriety of the soft matzah ball of the one versus the harder matzah ball of the other. Girls and young married women were considered incapable of making certain dishes; a lifetime of experience was necessary for concocting a proper *tsholent*. Only grandmothers made the *kreplakh* for major events.

Compounding these cultural and social levels of meaning are the special requirements for food among the aged and poor. Poor teeth and uncomfortable dentures, digestive difficulties, special diets for diabetics and those with high blood pressure mean attention must be given to every bite. The combination of "modern science" and ethnic dishes is considered both Jewish and healthy, as awareness grows of nutritional losses due to chemicals and processing. Organic squash is preferred for making *latkes* and brown sugar for making coffee cake, "to avoid modern poisons." But eating properly is harder and harder for them.

Most troubled by the need to eat properly are the single men, who are appalled at the necessity for obtaining their own meals. They find it difficult to get to restaurants and, when there, consider the food un-Jewish and expensive. Even worse is the prospect of cooking for themselves. "It isn't right for a man to do. It isn't natural. Who knows from cooking?" asked Abe when he talked about how unhappy he was. "It's the worst part of living alone." Mealtimes, unceremonial and lonely affairs, are reminders for everyone of their losses, physical and social.

Food is probably the single most important of their concerns, more charged than other necessities with meanings, emotions, and associations, and more capable of giving pleasure as well as pain. For all these reasons, the luncheons at the Center are important occasions, presenting the opportunity for eating in a suitably social and Jewish fashion. In view of the deep significance of food, it is not surprising that at meals, the old shtetl models of male-female roles and relations reappear at these times. There are three charitable organizations of Jewish women which hold the luncheons. The one described here, *Kahal,* is strictly kosher, hence more traditional, but all are very similar in form and purpose.

All raise funds to support various projects in Israel. Many of the Center women have belonged to one of the groups for ten to twenty years. Organizations provide opportunities for contact with non-Center people and with younger women and thus constitute an important extension of social ties. Among the three organizations at least one luncheon a month is held. Anyone who buys a ticket may attend. The meals are regarded as exceptionally good and good bargains, "a three-dollar meal for a dollar fifty, plus entertainment."

A typical *Kahal* luncheon began one Sunday at 11:30 A.M.—the hour and day chosen to maximize attendance. About twenty Center women belong to the local chapter of *Kahal*. They sponsor, attend, and participate in the affairs, and they are the luncheon hostesses. Another six to eight dignitaries from the national organization attend, as well as occasional guests and family members on whom Center women have pressed tickets. Altogether, about eighty people are served. The tables are carefully set by the hostesses, covered with bright oilcloth and fresh flowers. Everyone wears his or her best clothes—women wear gloves and men *yarmulkes*. The proportion of men attending is quite high, relative to other events. Seating is always a source of argument. The official hostesses attempt to distribute guests as they see fit, and the guests insist on following their own preferences. Tables near the kitchen are much desired for quickest service, and tables with two or more men are also much sought after.

Seating at these luncheons does not reflect the social structure revealed in the seating arrangements at other events. Hostesses who are generally not among the leaders can sit wherever they like for their luncheons. The few non-Zionists present—otherwise accepted—are shunned at these affairs, since it is assumed "they only came to eat, not to help Israel." Those with pleasant table manners and "dignity" are preferred company; more than a matter of etiquette, this reflects physical condition. No one is eager to sit near the very old or sick people, some of whom wear bibs because their hands are too shaky to manage the food without spilling. Others need to have their food cut up for them. (Since the "silverware" is the flimsiest plastic, cutting is difficult for everyone, but for the really weak it is impossible.) Members who are known to be wealthy are also not preferred company for the luncheons. It is considered inappropriate for them to take advantage of these inexpensive meals; they should give their money to the organization or buy a ticket for someone else, people feel. And the *shnorrers* ("beggars") who pocket extra rolls or pieces of cake are likely to sit alone. For other events or when eating at a restaurant, pocketing extra food is viewed as sensible. But here, they are cheating Israel. Thus the seating at luncheons held to raise money for Israel is an indication of a set of social and psychological factors specific to a particular event. Indeed, one of the important functions served by these affairs is its offering of an additional arena in which people can receive honor and display abilities and attitudes not provided for in the usual Center calendar of activities.

The assembled guests are welcomed by one of the Center hostesses, and the food is brought out by the other hostesses, two plates at a time. They distribute dishes in order of their friendship ties, with a few exceptions. Naturally, this causes considerable commotion and women object loudly when they are passed by in favor of another, but no one contests that the men are served first, and a little struggle may develop as to which woman will be the last to handle a man's plate. If a woman sitting next to a man can take it from the serving hostess's hands so as to be the one to put it down in front of him, she will do so. It seems as though the one who actually places it on the table before him is regarded as the real giver of the food. It is understood that women with male escorts will be served before the single women. The latter are served last, the order of service reflecting the social networks of the hostesses.

Throughout the meal, women seated near men watch over the latter's plates, sometimes giving them morsels off their own, reminding a man that the back of the chicken is the best, that bread crust is healthy and he should eat it, that he must not eat salt because of his heart, that he likes lemon in his tea, and so forth. Occasionally, a woman will take something from the plate of another woman and give it to a man, behavior that would never be tolerated if the food were taken for a woman. Throughout, the hostesses in aprons and scarves bustle happily, importantly overseeing everyone and checking to be sure that the dishes they have prepared are appreciated and identified. "Don't tell me you already had Jell-O, Jake. Sofie's Jell-O you couldn't eat—it's like rubber. Mine is made with pure fruit juice. No water. Taste." Though the menu varies little, women's expertise in cooking is asserted in finely differentiated terms. When luncheons fall on holidays, festivity is more intense, and the ethnic character of the dishes is more evident. The effervescence is palpable when the women bring out *gefilte* fish, *matzah brei, tsimis,* potato *latkes* and *kugel*. Special diets are ignored and the hall is redolent with the scents and flavors that originated in people's shared childhood culture.

Throughout the luncheon the nurturant role of the women is divided into the joint tasks of raising money for Israel and serving food. While people are eating, one of the hostesses circulates, selling raffle tickets. Then, when the main course is finished the program begins. This is always a troublesome moment, since the program is the main reason for assembling for the organizers but not for the majority of those attending. If the meal is completed before the program, people leave, so dessert and coffee are not brought out until after the program. This annoys them, and they express their irritation loudly, until they are reprimanded sharply by one of the hostesses. "I talk to you about Israel and you talk to me about coffee. You should be ashamed." After her exhortations about Israel's need for their help, the "entertainment" section begins. Bessie's son-in-law, newly returned from Israel, describes his and his wife's recent trip, circulating pictures of the children on the *kibbutz* being supported by the organization. Though he refers to "my wife and I" throughout his presentation, and his wife, seated beside him, is a member of the organization and daughter of a Center member, there is no doubt that he and not his wife should give the talk. In other circumstances, the woman would be the lecturer. But it would be inconsistent to follow that norm at a luncheon covertly oriented to serving food and deferring to men.

Throughout the program, the hostesses circulate among the guests, collecting coins in little boxes called, in Yiddish, *pushkes*. These containers were a staple fixture in the kitchen of shtetl women, used to collect pennies for charity. Before lighting the candles on Friday, she, the *baleboste*, would put in a few coins, and whenever a bit of extra money was brought into the house, she would skim some off for the *pushke*. Collectors regularly visited housewives, redistributing the funds to the needy. Many collectors had stable relations with certain women, and some of these ties were passed on between housewife and collector for several generations. The *pushke* was referred to by the women at the Center as "hungry little mouths," and as *pishke*, which also means "little pisser," an affectionate term for a small child, who requires care but is much loved. The use of terms such as these reflects the sentiments about Israel as needing the women's nurturance, requiring food and care; these are the areas of pride and expertise for the Jewish housewife in the Old Country and no less, in the New World.

Bessie's son-in-law passes around his photographs taken in Israel, telling the guests, "You see this *kibbutz?* You see these beautiful children, happy and well fed? You built this *kibbutz,* you are feeding them, with your little *pishkes,* with your little nickels and dimes. Without you, there would be no Israel." His tribute is a very successful conclusion to the gathering, an affair in which the women found an opportunity to exercise their traditional skills and enact their traditional female role, as givers and caretakers, and at which men likewise fulfilled their traditional male role, as the cared-for and as appreciators of women. It was reassuring, familiar, and satisfying, full of nostalgia for all involved.

Ritual and Food: Integration and Continuity

Ritual and food provide the occasions for resuming the original shtetl complementary sex roles for men and women. Both are, in this as in many cultures, completely associated with household life, embedded in the matrix of family ties, and evocative of the most formative and enduring experiences in the first home. Through ritual and food, the old people momentarily retrieve their past, as individuals and as a culture. A sense of continuity with the past is vital to all integrated adults, especially for the elderly, for immigrants, and for people whose society has been dispersed and whose original culture all but obliterated. Ritual offers an occasion of personal integration, in which one becomes aware that he/she is the same person now that he/she was long ago, despite so much change, in one's body and one's world. Ritual takes up the task of allowing for an experience of continuity, for it provides the opportunities for the most basic, cherished symbols to become vivified, active, and transformative.[2]

Bertha provided a particularly articulate statement about the personal integration made available to her in the course of the Sabbath ceremony of lighting candles:

Do you know what it means to me when I am called to the candles? I'll tell you. When I was a little girl, every Friday I would stand this way, beside my mother when she would light the candles. She cried and I cried. We would be alone in the house, everything warm

2. For a more detailed discussion of the capacity of ritual to alter time and communicate order, see Moore and Myerhoff (1977). —Ed.

and clean with all the good smells of the food around us. We were poor but we always had something special. We were fresh from the *mikve,* and I would save my best ribbons for Fridays. Mama would braid my hair very tight, to last through the Sabbath without being combed. We always wore our best clothes, whatever we had. To this day, when I feel the heat of the candles on my face and I cover my eyes and begin the prayer, I feel my mother's hands on my cheeks. Then we are reunited again.[3]

It is in the context of two domestic events—the Sabbath meal and preparing and serving food—that the childhood shtetl sex roles reappear. At these times, the contemporary adaptations of men and women are suspended and the old forms, practiced by the people's parents and grandparents, are observed. The men are in power on Fridays, controlling the participation of women in the religious ritual of the *Oneg Shabes,* and in turn, the women dominate and control the men in the luncheons. Both men and women recognize that power is sometimes abused, but that this does not necessarily lead to questions of legitimacy of the roles and of the rights and obligations associated with them. Abe's statement after the *Kahal* luncheon is illustrative: "Those women think that they can do what they want with us. They bring out a bowl of *tsimis* and expect us to fall over dead. And why not? Where else can a man get real *tsimis* these days? Not for a dollar fifty, not for a hundred and fifty!" This is the woman's opportunity to give and withhold, for who can do without her cooking? The men, like the women, vibrate with excitement during the meals. They are animated and bold. They encourage the women to rush about perspiring, carrying the heavy, steaming bowls. They demand their due portion imperiously, inflame the competition between women, and acknowledge their physicality with a kiss or a pinch, or an amiable slap on the bottom. Their pleasure has a boyish tone, and one can imagine their feelings when the aroma and taste of a rarely available, familiar, cherished morsel fill nostrils and mouths. Surely it brings them their past, a recollection of all the women in their homes who cared for them and bossed them around, blandishing them with food and love. Proust demonstrated beyond all doubt that food—like

---

3. Much Jewish ritual takes up the need to provide opportunities for experiencing a sense of being One People, despite geographical and temporal separations. For further discussion, see R.-E. Prell-Foldes (1973).

ritual—has the capacity to take one back to the past, unfolding an entire lost world, not only referred to but relived.

The original sex roles, retrieved from their childhood culture, are available for certain occasions. It is not unlikely that both men and women continue to value those old roles and would choose to follow them on a regular basis if given the choice. The old women have developed alternative roles now, as they did in the shtetls of Eastern Europe, in response to the circumstances in which they have found themselves. There is no consistent ideological support for the women's new roles; they do not seem to regard their autonomy and competence with particular pride. As always, they are merely "making do." But it seems that "making do" is a very suitable means for adapting to their status and situation as marginal, old, and poor. Inevitably, one contrasts them with the men, who seem to have more difficulty with many matters that the women take for granted. The question may be asked of these people and perhaps of others in similar circumstances: are old women better off than old men, and, if so, why?

Men and Women: Present Roles in Present Circumstances

Formerly, in shtetl culture, male and female roles were reciprocal and men and women interdependent, though men were more esteemed and ideally, at least, more powerful. In the present circumstances, it seems that the old woman's role has enlarged while the old man's has shrunk. The old woman has taken over many tasks and prerogatives previously belonging to the male world, particularly leadership functions. With the exception of a few religious rituals, the women are quite independent and have no need of the men, except in the token, rather superficial way described earlier. The women seem to thrive compared to the men, who grow quieter as the females become more energetic, robust, and self-directed, more engaged in the life around them and more involved with others. In discussion both men and women complain a great deal about their fates. Men are more often bitter, lonely, and depressed, whereas the women are more angry, but stoical and resigned to their difficulties. It does seem as though the women have made a better adjustment in old age than the men.

Women in the shtetl (and some would say women in all cultures) were emotional or expressive leaders *par excellence*.[4] They were responsible

---

4. Zelditch, Parsons, and other American sociologists believe that the expres-

for nurturance, for interpersonal relations, and for what might be called, in contemporary parlance, quality-of-life concerns. The women's specialty was maintenance of others, the emotional ambience in the home, the general and diffuse work of attending to the well-being of intimates, responding to the totality of their human needs. Men had the responsibility of providing for the family's worldly and spiritual state. In the middle years, women were withdrawn from public and economic affairs and the men became the exclusive link between family and society. The man's family leadership, psychology, and cognitive approach to life were more problem-oriented, more goal-directed, focused, and emotionally neutral than those of his wife. His responsibilities were instrumental where his wife's were expressive.[5]

Retired people generally have most of their difficulties with instrumental roles. Their essential link to the public sector, the job, has been severed. They lose all that goes with being identified with a job—money, of course, but also a sense of self-worth, social contacts, a schedule, location, and membership in the social structure. The life allocated to the retired in our society, for men and women, is expressive. Their entire time is expected to be spent in recreation, taking care of themselves, and socializing. These activities are often demeaned by men who regard them as trivial—women's work—and they rarely have had occasions for acquiring skills at such activities. The instrumental role of the husband/father in our society is completely demolished for the retired male. But the expressive role, regularly occupied by women, not only continues to be viable in old age but becomes *the* full-time role for both sexes in many communities of American retired persons. It is no wonder that women are better than men at being old.

There are other factors that account for women's seeming advantage over men. That these old women are marginal people thrice over could be important. All the people are marginal at present, being poor and old. And they have always been ethnically marginal, as Jews, in the Old

sive-instrumental dichotomy is a universal arrangement for allocating family roles to women and men, respectively. It is found in many cultures though several scholars question its universality.

5. Some psychologists, Bakan (1966) and Chodorow (1974) among them, describe male-female differences of cognitive style in a fashion that corroborates and reflects the Zelditch-Parsons instrumental-expressive distinction. Whether universal or not, innate or learned, the cluster of characteristics suggested for men's and women's roles in the family are certainly stable and widespread.

Country, where anti-Semitism was official, relentless, and overt, and in this country as "greenhorns." The men, however, were uniformly regarded as superior to the women of their own society and thus were caught in a conflicting set of hierarchies. They were exalted within their immediate group but disdained outside of it. In contrast, the status of the women was unambiguous: they were on the bottom, on all counts. Perhaps the simplicity and consistency of this made it easier for women to work out personal solutions. And certainly, it gave those who failed to do so every excuse necessary, all in terms of social definitions rather than individual shortcomings.

Compared to the women, the old men in this group are less connected, less needed, by each other, by women, by children. Moreover, they have not been prepared for recognizing their need for others, except in economic terms that are no longer applicable. The men are less enmeshed in social and kinship networks, less engaged in all kinds of interpersonal relations than the women. Indeed, the allotment to women of responsibility for expressive leadership has made them experts at relationships. Roles based on nurturant functions are durable and expandable. They can last a lifetime, and there is always someone around who needs taking care of. The nurturance role has two added advantages: putting the caretaker one-up in terms of never being the worst-off person in the world, and arousing obligations and sentiments in the cared-for which may develop into deep and long-lasting associations. By definition, expressive roles take account of the quality of people's emotions, and are more likely to expand than are narrowly construed instrumental transactions.

Another part of the nurturant role advantageous to old women is their experience in self-maintenance. If one's basic biological requirements have been provided by others, it comes as a shock to have to do these things for oneself. For the women, getting rid of their garbage, doing their laundry, mending, shopping, cleaning, cooking are not troublesome. On the contrary, this work is a steady source of satisfaction. (Bessie, for example, mentioned that her arthritis was growing worse. She did not mind too much that she was no longer able to carry heavy objects or hold a paint brush, even though she loved her art classes. But when she realized that she could no longer make her own bed, she said, that was when she wept.) The adage "A woman's work is never done" calls attention to the continuity of woman's tasks on a daily basis, but it applies no less to the continuity over a lifetime. In those instances where the old men have needed to perform maintenance tasks for others, usually their ailing or incapacitated wives, they are revolted and inept. But incontinent or invalid husbands present no surprises to the women. Changing diapers is not a shocking affair to these women, whether for a child or an old person.

Since childhood, the women have always been *bricoleurs,* as Lévi-Strauss (1966) calls the constructors of systems who use leftover materials, as does a handyman. These women have long known how to devise entire though miniature worlds out of their peripheral status and tasks. They were made of smaller and homelier materials but built in proportion, as complex and compelling as the external, male-dominated realm. In her own miniature world, the woman was in charge, using time and energy according to her own lights. Within the structured points of her day in the household, she did a great many highly diverse tasks, all at the same time, always expecting to be interrupted, never finding full closure, but hastening from one activity to the next, watching her work come undone as soon as it was completed. The standards for performance had to be more flexible and individually administered.[6]

Men did not usually work in isolation and thus were not as self-regulating as the women. The loss of the world of work for men meant they lost the arena that dictated their use of time and energy in an absolute and external manner. Within the household, it was true that women were often tightly tied to biological rhythms of small children and had to respond also to the outside scheduling of other adult family members. But within this framework there was considerable choice and discretion, and a gradual lifting of nonpersonally generated limits took place as the children matured. The nearest equivalent to male retirement is the mother's "empty nest." But this phenomenon is less abrupt and irreversible than is retirement from a job. Her children need her less in small increments. And even after they have physically left the home, they

---

6. Some men who are taking over women's nurturant roles evidently find the lack of clear-cut "performance standards" in child care among the more troubling parts of the job. At the American Psychiatric Association meeting in 1976, a young American psychiatrist delivered a paper in which he detailed his experiences as a "house-husband" when his wife went back to school. He described the continual interruptions in his work (or the expectation of being about to be interrupted) combined with never being sure when he had "done a good job" as being harder to bear than anything he had had to deal with in his years of medical practice.

return for her services, favors, meals, advice, baby-sitting, care of clothing, and the like. Before and after "the empty nest" she has more time
to adjust, to establish her independence, and then accommodate to the
changes.

Let us consider biology too. Perhaps women are more prepared for
the inevitable infirmities of old age by a lifetime of acceptance of their
bodily limits and changes. Initially, in this culture the little girl observes
herself to be physically weaker than her brothers and nothing she does
can alter the fact. With the onset of menstruation, again she finds that
her body intrudes itself on her wishes and must be taken into account
in her plans. Soon after, the cycle of childbirth and nursing begins, and
once more her projects perforce take her bodily limits into account.
Finally, menopause interrupts her activities and her fantasies; she must
always make choices, decisions, and self-interpretation with her physiological base.

All this is good schooling for what lies ahead. The old men in this
group have been able to indulge in more independent self-conceptions.
Among the most agonizing of the difficulties they face is their daily
awareness of being physically limited and, ultimately, dominated by
"forces outside themselves," beyond their control. Old age is a brutal
check on omnipotence fantasies. The discovery of their mortality, late
in life, it seems, shocks the male ego far more severely than the female.
The women have always known their bodies have a life of their own.
Women always knew about needing others (especially men) but often
the men (generously assisted by wives and mothers) have been able to
overlook the forms and frequencies of their corresponding dependencies.
It appears that for a woman to accept help from others has entirely
different meanings than for men. An old woman in this community is
more patient and grateful in allowing someone else to cut up her food,
help her rise from a chair, or take her arm over a rough spot in the
sidewalk. The men accept help when they must, but it is apparent that
it costs them dearly to do so.

One of the tasks and pleasures for the elderly is life review (see Butler
1963), during which they take stock of their histories, estimating what
went well, what could have been better, what remains, and what counts
in the end. The men have devoted most of their lives primarily to two
concerns, which "do not count" in their present reference group: making
money and religious study. The meaning of the latter has been lost along
with their religious community; life in America is a secular affair. The

money they made has been long gone. Some still have savings, but the norms of the subculture prevent them from conspicuous demonstrations of wealth. Money brings the well-off no rewards in superior standards of living or recognition in this community; indeed, they are often suspect and resented for not being poor. And they are not permitted to engage in one of the most enjoyable and prestigious activities of the group: bargain hunting. The person who appears well turned out in a thrift shop purchase is much admired, more for his/her acumen than for appearance. The well-off man who gives a large amount of money to charity is awarded less admiration than the poor one who, by discovering a day-old bakery within walking distance, benefits the whole group. The former is only doing what is expected.

What does count for these people, in reviewing the merits of a life? Above all, rearing children who are well educated and well married, good citizens, good parents in their own right, children who consider themselves Jews and raise their children to be Jews, and who respect their aged parents. Again the old women have the deck stacked in their favor. They have maintained closer ties with their children than have the men; moreover, the women are considered more responsible than the men for "how the children turned out." The men paid the bills, the women raised the children, and to them goes praise or blame. Since few women consider their children as complete washouts, they almost always gain more satisfaction than grief from considering their children as the important work of their lives.

There is a final comment to be made concerning the different bases for evaluation of one's lifework, comparing men and women. It is often said that the contingent nature of woman's work makes it intrinsically less satisfying, and that this is why it is consistently and permanently devalued by societies all over the world. Women are identified as responsible for the work of nature, and culture is officially the work of men. Women, it is felt, concur with men in viewing cultural projects as the more valuable enterprise. This opposition between nature and culture has been much discussed, by Lévi-Strauss (1969), by Simone de Beauvoir (1953), and by Sherry Ortner (1974). Women's projects are immanent compared with the lasting, transforming projects of men. Her works are concrete as opposed to male abstractness. Hers involve subjectivity, personalism, and particularism. Says de Beauvoir:

> ... in her heart of hearts [a woman] finds confirmation of the masculine pretensions. She joins the men in the festivals that cele-

brate the successes and victories of the males. Her misfortune is to have been biologically destined for the repetition of Life, when even her own life does not carry within itself reasons for being, reasons that are more important than life itself. (1953:59)

Is it surely true that women consider their work lesser "in their heart of hearts"? Woman's work is very complex and subtle, not made of the kinds of victories and successes celebrated in war dances and hunting parties. The work is not clear-cut; unequivocal successes and failures are relatively rare. Every mother is continually reminded as to how much of her "product" is beyond her control. She is facilitator, mediator, not maker. *Outcome* is not an accurate term in reference to people, who as long as they live offer surprises and are full of potentiality.

Women are kept humble by the nature of their everyday activities. They are immersed in unglamorous stuff—the mess of life itself, bodily excretions and necessities, transient and trivial details that vanish and reappear every moment. But this does not mean that a woman is not fully aware of the enormous importance of offering food, producing and raising children. Why, then, do we not hear about it? Why is there no public, general female statement vaunting these tasks? I would claim that there is a set of understandings, regularly stated and shared among women, concerning the meaning and value of their conventional functions. These are communicated but in a form not easy to recognize. They are enacted nonverbally in the quiet acknowledgments that pass between women in their work.

Because their tasks are particularized, concrete, embedded, and subjective, there is no natural desire (not to mention opportunity) to make them into platforms, public festivals, ideological treatises. They are known as part of living rather than discussions about living, and it would be inconsistent to formulate them as enduring, collective principles. These understandings are a kind of underground culture, quietly transmitted in situations, no less treasured than the starkly evident, grandiose cultural productions we customarily attend. They are real but rather easy to overlook. They continue through the life cycle, and it may be that they reemerge as essential aids in later life. These old women I have described communicate a quiet conviction and satisfaction with themselves. Perhaps because they did what had to be done, and knew that without what they did there would be nothing and no one. This is no scant comfort in looking back at one's lifework. Woman's work provided them with an end and a means. Perhaps this is the secret shared by these old women, who expected little and found more than did the men, who expected everything and are left now with much less.

Experience at the Threshold:
The Interplay of Aging and Ritual

Of the myriad forms of human ritual, it is those that mark transitions in the life cycle—rites of passage—that we might expect to yield the most valuable information concerning the interplay of aging and ritual. In his now classic study of these rituals, Arnold Van Gennep (1908) first outlined the three-part progression through which these ceremonies proceeded as they moved initiates through transitional states involving permanent transformations in status and age, first by identifying and segregating them (Phase I, separation), then by isolating and confining them to each other's company as marginal beings, at the threshold (*limen*) between categories (Phase II, liminality), finally by reincorporating them into full membership in the society (Phase III, reaggregation). In the course of these transformative rituals, the interaction of culture, humanity, and biology is most clearly observed, for these ceremonies occur most prominently at the edge of our animality, at the intersection of our creatural existence and our cultural pretensions: at birth, reproduction, and death. During rites of passage distinctions are made most clear between the fundamental categories that set humans apart and define them: young and old, male and female, living and dead. As humans, we all are born, mate, and die, but we manipulate these constancies endlessly, so that biology with all its imperatives and universals can often be only faintly distinguished beneath the templates of symbolic and ritual forms that overlap it. Here we confront one of the many paradoxes that rituals characteristically handle that we mortals belong as much to nature

This text was first published as a section on "Rites of Passage" in a five-part essay titled "Rites and Signs of Ripening: The Intertwining of Ritual, Time, and Growing Older." The omitted sections—on "The Work of Ritual," "Ritual as Cultural Performance," "Memory, Re-membering and Reminiscence," and "Time, Ritual, and Age"—repeat discussions that appear elsewhere in this volume.— Ed.

as to culture, that these conditions are inseparable, that we play seriously and perpetually with our joint membership in the human and animal kingdoms, now reminding ourselves, now denying the one element or the other; now transcending, now exploiting our ineradicable oneness with all other creatures, usually enjoying ourselves in the act of self-contemplation, realizing in the end that we seem to be the only creatures so much and long amused by our play with categorical distinctions and self-definitions.

Occasionally biology and culture are closely coordinated, as when a girl's marriageability is celebrated with the onset of menstruation. But often these personal physical changes are not acknowledged or are out of synchrony with cultural identities. A thirteen-year-old boy bar mitzvahed in the Jewish religion may be sexually immature though he is socially transformed into a man by this rite of passage. Menarche, one of the clearer physiological changes in the human life cycle, seems to be little acknowledged formally, though older women as a category are often accorded special privileges and considered to have special powers. But again, sociological indicators that accord privileges may or may not coincide with the physical condition of a particular woman at a particular moment.

In contemporary industrialized nations, old age as a life stage seems particularly to be dominated by social rather than physiological criteria. In such societies, the "old" retire at a specific, legal moment, chronologically rather than functionally determined. Ever after, they are sharply separated from the "useful," fully participating members of the society, for the most part without reference to individual desire or capability. Here nature and culture stand at great remove from each other. Among the Eskimo, in earlier times, the closeness of fit between function and retirement was especially striking: when people could no longer help others or support themselves, they were put out onto the ice. The discrepancy between individual capacity and cultural/legal definitions of old age are sharp in Western modern societies, for many well-known reasons, including the dominance of technological tasks; formal, universalistic social definitions; and the complex, specialized division of labor, with all it implies. The fact that old age is a period of growing duration in absolute terms, given everlengthening life expectation, means that more and more people are older and older. This situation makes our ill-defined conflicting attitudes and dearth of expectations and rituals surrounding and punctuating the latter part of the life cycle all the more serious. That "old age" may last for three decades, lacking even demarcations provided by clearly named phases, goals, or features, is astonishing. Within the immense category we call "the old" there are "young old" and "old old," fit and frail, strong and invalid, independent and destitute, powerful and isolated, but none of these features is regularly specified by our social and legal conceptions.

Certainly anthropologists have not rigorously studied the phases and rites, the conceptions and ceremonies that characterize the latter part of the life cycle—neither in their own societies nor in those more remote in which they have worked. Nevertheless, one gets the impression that the degree of social and ceremonial specificity surrounding old age in most societies, of all levels of technological complexity, is generally less than that accorded earlier phases in the life cycle. While this cultural vagueness often creates anomie and isolation, at the same time it offers calculating, resourceful elders in many settings occasions in which they may innovate and exploit the rolelessness, a set of fruitful possibilities. Often freed from heavy social obligations and prohibitions for the first time, the elderly may become deft manipulators and entrepreneurs, justifying stereotypes concerning their unconventionality, originality, and wisdom. The wily old man, the truly frightening powerful old witch, the curmudgeon recluse in the hills, the mysterious, unpredictable old crone are types of exploiters of cultural freedom and confusion. If culture is conceived as a cognitive map, the inconsistencies and incomplete areas are not merely the unknowns; they are also contingencies—invitations to culture making and innovation—and in this light the relative normlessness surrounding the aged and old age holds promise as well as penalties.

But the disadvantages of the lack of rituals for the latter part of life probably outweigh the advantages, for rites of passage are moments of dramatic teaching and socialization, occasions that a society constructs to inculcate and clarify, to make its members most fully and deeply its own. Rites of passage in later life could go far toward teaching the elderly and their juniors the meaning of their existence, the justifications for their continued being. Such rites would surely minimize the existential uncertainty that is one of the hardest states to bear at any time of life. Rites of passage present a society's members with a paradigm for the future, for the individual and the social order. Such rites are held at moments of great anxiety and social-biological tension.

Inevitably, rites of passage arouse self-consciousness in their subjects and invite profound self-questioning, at the very moment when they are pressing their designs and interpretations on the subjects, sometimes literally inscribing symbolic codes on the bodies of initiates in the form of tatooing, scarification, and mutilation. The Balinese who reaches maturity must undergo a tooth-filing ceremony during which the canine tooth, the mark of the beast in humanity's heritage, is smoothed, to make the smile less reminiscent of an animal's snarl. And in some African societies, according to Victor Turner (personal communication), a youth being initiated into manhood may ingest a powder made from the foreskins of previous initiates, incorporating and sustaining in his own body the vitality and power of his predecessors. James Fernandez (1980) describes an initiation ceremony in which a neophyte stares into a looking glass until the face of an ancestor appears and merges with his own. The identification between the ancestor behind the glass and the living descendant in front of it presents, literally, a picture of genealogical continuity between the living and the dead and allows the initiate to pass into a new state of being. In such instances the human body itself is a symbolic statement, presenting to the society and the individual the message that the group and its members are inseparable, that they are vehicles for each other and must coexist. The fundamental, recurrent theme that appears in so many teachings during rites of passage is reducible to that: the interdependence of the collective and the individual; the group and the separate people who are to carry its purposes forward.

Because rites of passage occur at moments of great anxiety, at naturally transitional, dramatic moments, exaggerated by the society, the subjects are considered most malleable. Yet it is during such rites, when the group most avidly presses its messages upon members, that it also invites doubt and questioning. Self-consciousness is likely to be aroused through the regular play with mirrors, masks, costumes, and novelty so often found in rites of passage. Borders are crossed; identity symbols are stripped away, familiar roles and customs suspended. These are the very conditions under which one is likely to experience the sense of radical aloneness and uniqueness, freedom and awareness, the irreversible moment of reflexive consciousness, in the middle of the group's efforts to persuade initiates of its purposes. Thus rites of passage both announce our separateness and individuality and at the same time remind us most vividly that existence apart from the group is impossible. This paradox expresses one of the basic truths of the human condition: that while all societies attempt to absorb the individual and shape him or her into a bona fide self-regulating member, they never wholly succeed. Even in the most highly integrated, small, stable tribal societies there are distinguished individuals: old or outstanding men and women whose traits and thoughts go beyond those required by their offices, roles, and circumstances.

Victor Turner (1975) has elaborated Van Gennep's early study of rites of passage, focusing on the middle phase, liminality, when the individual is in transition between known states. This phase may be a period of marginal existence that passes, or it may become a role extended through a lifetime entirely given to the principles and practice of uncertainty, exploration, innovation, rebellion, and many varieties of nonbelonging. Then we may speak of specialists in disorder: the ritual clowns, transvestites, shamans, poets, rebels, mystics, and vagabonds who move perpetually at the borders of known categories and agreements. Whether viewed as a phase in the life cycle, as a state of mind, or as a full-time role, liminality is conducive to the generation of social criticism, creativity, and play, with its built-in affinity for paradox, symbolic and social opposition, and disorder. It is not unusual to find old people who are liminal beings, living beyond the fixed and regulated categories, beyond the constraints of the superego, which can effectively warn against penalties for transgression. Such penalties have diminished bite when the future is short and uncertain. Often, the less future, the less to lose, from the point of view of the individual, and from the point of view of society; often old people are dispensable, their conduct a matter of little consequence, their controls a matter of diminished importance. It may be, then, that the often-noted but little-studied toughness, fearlessness, idiosyncrasy, and creativity among the elderly in many societies result from this combination of social irrelevance and personal autonomy. Carl Jung's term "individuation" refers to the personal evolution that may come with time and age, as older people free themselves from the conventional fetters that tightly bind younger, productive, structurally essential members of society. Folk wisdom has it that old people "are the same as they have always been, only more so." Liminality—being socially in limbo—anomie, rolelessness, neglect, and social irrelevance may have the complex advantage of leaving old people alone, to be themselves only more so. It is with affection and nostalgia that adults regard the innate creativity of unsocialized children. But usually they are blind to the creativity of *de*socialized elders at the other end of the life cycle, people whose reemerging originality—stemming from social detachment, long experience, the urgency of a shortened future—may be as delightful, surprising, and fruitful as anything to be found among the very young. Among them are personal and social resources that have yet to be mined and appreciated.

Intolerance for "bad behavior" among the elderly is part of our blindness to their gifts. Margaret Clark (1967) has documented what we all perhaps sense. In our society we assign the elderly roles that represent a limited range of stereotypes—serene, detached, disengaged, wise, and so on—all closely related to maintaining a manageable problem population, easily institutionalized and patronized. Traits that in middle life often lead to worldly success—aggressiveness, independence, individualism, competitiveness, initiative, future orientation, and the like—bring to the old people who manifest them the label of "maladjusted."

Ruth Benedict (1953) called such reversals in expectation "discontinuity in cultural conditioning." Such discontinuity between adulthood and old age is especially severe in our society. At the same time that we lament such inconsistency, it is impossible to release the elderly from all standards of reasonable behavior. That ultimately is the most degrading position of all, with the final effect of reducing old people to nonpeople. Ronald Blythe puts this idea felicitously: "Just as the old should be convinced that, whatever happens during senescence, they will never suffer exclusion, so they should understand that age does not exempt them from being despicable." We must not allow the old to fall into purposelessness, for "this is to fall out of all real consideration. . . . To appreciate the transience of all things is one matter, to narrow the last years—and they can be numerous—down to a dreary thread is another." But it is to this dreary thread that we often confine the elderly, and then we are appalled at the self-indulgent mindlessness of old age, which Blythe calls "its most intolerable aspect." Both young and old are uninformed in the management of old age; neither knows what it may or may not ask and expect of the other. "Perhaps," says Blythe, "with full-span lives the norm, people may need to learn how to be aged as they once had to learn to be adult" (Blythe 1979:22).

Rites of passage that socialize, clarify, and demarcate phases of old age exist in many societies in nascent and nonsystematic forms. In our own society, we do acknowledge some transitions: fiftieth wedding anniversaries, great-grandparenthood, special birthdays. These occasions are usually celebrated. We have no comparable rites for losses: giving up the family home, transferring property and privilege to children, completing menopause, relinquishing one's driver's license, moving into an institution, accepting a wheelchair or hearing aid, and the many large and small events that are usually thought of as failures and signposts indicating that the end is ever nearer. Even the gross forms of change, such as senescence and becoming a legal ward, are but crudely acknowledged. While these are undeniably negative and painful events, the clear public acknowledgment of them by others who accept and care about them has clarifying, healing consequences that redefine relationships and identities for all those involved. Retirements and funerals are crude markers for the stark beginning and end of old age; in between there is a universe of differentiation that remains a cultural wasteland for each to calculate and navigate alone, without the aid of ritual, ceremony, or symbol.

There is some irony in this absence of public social rituals during later life, since a great many older people create their own private rituals with enthusiasm, even obsessiveness. Just as children fastidiously work to bring some cosmos into the chaos of their emerging world of boundless complexity, so older people are often noted to fuss obsessively with trivial items, ordering a life that is ending, using the predictability and certainty that ritual provides during times of anxiety and helplessness. When things are finally coming undone, when the last rupture is imminent, the old often set about putting their house in order. It is an activity akin to the nesting that mothers-to-be engage in late in pregnancy, a nesting that is also a cleaning, sorting, classifying preparation for a drastic change. Among the very old, often it is memories and mementos that are sorted and integrated, a last look at what has been, combined with moving objects about, discarding and arranging papers and things: a final imposition of one's human purpose on the last random, untidy event of all.

In sum, it seems that the life sequences are segmented in all societies, with varying fineness. The life cycle is recognized in large part through ritual. The earlier stages in general are more highly defined, and adolescence in particular is abundantly celebrated and acknowledged. Later, at the end of life, mortuary rituals are often quite rich, as Richard Huntington and Peter Metcalf (1979) demonstrate, but between the rites that mark the beginnings of social-sexual maturity—puberty and marriage—and those that mark the end, distinctions are less rich and rituals more sparse. Lately some attention has been given to the dearth of literature on the adult life cycle in our society. Gail Sheehy (1974) and Roger L. Gould (1978) have written in some detail on the necessity for conceptualizing the phases of maturity in terms of predictable, normal adult crises. Bernice Neugarten (1980) has suggested some refinements in our approach to the phases of adult life, emphasizing the crudeness of our view of aging. She suggests that at the very least we make a distinction between the young-old and the old-old. The former have much to offer society, and our task as a group is to find ways they may make a meaningful contribution, though they may be occupationally retired. The old-old are frail and in need of care. The problems they present are entirely different.

Helpful as such theories are in suggesting a less simplistic approach to the life cycle, none of them draws our attention to ritual. The authors provide some guidance in making clear the characteristics of each age and, implicitly, the nature and meaning of a change from one to another. But they do not help us to identify *ceremonies* that define and accentuate the changes. But then, psychologists should perhaps not be expected to cast their studies in the form of rituals, which are, ultimately, social matters, even though they are enacted individually. It seems more appropriate to look to anthropologists for insights as to how ceremony and ritual might be usefully considered as part of the life cycle; but even anthropologists do not agree on the importance of rites of passage. Martha and Morton Fried (1980) cast doubt on the utility of these rites. They examine four critical transitions—birth, puberty, marriage, and death—in cultures deliberately selected to provide variation in geographical distribution and technological and social complexity. All the societies they examine celebrate some transition points in the life cycle, and all place a symbolic template over the facts of biology, treating it as socially manipulable. It is often thought, they note, that societies without profound rituals, particularly adolescent rites, are asking for trouble. But in their survey they find no association between the absence of ritual and the presence of social problems, as indicated by high rates of delinquency or suicide. They remark (1980:268): "It is possible, then, for cultures to survive with relatively small attention to ritual and also with extraordinarily rich preoccupation with ritual, including life transition ceremonies. We cannot say for sure that a culture cannot exist unless it has a bare minimum of such rituals. But we have no record of societies up to the present that have existed without ritual, hence if such existed they did not survive." They therefore assume that rituals play some adaptive role in the process of cultural evolution. They claim that human— that is, cultural—life came into existence considerably in advance of the first clear evidence of ritual. The latter is dated by the Frieds at roughly

40,000 B.C., in the flower-strewn remains of Neanderthals who used flowers to acknowledge and celebrate death. Since culture is now regarded as definitely manifested by the appearance of tools, two million years ago, it may be that rites of passage have existed for only two percent of the history of culture—a relatively recent, hence optional development, as things go (1980:269–70). Rites of passage may be functionally adaptive at the social level but probably are not necessary for the survival of individuals, the Frieds conclude.

But can we be so certain that individuals and social evolution are as separable as the Frieds maintain? Surely the ability of individuals to cope with increasing complexity, conflict, and isolation contributes to the evolution of society. Human beings are the carriers of culture, and they may transmit their culture more or less successfully, in confusion and disarray or with a sense of coherence and well-being. The well-being of the units of a society, the living people, surely cannot be so sharply severed from the success of the society, even in terms of mere survival and evolution. Emile Durkheim's classic study *Suicide* (1952) long ago indicated that social anomie may be expressed by the individual in the form of suicide. Rites of passage certainly do not *cause* social integration; rather they may be expected to reflect and enhance it.

Part 3
Re-membered Lives

Life History among the Elderly: Performance, Visibility, and Re-membering

> Slowly it comes out from them their beginning to their ending, slowly you
> can see it in them the nature and the mixtures in them, slowly everything
> comes out from each one in the kind of repeating each one does in the
> different parts and kinds of living they have in them, slowly then the
> history of them comes out from them, slowly then any one who looks
> well at any one will have the history of the whole of that one. Slowly the
> history of each one comes out of each one.
>
> —Gertrude Stein, *Lectures in America*

Karl Mannheim observed that "individuals who belong to the same generation, who share the same year of birth, are endowed, to that extent, with a common location in the historical dimension of the social process" (1969:290). Often, however, membership in a common cohort is background information, like grammatical rules, more interesting to outside analysts than members. Outsiders find and want explanations where the subjects continue unself-consciously in the habits of everyday life. Sometimes conditions conspire to make a generational cohort acutely self-conscious and then they become active participants in their own history and provide their own sharp, insistent definitions of themselves and explanations for their destiny, past and future. They are then knowing actors in a historical drama they script, rather than subjects in someone else's study. They "make" themselves, sometimes even "make themselves up," an activity which is not inevitable or automatic but reserved for special people and special circumstances. It is an artificial and exhilarating undertaking, this self-construction. As with all conspicuously made-up ventures (rituals are perhaps the best example), acute self-consciousness may become destructive, paralyzing actors in a spasm of embarrassed lack of conviction. But occasionally self-consciousness does not interfere with personal and cultural construction; rather it provides another, fuller angle of self-understanding. *Then*

231

the subjects know that their knowing is a component of their conduct. They assume responsibility for inventing themselves and yet maintain their sense of authenticity and integrity. Such people exercise power over their images, in their own eyes and to some extent in the eyes of whoever may be observing them. Sometimes the image is the only part of their lives subject to control. But this is not a small thing to control. It may lead to a realization of personal power and serve as a source of pleasure and understanding in the workings of consciousness. Heightened self-consciousness—self-awareness—is not an essential, omnipresent attainment. It does not always come with age and is probably not critical to well-being. But when it does occur, it may bring one into a greater fullness of being; one may become a more fully realized example of the possibilities of being human. This is not small compensation in extreme old age.

The group described here is such an acutely self-conscious one, making itself up, knowing that this is going on, doing it well, and appreciating the process. This is a subtle but distinctive state of consciousness, revealed in their personal and collective concerns. Many factors enhance this self-consciousness, not the least of which is their sense of bearing what Tamara Hareven calls "generational memories." She uses this term to refer to "the memories which individuals have of their own families' history, as well as more generational collective memories about their past" (1978). The subjects of this paper are heirs to a set of memories of a culture and society extinguished during the Holocaust. Very old and close to death, they realize that there will be no others after them with direct experience of their natal culture. And because intergenerational continuity has not been sustained, there are no clear heirs to their memories. The old people's sense of being memory bearers, carriers of a precious, unique cargo, heightens generational memory and intensifies cohort-consciousness, giving a mission to the group that is at once urgent and at the same time unlikely to be realized. Their machinations to accomplish their task, delivering themselves of their memories, establishing, then making visible their own identities, illuminates several matters: the nature of *performed* individual and collective definitions, the uses and kinds of witnesses needed for these performances, and the nature and uses of memory. *Life histories are seen here as giving opportunities to allow people to become visible and to enhance reflexive consciousness.* For the very old, in this population in particular, this may be construed as work essential to the last stage in the life cycle.

Self-Presentation and Performing: Becoming Visible

The old people with whom I worked were a group of elderly Jews who had emigrated from Eastern Europe in the early twentieth century. They were an invisible people, marginal to mainstream American society, an impotent group—economically, physically, and politically. But they knew they were irreplaceable and their consciousness of being the people who remembered a culture destroyed by the Holocaust fed their determination not to be extinguished until the last possible moment. Nevertheless, they knew they would lose in this struggle. Death, impotence, invisibility were omnipresent threats. But the atmosphere in the community was not one of defeat or despair. On the contrary, in it there was intensity and vitality, humor, irony and dignity. Always the people exuded a sense of living meaningful lives. Despite the evidence of their insignificance offered by the outside world, they were quite clear about their own importance. It is my interpretation that their self-consciousness, promoted by collective performances and private self-narration, their recounting of stories and life histories, influenced and nourished their success as old people.

Cultures include in their work self-presentations to their members. On certain collective occasions, cultures offer interpretations. They tell stories, comment, portray, and mirror. Like all mirrors, cultures are not accurate reflectors; there are distortions, contradictions, reversals, exaggerations, and even lies. Nevertheless, self-knowledge, for the individual and collectivity, is the consequence. These portraits range from delicate and oblique allusions through fully staged dramatic productions in the course of which members embody their place in the scheme of things, their locations in the social structure, their purposes and natures, taking up the questions of who we are and why we are here, which as a species we cannot do without. Such performances are opportunities for appearing, an indispensable ingredient of being itself, for unless we exist in the eyes of others, we may come to doubt even our own existence. Being is a social, psychological construct, made, not given. Thus it is erroneous to think of performances as optional, arbitrary, or merely decorative embellishments as we in Western societies are inclined to do. In this sense, arenas for appearing are essential, and culture serves as a stage as well as mirror, providing opportunities for self- and collective proclamations of being.

Since these constructions are intentionally designed, they are not only reflections of "what is"; they are also opportunities to write history as it should be or should have been, demonstrating a culture's notion of propriety and sense. History and accident are not permitted to be imposed willy-nilly, those badly written, haphazard, incomplete recordings of occurrences that are so unsatisfactory. Rather performances are shaped and groomed justifications, more akin to myth and religion than lists of empty external events we call history or chronicle.[1]

The performative dimension of culture seen most often in rituals, ceremonies, festivals, celebrations, and the like is properly understood as both instrumental and expressive. It blurs our overstated dichotomies between art and science, myth and reality, religion and work, subjective and objective.

When such performances are successful, we receive experience rather than belief. Then the invisible world is made manifest, whether this is a prosaic affair such as demonstrating the fact of a rearranged social relationship, or a grander more mysterious presentation involving supernatural beings or principles. In all events the performed order is explicit, realized, and we are *within* it, not left merely to endlessly wonder or talk about it.[2] Any reality is capable of being made convincing if it combines art, knowledge, authentic symbols and rituals, and is validated by appropriate witnesses.

Cultural performances are reflective in the sense of showing ourselves to ourselves. They are also capable of being reflexive, arousing consciousness of ourselves as we see ourselves. As heroes in our own dramas, we are made self-aware, conscious of our consciousness. At once actor and audience, we may then come into the fullness of our human capability—and perhaps human desire—to watch ourselves and enjoy knowing that we know. All this requires skill, craft, a coherent, consensually validated set of symbols, and social arenas for appearing. It also requires an audience in addition to performers. When cultures are fragmented and in serious disarray, proper audiences may be hard to find. Natural occasions may not be offered and then they must be artificially invented. I have called such performances "Definitional Ceremonies," understanding them to be collective self-definitions specifically

---

1. Charlotte Linde distinguishes between "narrative" that implies an evaluative dimension and "chronicle," a list of events that does not imply evaluation (1978).

2. For a fuller discussion of the capacity of ritual to redefine social relationships, see Myerhoff and Moore (1977).

intended to proclaim an interpretation to an audience not otherwise available. The latter must be captured by any means necessary and made to see the truth of the group's history as the members understand it. Socially marginal people, disdained, ignored groups, individuals with what Erving Goffman calls "spoiled identities," regularly seek opportunities to appear before others in the light of their own internally provided interpretation.

Attention was the scarce good in the community I studied. Everyone competed for it with astonishing fierceness. The sight of a camera or tape recorder, the mere possibility that someone would sit down and listen to them, aroused the members' appetite to have themselves documented. One of the members was heartbroken when she was not elected to the Board of Directors. "How will anyone know I am here?" she asked. If possible, the attention should come from outsiders who were more socially prestigious and therefore more capable of certifying their existence. And if possible, these should be younger people, because peers would soon be gone. Who then would be left to recall their existence? What Sir Thomas Browne said in 1658 is still true. The threat of oblivion is "the heaviest stone that melancholy can throw at a man."

Performance is not merely a vehicle for being seen. Self-definition is attained through it, and this is tantamount to being what one claims to be. "We become what we display," says Mircea Eliade in discussing the transformative power of ritual performances. The imposition of meaning occurs when we select from the myriad possibilities a particular formulation that summarizes and epitomizes. Enactments are intentional, not spontaneous, rhetorical and didactic, taming the chaos of the world, at once asserting existence and meaning.

Meaning and "Re-membering"

The necessity for meaning is probably ubiquitous. In the Center population it was elevated to a passion. The old people were inclined naturally toward self-consciousness by their tradition's emphasis on their unique status as a Chosen People. The historical facts since the dispersion from the Holy Land exacerbated this tendency, since Jews have spent so much of their history as a pariah people surrounded by hostile outsiders. The Holocaust further intensified their awareness of their distinctiveness and promoted among survivors a search through the events of their private and collective lives for an explanation of their destiny. Lifton has suggested that survivors of mass destruction often become "seekers after justice." They carefully examine events for evidence of something aside from chaos to account for their sufferings. Indications of a moral and sane universe become imperative to ward off despair. Sense must be resurrected by means of an explanation. Any disaster becomes more bearable once it is named and conceptualized, once support is found for the belief in the "relatively modest assertion that God is not mad," to paraphrase Albert Einstein's minimum definition of religion (cited in Geertz 1973:100–101). Lifton speaks of survivors of the Holocaust and of Hiroshima as restoring sanity to themselves through "the formulative effort. Any experience of survival—whether of large disaster or intimate personal loss . . . involves a journey to the edge of the world of the living. The formulative effort, the search for signs of meaning, is the survivor's means of return from that edge" (1967).

The survivors of catastrophe, like the victims of disaster, must account for their escape. Job-like, victims petition the gods to know their sins, asking for explanations as to why they deserved their fate. But we often overlook the fact that those who are not afflicted when all around them are also ask the gods, "Why me?" The sorting through collective and private histories for answers was for some Center old people nearly an obsession, and often exceedingly painful. But the members were committed to it nonetheless. "The one who studies history loses an eye," said Moshe. "The one who does not loses two eyes." More formally, Wilhelm Dilthey says, "Both our fortunes and our own nature cause us pain, and so they force us to come to terms with them through understanding. The past mysteriously invites us to know the closely-woven meaning of its moments" (Hodges 1952:274–75).

Surviving and survivor's guilt, then, can serve as transformative agents, taking the base materials of ordinary existence and disaster and working the alchemical miracle upon them until they result in consciousness. The consequence is a development of the capacity to lead an examined life. This includes the construction of an explicable, even moral universe despite crushing external evidence to the contrary. The Center members had achieved this, and their use of rituals and ceremonies to enliven and interpret daily life was remarkable. Every day, even every minute, was focused in the light of all that had been extinguished and lost. "If we lose ourselves now, if we give up our traditions, if we become like everyone else, then we finish ourselves off. We finish Hitler's work for him," said one of the old women. They felt that they owed living fully to their beloved—always the "best of us"—who had perished. Thus were despair and depression held at bay. The old people also felt a certain sense of triumph at having persisted despite the attempts of so many to extinguish them. Outliving their enemies was a personal accomplishment for which they took responsibility and in which they took pride, flavored often as not by bitterness.

Overcoming physical handicaps and poverty were also moral accomplishments. The ability to remain independent and take care of themselves was closely attended and valued collectively by the elders. Senility and loss of autonomy were more feared than death. Their accomplishments were finely calibrated, nearly inconspicuous to younger, healthy outsiders. Basha succinctly stated her sense of achievement, even power, when she said:

> Every morning I wake up in pain. I wiggle my toes. Good. They still obey. I open my eyes. Good. I can still see. Everything hurts but I get dressed. I walk down to the ocean. Good. It's still there. Now my day can start. About tomorrow I never know. After all, I'm eighty-nine. I can't live forever.

Center members' attitudes toward time were colored by extreme age, the closeness of death, their sense of accomplishment at outliving catastrophe, and an often righteous determination to be themselves. They were alone and angry at being alone. They were no longer willing to trouble themselves to please others or pretend to be what they were not. Decorum, grace, and courtesy were not for them; truth was permitted to this stage of life. Time was an issue that flickered in and out of discussions often. On the one hand, the elders felt they had plenty of it, due to their enforced leisure. But on the other, every remaining day counted. This was illustrated by an exchange between some of the members discussing the existence of God.

> *Nathan:* If we start to talk about God now we'll be here for five thousand years. These questions you could keep for posterity.
> *Sonya:* Have you got better to do with your time than sit here and talk?

Sadie interrupted and began to talk about her ailments . . . "Even the doctors don't know how I survive. I could list for you all my sicknesses." Nathan retorted: "For *this* we don't have enough time."

Jacob Kovitz, the Center's president emeritus, often wrote essays on the proper way to age and use time. His writings included a piece called "Ten Commandments for the Elderly." Gentle irony and a delicate sense of the preciousness of time remaining are apparent. No future exists, so time should be neither rushed nor rigidly saved—the sense is there of fully using what is left but not expecting or demanding more.

Dress neatly and don't try to save your best clothes, because after you leave this world you won't need them anymore. Keep your head up, walk straight, and don't act older than your age. Remember one thing: If you don't feel well, there are many people who are feeling worse. Walk carefully, watching for the green light when crossing. If you have to wait a minute or two, it doesn't make any difference at your age. There is no reason to rush.

Time is abolished not only by myth and dream but occasionally also by memory, for remembering the past fully and well retains it. Life experiences are not swept away as if they had never been. They are rewoven into the present. Memory was problematic very often and forgetfulness experienced as very painful. Forgetting a person, an incident, even a word was often a torment. Shmuel explained the seriousness of this. "You understand, one word is not like another. . . . So when just the word I want hides from me, when before it has always come along very politely when I called it, this is a special torture designed for old Jews."

Memory is a continuum ranging from vague, dim shadows to the most bright vivid totality. At its most extreme form, memory may offer the opportunity not merely to recall the past but to relive it, in all its original freshness, unaltered by intervening change and reflection. All the accompanying sensations, emotions, and associations of the first occurrence are recovered and the past recaptured. Marcel Proust more than anyone analyzed how this process works and how exceedingly precious such moments are. The process does not involve will, volition, or the conscious, critical mind. It cannot be forced. Such moments are gifts, numinous pinpoints of great intensity. Then one's self and one's memories are experienced as eternally valid. Simultaneity replaces sequence, and a sense of oneness with all that has been one's history is achieved.

These moments very often involve childhood memories, and then one may experience the self as it was originally and know beyond doubt that one is the same person as that child, still dwelling within a much-altered body. The integration with earlier states of being surely provides the sense of continuity and completeness that may be counted as an essential developmental task in old age. It may not yield wisdom, the developmental task that Erikson points to as the work of this stage of life.[3] It does give what he would consider ego integrity, the opposite of disintegration.

Freud (1965) suggests that the completion of the mourning process requires that those left behind develop a new reality which no longer includes what has been lost. But judging from the Center members' struggle to retain the past, it must be added that full recovery from mourning may restore what has been lost, maintaining it through incorporation into the present. Full recollection and retention may be as vital to recovery and well-being as forfeiting memories.

Moments of full recollection are often triggered by sensory events—taste, touch, smell. Often physical movements, gestures, and actions—singing, dancing, participation in rituals, prayers, and ceremonies rooted in the archaic past—are also triggers. Actors in the method school use these devices to re-arouse emotions, speaking of this as "kinesthetic memory." The body retains the experiences that may be yielded, eventually and indirectly, to the mind. Often among Center members it was possible to see this at work. In the midst of a song, a lullaby that had been sung to the old person as a child, a dance that seemed to dance the dancer, the past became present and produced changes in posture, a fluidity of movement or sharply altered countenance in which youthfulness was mysteriously but undeniably apparent. And Center members were articulate about these experiences. When reciting the ancient prayer for the dead, one old man brought back the entire experience of the original context in which he first heard the prayer: Once more he felt himself a small boy standing close to his father, wrapped snugly in the father's prayer shawl, close against the cold of the bright winter morning, weeping, swaying over an open grave.

---

3. See especially Erikson's discussion of old age in "Reflections on Dr. Borg's Life Cycle" (1978).

To signify this special type of recollection, the term "re-membering" may be used, calling attention to the reaggregation of members, the figures who belong to one's life story, one's own prior selves, as well as significant others who are part of the story. Re-membering, then, is a purposive, significant unification, quite different from the passive, continuous fragmentary flickerings of images and feelings that accompany other activities in the normal flow of consciousness. The focused unification provided by re-membering is requisite to sense and ordering. A life is given a shape that extends back in the past and forward into the future. It becomes a tidy edited tale. Completeness is sacrificed for moral and aesthetic purposes. Here history may approach art and ritual. The same impulse for order informs them all. Perhaps this is why Mnemosne, the goddess of Memory among the Greeks, is the mother of the muses. Without re-membering we lose our histories and our selves. Time is erosion, then, rather than accumulation. Says Nabokov in his autobiography, ". . . the beginning of reflexive consciousness in the brain of our remotest ancestor must surely have coincided with the dawning of the sense of time" (1966:21).

The process is the same when done in individual lives or by a culture or a generational cohort. Private and collective lives, properly remembered, are interpretative. Full or "thick description" is such an analysis. This involves finding linkages between the group's shared, valued beliefs and symbols, and specific historical events. Particularities are subsumed and equated with grander themes, seen as exemplifying ultimate concerns. Then such stories may be enlarged to the level of myth as well as art—sacred and eternal justifications for how things are and what has happened. A life, then, is not envisioned as belonging only to the individual who has lived it but it is regarded as belonging to the world, to progeny who are heirs to the embodied traditions, or to God. Such re-membered lives are moral documents and their function is salvific, inevitably implying, "All this has not been for nothing."

The extraordinary struggle of survivors to recount their histories is explicable in this light. Again and again concentration camp literature describes inmates' determination to come back and tell the living their stories. This is seldom with the expectation of bringing about reform or repentance. It is to forge a link with the listener, to retain one's past, to find evidence of sense—above all it is an assertion of an unextinguished presence. The redemption provided by re-membering is well understood by the storyteller Elie Wiesel, who struggled back from hell to recount the voyage. In the dedication of his book on Hasidism (1973) he says:

My father, an enlightened spirit, believed in man.
My grandfather, a fervent Hasid, believed in God.
The one taught me to speak, the other to sing.
Both loved stories.
And when I tell mine, I hear their voices.
Whispering from beyond the silenced storm.
They are what links the survivor to their memory.

A young actress, Leeny Sack, working with the histories of her parents as concentration camp survivors, has recently developed a theater piece. The recurrent phrase that punctuates her narrative begins, "My father told me to tell you this. . . ." The substance was unbearable, but she explained the only pain worse than recollection was the pain of considering the possibility that the stories would be untold.[4] His anguish, we may assume, was assuaged by capturing his daughter as audience and giving her the task of transmitting his account. The usual feelings aroused in the teller are gratitude and relief.

A student working with one of the Center members noted this when she completed a series of life history sessions with one of the old women. The old woman was illiterate and completely alone. She never envisioned an opportunity to find a proper listener. When the project was complete, the younger woman thanked the older profoundly, having been exceptionally moved by the older woman's strength, the range of her struggles, her determination to rise to the challenges of her life. The older woman declined the thanks saying, "No, it is I who thank you. Every night before I fall asleep here on my narrow bed, I go over my life. I memorize it, in case anyone should ask."

The prospect of death for many of these elderly was often less fearsome than that of dying without having had an opportunity to unburden themselves of their memories. Their stories did not have to be complete or accurate. They realized that younger listeners who could pass them on would not be capable of comprehending what they had not lived through. But the mere remembering that there had been a history, a

---

4. Ms. Sack presented her work-in-progress to a session of the seminar on "Performance and Anthropology," conducted by Richard Schechner at New York University.

people, a culture, a story, would suffice. Characteristically, Shmuel made this point by telling a story. He recounted a parable concerning the founder of Hasidism, the Baal Shem Tov.

> When the great Hasid, Baal Shem Tov, the Master of the Good Name, had a problem, it was his custom to go to a certain part of the forest. There he would light a fire and say a certain prayer, and find wisdom. A generation later, a son of one of his disciples was in the same position. He went to that same place in the forest and lit the fire but he could not remember the prayer. But he asked for wisdom and it was sufficient. He found what he needed. A generation after that, his son had a problem like the others. He also went to the forest, but he could not even light the fire. "Lord of the Universe," he prayed, "I could not remember the prayer and I cannot get the fire started. But I am in the forest. That will have to be sufficient." And it was.
>
> Now, Rabbi Ben Levi sits in his study with his head in his hands. "Lord of the Universe," he prays, "look at us now. We have forgotten the prayer. The fire is out. We can't find our way back to the place in the forest. We can only remember that there was a fire, a prayer, a place in the forest. So, Lord, now that must be sufficient."

Upon completing a recording of his life history, Shmuel reflected on what it meant for him to face his death knowing his recollections of an entire way of life would be lost. His town in Poland that he had loved in his childhood no longer existed; it was destroyed in the Holocaust.

> ... It is not the worst thing that can happen for a man to grow old and die. But here is the hard part. When my mind goes back there now, there are no roads going in or out. No way back remains because nothing is there, no continuation. Then life itself, what is its worth to us? Why have we bothered to live? All this is at an end. For myself, growing old would be altogether a different thing if that little town was there still. All is ended. So in my life, I carry with me everything—all those people, all those places, I carry them around until my shoulders bend.
> ... Even with all that poverty and suffering, it would be enough if the place remained, even old men like me, ending their days, would find it enough. But when I come back from these stories

and remember the way they lived is gone forever, wiped out like you would erase a line of writing, then it means another thing altogether to me to accept leaving this life. If my life goes now, it means nothing. But if my life goes, with my memories, and all that is lost, that is something else to bear.

The Life History Classes

Not long after I began my work in the Center, I began to look for some appropriate means of reciprocating the members for the time they spent with me often talking about what I wanted to learn. It was soon evident that providing them with an opportunity to be heard, to recount their histories and tell stories, was ideal. This would constitute another arena in which they could appear in their own terms, and I would serve as audience, conspicuously listening and documenting what was said. I hoped also that some satisfaction would come to them from listening to each other in formal circumstances, that they would validate one another's accounts, and at the same time stimulate and encourage each other's memories. These hopes were fully realized in the form of a set of "Living History" sessions, as the members called them. Members were invited to attend "a class" that met for two hours or more each week. The series ran for five months, broke for the summer and resumed for four months. Before long a rather stable group of about twenty people formed itself and attended regularly.

There were few rules. People were required to abstain from inter- rupting each other. Everyone would have some time to speak at each session, even briefly. Any content was acceptable. I reinforced the appro- priateness of anyone's offerings, discouraging the members from chal- lenging the speakers on matters of accuracy. The content discussed varied greatly but loosely fell into four categories: Being Old, Life in the Old Country, Being a Jew, Life in America. In time, people's offerings grew more emotionally varied and less guarded. They brought in dreams, recipes, questions about ultimate concerns, folk remedies, book reports, daily logs, and the like. I encouraged them to keep journals, providing notebooks and pens, and many did so with considerable pleasure.

Their Life History sessions paralleled the Definitional Ceremonies in their presentational format. They were intended to persuade, and enact- ments were inserted as often as possible. Illustrations of points people wanted to make were taken to class in the form of objects. They brought mementos, gifts, plaques, awards, certificates, letters, publications, and photographs from all periods of their and their families' lives. One woman brought her sick husband who had grown senile and could no longer speak coherently. She spoke for him, recounting his stories, and along with them, the place he had filled in her life. Another woman brought her retarded grandson "to show you what I am talking about when I tell you about him." He was a kind of badge of honor, for she handled him with dignity and patience, an injury transcended but for which she wanted credit. Still another man brought in a yellow felt star bearing the word "Jude." It circulated throughout the room in silence. Words were not needed. The star dramatized a major facet of his existence. A number of the women regularly brought in food, demonstrating their claimed skills as cooks. Songs were sung, and from time to time there was dancing. Poems were recited frequently in many languages, demonstrations of erudition and memory. Learned quotations, of Marx and Talmud, folk and fine literature also adorned people's accounts. The sessions, then, were not merely verbal. Insofar as possible they were made into performances. People displayed the qualities they wanted seen as much as they could and became what they displayed.

The importance of storytelling and a strong oral tradition among the Center members were significant factors in accounting for the vitality of the Life History sessions. Though profoundly literate, the oral tradition among Jews is also highly developed, particularly in those exposed to Hasidism. The recognition that words spoken aloud to another person have particular power is a notion that weaves in and out of Jewish culture. Shmuel spoke of the esteem for the "wonder rebbes," the Hasidic teachers who traveled from one town to another in Eastern Europe.

Oh the stories they would tell us, full of wisdom, full of humor. It was immense. . . . All of us, little boys by the dozens, would follow them when they came into the town. You could always tell them by the chalk on their caftans, this they carried to mark around them a circle of chalk that would keep out the spirits. My father did not approve of me listening to them, but I would sneak out whenever I could, because what they brought you was absolutely magic. This experience was developing in me a great respect for telling stories. This is why it is important to get just the right attitude and just the right words for a story. You should get everything just right because no matter how pleasant, it is a serious thing you are doing.

The sessions were not cosmetic. Catharsis occurred and often more than that. Re-evaluations were clearly being undertaken, too. Having witnesses to this work proved essential. The elders found it hard to convince themselves of the validity of their interpretations without some consensus from the listeners. In time, they became better listeners. Though they knew their audience of peers was going to die out with them, members of the same generational cohorts have advantages as witnesses. They knew the reality being discussed through direct experience. Less had to be explained and described to them, but the work of persuasion was often all the more difficult because deception was less likely to be successful. When Jake quoted his father to demonstrate the latter's wisdom, one of the members promptly corrected him. "This you are getting not from your father. It comes from Sholom Aleichem." "And don't you think Sholom Aleichem learned anything from ordinary people?" he persisted. But no one was impressed.

A story told aloud to progeny or peers is, of course, more than a text. It is an event. When it is done properly, presentationally, its effect on the listener is profound, and the latter is more than a mere passive receiver or validator. The listener is changed. This was recognized implicitly by Rabbi Nachman of Bratzlav, who ordered that all written records of his teachings be destroyed. His words must be passed from mouth to ear, learned by and in heart. "My words have no clothes," he said. "When one speaks to one's fellows there arises a simple light and a returning light." The impact of the stories told by the old people to outsiders who would stop to listen was consistently striking. Among those old people embarked on the deep and serious work of re-membering, struggling toward self-knowledge and integration, it was especially clear that something important was going on. Sensitive young people, students, and grandchildren, often found themselves fascinated by the old people's life histories. The sociological shibboleth that claims in a rapidly changing society the elderly have nothing more to teach must be reconsidered. Anyone in our times struggling toward wholeness, self-knowledge based on examined experience, and clarity about the worth of the enterprise exerts a great attraction on those searching for clarity. In the company of elders such as these, listeners perform an essential service. But they get more than they give, and invariably grow from the contact.

When the sessions were at their best, the old people were conscious of the importance of their integration work, not only for themselves but for posterity, however modestly represented. Then they felt the high satisfaction of being able to fulfill themselves as individuals and as exemplars of a tradition at once. Then they were embodiments of the shared meanings—true ancestors—as well as individuals in full possession of their past. Rachel described such a moment most eloquently when she talked about what the sessions had meant to her.

All these speeches we are making reminded me of a picture I have from many years ago, when we were still in Russia. My brother had been gone already two years in America. I can see my mother like it is before me, engraved in my head. A small house she goes out of in wintertime, going every morning in the snow to the post office, wrapped up in a shawl. Every morning there was nothing. Finally, she found a letter. In that letter was written, "Mamalch, I didn't write to you before because I didn't have nothing to write about." "So," she says, "why didn't you write and tell me?"

You know this group of ours reminds me of that letter. When I first heard about this group, I thought to myself, "What can I learn? What can I hear that I don't know, about life in the Old Country, of the struggles, the life in the poor towns, in the bigger towns, of the rich people and the poor people? What is there to learn, I'm eighty-eight, that I haven't seen myself?" Then I think, "What can I give to anybody else? I'm not an educated woman. It's a waste of time."

That was my impression. But then I came here and heard all those stories. I knew them, but you know it was laid down deep, deep in your mind, with all those troubles mixed. You know it's there but you don't think of it, because sometimes you don't want to live in your past. Who needs all these foolish stories?

But finally, this group brought out such beautiful memories, not always so beautiful, but still all the pictures came up. It touched the layers of the kind that it was on those dead people already. It was laying on them like layers, separate layers of earth, and all of a sudden in this class I feel it coming up like lava. It just melted away the earth from all those people. It melted away, and they became alive. And then to me it looked like they were never dead.

Then I felt like the time my mother got that letter. "Why don't you come and tell me?" "Well, I have nothing to say," I think. But I start to say it and I find something. The memories come up in me like lava. So I felt I enriched myself. And I am hoping maybe I enriched somebody else. All this, it's not only for us. It's for the generations.

Life History as Integration: Personal Myth and Aging

Barbara Myerhoff and Virginia Tufte

One of the concerns of the elderly, encountered so frequently that it may be considered universal, is the desire to make a life review.[1] Their passionate affinity for reminiscence, for recalling their past, evaluating their personal experiences and integrating them with their present lives is often unfortunately viewed by many—professionals and lay-people alike—as a pathological phenomenon, expressive of the wish to escape the realities of the present, indicative of the loss of sensibilities and a compensating inward turn to the world of dreams and wishes. As Butler (1963) points out, reminiscence may as often be indicative of growth and change as symptomatic of disturbance. In the life review, the old person, living with intimate knowledge of coming death, may undertake the construction of a sacred account, providing him/herself with a formulation about what, ultimately, life has been about. Mythology is an essential human concern, and where societies no longer provide ready-made interpretations, individuals may develop their own, taking up the basic and enduring questions about the coherence and worth of their own time on earth.

In traditional societies where change is imperceptible, opportunities for life review are intrinsically provided, and it is a truism that in lieu of writing, knowledge is passed on orally by the old and valued by the young as guidelines for the future. But in our world, the old are neither providers of philosophical wisdom nor sources of practical information, and occasions for them to present their life stories must be artificially and deliberately constructed. Among us, it is usually only the great and articulate people who leave behind accounts of their histories. The need for the elderly to review their lives is exacerbated when they are an

---

1. There is considerable controversy as to the universality of the life review process. For a discussion of this issue, see Kaminsky, 1984. —Ed.

immigrant population whose participation in two or more different cultures constitutes internal discontinuity and also results in sharp discontinuity with the experience of their progeny. Where old people's knowledge is treated as irrelevant and obsolete, the natural inclination toward reminiscence may become exaggerated. Add to this, living in a secular world which provides no shared, sacred eschatological tradition, where death means only complete obliteration, in such circumstances the question naturally presents itself, "How may I be sure that my life has mattered?" and the even more terrifying unspoken preoccupation, "Can I be sure that I exist at all?" When one's name is assured of remembrance neither by God nor by one's fellows, who then is there to provide even a small measure of immortality?

To such profoundly troubling concerns, there are occasionally surprisingly simple remedies, and one of these, the Life History technique, is a tool responsive to the need for life review. It is often trying to listen to the stories told by the very old. Their dentures click, words are lost or offered in a foreign language, memories fail, they don't hear questions, refuse to respond to direction, and if one's goal is to teach, counsel, soothe or change them, frustration is inevitable. But in a setting where the only task is helping them record their own version of their history, unexpected rewards may accrue for the listeners.

A project designed to allow old people to tell their life stories was undertaken at the University of Southern California by two professors, of English and Anthropology, who joined their classes and their different skills and perspectives in an experimental Life History class. The English professor had found that a successful way of teaching writing skills was to involve students in writing projects that were concentrated on the gathering of data on family sagas, using first-hand information derived by interviews. But the students needed additional interviewing and fieldwork training for the project. Similarly, the anthropology professor had found that her students lacked basic writing skills for their work. It was logical to combine their classes and teach jointly writing and fieldwork techniques. The anthropologist provided, in addition to concrete fieldwork methods, the perspective which defines the basic task of the discipline as entering and comprehending the internal world of the subject. Anthropologists naturally gravitate toward the elderly as a result of their tradition of work in preliterate societies where the old are learned and esteemed. And anthropology treats every "native" as a carrier of culture, an expert on the "Little Tradition,"[2] which is less conspicuous but no less valuable than the knowledge of the elite who are conveyors of the great, literate traditions associated with advanced civilizations. It is an intrinsically humanizing perspective, validating the point of view of Everyman.

Students were asked to locate an older person with whom they had some rapport and to undertake a lengthy life history. They located old people in various ways. Many chose their grandparents. Others picked employees in family businesses, landlords, housemothers in sororities, servants, neighbors—people whom they had long known but had paid little attention to. Students were encouraged to ask for supplementary documents—photographs, diaries, treasured objects, letters and the like—to augment the interviews. They were urged to enlarge their understanding of their subjects by library research on the specific social and historical contexts in which they had lived. Students were asked to provide subjects with a copy of the final paper to keep and use.[3] The papers were actually collective documents since we had recommended that students carefully preserve the distinction between the subject's and writer's interpretations. The final interviewing session between student and old person was devoted, wherever possible, to a joint review of the document, explaining, changing, putting the final stamp of approval on the now-authentic statement which was a version of the subject's life in the form of a durable and tangible object.

The value of the activity for the young people was clear. For many, it was their first encounter with history as a meaningful concern in human terms. Countries, wars, social changes, became more than mere names and dates to memorize for a test. They saw something of the life of peasants, and of people whose preoccupations were utterly basic but

---

2. For a discussion of this concept, see "We Don't Wrap Herring in a Printed Page: Fusion, Fictions, and Continuity in Ritual Drama," in this volume. —Ed.

3. Previously Professor Tufte had experimented in teaching creative writing and composition to her students by arranging to have them work with ghetto elementary school children. There she came to appreciate the importance of providing concrete written documents to the children as the work progressed. She also became aware of this approach as a means for heightening esteem for self and for one's cultural experiences among devalued peoples who might otherwise regard their ethnic, class, or in this case, age membership as an individual, unfortunate, accidental affair, rather than an internally rich, adaptive set of collective responses and solutions to shared problems.

utterly outside their experience: the old people described struggles to assure mere subsistence and safety for their families, coping with extreme hardships and adjusting to a new country in the hope of finding religious freedom for their progeny (who turned out to be more interested in other things).

Many young people chose to work with old people who represented and strengthened their connections with their ethnic origins. These students were able to establish some sense of continuity with their own cultural heritage and history. Even more important, though, was the opportunity to identify with their future, as aged, infirm individuals facing that critical ingredient of life which had hitherto been no more than an abstraction—mortality and death. This assignment provided them with the opportunity for envisioning their own destiny, for completing themselves, and thus overcoming that alienating and dehumanizing perspective which treats old age as something that happens to a disparate and unfortunate segment of the population, "them" as opposed to us all. For these young people, most of whom had lived always in two-generational families, the encounter with the aging process in all its specific forms was often a startling revelation, these days not typically provided at home or in the classroom.

It was not difficult to train students in the essentials of this work: being reliable in arranging meetings, not interfering with the flow of memories and stimulating it when it was slow, learning that it was all right to let their subjects cry, and above all listening: visibly, sympathetically, and with great attention. No fixed format was recommended for data collection. Subjects were to provide their own sequences of presentation, based on the assumption that the priorities for discussion would probably reflect the significance to the subject of material recalled. Coverage was inevitably uneven, major life episodes were often garbled or lost, and students often needed considerable reassurance that this did not reflect inadequacies in their work. Always evident was the natural affinity between people of alternate generations, so often observed by anthropologists (Radcliffe-Brown 1950). Between grandparent and grandchild the strains of rivalry, authority, guilt, and ambivalence are nearly always minimized. It was soon clear that a dyadic relationship between a young and an old person was the best arrangement for the taking of life histories. The work cannot usually be done alone. A recipient is necessary to assure a coherent flow. Work with individuals of adjacent generations is not nearly as gratifying to either party. And among peers, it is usually impossible, not only for lack of mechanical and sensory means, but also because competition for attention is often too keen to allow for free listening and compassion. Younger people, in the end, represent another generation to whom old people can entrust the treasure of their life experience with the expectation of continuity, and the corresponding assurance that they have been heard by those who will follow.

The experimental class was a success for everyone involved. The old and young people often became friends and maintained a relationship after the class work had been completed. The students rated the experience as one of the most meaningful assignments that they had had in their university careers. And the work they produced, in form and substance, much exceeded their teachers' hopes.

So clear was the need among the elderly to make a life review that the anthropologist was inspired to undertake a Life History class in the senior citizens' Center where she was doing research on aging. Here, the format used was that of a class in "Living History," lasting several hours on a weekly basis, offered over a five-month period, attended by several dozen people. The topics discussed were selected by the senior citizens and ranged widely, touching on sacred holidays, childhood memories, thoughts about being a Jew, the meaning of death, the use and interpretation of dreams, folk medicines, disappointments and pleasures in their progeny, and the like.

In the beginning the sessions were chaotic. It was necessary to use a rigorously structured format which prevented interruptions and assured each person an opportunity to talk for a specified period of time. The meetings were tape recorded, so that we could collect the members' statements in a volume which each person could keep. Members were given notebooks in which they kept their poems, dreams, concerns, fears, philosophical and polemical pieces. In these ways, participants were given evidence of the importance of their recollections.

The conscious modeling of listening was actively promoted. Gradually, the pressure to talk and receive attention diminished enough for the old people to be able to listen to one another. In this stable and supportive atmosphere, intimacy grew and acquaintances deepened into friendship, a development which had not occurred spontaneously despite their long association with each other. Members stimulated each other's memories, and collectively were able to re-evoke long buried early experiences. This was exceptionally valuable to them, allowing them to relate to themselves when they were young and to experience themselves as the same person they had always been, despite great changes and the passage of so much time.

The class meetings gave many an occasion for catharsis, but in passing. More important, it seemed, was their effort to provide for themselves and one another, an agreed-upon interpretation of their lives, imposing form on what would have otherwise been chaotic and haphazard, and consoling them by disclosing sense and coherence in the series of choices and accidents that make up a life. This process of reviewing one's life results inevitably in self-scrutiny and heightened self-awareness.[4] The quest for personal and collective patterns goes beyond catharsis; it is a fundamentally curative act and leads to that enrichment and growth that characterizes, potentially, all the stages of life.

The sessions were not therapeutic in intent, though occasionally the depths plumbed and the re-evaluations accomplished might earn them that label. But it was important to the elderly attending that they not regard the meetings as directed toward solving personal problems. Their pride and traditions did not allow them to work comfortably with a therapeutic model. Clearly, however, group interactions improved; with time and continuing attention, all members became more responsive to and supportive of each other, and all appeared to have gained some heightened sense of their importance and visibility.

Too often, our concern with decline and loss among the elderly inclines us away from attending any positive changes which may also accompany aging, as Butler (1963) has observed. Impending death and extinction are a formidable impetus toward self-scrutiny. It may well be as characteristic of the aging to reflect and introspect as it is to obsess about past and present losses.

The life review provides an opportunity to accomplish several kinds of integration simultaneously. First, it offers to the elderly what is certainly their due, the chance to be heard, be seen and recorded as having

---

4. Here, the argument crosses the boundary between well-founded advocacy and overzealous polemic: this statement is unsupported by the clinical literature and by everyday observation of reminiscence-based groups of older adults. In the article that Myerhoff frequently cites, Butler (1963) writes: " . . . the many and varied behavioral and affective states resulting from the life review can include severe depressions, states of panic, intense guilt, and constant obsessional rumination; instead of increasing self-awareness, one may find increasing rigidity."
—Ed.

existed, and through this attention, to integrate their historical experiences and thus construct and manifest a valuable identity, a personal mythology. It affords for the younger people taking a life history an occasion in which they may identify with historical time and thereby become connected with their own traditions and past. It gives an opportunity, too, for the younger people to see and know a model for the future, thus complete themselves, and to recognize the full scope of the human life cycle with all its limits and possibilities. Finally, it provides intergenerational continuity, integrating the teller and the listener into a web of common meaning.

"Life Not Death in Venice":
Its Second Life

The whole earth is the sepulchre of famous men and ordinary men, and their story is not graven on stone, but lives on woven into the stuff of other men's lives. . . .

— Pericles's funeral speech

The power of breadth of our own life, and the energy of reflection upon it is the foundation of the historical vision. It alone enables us to give second life to the bloodless shades of the past.

— Dilthey, *Pattern and Meaning in History*

In a recent article on "the refiguration of social thought," Geertz (1980:178, 167) points out the growing vitality of interest among social scientists in "the anatomization of thought" as indicative of "a move toward conceiving of social life as organized in terms of symbols . . . whose meaning we must grasp." How people make sense out of themselves, for themselves, and how we as anthropologists develop our interpretive skills in unpacking their symbolic systems becomes a central concern in our discipline.

One of the most persistent but elusive ways that people make sense of themselves is to show themselves to themselves, through multiple forms: by telling themselves stories; by dramatizing claims in rituals and other collective enactments; by rendering visible actual and desired truths about themselves and the significance of their existence in imaginative and performative productions. Self-recognition is accomplished by these showings and is, as George Steiner says, a "formidable, difficult, and perpetual task." More than merely self-recognition, self-definition is made possible by means of such showings, for their content may state not only what people think they are but what they should have been or may yet be. Evidently, interpretive statements are mirrors for collectivities to hold up to themselves; like mirrors, such statements may lie, reverse, and distort the images they carry, and they need not be isomorphic with "nature."

In this paper, I will present two instances of cultural mirroring, one event which I call a "definitional ceremony," the other an inscribed text, a self-portrait of a collectivity. Both of these are found in a highly self-conscious community which continually interprets, depicts, and performs its self-determined reality; both forms are strikingly symbolic and can be unpacked to elucidate the community's understanding of itself; and both are reflecting surfaces and reflexive, demonstrating the creators' consciousness of their own interpretive work.

The cases I cite, ceremony and inscribed text, were exceptionally successful in the persuasions about the reality they asserted. Their success may be judged by the fact that they reached beyond convincing and moving their own members about the claims they made. They succeeded in interesting and captivating outsider-witnesses as to the validity of the interpretations. These outsider-witnesses—anthropologist and the media—served as further reflecting surfaces, broadcasting, re-presenting what they had been shown, and thus enlarging the people's original interpretations and giving them a greater public and factual character than they had in their primary form. By pressing into service others who believed, to restate their versions of themselves, they amplified their claims. The people involved eventually succeeded in bringing about actual changes, in reversing to some degree their political impotence and invisibility, by the canny deployment of their symbols, consciously manipulated; by their skillful operation on public sentiments; and by their sheer conviction that although they understood their manipulations fully, they were innocently, utterly correct. Ultimately, they displayed "facts" of their life and their meaning, knowing full well that the facts they portrayed were about life not as it was but as it should have been.

"Life Not Death in Venice": Background

In 1972 I began an anthropological study of aging and ethnicity at the Israel Levin Senior Center in Venice, California.[1] My work there brought

---

1. After much deliberation I decided to use real names in this paper, for the Center, the community, and the pertinent individuals. This is not consonant with general anthropological practice, which seeks to preserve the anonymity of the populations it studies. In this case, however, the group's urgent desire to be recorded suggests that it is appropriate to name names; it is also consistent with the approach that they have pressed me to take and that I have agreed is suitable. In view of the wide distribution of the film about them, anonymity is not

to my attention a singular and dominant theme: the people's severe invisibility and the consequent disturbing psychological and social consequences of being unnoticed. It is a truism that severely marginal people are stigmatized and neglected by the mainstream society, subject to dismissal that is usually not even the result of hatred or conscious disdain. Often, it is merely that such people are not *seen;* they are treated as invisible.

It became clear to me that these particular elders were intent on presenting themselves to the world and being noticed; on interpreting the meaning of their history and culture to a wider outside world that would remember them after they had died; on possibly transmitting something of their lives to younger people. Many of their struggles were intractable: extreme poverty, poor health, inadequate housing and transportation, insufficient medical care, dangerous surroundings, loss of social roles, and outliving spouses, family, and friends. But their invisibility proved not to be irreversible. Through their own ingenuity, imagination, and boldness, aided by outsiders who publicized their activities, they learned to manipulate their own images, flying in the face of external reality, denying their existential circumstances. They displayed and performed their interpretations of themselves and in some critical respects became what they claimed to be. By denying their invisibility, isolation, and impotence, they made themselves seen, and in being seen they came into being in their own terms, as authors of themselves.

The elders had created an entire culture of their own making, one of great complexity and richness that was shot through with contradictions, paradoxes, and fantasies. It had been built up over the course of some three decades spent together on the beach in Venice. Here, in an age-homogeneous ethnic enclave, surrounded by the carnival-like life along the boardwalk, they revived some features from their childhood history in the cities and shtetls of the Old World. Particularly important was their return to their natal language and culture, Yiddishkeit, and to some extent to the religious practices they had discarded on arriving in America, when rapid assimilation for themselves and education for their children were their most singular concerns.

---

genuinely possible, in any case. Since I live in close proximity to these people and continue to be in contact with them, I regularly submit my writings and photographs to them for comment. There is usually some disagreement about my interpretations; sometimes I amend the original statements, sometimes I merely note that our views do not concur.

The culture they had invented to meet their present circumstances in old age was bricolage in the best sense—an assortment of symbols, customs, memories, and rituals, blending in a highly ecumenical spirit; they used something from all the layers of their history: Old World, Yiddish, Jewish, modern, American, Californian, secular, and sacred. They knew that improvisation and invention were essential, but like all people they also needed to convince themselves that these solutions were proper, authentic, believable, and occasionally traditional. Their need for such persuasions, and for being visible, coincided with their naturally performative bent, resulting in a highly dramatic self-presentational culture that was extroverted and often touched with the frenzy of desperation. (And, of course, things had to be loud, clear, and exciting since most of these people were in their mid-eighties to mid-nineties; it was often difficult for them to see and hear some of the quieter displays.) The way of life devised by these elderly Jews was a major accomplishment, one that proved successful in dealing with their everyday circumstances and with numerous internally and externally generated crises.

Exegesis and self-examination were ancient religious and secular customs for the elders; textual analysis was taught them as part of the Scripture. A long history as pariah people, at least since the biblical Dispersion from Israel, in the Old World, and repeated now in their old age, further heightened their self-consciousness. Performance and self-commentary were natural to them. Life in a constructed world (one that they knew to be constructed) was characteristic of their past as well as their present. The power of the imagination, when publicly stated and collectively experienced, was understood by many to be a necessity, a gift, and a potential danger.

The dangers of a life lived imaginatively were discussed vividly by Schmuel, who described his childhood in a little town in Poland:

> Now it is strange to say that we belonged there. . . . The beautiful river, forests, none of these are ours. What did we have but fear and hunger and more hunger? Hidden in a foreign land that we loved and hated. A life made entirely from the imagination. We say our prayers for rains to come, not for us here in Poland but for the Holy Land. We pass our lives to study the services in the Temple. What Temple? Long ago finished. Where do our priests make offerings? Only in our minds. We feel the seasons of Jerusalem more than the cold of Poland. Outside we are ragged, poor, nothing

to look at, no possibilities for change. But every little child there is rubbing elbows with the glorious kings and priests of the Holy Land. . . . In this we find our home. . . . Would you say this is insanity? It could be. If we lived more in Poland and not so much in the Holy Land, would all our people now be buried in pits along the river? (1980:68–69).

Here, then, is an illustration of the group's capacity to describe their lives imaginatively and consciously, questioning their own inventions while proceeding to believe in and enact them. Alongside their verbal reflections, however, was their often startling capacity to shape their physiological lives no less than their thoughts and acts. It was remarkable that they continued to survive, as individuals and as a collectivity, far beyond the norm, beyond predictions of sociology, history, and physiology. And not a few proved able to tailor their deaths as well as their lives, according to their own designs, dying naturally but precisely in the moments and manners of their choice. These people inscribed their self-interpretations on the spaces and surfaces they touched—walls, neighborhoods, media—sometimes even pressing their own bodies into service as statements of meaning, the most final and most dramatic of all.

Definitional Ceremonies

Definitional ceremonies are likely to develop when within a group there is a crisis of invisibility and disdain by a more powerful outside society. Let me state briefly why visibility was such a critical issue among these people. As immigrants, they had no natural witnesses to their past lives and culture. They lived in a world of strangers who "had to be told everything." Moreover, since the Holocaust had eliminated their natal culture, these elders felt an especially great obligation to transmit their firsthand experiences in Eastern Europe to others. They were the last ones who could explain "what it really had been like." And because their children were assimilated into another culture, there was often no one to receive and preserve their memories and tales. Also, because they were marginal, disdained people, outsiders knew nearly nothing about them. The absent witness/missing progeny feature, then, was a serious, multidimensional problem.

While marginality, extreme age and the proximity of death, the shock of immigration and the loss of a natal culture (suggesting personal and collective obliteration) all contribute to a sharp self-consciousness, pain and discontinuity are essential contributors as well. Only through the assimilation of experience into a form that endows meaning can such a history be rendered bearable. But the sense of continuity, of being a member in a chain of being with an inherited history that can be transmitted, may contribute as much to reflexive consciousness as rupture, pain, and loss.

This point emerged very clearly in a discussion with some of the elderly artists who participated in the cultural festival.[2] Sherrie Wagner, a graduate student in history, queried the artists about their sharp awareness of being "in history," saying:

> One of the things that I often asked my grandmother was what she thought about historical events, like Pearl Harbor, the Second World War, and things like that. She never really had a sense of having been a part of history or a part of the important events of her time. I could never get her to talk about where she was or what she felt. It was as though they had no impact on her. But the people sitting here today seem to have a much clearer sense of history and I wonder if it is because they are painting and sculpting and that makes them more aware? Or is it being in this show? Do you now have a greater sense of being part of history?

Ida Bernstein replied: "Well, to tell you the truth, I had it before, I always had this very strongly. This may sound very pompous, but I have to say I am very conscious of the fact that I have certain traditions, values that I can transmit."

---

2. The "Life Not Death in Venice" art and cultural festival held at the University of Southern California in 1980, where the elderly and their art works, and scholars and artists who had worked in the same Eastern European cultural traditions, were brought together. The older people served as docents to their art works, and their life histories, collected by students, were presented along with the art. The subtext of this festival was to provide circumstances not only for the elderly to be seen and appreciated, but for them to be there when this occurred, seeing the public, artists, and scholars *seeing them*, thus assuring them of some of the cultural transmission which they so ardently sought.

The discussion was organized and videotaped in connection with a grant from the California Council for the Humanities, to assess the impact of the artists and scholars involved in the festival on one another and to evaluate the effects on the artists of both themselves and their works being displayed in public.

Not being noticed by children or the outside "serious world" was exacerbated among these elderly by the loss of some of their sensory acuity. Clarity of consciousness tended to fade, memories fused with the present, dreams with desire, sleep with wakefulness. There were few kinesthetic cues as to their continuing vitality since there were no kin, spouses, or children to hold, and it was not their custom to embrace each other. Sensory deprivation was often severe. When both the outside and the inner world deprive us of reflections—evidence that, indeed, we are still present and alive, seen and responded to—the threat to self-awareness can be great. Definitional ceremonies deal with the problems of invisibility and marginality; they are strategies that provide opportunities for being seen and in one's own terms, garnering witnesses to one's worth, vitality, and being. Thus, it was the custom for Center members to display and dramatize themselves in many forms, informal and formal, planned and spontaneous: by storytelling, creating difficulties, making scenes; by positioning themselves to be noticed, recorded, listened to, and photographed.

Definitional ceremonies were the elders' most regular and formal patterns of display. These were quite predictable, marked by considerable momentum leading up to a crisis, after which, when things had settled down, it appeared that nothing had been accomplished. No internal conflicts were settled, no social realignments made. At first these events seemed to resemble what Turner (1974) described as social dramas—they had a natural sequence, a beginning, a middle, and an end, and there was the same progression from breach of a norm to crisis and resolution, with displays of common, powerful, binding symbols. Certainly the style was agonistic; much adrenaline had flowed and a good fight indeed offered clear-cut evidence of continuing vitality. Heroes emerged, pro- and con-, and there were antagonists, accessories, and always a sizeable chorus. Parts were discovered and developed so that everyone was heard from, seen, authenticated. And as with Turner's social dramas, the ends of these affairs were always marked by the enunciation of the participants' collective symbols, reiterating their common membership and deepest shared commitments. That the ceremonies changed nothing was signal, and is what distinguished them from social dramas. It seemed, in fact, that their purpose was to allow things to stay the same, to permit people to discover and rediscover sameness in the midst of furor, antagonism, and threats of splitting apart.

Here, the performative dimension of definitional ceremonies was the critical ingredient. Within them claims were made that were frequently unrelated to any palpable "reality," which was often evident to all of those involved. To merely assert such claims would be ludicrous and utterly unconvincing; but to enact them was another thing. Mounted as dramas they became small, full worlds, concrete, with proper masks, costumes, gestures, vocabularies, special languages, and all the panoply that made them convincing rituals. Like string quartets and Balinese cockfights, as Geertz (1973) points out, such symbolic dramas are not "mere reflections of a pre-existing sensibility, analogically represented"; they are "positive agents" in the creation and maintenance of the subjectivity they organize into a proper, coherent tale. Considering the frequency with which this particular population engineered such opportunities for appearing and enacting their dreams, we are tempted to describe definitional ceremonies as more like stages than mirrors. They did not merely show the people to themselves; rather, they provided scenes into which the people could step and play their parts. If others were watching, so much the better. Their attention, belief, and possibly recording would become evidence in the future of the "truth" of the performance, solid corroboration of what began as desire and through enactment came into the world as fact. If no one else noticed, the Center members watched each other and themselves, bearing witness to their own story.

The Parade

The boardwalk which the Center faces had been used for some time by bicyclists, though a local (unenforced) ordinance prohibits wheeled traffic. Then roller skating enthusiasts joined the stream of bicyclists, making the boardwalk as heavily trafficked and dangerous as a major street. Several collisions occurred; old people were struck down and injured. All of them were growing frightened and angry, but no one succeeded in seeing to it that the law against wheeled traffic was enforced. Old and young competed fiercely for space, dramatically enacting their opposing concerns in regular shouting matches:

> "This isn't an old people's home, you know!"
> "I worked hard all my life. I'm a citizen. I got to have a place to put down my foot also."

Thus the stage was set for the precipitating event that led to a crisis.

A bicyclist struck Anna Gerber, aged 86, as she left the Center one Sunday morning. The youth who hit her was reported to have said in defense of himself, "I didn't see her." His statement outraged the old people, for Anna evidently had been directly in front of him. Clearly, it seemed a case of "death by invisibility." When Anna died as a result of her injuries, the Center members organized a protest march. The event was carefully staged and described in advance to the media, which appeared to cover it. An empty, unmarked "coffin" made from a paper carton painted black was in the middle of the procession. Members carried placards reading "S.O.S. = Save Our Seniors," "Let Our People Stay," and "Life Not Death in Venice." Two blind men led the procession, and people with walkers and canes placed themselves prominently alongside the coffin. The members dressed in particularly bright, nice clothing, "so as not to look poor or pathetic," said one member.

Roller skaters, bicycle riders, and the concessionaires who rented skates and bikes all heckled the elders, who spoke up sharply to be sure that the television cameras and microphones caught the moral outrage they articulated: "See this sign, 'Let Our People Stay'? That goes back to the Bible, you know. We were driven out from Europe already. We don't want to be driven out from here." The group proceeded several hundred yards down the boardwalk, to the small orthodox synagogue that recently had been acquired by a group of young people. The elders did not regularly visit the synagogue because most were not observant and many objected to the orthodox practice of separating women and men during prayer, regarding it as "too old-fashioned, the kind of thing we got away from when we left the Old Country." Now everyone crowded into the little shul. Men and women were seated together, Jew and non-Jew, young and old, members and media people, as many of those who had joined the parade as could fit inside. It was a splendid moment of *communitas*, a profound and moving celebration of unity, as the prayers were said to "bind up the name of Anna with the ancestors."

The ceremonies did not end there, however. The members returned to the Center for an afternoon of dancing to celebrate the birthday of Frances Stein, aged 100, a woman of singular strength, a symbol of successful longevity, always in good spirits, clear-headed, unencumbered by cane, hearing aid, or illness. The continuity of life was acknowledged as vividly as the presence of death had been earlier in the day. "It's a good way to finish such a day," people agreed, clearly aware of the symbolic propriety of juxtaposing a funeral and a birthday to assert their continuing vitality and power despite injury and loss. The ceremony had been an enactment of their historical vision and their rejection of the assigned position of helpless victim. It was a profoundly reflexive occasion, the kind that, as the opening epigraph by Dilthey notes, gives human experience its "second life."

What were some of the specific symbols deployed in the definitional ceremony? Most were clearly identifiable with the people's layered, long history, ranging from ancient times to the most recent developments. "Let my people stay," the reference to the Jews' exodus from Egypt, came from the oldest layer of history, signifying their capacity to achieve freedom and leave slavery behind in a return to their homeland. Certainly the motto referred as well to the repeated form, a procession, or in recent terms, a protest march, a demonstration. That freedom in ancient times meant "going out" and in contemporary times meant "staying put" was a satisfying bit of opposition that gave that motto a pungent, ironic flavor. The placard that became "the name" for the parade, "Life Not Death in Venice," similarly reasserted the life-over-death message and was in response to a newspaper clipping announcing the coming protest march under the heading "Death in Venice." Some members became irate by this suggestion of defeat and, recognizing its danger, used a counter-slogan; they employed placards, printed words speaking to other printed words (the newspaper headline), as a means of erasing or out-shouting the statements made by outsiders about them. It was another instance of literally "making a scene" to make sure that their message was seen and heard.

The use of the prayer for Anna, "binding her up with the ancestors," came from a historical layer that was equally old. The Jewish prayer for the dead, Kaddish, makes no reference to death. It is a statement only about continuity and perpetuity; it elevates the individual who has died to the quasi-sacred position of the Patriarchs and Matriarchs, mythic figures with whom he or she becomes bound, suggesting the removal from history and time, sounding again the theme of renewal and transcendence, of deathlessness. Note as well that no official reference was made to the most recent and powerful historical episode of all: the Holocaust. While it was briefly, obliquely cited verbally, it was not used on a poster or displayed in any way. It is my impression that, as a rule, these people avoid using that experience or exploiting it, except in rare circumstances, and then usually to each other but not outsiders. The experience seems too strong and sacred to put to immediate practical purposes.

The note of renewal and denial of death were repeated in the association of a coffin and a birthday party. The incorporation of the synagogue into the procession was a fortunate choice, for it symbolized the inclusion of all of Judaism in this local event and touched the particular circumstances with sacrality. That outsiders and nonmembers were included within the synagogue was a fine symbolic note that their cause went beyond them, beyond other Jews or old people. It was essential that outsiders be brought into the protest for the definitional ceremony to succeed. If it were limited to only those like themselves, there would have been no audience to register the elders' message. While they might have succeeded in convincing themselves, there would have been no hope of making the impact they aimed for on the outside world.

Finally, within the procession the elders displayed themselves as symbols, dramatizing precisely how they wished to be and how they wished to be seen. They exploited signs of their fragility—canes, walkers, blindness—but deliberately dressed well. They wished to be viewed as strong presences, angry but not defeated; yet they were too cagey to omit the message about their vulnerability and the implicit accusation it stated. At once they dramatized strength and weakness in a brilliant, accurate paradox. Moral superiority and structural inferiority so commonly deployed by liminal people, as Turner has pointed out, was particularly well stated here.

The comment made by the youth on the bicycle after he struck Anna was often repeated and called to the attention of outsiders as highly symbolic. All the old people knew why he hadn't seen her; their determination to make themselves visible was the specific impetus for the parade. That they succeeded in altering more than their own version of themselves was beyond question when a few weeks later barricades appeared on the boardwalk, on either side of the Center, providing a four-block section where the old people could walk without fear of traffic. A limited but decisive victory. The elders had transformed their assigned role as helpless, unseen people into their chosen one as people to be reckoned with. The definitional ceremony had defined them as such and was sufficiently convincing to outsiders as well. All entered into collusion to agree that the elders did indeed exist and should be seen.

It was, of course, real or anticipated popular pressure that finally caused local politicians to erect the barricades. This pressure was generated by media coverage that amplified the elders' visibility, making it larger, clearer, and more public than it would otherwise have been. Hence, the media must be included in this analysis of reflecting surfaces. Publicity afforded by the parade was a significant mirror that showed the old people's culture to themselves and to outsiders. Nevertheless, the elders originated the image that was broadcast, and it was to their image that they successfully drew their witnesses. They not only created an imaginary existence for themselves but for those who watched them. Geertz has described ritual as that form which allows the "dreamed-of" and "lived-in" orders to fuse (1973:112). Indeed, they fused in this event. The authors of the ritual stepped into the single reality made of the two orders and took part of their audience with them.

The Center Mural: An Inscribed Text

Paul Ricoeur tells us that "inscriptions fix meaning." A social event read as a text is slippery, as though the words flew off the page before we could finish reading them. An "inscribed" social text is easier to read, however. Like an object, it sits still while we look at it; it allows us to re-present it to others, as I do here in discussing the meaning of the second symbolic form used by the group of elderly Jews in California.

The Center members all came from a tradition that forbade portraiture and the depiction of images. Nevertheless, many were attracted to visual art and themselves enjoyed painting. Their self-expression in this form was encouraged by their art teacher, Mrs. Betty Nutkiewicz, herself an Eastern European Jew and a refugee from the Holocaust, somewhat younger than most of the members but still what Americans would call a senior citizen. She organized some of the most enthusiastic students in her regular art classes in the Center to paint a mural the length of one hall there. Many people participated in the project, but three of the members were the major designers and artists. Those who did not paint instead witnessed, criticized, kibitzed; and finally the painting took shape. It is not possible to determine precisely how many or who contributed particular themes and ideas, though Mrs. Nutkiewicz remembers some especially striking contributions. The mural is unquestionably a collective self-portrait, showing the elders' social history freely interspersed with their myths.

The mural begins at the west end of the hall with a drawing of the

Mayflower. An American flag flies on top, jutting out of the confining frame. Mrs. Nutkiewicz notes: "This was Bessie Mintz' idea though I do not think that most people in this group came over on the Mayflower. She made the boat very big because it had to carry so many Jews here."[3] The next scene depicts the Statue of Liberty, like the American flag a beloved symbol to these immigrants, marking the beginning of a new life of freedom. Mrs. Nutkiewicz comments: "You notice they made Miss Liberty a little heftier than usual. You might think that is because she is strong. That's true, but also because the artist who made it thought that women who were a little bit fat looked healthier, more attractive."

A market scene in a village square, fusing New York and Eastern Europe, follows, prompting Mrs. Nutkiewicz to tell us: "What is interesting here is that these little houses you wouldn't really find in New York. They brought them from their past probably. They carried these ideas and memories from their little shtetls and put them right up here on the wall." The secular associations of Yiddish and the sacred associations of Hebrew are eluded to by two written signs in the scene: "Fresh herring can be bought here" in Yiddish over one of the stalls in the marketplace scene; "Synagogue" in Hebrew over the House of Prayer. She continues: "This scene you would find in the Lower East Side, all right, it's mixed up with Europe. [The Center elders] identified themselves with these people. Some had sisters, mothers like this, sitting all day in front of a little pile of fruit, vegetables. And of course, there are peddlers. You see one very talented artist made that horse, a beautiful skinny horse, had to be skinny because it shows that everyone was poor."

Next is a segment on the elders' middle years in America, in the sweatshops where so many passed most of their working lives and which represents a significant portion of their collective social history; whether or not experienced individually, the experience is "borrowed" as a historical moment and regularly incorporated into accounts of personal histories. (The same is true for having lived as a member of a shtetl rather than in a town or city. When pressed, many members indicate that they were not actually born or raised in shtetls, those largely Jewish hamlets and villages of Eastern Europe. Rather, they use the term to signify their childhood experiences as members of a religious community of their own people, in contrast to their later lives in secular, pluralistic

---

3. This commentary was recorded on videotape and transcribed for inclusion of excerpts in this essay.

America.) Mrs. Nutkiewicz remarks: "And this is, you know, the Liberation movement. It started to grow up at this time. Here are the suffragist women with their signs, 'Strike,' 'Fight,' 'Eight Hours of Work,' 'Arbeiten,' all in Yiddish. You see, they are in long dresses, heels, the old-fashioned dress but they are modern people, fighting for the improvement of their working conditions. Because after the sweatshops come the unions. That was their doing. They fought for themselves, for freedom and social justice, but everyone benefited." The merging of strikers and suffragettes is an interesting note, suggesting the people's identification with common causes for which they must struggle in their pursuit of freedom and social justice. Trade unions and the fight for women's rights merge here. That primarily women are depicted in the protest march is not unusual when we consider that all the painters of the mural were women. Clearly, it is the privilege of artists everywhere to personalize and localize their great themes, imbuing the Great Tradition with the specific forms and personnel that give the Little Tradition its vivacity.

The portion of the mural that follows this displays the citizens as middle-aged people in the sweatshops. "This has a great history in the life of the Jewish people," says Mrs. Nutkiewicz. "Because you see here the worker sewing, in very poor conditions, on the sewing machine. And you see standing over them, the foreman who is supposed to be very strict, selfish. You can see how hard everyone works. But at least we are together."

Then come the elders in Venice, already retired, dressed in modern American garb and seated outside the Israel Levin Center on the boardwalk benches.

Here you see the people sitting on the benches. Look, one is feeding a hungry dog. You see the woman is almost falling down but she didn't want to sit because she had to feed the dog. They painted this picture but they were unhappy with it because they identified themselves with this picture. You see they are a little apart from each other and they look kind of desolate. So what can we do to make the picture happy and the conditions happy? So somebody said, "Let's make the Israel Levin Center." And here we began to build a center.

Now here is something interesting, I would say almost surrealistic. People walk through the Center and the Center became almost transparent. You see one figure is inside, one figure is half outside.

But they show that they are going through the Center. Even the figure is still in the Center but we can see it. And naturally, they dance, the "eternal Hora" dance, and they're all happy. And it was Friday. We finish with the *Oneg Shabes* [the welcoming of the Sabbath] with the blessing of the candles. The challah [braided Sabbath loaf] is there, and the beautiful table cloth with fringes.

The half-inside-half-outside figures are two individuals who are holding hands, drawn in outline, not colored, shaded, or given any detail. They look unfinished. Indeed I assumed that someone had simply failed to complete them, until I heard them referred to as the "ghosts" or "spirits" in the mural. Explained one of the members: "We have here ghosts because, you see, even though we are old, we are not yet finished. We still come into new things and could change yet a lot before we die." Intrigued, I asked several other people about the possibility of ghosts, and there were various interpretations: "These are not ghosts. No, it's because you see, people don't come fully into their life without holding their comrades' hands. This we learn from our history. United we stand. You can see how lonely they look over there [on the benches] before they took hold of each other."

A woman standing nearby overheard our conversation and countered: "You always got to put politics into things. It was much simpler. I know the woman who did this part of the painting. Esther Wolfe was her name. You would be standing outside and so naturally you couldn't see the people inside the Center already. So you have to show them coming out into the world, which they couldn't do with their bodies. So they don't get their bodies until they come out into the sunshine." Mrs. Nutkiewicz didn't like the suggestion that these outlined figures were in any way "not real":

Oh no! They are not ghosts or spirits. They're very real. They are the people going through the Israel Levin Center. And our artists are primitive, I would say. They didn't know how to solve the problem to show that the person is inside and you can see the person, half in and half out, if you are standing outside looking in. But they are real. Real living members of the Center, not ghosts, everything is real. If someone wants to say they see ghosts, all right, but that would be gloomy. They are very much alive.

Here's another thing. You can be naive but it doesn't mean you are always realistic. Chagall would have a cow flying in the sky. That doesn't make it senseless. So maybe if the people weren't inside or weren't dancing the Hora, they are pale, a little anemic you could say. They became alive when they join hands and danced in a group. This could be, too. Esther said that in the Center when they participate in the activities, they look much brighter. I thought this was very interesting. You see, one person inside is really pale, like a shadow, and the other one joined hands and became already colorful. It is like a little fantasy.

This carries over into the *Oneg Shabes*. You see how everyone here is inside now. Everyone is together and peaceful and very happy.

This is a significant set of comments. The overall discussion at several points makes explicit the elders' free interpretation of history, shaping and idealizing it, bringing it to the level of near-myth. Many of their most strongly held ideals are portrayed, particularly working for others through social change and philanthropy, which is somewhat pathetically expressed by the woman feeding a hungry dog even though she herself was too frail and poor to stand alone. Another important theme is the returning to the peace of the Sabbath, the sacred, expressed primarily in the realm of women and the home, usually at a heavily laden table. The importance of community is another theme that is implicit throughout the mural. And Mrs. Nutkiewicz's statements are interesting for their near explicit claim that the mural does not merely reflect, it actually creates the people's reality: "They painted this picture but they were unhappy with it because they identified themselves with this picture"; and later, by "making the picture happy the conditions depicted are also made happy."

The argument about ghosts is, however, the outstanding element here, establishing with certainty a truly reflexive attitude on the part of the creators of and witnesses to the mural. Their analysis and argument, sorting among the possible symbolic implications of the empty figures, is a metatext, a commentary on the original commentary. In more abstract terms, it is a second-order signification. The mural becomes fully contextualized in this argument, for we hear the creators' exegeses of it. Texts require multiple contextualization to be well read (see Geertz 1980:176–77). In this segment we have such contextualization: the relation of the parts to each other within the text; to the creators of the texts; to the realities lying outside the text; and to those associated with it. What, then, is the meaning of the ghosts? All the suggestions made are valid and germane: the people are unfinished; they continue to grow and change and therefore have a future, for which they need each other, coming fully into their humanity only when they are seen in public, though they never stray too far from the place of their beginning, to which they always return—the Center and all that is associated with it: Yiddishkeit, home, hiddenness, and community.

The Parade Comments on the Mural, and Vice Versa

Since both the parade and the mural are regarded here as symbolic statements, as texts to be read, it is suitable now to read each in relation to the other, intertextually. Do they merely repeat the same message? Do they distort, contradict, reinforce, expand, refine, or shift each other's messages? Do we find in them any information about differences between performed and inscribed texts? Since one is behaved and the other is a picture of ideas, can we draw any conclusions about the relations between action and ideas? Can we go beyond considering both as mirrors and attribute causality or influence of one statement to the other? Finally, can anything be said about the relations of these texts to the existential circumstances in which they occur? These are some of the more interesting questions raised by the data, and they are worth noting, though not all of them can be fully answered or explored in depth with the materials on hand.

Both statements, Parade and Mural, were made for the same purpose— self-knowledge, self-creation through display—and roughly by the same people. Presented diagramatically (see fig. 1),[4] it is clear that both the mural and the parade have a parallel form. In each case the members depart from the safety and familiarity of home, here associated with

---

4. I have begun this reading with the New York/shtetl scene instead of the Mayflower/Statue of Liberty because of the fusion of New York and shtetl, New World and Old. The story which the mural tells is about America, but it suggests the people's reluctance to omit or leave behind their past in Europe. Read as a pilgrimage, the mural suggests a set of nesting circuits: from the Old World to the New, from the East Coast to Venice; and in miniature, the same form is enacted whenever they depart from the Center for an outside public event in which they enact their self-definition, and then return to the Center. The format and message are reiterated.

	Departure from "home" Primary ties Exclusively Jewish Sacred; familial	Protest for social justice Public activity Secular, amid strangers	Liminal zone Venice community Neighbors, lantzmen Strangers, intimates	Return "home" Primary ties Exclusively Jewish Sacred; familial
PARADE	Center	March with coffin, placards	Synagogue	Center: celebrating life (birthday party)
MURAL	New York/shtetl	March with placards	Boardwalk benches	Center: celebrating life (Sabbath)

Fig. 1. Diagram of the parade and mural

childhood, family, and exclusively Jewish communities and made sacred through local custom and deep embedding in culture. These are the profoundly familiar and intimate settings in which daily life takes place. With all its limits, poverty, and conflict, unquestionably it is *home* in the fullest sense. The people depart for a zone of strangers, a secular world to which they do not truly belong but which they try to improve nevertheless through protest for social justice. They are active, resolute, and performing. Then they pass into a liminal zone, betwixt and between, partaking of public and private, strangers and intimates, in their made-up community in Venice where they live with neighbors and *lantzmen* (fellow immigrants). They are midway between inside and outside, somewhat lost. The benches are not truly theirs, nor is the synagogue (for reasons too complicated to discuss here; see Myerhoff 1980). They are described and depicted as "desolate," sitting apart from each other in the mural, not yet having established the Center. In the synagogue they are similarly uncomfortable, partly because they are not habitual visitors, partly because it is being used for secular as well as sacred purposes and includes a great many non-Jews. In both cases the elders are passive, witnessing the activities of others rather than performing themselves.

The circuit is completed in both cases by a celebration back "home" in the Center. At the end of the march a birthday is marked, that of an exceptionally vital, exceptionally old person, a clear rejoicing in ongoing life. Similarly, the end of the mural shows a celebration, the *Oneg Shabes,* a holiday customarily celebrated at home which includes women and children and is associated with all that is intimate, safe, and loved. The Sabbath begins when the woman of the house lights the candles, bringing in the Sabbath and with it a foretaste of Paradise, for a Jew enters Paradise for this twenty-four-hour period.[5]

Together, the mural and the parade sketch the same shape: birth, struggle, and death; movement from home, into the world, and returning home; a rite of passage showing separation, liminality, and reaggregation. These are variations on the same theme, marking the movement through the primary stages of life, individually and collectively, macro- and microcosmically.

Clearly, we are justified in noting that the mural and the parade replicate each other; the mirrors show the same image. As texts, they are redundant. The performed text, the parade, was preceded in time by the inscribed one, the mural, which may have had some influence in shaping behavior. Certainly, no one consciously constructed the parade to conform to the mural. But remember that these people spend all day, every day, within walls that broadcast messages about who they are, what they do, how they do it, where they have come from, and where they are going. This must make a silent, steady impact on them. One might say that the idea of the mural shaped the behavior of the parade; but it is more fruitful, I think, to see them both as symbolic statements, performance and icons ricocheting off each other, dual reflecting surfaces that do more than merely mirror. The parade and the mural are mutual shapers of thought and action.

In these texts we see a group of people creating themselves. The inner world, the more real one, they know they have made up. It is invisible to the outside world, sometimes even invisible to them, as many of its most important features are shadowy memories from the remote past. The membrane that separates the real invisible world from the unreal daily world of the present is permeable, like the curtain that separates the Balinese Topeng dancer from his audience, or the Indonesian *wayang kulit* screen on which shadows appear and dance, reflections of the "real" invisible world of heroes, gods, and demons. Just before he leaps into

---

5. The association of fire, the lighting of the candles, with entering Paradise is very widespread. Here Paradise is clearly associated with a symbolic set: renewal, the transcendence of time and change, *illud tempus,* the return to eternal beginnings and origins, completion, fulfillment, and finally death, at least in mortal, temporal terms.

view, the Topeng dancer daringly shakes the curtain that separates the daily world from the world of illusion. When he bursts forth, we are reminded of the fragility of such boundaries. The imagination incarnated in action does not give us time to pause and consent. It is palpable and must be addressed. No matter how secular the setting, stepping from one world into another is a numinous moment, a hierophany, when the sacred shows through.

These old Jews know exactly what they are doing. Their highly developed reflexive consciousness does not impede their capacity to believe in their creations. Long ago they learned to make hidden, safe, self-determined worlds from within. To quote Shmuel again on his little town in Poland: "In that little town, there were no walls. But we were curled up together inside it, like small cubs, keeping each other warm, growing from within, never showing the outside what is happening, until our backs made up a stout wall." This was an important lesson, one that serves them well in America in their old age. Here, they do not remain inside, however. By enacting their dreams publicly, they have altered the world in which they live. As a result of their ceremonial parade, something has changed externally; through self-display, their commentary has persuaded outsiders to their own truth. Skillfully using strong symbols drawn from relevant, abutting social fields, the old Jews have managed to convey their statement to outsiders, to witnesses who then amplified and accredited their claims. Quite literally, they were taken in. A self-fulfilling prophecy and then some: the reality created by the elders' imaginative statements is not limited to their own minds and beliefs but has become true for nonbelievers, for nonmembers. As a result, the real world has been brought into conformity with imagination, by means of imaginative statements.

Lansing (n.d.) describes the Balinese as remarkable for their ability to "make up an invisible world, watching themselves make it up and still believe in it so strongly that they can enter it." These old Jews do likewise, separating the curtains between real and unreal, imagined and actual, to step across the threshold and draw with them, pulling behind them, witnesses who find, often to their surprise, that they are somehow participating in someone else's drama. They may not "believe" in the claims being made, nevertheless they are incorporated. Having stepped over the threshold, they become the "fifth-business," witnesses who push a plot forward almost unwittingly; their story is not wholly their own but lives on, woven into the stuff of other people's lives.

Surviving Stories:
Reflections on *Number Our Days*

Ernest Hemingway is reputed to have remarked that all stories that go on long enough have the same ending. The question, then, is not how things finally end, but how they unfold, and how much time there is for the unfolding. This essay is the story of how things have unfolded in the allegedly doomed, small community of elderly Eastern European Jewish immigrants who live at the edge of the Pacific Ocean in Venice, California. Their social life has long been focused on the Israel Levin Senior Adult Center, a Jewish community day center, sponsored by Jewish Federation of Los Angeles, directed by Morrie Rosen, whose dedication to this group qualifies him for designation as one of the *lamed vov,* the thirty-six just men who exist in each generation and who by their compassion and generosity help hold up the world.

The community has been amply documented, and in many media. In 1972 I began an ethnographic study there, funded in part by the National Science Foundation. This study was the basis over the next ten years for a film, book, play, and cultural festival. The film, called *Number Our Days,* appeared in 1977; it was directed and produced by Lynne Littman for KCET, the public television station in Los Angeles, and to everyone's astonishment it won an Academy Award for Best Short Documentary Film, assuring it wide visibility. My book by the same name was published in 1979.[1] In 1980 the University of Southern California Center for Visual Anthropology mounted an exhibit of the elders' art works and folklore as part of a cultural festival of Yiddishkeit. And in 1981 the Mark Taper Forum of Los Angeles dramatized and performed

---

1. *Number Our Days* was first published in 1979 by E. P. Dutton; this edition is out of print. A paperback edition was published in 1980 by Simon and Schuster. Myerhoff usually cites the later edition, and this practice has been followed throughout this volume, except for this chronology of the forms in which Myerhoff documented the Center members' community. —Ed.

the play *Number Our Days,* directed by John Hirsch. I have lectured widely about the Israel Levin Center people, conducted scores of discussions, received hundreds of letters.

Everyone eagerly asks: "How does the story end? What has become of them?" If the discussion goes on long enough, they also ask: "How did they respond to seeing themselves portrayed? How has the publicity affected them?" Then: "How has the work changed you?" These are among the questions that I explore here, in 1984, twelve years after the work began. At first I was reluctant to look back and plow well-furrowed fields, but the longer I considered it, the more I realized that the unfolding of their story concerns more than the mere passage of time. It concerns the way they have lived and changed and stayed the same. It is full of teachings: about the importance of stories and visibility as essential to meaningful survival; about the values and problems of participatory anthropology; about the nature and process of cultural invention and transmission; about the necessity and power of performance and witnessing. None of these ideas is new; all are implicit in the book, but they have become clearer and stronger for me and easier to document over time. That is the unusual benefit of having such a long time frame within which to observe a group: change can be seen in the making, rather than inferred from the before and after.

What has become of them? They have not died out. This, then, is a collection of surviving stories, which tell how the elders have survived; a collection of persisting, not-yet-told stories, offered in response to the questions these studies and portrayals have raised. All stories of surviving are miracle tales, and these are no different. The seniors of the Israel Levin Center were expected to have died out years ago. How could they continue? From the beginning their circumstances were perilous. Twelve years later, they are more burdened and imperiled than ever. Housing is more expensive. They are older—now in their nineties and up—more cross, more frightened and fragile with each passing year, but sharpened, honed by the burden and blessing of knowing how remarkable they are in their heroic and improbable persistence. They have outlived statistics and enemies.

Morrie Rosen has allegedly retired and that worries everyone, but the Center has more members than ever. No one knows exactly who they are or where they come from, because no new members can move into the area, given the unavailability of housing. Perhaps the isolates among the original people have been flushed out of their rooms by needs made more extreme by age. Perhaps those who previously were marginal have decided to join and participate, since the Center is livelier than ever before and locally famous to boot. Perhaps those who remain are so strong, biologically and psychologically selected for survival so many times, that they constitute a genuine elite, a blessed group that like their biblical predecessors are meant to live to be a hundred and twenty. One becomes very humble in making any predictions in such circumstances. All that can be said definitively is that the Center membership has slowly but steadily continued to rise and that the new members are like the old members, culturally and socially. There is a contingent of younger members, in their seventies for the most part, but there are not enough of them to have substantially altered the face of the Center population.

Somehow, the Israel Levin Center still brings in close to five hundred people for major events. The boardwalk and benches along the beach still accommodate the arguing Zionists, socialists, agnostics, Orthodox men and women who have not ceased to participate in local and national political and cultural events, as if their debates and critical evaluations are all that keep public life on course. And still in the Center there are singers, poets, musicians, declaimers, dancers, teachers, artists, those who circulate *pushkes* and hold rummage sales for charity, always on the lookout for ways to raise money for Israel, for the poor and the needy. That they themselves are alone, poor, in delicate health, ill-housed, threatened with expulsion by developers, rapacious landlords, and entrepreneurs, physically endangered by winos, muggers, self-absorbed youths on bicycles and skateboards—this in no way alters their sense of commitment to their community, defined as anyone in need, preferably but not necessarily Jewish.

Of course, many individuals have died; many have left for board and care, old age homes, or convalescent hospitals. But the number of familiar faces—people that I have recognized or known well since 1972—is endlessly reassuring, whenever I return.

Since these people do not die when predicted, the problem of severing relations with them becomes very complex and painful. Lynne Littman and I struggled with it continually. After our documentary film, Lynne went on to work on feature films (considered a defection by the elders), and I to study the larger, more complex regenerating Jewish neighborhood of Fairfax (considered as choosing youth over age by the members). Both of us return periodically and experience culture shock each time we come back. Reentering this arena resonant of our own grandmothers, filled with people who continue to inform our choices and imaginations, is a wrench: always the fear that a cherished face will be missing, a lively friend confined to a walker. And there is always their anger if we have stayed away too long; there are accusations of infidelity. (Who has replaced them in our affections? Now that we are "rich and famous," do we no longer need them?) The rush of grateful familiarity and the sense of belonging are always accompanied by floods of guilt. We are children again, eager for their approval, achingly imperfect and vulnerable. And for me, the anthropologist, there is always the problem of having missed information as well as people whenever I am away. It is only our monographs that end. The lives of our subjects persist after we have stopped looking and listening.

The elders somehow have become our touchstones, the fixed and reliable planets by which we navigate our lives and morality. After a particularly materialistic and vulgar bar mitzvah or a skeptical, shallowly felt religious service, I find myself rushing back to the Center to reground myself in their changeless, fully lived, deeply embedded forms of Jewish practice. Lynne returned there for a blessing before her marriage, and although it was not spoken, she wanted their acceptance of her non-Jewish husband. Their children would be raised as Jews. The elders liked her husband's socially committed politics, which he practiced at that time as an investigative reporter. Lynne was called to light the Sabbath candles that day. Their union was approved. To whom else would Lynne go for a blessing? Her mother lives in New York. Her grandparents are dead. We need the grandparental generation for such occasions, and if we do not have our own, we borrow them. It reminds us of Foucault's remark that when we trace our forebears back far enough, they diffuse and dissolve. Genealogy branches out and results in a wider commonality. *Mishpokhe,* the family, expands as the directness and limitation of lineality fades.

I returned on one memorable day to touch base before undergoing surgery. It was to be a hysterectomy, a personal operation. I whispered news of this to Morrie, who, to my astonishment and acute embarrassment, announced it over the loudspeaker and asked people to pray for me. It took all my self-control to sit through the little ceremony, reminding myself that all prayers are statements of good will and, as such, useful, even powerful. Anyway, I was an anthropologist, trained to locate objectivity when I needed it. As I left, several women shouted to me that all would go well, they or their daughters had had such an operation, it was nothing. "Besides," yelled Manya, "how could you fail to recover when you got two hundred atheists praying over you?" Thus they gave me their blessings, laughed at themselves, and demanded a little gratitude, all at the same time. Theirs is not a world in which something is given for nothing. Everything is built around exchange. There are no beggars, no charity, only webs of donors. And so their irony made me laugh, restoring my perspective, mending my embarrassment. We were in this together, and I left them knowing why I had come. This attitude of theirs was what I had so often seen carrying them through the worst of times; it was the subtle, sturdy stuff of surviving.

In April 1984, Lynne and I attended Morrie Rosen's retirement party at the Center. This was the really serious separation. It was inconceivable that he could continue without them or they without him. Over five hundred people attended. The senior chorus sang. People recited their poems and tributes. There were plaques and mountains of gifts. Morrie was given a piece of luggage by the members. "You should really try to get away, Morrie. Get some rest. It will be hard for you to leave us, but you should try." They were still his teachers, his elders. They would make out on their own.

A month later, news came to me from a legal aid society. Morrie had led a delegation to a meeting at City Hall, protesting an attempt to evict Center members from the Cadillac Hotel in violation of zoning restrictions. Was I willing to be called in as an expert witness and testify to the damage done to the community and to the well-being of the elderly, displaced from their homes? Was the man I called "Abe" in my book Morrie Rosen? Was the hotel in which Basha lived the Cadillac? Would I waive the anonymity I had tried to preserve in order to testify? Of course I said yes. It was reassuring to know that Morrie still hadn't retired and would probably be on duty as long as he was needed. And, as usual, the request raised some important anthropological issues. Here was a major one—the importance of attaching names to stories, of allowing witnesses to proclaim what they had seen and lived through, not anonymously, but personally.

Their names and images needed to be recorded to attest to their continuity. This is a particularly sensitive issue to elders whose children have not carried on their heritage, whose peers and natal culture have been extinguished by the Holocaust. And just as important is their perpetual struggle to be noticed in the simple, basic sense of being still among the living, members of a society that tries so often to push them off their little edge of land, from neglect into oblivion. In our society, perhaps all societies, unwanted members are rendered less disturbing by being overlooked, made into nonpersons, erased; and here were people who were pariahs three times over—old, poor, and Jews. Their ceaseless determination to perform their own lives, garner audiences, and be noticed was not mere petulance or immaturity. It was the very expression of their life force, which dictates that one must be seen by others to experience oneself; existence, to be experienced, depends upon membership in the human community. In *Number Our Days,* I talked about the search for "arenas of visibility" in which elders could present themselves to each other and outsiders; this necessity became clearer, fiercer, and more difficult to obtain with the passage of time.

This bore directly on the problem of anonymity and the protection of people's privacy. As an anthropology student, I had always been taught that subjects' names should be changed in one's publications and insofar as possible, their circumstances carefully disguised in order to avoid identification, for legal and ethical reasons. This is not too difficult when one is studying distant peoples, isolates, or nonliterate groups. Disguising people in one's own backyard is another thing. And it was for my sake as well as theirs that I attempted, in the book, to detach their stories from their personal lives and names. My subjects wanted the last word on how they should be understood, and I had decided to reserve that interpretation for myself. Anything else would have resulted in each one writing his or her own book. Some people's stories or personalities could not be disguised, but all of these were dead at the time of writing. Still, I changed their names. Then there was the problem of the existence of the movie. There, real names and faces appeared. The Center, Morrie, the Center president, Harry Asimov (called Heschel in the book), the student rabbi, Andrew Ehrlich, were all identified.

What I had not been taught was that there are circumstances when ethics call for identification rather than disguise. The anthropologist is a witness, must bear witness, when no one else is available. The question "How did the publicity, the many portrayals of these people, affect them?" is complex. If there is a single truth to be offered, it is that they would always rather be seen than be invisible, even if they disagree with the portrait. This was borne out repeatedly. During the Festival of Yiddishkeit presented at the University of Southern California in 1980, one of our presenters, Tillie Olsen, was determined to read her entire novella, "Tell Me a Riddle," to the elders, who had been bused in for a series of performances. I pleaded with her not to. "They are too old to sit still so long. And how will they bear hearing a story about an old woman dying of cancer?" "You'll see," Tillie answered. "They will be rapt. I know what I'm talking about." I was dreading the evening, but Tillie was right. The several hundred Center members in attendance sat more quietly, for longer, than they had done in all the time I had known them. They were enthralled. Afterward, I asked one of the elders if it was not hard to bear. "Of course it was painful. Who likes to look at his own death? But after all, it was well written. And it was about *us*."

This teaching recurred, most dramatically and poignantly, when I discovered that in order for the Mark Taper Forum to present the play *Number Our Days,* Rebekkah Goldman, Shmuel's widow, the only living, identifiable person in the piece, had to sign a new release form giving permission for her portrayal. The release form would allow the theater to present her "fictionally, anonymously, without any claims." I was uneasy from the start. For so many of the elderly, their very lives depended on making claims, on not releasing their identity. I sensed trouble. I searched everywhere for Rebekkah. She had not been seen at the Center for months. I left the permission form with Morrie while I was out of town for a couple of weeks. When I returned, Morrie greeted me with the devastating news. She wouldn't sign. She wanted money, a thousand dollars or maybe fifty thousand dollars. "After all, my husband's writings and my life are priceless. And these are the real heroes of *Number Our Days.*"

The day before Thanksgiving I reached her by phone. "May I come and talk to you, Rebekkah? Is Friday okay?"

"You can come any time," she said. "What about 11:00 A.M. Friday?"

"Okay, Rebekkah, I'll be there."

"But that will only give us two hours."

"Tell me what time, Rebekkah. I'll be there."

I remember Rebekkah scolding me for spending so much time with Shmuel.

"Don't you think my life is interesting too? Have you ever heard me read Peretz? I can bring poetry to life like no one else. . . . You gave me Shmuel's tapes to keep, but I can't work the tape recorder. Also, I can't listen to them alone. Come sit with me to hear them."

"But Rebekkah, there are thirty hours of tapes there." Her demands always escalated. Later: Rebekkah told me she could no longer go to the Center parties because the clothes Shmuel made her were wearing out. My long skirts were so lovely. Did I have any others? I brought three, one an orange velvet, one from Lynne.

"The ones you gave me were so drab, not like the one you are wearing." Did she want me to take it off there in the Center and give it to her? Another time: We are videotaping an interview with a Center member. There is much excitement. Rebekkah looks on, scowls, then plucks at my sleeve. "You should come over today. I found more poetry of Shmuel's. Come *now*. I will show it to you."

I had long known that the worst thing we had done to the Center people was to exclude them from the film, to change their names in the book. Manya was incensed. "You interviewed me for hours, I told you everything. Then you left me out of the movie." Contrite, I gave Manya an immense photograph of herself, publicly, with honor, in front of her friends, and I asked her pardon. "It's no good," she said. "I don't forgive. It's wrong of you to ask me to forgive now, between Rosh Hashanah and Yom Kippur, the Days of Awe, when not to forgive is a sin." Then the film was shown on national TV. She was more annoyed and hurt than before. "I still don't forgive. It wasn't enough you left me out of the film when it showed in Los Angeles. Now it showed in Detroit where my children live. You left me out also in Detroit."

Nervously, I arrived at Rebekkah's apartment. Two television sets sat one on top of the other, neither working. But she didn't like TV. She preferred reading. "These things I read: *Jewish Currents, Spanish for Beginners*"—she still worked on behalf of Mexican migrant fruitpickers— "petitions, political journals, books by Balzac, Chekhov."

"I don't take *The People's World* anymore. Too politically narrow. Will you eat breakfast? I made fresh squeezed orange juice. Myself, I can't eat. I've been so aggravated about all this, I didn't sleep all night."

It dawns on me. Of course. It isn't money she wants, it's my time. "You never come and see me. Let me tell you the trouble I have been having with my lower dentures." We talk for forty-five minutes about her teeth. I drink my orange juice, resigned, summoning patience. Then there is a sudden turn from teeth to politics. "You know, I still work with the Emma Lazarus Club. We were never, what do you call it, subversive. Only for freedom. All my lower teeth were broken out when those boys tripped me last month."

"Rebekkah, wasn't that last year?"

"Whenever it was, I haven't been able to eat meat since then, because of the lower dentures. . . . You always spent so much time talking to Shmuel. He knew a lot, but I too know a lot. Do you remember the first time you met me? I was reading Mendele for the Emma Lazarus. How I can read Yiddish, it is as if you never heard the words before. I don't get myself between the poet and the words. I bring a life into it. I could have been professional." Her hands tremble as she makes me coffee. Her blouse is soiled. Her reading is powerful and her Yiddish is indeed a poem. My heart breaks again along different fissures.

After two hours, we begin to discuss the issue of the release. "You don't know what Morrie did to me, in front of everybody. He made it sound as though I wanted money. Money, for Shmuel's work. I was so embarrassed. No one else in the book is like Shmuel. Everyone says so. Do you know, some of my relatives won't read it. Too narrow. No vision. I didn't spend Thanksgiving with them. I sat here in my apartment and brooded about these things. The Center was closed."

I go over the release word by word. There will be a character based on her, fictionalized, an actress portraying her who may or may not look like her. No claims. Everything is all right until we get to the part about changing her name. "You mean you wouldn't use my real name? How would anybody know it was me? My children, my grandchildren. It will all be lost. You and I know Shmuel's greatness. Without your book, it would have remained hidden. By your work, you put it out to the world. Now, you take that away if you change the name. Why couldn't you use our real names?" Because the Taper requires a release that calls for anonymity. Because there would be Byzantine legalities, issues of invasion of privacy. I explain that this is to be a work of fiction, based on the Center people, but not exact copies. Liberties would be taken. It was moving from anthropology to art. "Rebekkah"—I am pleading now— "you will come to the play. We will invite your son and the Center members, and they will see and know your part in this. Opening night you will come with Morrie, in a long, beautiful skirt. You won't be anonymous. I can promise you that. You will be honored. But I can't promise you will be named in the play." "But if you don't put in my name it passes away. Anyway, Morrie is now mad at me. Will you fix it up with him? Otherwise I can't go back to the Center. It's too hard. I can't eat there if Morrie is mad at me. What will I do?"

"Rebekkah, please just sign this, and I'll go right now and explain to Morrie. He won't be mad at you, I promise."

Her hand hovers endlessly over the page. "Won't I get any money for this at all, even if it goes famous? If it's commercial? What do you mean people don't make money, it's nonprofit? Don't they pay an actress for being me?"

"Rebekkah, if you don't sign this, there will not even be a play. Or there will be a play with you left out altogether. The play will bring attention to the Center, and that brings in the meals on Sunday mornings, the donations for food from the temples. The Weiss family, Mickey Katz, and the Eddie Cantor B'nai B'rith Lodge—all those people have told me they knew about the Center because of the movie. The publicity brings in money, meals, programs. We *need* the play, not just for you and Shmuel but for the Center, for the other older people, and not just for Jewish people—for Mexicans, for all the poor old people, for the grape workers. So sign, or there will be nothing."

"Will this be a good play? Will it be correct? How can you be sure it will be true, if they make it a fiction?"

"I'm working very closely with the writer and director, Rebekkah. They love the material. They love you and Shmuel and are making it very carefully, full of respect and understanding. Art has its own truth. Trust me, Rebekkah. Sign. It's getting late. Morrie will be gone."

"But the name you will use in the play—it must be my real name. It should say 'Rebekkah and Shmuel Goldman.'"

"But those are the names in the book that I substituted for yours."

"That's right. That's where the story is. My own name, no one knows. What difference would it make. In the book I am known. I can show that's me. Let them use those in the play."

"I don't know if they will. Let's try. I'll put down that this is your request, that we use Rebekkah and Shmuel Goldman, not your actual names or any others. I can't promise, but we'll try."

"How should I sign this paper? I'm also known as Regina, it was my name when I lived in Paris."

At noon she signs. I dash to the Center. There is chaos in the kitchen. Morrie had to argue with the mayor to get meals served on an official holiday, the day after Thanksgiving. Everyone is shouting, three hundred old people waiting for lunch, having lived through Thanksgiving alone. Morrie is furious. "Do you know what Rebekkah did to me? Do you know what you have asked me? This is the most difficult thing I have done for you. Three hours I spent with her. I pleaded, threatened. The others were there. They advised her not to sign. 'You're giving away everything. You'll lose a fortune. Everyone else will get rich on your life.'"

"Morrie, never mind. She's on her way over. She signed and I promised you wouldn't be mad, I promised I'd make it up between you two."

"You want me to make it up. *I'm* not even in the play. I'll tell you what *I* want. After the performance when they applaud and call up the author, I want to be up there with you, alone, on the stage."

Rebekkah appears at the kitchen door. The soup has been lost. Was it thrown away as dishwater? Morrie approaches Rebekkah. She has put on lipstick. She wears a gray knitted pilot's cap. She is four feet ten or less. She stands, silently, apprehensively looking at us. Morrie kisses her. "Rebekkah, it will be wonderful. I will take you out to dinner beforehand. I'll drive you opening night. You and Barbara and I will sit together in the front row." I love Morrie all over again. I blush for my own complaining and anguish. Four people accost him, asking for their soup. Bessie wants to know if he knows who took her umbrella. "You see, Rebekkah, Morrie isn't mad at you."

"That's fine. Now would you go out and tell the others, the people out there, that I wasn't just out for money. I have principles, I have ideals. They should know."

"No, Rebekkah, actually I won't. I'll write to invite your son to the play. Now I'm going home."

Morrie walks me to the car. "I'm retiring in a year and a half."

"You can't, Morrie. They can't live without you. I can't live without you. Morrie, how can I thank you?" We embrace. We laugh and cry.

"Isn't she wonderful?" Morrie says. "Look at her, at this age, in these circumstances. How she still has all this power. She's not a victim. You have to admire her."

The play was a qualified success. The audiences loved it; the critics had reservations. The Center members, bused in for a benefit performance, took over as usual. Jennie informed one of the wealthy patrons in the front row that he should change seats with her. It was wrong that the Center members were given seats farther back, with their problems in hearing and seeing. He agreed with some embarrassment and soon the first few rows of patrons had been replaced by the elders. As soon as the play began, Bessie shouted to the actors that she couldn't hear them. "Speak up. We don't hear so good." "Good," echoed John Hirsch, the director. "It's what I've been telling them all along." After intermission, the sound of crackling cellophane was heard from all over the theater. The elders had come from a breakfast in their honor just before the play and had brought along extra lox and bagels for a snack later in the day.

They unpacked their leftovers, and the theater was pervaded with the unmistakable smell of fish. The play continued with a heightened atmosphere of realism. At the end Morrie and I did indeed stand up on the stage together and were given flowers. And at a formal and glorious reception afterward, Rebekkah entered on Morrie's arm, flashbulbs going off, in a room full of elegant and admiring people. The actress who played Rebekkah rushed up to her to tell her how inspiring she found her character. Some of the audience members complained about the "unnecessarily exaggerated immigrant characteristics" of the people in the play. In one of the scenes, a newcomer complained about the elders to the anthropologist. "But why must they always shout and gesture?"

"Because they can't hear," she replies in exasperation. Nevertheless, at the reception, a well-dressed, late-middle-aged Jewish gentleman could be overheard complaining to his wife, "But I still don't see why they had those terrible accents. And why do they have to shout all the time?" And the Center elders argued all the way home on the bus as to whether the representation had been faithful to them. "We don't really argue that much, do we?" "Some would say yes, some would say no. . . ."

The selective identification and recognition of themselves by the elders, by other Jews portrayed in the play, and by the audience was a fascinating phenomenon. The elders wanted more control over their portrayals, though they more or less agreed that the depiction of them was faithful. Still, they wanted the play as a platform upon which to mount their ideals. Younger Jews in the audience reacted to the elders in ways that suggested a reflection of their accommodations to the immigrant generations of Jews in general and to their own immigrant past. Those who had eschewed it were embarassed and annoyed. Those for whom it struck a nostalgic and sentimental response were warmed, even thrilled, rather than dismayed by the overt display of Jewish "ethnic" markers of identity. More than was the case with the film or book, it was possible to read Jewish responses to the play as a kind of barometer of people's adaptation to their social history, their degree of assimilation and, at a deeper level, their attitudes about very complex and personal issues such as their relationships with parents, grandparents, the elderly in general, and the prospect of their own aging.

Later, what stood out in my mind as I assessed the play's impact on the Center people was the subject of Rebekkah's release. In the beginning, her resistance had seemed some combination of narcissism and stubbornness, a desire for power by a person who had, as Morrie pointed out, few occasions for being able to give or withhold something of value. Slowly, it dawned on me that there was something loftier than that involved. She wanted the stories remembered more than her name. She was willing to keep the name I had given her in my book because that was the name attached to her and Shmuel's tales. The tales were her chance for an enduring identity, more than her personal, actual unknown name. She could make it clear to her immediate friends and family that they were hers, using her real name. The protracted and careful rendering of hers and Shmuel's stories presented in the book must remain attached to the names used there. That was where her identity and her chance for some immortality were located. To substitute another name, or to use her "real" name in the play, where the stories would inevitably be changed and abbreviated, would be a loss for her. The character in book and play must be the same, that woman and the stories inseparable. She had become Rebekkah, not in any blind or confused fashion, but because she agreed to let herself be rendered as Rebekkah. She had authenticated that rendering and identified with it. She had few choices. She could remain anonymous or call herself Rebekkah Goldman, since she could not write, publish, and distribute her own interpretation of herself. Thus whenever I brought a stranger or guest to the Center, she introduced herself not by her real name, but as Shmuel Goldman's widow, Rebekkah, so that she would be "recognized."

Members' reactions to their portrayals often demonstrated an almost bewilderingly close identification with them. This was particularly evident in Center people's responses to the film—by its nature the most concrete, repetitive, public, and affective of all the portraits we made of them.

Film and photographic images are overwhelmingly persuasive mirrors, relatively recent inventions in the array of reflecting surfaces people have used to know and identify themselves. There have always been many kinds of reflecting devices used for this purpose. The importance of mirrors for human self-recognition has been widely explored in studies of performance, reflexivity, and ritual, all topics bearing on the nature of observation and the emergence of self. When it was discovered that higher primates could recognize and respond to themselves in mirrors and could distinguish themselves from fellow apes, it was argued that they were closer to human consciousness than scientists had previously expected. Self-recognition is requisite to self-awareness, an attribute humans usually think is reserved for their own species. Pictures, mirrors, and movies are known to allow primates to identify or, perhaps, create "a self," that unique, steady bundle of distinctive attributes, appearances, and behaviors that allow one to say "I am I." This is, of course, true of humans, who recognize and reflect on themselves through performances in all the rituals, ceremonies, and religious and aesthetic forms they invent to tell themselves who they are (and by extension what they are doing there, and what the point is, in the end, of their existence).

Perhaps the most powerful reflecting surfaces that provide self-recognition are other people, as social interactionist theory has long indicated. We see ourselves in others' eyes. We can erase, even slay, a fellow by looking away often enough or looking with eyes that mirror hate; thus curses and the "evil eye" can be efficacious even without words.

In simpler, stabler times, occasions for reflection were assured, the birthright of all who lived within the web of meanings and tales that constitute a coherent culture. Then all the heroes and demons, animals, deities, plants, and stones are variations of oneself, like a dream in which a single dreamer retells versions of himself/herself in all the characters and situations imagined and envisioned. Then every story told is "my" story, about my family and predicaments, past and future. But now surfaces and stories are provided not from within the indigenous reservoir of agreed-on understandings in the group; they are given, and withheld, by outsiders. Accidents, displacing people from their native countries and cultures, may loosen the web of meanings that held people together and thus may destroy the occasions in which they find themselves "properly" (familiarly and appropriately) understood and reflected. And politics plays an immense role in this destruction: disenfranchised, disdained, marginal people are at a loss for mirroring media, and thus often cannot recognize themselves anywhere. If they are seen at all, it is likely to be in caricature, in simple and negative stereotypes that are disorienting and damaging.

In our time, the stories we hear and the pictures we see that give us images of ourselves are most often out of our hands; they have been centralized, packaged, mixed, and sold. It is not unusual to meet, as I did lately, an educated, very intelligent young woman who confessed that she was addicted to television soap operas because "they are realer than my own life." The characters move faster; they are more sharply etched, simplified, exaggerated; they come right to the point; the plot unfolds more powerfully, dramatically, coherently; motives are clear, emotions unmistakable. Whether she likes it or not, those tales have more punch than her own meandering, erratically unfolding story in which the plotline and the outcome are obscure and slow in their revelation. The television image holds the experienced reality of a life, and we, the "originals," are the faded, bored copies.

People's responses to themselves on film have long fascinated ethnographic cinematographers for ethical as well as theoretical reasons. When people who are unsophisticated about technology die after their "images have been taken," their survivors sometimes ask: has the photographer stolen their souls? If a whole village disappears in a slow pan shot across a horizon, how is it to be brought back? When people are shown photographs, or more powerfully, movies, they can often be observed to shape themselves kinesthetically into the person they see on film, verifying the "authentic" filmic version. The French cinematographer Jean Rouche has written on this subject extensively, noting that among Africans he was filming in a documentary on trance behavior, individuals who saw themselves in a possessed state on film were likely to fall into trance again. The replay of the original trance triggered a secondary one. What is the relation between them? Is the original behavior authentic and the second trance a replication, somehow false because it is not spontaneous? Is one real because it is unself-conscious, and the other more real because it is more conscious? Societies tattoo certain markings on their citizens to show them to themselves in a new light: "Now you are an adult, you are marriageable, a full member." These are lessons made palpable, literally embodied. We become emblems. Likewise, the secondary trance, induced by the camera's presence, inscribes society's teachings and, at the deepest physiological level, recreates its images. Perhaps it is a "cine-trance," manufactured by the camera's eye, or an "ethno-trance," an expression of a culture's interpretation of itself, made more sharp, triggered by the heightening of reflexive consciousness that is one of the hallmarks of human experience and one of the points of all cultural performance.

The same process can be observed in interviewing. When one takes a very long, careful life history of another person, complex exchanges occur between subject and object. Inventions and distortions emerge; neither party remains the same. A new creation is constituted when two points of view are engaged in examining one life. The new creation has its own integrity but should not be mistaken for the spontaneous, unframed life-as-lived person who existed before the interview began.

This could be called an "ethno-person," the third person who is born by virtue of the collusion between interlocutor and subject.

Subjects know this intuitively, and for some, the emphasis comes to be on how they are changed by being interviewed, while for others the interest is on how the interview changes the interlocutor. One of the Center members whom I had chased for nearly a year, trying to pin him down to do a life history session, faced me at last and explained his refusal. What I wanted was a serious thing, almost like making a *golem*, an idol, he said. It would forever alter both of us.

"If I would tell you my life and you would really listen, it would change you, and what right have I to do that? On the other hand, if I would tell you my life and you would really listen and not be changed, why should I waste my time?" For him, it was not worth the risk, but that was unusual. Most Center members wanted desperately to be included. They had very few remaining opportunities for being seen, remembered, attended to. And being left out, particularly being left on the cutting-room floor, was a real trauma.

"It's bad enough that you left me out in Los Angeles. Now the movie shows in Detroit where my daughter lives, and you left me out all over again." Manya never forgave us. Each replaying was a fresh erasure of her existence.

Mr. Stoller, on the other hand, was thrilled. "You gave me back my wife by this film." He was referring to the close-up of a photograph of his wife of nearly fifty years, focused on during an interview with him in his room. "After all this time, she comes back to me." The photograph sat on his dresser in his room facing him every day. How, then, had we given it back? It could only be that seeing it blown up so very large had an impact on him, making it more alive than the version in his room. But more than that, it seemed to me that viewing his wife's picture in a public setting, seeing her being seen by all his friends and fellows there in the Center gave her image a heightened reality. Additional life was breathed into her photograph when it was held up to the watching world. There were witnesses who could attest to her existence, to their marriage, who could see his continuing love for her. The audience cospectatorship brought her back into living society, and briefly, magically, returned her to him with a power the picture lacked when, standing mutely on the dresser, it was viewed by him alone.

Whenever we showed the film in the Center, we were struck with people's consistency. Those who watched themselves clapping in the film were clapping in the room. Over and over the same people got up and actually left the Center at the point they were shown departing in the film. And after the first time we showed it, three of the women, having just heard me reflect on how often I was asked, "Who's with your children, madam Professor?" called me aside, said they liked the film on the whole, then asked me who was with my children.

Everyone was happy about the Academy Award and the public validation of them it offered. But Lynne and I were urged not to become too inflated about it. They had, after all, told us on the first day we began filming that if we did our work well, we would get an Oscar. It was clear that we were only the recorders, and it was *their* lives, *their* survival, that was the material to be acclaimed. (And of course if we had failed, it would have been just as clear whose fault that was!)

The film brought the Center immediate attention—visitors, donations, the establishment of programs, some of which went on for years. The capacity of film to change consciousness has always been clear; what had not been so clear to me previously was the extent to which film can be a service as well as a record. And it was and continues to be a source of research information. Now, years and hundreds of viewings later, I still find things in it I hadn't noticed before. And watching people's responses to particular moments is also a source of research data. In one scene, an older woman without a partner dances tentatively at first, then picks up momentum and ends up dancing with great verve, alone and grave, slapping her thighs to the music. It is an emblematic moment in which one can see the crystallization of years of experience: the steps, leading up to the courage to be so alive though alone, are laid out like pebbles marking a path. Audiences of all ages and both sexes often gasp at that image. And Gita, the proud ballerina who is accompanied in her dance by her blind husband, becomes another such emblem. He holds her wrist with reverence, and it is evident that he still sees her beauty. They demonstrate the way two people can use all their artistry and love and years of experience in living together to display *her*, a tiny bent woman, still a coquette, eternally feminine; they execute their routine with the dedication and care one sees in the partnering of Margot Fonteyne by Rudolph Nureyev. At this instant, the Center is no longer a miniature arena; it swells to become as immense as the grandest stage in one of life's most exalted enterprises. The common human impulse for beauty and an exhibition of grace are identified; the couple is not any longer cute or endearing but magnificent. Such a transformation can only be *felt* through film, and audiences consistently find that a mysteriously moving moment.

Some acute observers notice the saxophone player's hands in the dance sequence: he is crippled with arthritis. He has no lower teeth. Yet the music we hear is wild and sweet. Viewers respond to this subliminally, moved by more than the music but unable to say why. Jewish audiences laugh or weep at certain words, certain events that do not similarly move non-Jews. But to our amazement the film managed to cross the ethnic barrier. "That's my Armenian grandmother!" "It's just like my Greek grandfather!" We hear this over and over. It has seemed that the commonalities of the immigrant experience over-ride the ethnic specifics.

One of the lessons of the film emerged from my decision to include myself overtly as part of the story I was telling. The decision to include me had been made on strictly utilitarian grounds: it sped things up and allowed us to discuss some of the invisible issues. Serendipitously, exposing the way I learned about the elders' lives and how theirs affected mine turned out to be of great interest not only to anthropologists but to lay people as well. That the observer is a part of all she witnesses has long been a truism. That the process of the witnessing is very interesting and instructive was not as clear when we began. Unexpectedly, the film's presentation of my discovering and responding to the members' lives proved to be a model and a teaching. Somehow, audiences were less removed from the elders because I was a more familiar figure—American-born, middle-aged, a bridge. Since so much of the receiving of cultural traditions requires a witness, since so much of what the older people lacked and needed were witnesses, it was absolutely right that I filled that role in the film. None of this was evident to us at the time. In retrospect, the showing of the listening and receiving was as important as showing the offering and telling of stories and traditions. The transmission of culture requires two parties in a complex process, and the role of both parties should be made explicit.

This lesson from the film was incorporated into the book. The decision to include myself was immensely liberating. I was able to expose and explore my conflicts and choices instead of presenting them as hardened, closed states or facts; I could unfold them as processes, resonant with elements originating from the research situation and my own personal reactions. It felt more honest, deeper, and finally simpler than any anthropological work I had ever done. I felt more of my reactions being used, wholistically, the way we are taught to study societies. I was thinking with my viscera, feeling with my brain, learning from all my history and hunches and senses. This notion of wholistic knowledge was part of the lecture I was used to giving my students when introducing them to the idea of participant-observation, but it felt as though I was practicing it for the first time, and I could never imagine trusting my own or anyone else's work as fully again without some signposts as to how the interpretations were arrived at and how the anthropologist felt while doing so.

The book was much less important to the Center people—another sort of disappointment entirely. People were either in or out of the film. In the book, such absolutes did not obtain: people were disappointed not to be able to find themselves easily. The careful observers among them noted that the film was the simpler portrait. It was, in fact, a more idealized portrait—the elders seen more as they wanted to see themselves—edited so that there would be no fools or even people who were simply mean. But, of course, such people existed. And the film downplayed the extent of quarreling and dissension within the community. This was a conscious choice. In thirty minutes, it is not possible to present a sufficiently complex picture of an entire group of people; simplistic images, spontaneously presented by "real-life" appearances and performances, are inevitably transmitted. The very concreteness of film presents a clearer, misleadingly precise version of reality. It is much more difficult to control, to shade, to turn over for another perspective. That multicolored interpretation was reserved for the book. Both had different messages. The subjects enjoyed the film much more; it was really theirs. Outsiders, social scientists, younger people were more affected by the multiplex and more protean situations found in the book. And they attached themselves to Shmuel—who was in the book but not the film—with intense devotion and even inspiration.

Disguising people in the book was always difficult, a conventional and practical choice originally, but finally futile. Shmuel's son telephoned me sometime after the book came out. "Is the man you call Shmuel in fact my father?" "Yes it is," I confessed, my heart pounding. Would he recognize and approve of this portrayal? Had I really understood the man? The son was as nervous as I was, and about the same issue. Had *he* really known his father? Had his father been closer to me, confessed more to me than what had appeared in the book? Had his father known he was going to die, and had he, the son, somehow been unaware of that? I was immensely relieved to be able to tell him the only one who really knew his father, to whom Shmuel really opened himself, was his wife, not me, an outsider. And no, his father had not known he was going to die. The son had not missed the reality of the man, Shmuel, that showed in my sustained portrait; it matched, but it was not identical with the man the son experienced in the course of ordinary living. "Your picture of him is not false, but it is too sharp. Distilled. My father was an outstanding man, but there was so much else, so much of no clear consequence. You left out the mundane." "Yes," I agreed; as Shmuel said, "I exaggerated." That is the purpose of framing an individual or an event; there are only choices, no faithful copies.

The final arena of visibility in which the elders "appeared"—an exhibition and celebration titled "Life Not Death in Venice: From Victims to Victors"—grew out of an incident I have described elsewhere.[2] One of the Center members was killed by a bicyclist who ran her down. "I didn't see her," he said, though she was directly in front of him. It was emblematic of all that had grown increasingly apparent to them over the years— the elderly were invisible. After the extensive coverage and attention provided by the film, many members had become very sophisticated about manipulating their images and had grown sensitive to the power they could mobilize by reaching a broader, sympathetic outside public. An article in the newspaper titled "Death in Venice" decried the death. The elders took up the headline as a battle cry, made placards reading "Life Not Death in Venice," and led by Morrie Rosen's always deft political sense, they arranged a procession down the Boardwalk, accompanying a mock coffin (a refrigerator carton painted black, carried on a child's wagon), calling attention to their need for some safety zones where they could walk without being imperiled by bicycles and skateboards. Much media coverage assured them the attention they desired, and indeed, they were successful. A city ordinance prohibiting wheeled traffic in the area was enforced. The photograph of the parade became the logo for an exhibition of folk art and a celebration of Yiddishkeit that we mounted at the University of Southern California in 1980. The title was our own mnemonic device for remembering how important it was that these people were learning to empower themselves by appearing in public and commanding attention.

2. See "'Life Not Death in Venice': Its Second Life" (this volume) and *Number Our Days*, p. 275. —Ed.

Increasingly fascinated by their self-depictions, I began to pay more attention to a mural painted by the elders along one entire wall of the Center, portraying their peregrinations, from the shtetls of Europe, through the sweatshops of New York, ending up at the beach in Venice. It is a complex piece of self-portraiture. For our purposes here, two features are striking. At the heart of the mural they had painted a picture of themselves as young people, parading, marching in union demonstrations, picketing, carrying placards, much as they had done in response to the Venice death. Here, then, was an old model, one that existed on their very walls, alive in their history and imaginations as painting and performance. Second, two of the figures in the last panel were mere outlines, empty of color. I had assumed that the mural was simply unfinished at that point. Then I overheard two women discussing it. "It shows us before we came together, so we really didn't exist completely." "No," the other woman rebutted. "It's because we are unfinished. No matter how old, we are still growing and new things can come in."

We underestimate folk art. I had looked at this piece for years without fully understanding it. How much else would they have to say about their paintings and drawings, which hung about on the Center walls? What were the visual images that accompanied or elaborated the stories that I knew in much greater detail? Periodically, some of them would bring in a few paintings. I had known them as consummate storytellers. Now I became aware that their visual pictures were rich and vivid too. Completely self-taught, overcoming a religious tradition that forbade portraiture and the depiction of images, nevertheless, they made art objects.

I became even more intrigued on the day I accompanied the members to an exhibition of the works of Marc Chagall at the Los Angeles County Art Museum. The docent led us through the corridors, politely reciting the text that had been provided for her. When she got to one of the last paintings, she announced that what we saw was an example of "true art," a work, in short, which was incomprehensible. "You see, there is a tablecloth, floating upside down in the air. Only the free and inexplicable imagination of an artist would have thought of such a thing."

"Excuse me, Miss," Beryl interrupted politely, "but on this I would explain a few other things. What you see here is on the day we call *Simkhes Toyre* [Simhat Torah]. We celebrate the joy that comes when we begin to read the Torah all over again. It means the Torah has no beginning and no end, neither is there an up or a down. So everything is backwards and upside down, or the opposite, to show how special it is, to show the wonder and the happiness and that it is a day unlike any other. This thing that you call a tablecloth, we call a *talis,* a prayer shawl. The painting is not so mysterious as you think. Maybe it is even a little bit familiar."

"But none of this is in my guidebook. How do you know it?" she asked him.

"Myself, I am from Vitebsk, which is Chagall's town, and we knew him. So if you have the time I will take the liberty and show you a few other things you have overlooked." And he did, with the members following along approvingly, full of additional interpretations.

If there was this kind of knowledge inside these people about the visual arts, what else was there to be fathomed? I began to sense the importance of looking more closely at their drawings and hearing their interpretations of them. They were portraying a vanished world, personally felt visions with profound cultural correlates. Their techniques and symbols were not at all self-evident, despite the seeming simplicity and rough technique.

And just at this time, as I was becoming more aware of the meaning of their visual images, the opportunity arose that would provide an arena in which to exhibit their art works and give them a chance of offering a public exegesis, for they would have to be their own docents. The Skirball Museum of Hebrew Union College (HUC) at the University of Southern California (USC) announced an exhibition about the elderly of Venice ("The Golden Age of Venice"), by a photographer, Bill Aron, and a fine artist, Carol Tolin. I felt it was essential that we also provide a space where the elderly could present their own depictions of themselves, to complement and complete the HUC show. The USC Davidson Conference Center, which specializes in programs for adult students, offered the space, its lobby upstairs and auditorium below. Locating and collecting the art work began in earnest in March 1980.

At that time we began to develop a cadre of young people, students in my anthropology life-history class, whose semester's work would be to locate elderly artists and storytellers and document their lives. The young people gathered the elders' life histories, preserved in written form, and at the same time trained them to interpret their art and experiences to the unfamiliar audience of outsiders that we hoped would attend the exhibit. The search was not too difficult; using local teachers in senior citizens' centers and classes we soon found seventeen people between the ages of sixty and ninety-two, all of Eastern European background, all self-taught and nonprofessional, with one exception. Over a hundred pieces were gathered and displayed, representing a great range of styles and media, but all depicting some aspect of the culture of Eastern European Jewish life in the old world and in America.

During the spring, we ran a series of all-day workshops in traditional storytelling, intergenerational journal work, and intergenerational dramatic improvisation. In these we included the elderly artists whose works we had selected for the exhibition as well as those whose works were not used but who expressed a desire for contributing to making a record of their lives.

Young people enrolled, some volunteers, some relatives and friends of the elders, along with other university students interested in art, anthropology, history, Jewish studies, and social work.

The second phase of the project took place over a six-week period in May and June during which we developed a folklife celebration: a series of weekly performances to accompany and interpret the art work. These consisted of a set of rather glamorous events, held in the downstairs auditorium, designed to attract the widest possible audience, which would have to pass through the elders' art exhibit upstairs to attend the evening events. It was a way of gaining a captive audience of people who, we felt, would not ordinarily pay attention to the artists or folk art of the kind we had assembled.

The events consisted of the works of scholars, fine artists, and performing artists that drew upon, interpreted and universalized the original Yiddish sources portrayed by the elderly folk artists. The refined, inflected expression of the Yiddish themes—in the form of films, stories, readings, concerts, lectures, and plays—were readily available to those who were estranged from or strangers to the "Little Tradition," the basic, mundane cultural life of the shtetl that was the living experience of the elders. The folk art exhibit and the cultural events juxtaposed origins and interpretations, actual historical experiences of the elderly and the assimilated, imaginative versions of those experiences by people who had lived it for a short time as children or at one remove through their parents' or grandparents' memories and stories. The performances were selected to show the immense richness and variety distilled from the culture of Yiddishkeit. Abba Eban opened the art exhibit. Isaac Bashevis Singer told stories of his family life in pre-Holocaust Poland; Lee Strasberg reminisced about the klezmer music of his childhood; Barbara Kirshenblatt-Gimblett showed home movies of Poland between the wars; Jerome Rothenberg read poetry from his anthology, *A Big Jewish Book;* Mickey Katz and His Octogenarians offered Catskill and vaudeville music and humor of America in the 1920s and 1930s; The Traveling Jewish Theater performed stories of the Hasidic master, Reb Nachman of Bratzlav; Tillie Olsen read "Tell Me a Riddle"; Georgie Jessel and Baruch Lumet gave stand up one-man shows, comic and dramatic readings in English and Yiddish, respectively. The Israel Levin Senior Adult Chorus opened and closed the series.

Audiences were large, enthusiastic, and heterogeneous. Many were young people who were astonished at finding themselves for the first time among so many old people. "I never dreamt they had so much energy!" was a commonly heard remark. "Where did this stuff come from?" was also a staple comment. "Grandma, you never told me you could draw!" "You never asked," was the reply. The exhibit was full of discovery and surprise, particularly when the young found themselves pressed into providing transportation for old people who found it easier to ask for concrete services than for a more direct and open form of attention. We capitalized on this development by providing free admission to all intergenerational couples who came to the events together. Some lasting unions were established, and our audiences soon included many more elderly people than we were able to bring to the exhibit on our own.

The audience was broadened further when PBS produced a special segment on the exhibit as part of its *Over Easy* television series aimed at the elderly. The visibility we had hoped for allowed us to present the exhibition and celebration as a model, adaptable to people of any cultural group. There is no doubt that there are ethnic elderly people all over America, waiting to be asked, to be discovered, whose art works sit on boxes in the cellar, in trunks, in the attic, whose poems are jammed in drawers, whose reminiscences need to find a witness, a receiver, so that they may complete the interchange that is requisite to all cultural transmission.

In our time we have come to realize that the concept of "image" is not a shallow or trivial affair. Images are the coins in terms of which we are known and valued by the world, and ultimately they are internalized; as such they become the basis for self-evaluation. Appearance becomes "reality," and nonappearance may mean oblivion. When disdained or ignored, people are taught how to control their images, to shape them

in accord with their view of themselves and life, despite often contradictory views presented from outside, they acquire a set of skills that
are nothing less than the means for gaining enhanced power and self-
determination.

Work that is built around portraying a people's interpretation enriches
the society to which it is addressed. We have come to accept our multi-
cultural, multiethnic world as a richer one than the imaginary homogeneous "melting pot" once desired. We enrich the total culture and the
members of ignored groups when we aid them to "be themselves," publicly
and powerfully. It is significant that the elderly provide a model here,
since they represent a human universal, cross-cutting specific ethnic and
regional membership. Assisting them in their movement from victims to
victors is a fitting way to bring about internally generated social change.

We were able to demonstrate the use of folk art as a means by which
the elderly communicate to successor generations and establish autonomy
over their own images, creating their own artistic works and interpretations of their culture in a context in which they see themselves as major
figures. They became, for themselves and the outside world, people who
must be seen, with important images to show and stories to tell, and
so they escaped, however briefly, from their position as invisible victims.
The exhibition also called attention to the riches they provide in their
role as repositories of history and vanished cultures. The entire body of
work provided occasions when young and old came together, to face
each other in the giving and receiving of the lore, the lives, which
ultimately link the generations; and it is only through exchanges of this
kind that we become part of the ongoing stream of history, which makes
our lives comprehensible, coherent, and finally gives us the consolation
to continue.

We did not, unfortunately, have the means or facilities to publish a
catalogue of the artists' works and excerpts of their comments on the
meaning of their art and their artistic process. The closest approximation
to conveying the discoveries of the project can be seen in some of the
captions selected to accompany particular art works. Here are some
examples:

> "This is a self-portrait, how I look to myself. My friends say, 'Sadie,
> look in the mirror.' I see my face and it's wrinkled. But the heart,
> the heart is not wrinkled. Could you see that in the painting?"
> "What I find worthwhile in this effort is a sense of identity and

self-worth, and to be able to say I have made a contribution, however modest, to the enrichment of the human spirit."

"In drawing, like music, you're trying to express. When you're drawing a face you try to bring out something in the face, like you want to say something in music. After all, there you have black notes on white paper and have to make those notes come alive. Now it's the same thing in drawing. You have black lines on white paper and you have to make those lines say something. A curve, even a twinkle in the eye can say something. I like faces because every face is like an unopened box. But each one has to be opened. Each has something to say. Of course, some you open and they are blank."

"When you look at this picture of Anatoly Shcharansky's mother, you see a mother in grief. As a mother, anyone can understand, all the mothers whose children have suffered. You understand? It is perhaps a Jewish theme but it is about yourself. You have that experience. So you don't have to be Jewish to be Jewish."

"My chief aim in sculpture is to express my fellow man with dignity, understanding, and with as much perfection as I can command. I hope that I am able to give others some measure of joy and pleasure through my work."

"When you design, you are an artist. So many things in your head, and you could yourself create the style. An architect, a tailor, and it's the same thing. There are patterns in things, like blueprints. When you put it together, you have made it for the first time. Do you understand what I am saying? Everything has a pattern. You didn't make it, but you brought it out, so you make something new in the world."

"I've been drawing as long as I could remember. We used to live upstairs from my papa's bakery, that was in New York. I remember—he would close the store about 11:00 P.M. at night and come upstairs and shake his head. However tired, there I would be—sitting, drawing still."

"Art to me is life itself, like the children is to the parent. It is my history. It tells a story and I love it."

"A person who works only with her hands is a laborer. A person who works with hands and head is an artisan. But a person who works with hands and head and heart is an artist."

"Painting for me is turning inward. It is how I find who I am. I may start a painting with an idea but in the process that gets lost and I just permit myself to be led by what's happening on the canvas. Most start one way and become something else."

"This what you see is a dead tree, found in Hollywood, come back to life. This particular tree represents the beginning of life. What I have carved from it is the statue of Adam and Eve, inside the trunk of the dead tree. It is placed to overlook the playland of Hollywood, right in our garden—the garden which my wife made our Garden of Eden with all kinds of fruit trees, vegetables and beautiful flowers. So I put this in. It is a real Garden of Eden."

"What does it mean to draw my shtetl? It means you can't forget. They always said to me, 'You should not forget our history, ever, you must remember.' There's sadness in this scene, sure, but also happiness too, because you see I did my job. I survived."

"Let the person who looks at my paintings interpret for their own. I have nothing more to say."

The Center members, I am convinced, will remain indomitably themselves, impervious to outsiders and to intrusions on their customs and morality as long as they live. One of my most vivid memories of a recent visit with them reinforced my realization of the extent of their self-determination. I was going to Jerusalem, where I had agreed to take their messages to put in the *kotel,* the Western Wall of the Temple, along with their notes to relatives, used clothing, old jewelry, a used set of dentist's tools, a pair of drapes, and other miscellaneous items to be given to friends and family. As I was trying to juggle the implements, feeling very much like a refugee myself, Beryl called me aside. "I will give you here one dollar. When I left Russia seventy years ago, my father did this for me. 'Beryl,' he said, 'take these ten rubles and find a poor man in America who needs them. That way your trip will be safe. You will be a *shaliekh mitzve,* a blessed messenger on a sacred journey.'" Others overheard him, and before I knew it, I had nearly two hundred dollars in crumpled bills to deliver to the needy in Israel. An intense argument immediately began as to who should receive the donation. "Not the anarchists!" "Whatever you do, not the ultra-Orthodox. They're against Israel!" "You should find the Arabs who need it the most—that's true charity!" The blind, war orphans, for education—all were passionately urged on me as the proper cause. With no consensus, I felt free to decide for myself, realizing that no one would be happy with my choice.

After much searching, I settled on an organization that provided care and work for elderly Jews and non-Jews who were unable to live on their own, "Lifeline for the Elderly." Founded by Miriam Mendilow, the original group had been comprised of homeless and helpless elderly people, caught in the crossfires of various wars. They knitted, crocheted, embroidered, bound old books, made cards, and raised funds to support themselves in a sheltered workshop. They were very appreciative of my offering and insisted on giving me dozens of items they had made to return to the Jews in Venice who had kindly sent them the donation.

I came back to Venice, bearing the return gifts and filled with apprehension. "What do you mean you gave it to the elderly? What good does that do anyone? You must support youth, they carry on the future. Besides why have you brought these things back? Don't those people know we don't take charity? We were giving to them!" In the ensuing commotion, I slipped away, but not before I heard a discussion developing as to how they could auction off the gifts I had brought back and use the funds to send money to Israel, to the really needy people, and the ones who wouldn't try to send back anything in return.

This, then, has been a reprise of some of the stories of survivors, the surviving stories not elsewhere recorded. There are scores more; it is endless. There is no telling how much more unfolding will occur or how long it will take. It cannot be called a tragic tale or a predictable one. On the contrary, the people seem to have a boundless capacity for passionate, meaningful, self-determined lives, full of irony, dignity, humor, and conscience. No one who has spent sufficient time among them or looked very closely at their lives can feel anything save delight, wonder, and finally awareness that it is a privilege to have shared this time and this place with them.

Part 4
Reflexive Genres

A Crack in the Mirror: Reflexive Perspectives in Anthropology

Barbara Myerhoff and Jay Ruby

Reflexivity and Its Relatives

There is a thick tangle of terms clustered around the idea of reflexivity. Such confusion often accompanies a technical term used in many disciplines and in everyday language as well. In this case it is worsened by the very nature of the activity indicated by the term: consciousness about being conscious; thinking about thinking. Reflexivity generates heightened awareness and vertigo, the creative intensity of a possibility that loosens us from habit and custom and turns us back to contemplate ourselves just as we may be beginning to realize that we have no clear idea of what we are doing. The experience may be exhilarating or frightening or both, but it is generally irreversible. We can never return to our former easy terms with a world that carried on quite well without our administrations. We may find ourselves like Humpty-Dumpty, shattered wrecks unable to recapture a smooth, seamless innocence, or like the paralyzed centipede who never walked again once he was asked to consider the difficulty in manipulating all those legs. Once we take into account our role in our own productions, we may be led into new possibilities that compensate for this loss. We may achieve a greater originality and responsibility than before, a deeper understanding at once of ourselves and of our subjects.

Though reflexivity takes on different shades of meaning in various disciplines and contexts, a core is detectable. Reflexive, as we use it, describes the capacity of any system of signification to turn back upon itself, to make itself its own object by referring to itself: subject and object fuse. A long tradition exists in which thought has been distinguished from unconsidered experience: where life is not merely lived naively without being pondered but regarded with detachment, creating an awareness that finally separates the one who lives from his history, society, from other people. Within the self, detachment occurs between self and experience, self and other, witness and actor, hero and hero's story. We become at once both subject and object. Reflexive knowledge, then, contains not only messages, but also information as to how it came into being, the process by which it was obtained. It demonstrates the human capacity to generate second-order symbols or meta-levels— significations about signification. The withdrawal from the world, a bending back toward thought process itself, is necessary for what we consider a fully reflexive mode of thought. To paraphrase Babcock (1980), in order to know itself, to constitute itself as an object for itself, the self must be absent from itself: it must be a sign. Once this operation of consciousness has been made, consciousness itself is altered; a person or society thinks about itself differently merely by seeing itself in this light.

Reflexivity can be individual or collective, private or public, and may appear in any form of human communication: arts, natural science, the science of humanity or any other contrived uses of, or comments on, experience. Though it may seem modish and new, the idea of reflexivity is indeed very old, existing in the natural as well as the social world. As an example, consider storytelling, an ancient and apparently universal human occupation. In all cultures and times we find embedded tales, stories about storytelling. Scheherazade's *1001 Nights* is a famous example; Sinbad's version of Scheherazade's exploits is a story about a storyteller telling stories. And usually there is a satisfying replication between stories and their frames; we learn about Sinbad by observing Scheherazade and vice versa. Lest one is inclined to regard reflexivity as confined to the intelligentsia, it should be noted that Norman Rockwell, a popular artist, was fond of using this technique. One of his *Saturday Evening Post* covers shows him painting the cover in which the magazine itself appears with a picture of him painting the cover.

Reflexivity is found in the universal activity of dreaming, a story the unconscious tells to the conscious mind. (Among the Dinka of Africa, the word dreaming is translated as a story the self tells to itself.) It is not unusual to dream about dreaming; we awaken wondering not only what the dream meant to say but also what it says about dreaming itself.

"Reflective" is a related but distinguishable term, referring also to a kind of thinking about ourselves, showing ourselves to ourselves, but without the requirement of explicit awareness of the implications of our display. Without the acute understanding, the detachment from the process in which one is engaged, reflexivity does not occur. Merely holding up a single mirror is not adequate to achieve this attitude. The mirrors must be doubled, creating the endless regress of possibilities, opening out into infinity, dissolving the clear boundaries of a "real world." Babcock refers to this as "identity with a difference" (1980:2):

> Narcissus' tragedy then is that he is not narcissistic enough, or rather that he does not reflect long enough to effect a transformation. He is reflective, but he is not reflexive—that is, he is conscious of himself as an other, but he is not conscious of being self-conscious of himself as an other and hence not able to detach himself from, understand, survive, or even laugh at this initial experience of alienation.

All societies have created occasions for reflecting upon themselves: regularly engineered crises, collective ceremonies, celebrations, rites of passage, rituals, public performances, and the like; times when the society tells itself who it is (or how it would like to be or should have been). But these interpretations do not necessarily call attention to themselves as interpretations. Often they parade as other versions of "reality," no matter how fabulous. They masquerade as different versions of truth into which individuals may come and go without realizing how contrived it all is. Rituals in particular may generate sentiments that mostly discourage reflexivity, requiring a mindless and frenetic, repetitive activity that keeps the body too busy to allow the mind to criticize. This occurs even while the event may be precariously fiddling with the frames, mirrors, masks, reversals, screens, clowns, transvestites, and all the other commentators that threaten the sanctity of the order of things being presented. Precariously, a ritual may march along the edge of discovery of its own contrivances, producing not reflexiveness but reflections. These two ideas are capable of coexisting without penetration. The sleep of the unexamined life is one extreme, the achingly clear realization of the nature and process of understanding the other. No doubt most people and events range in between. For both attitudes the devices we call metacommunication are necessary. Markers, frames, keys, clues, and disruptions remind us not to be content with how things seem; something more important is going on. The world as it is being presented is not to be taken at face value.

The term reflexivity is in need of many fine distinctions. We have touched on the fact that it may be public or private, collective or individual, displayed openly or pondered introspectively. Cultures have moments of self-commentary as do people; these moments may be performed in a fully exposed fashion or quietly noted almost sotto voce. The commentary may be sustained or abbreviated, mere moments or protracted examinations. When in a film, conventions of realism are mocked, as, for example, when the main character is a film director making a film (François Truffaut's *Day for Night* or Mike Rubio's documentary on Viet Nam, *Sad Song of Yellow Skin*), we are thus reminded that we are seeing a film, not reality or even a pretend version of reality. But this can be merely an aside, read as a comment on the film's character and the director's work. We can proceed to forget that illusion and reality have been severed and return to the conventional suspension of disbelief, enjoying the film as if we had not been told it was not what it pretended to be, or was pretending not to be what it, in fact, turns out to be.

In more protracted reflexive works, we are not allowed to slip back into the everyday attitude that claims we can naively trust our senses. We are brought into a different reality because the interplay between illusion and reality continues. The frame is repeatedly violated, and the two stories, commenting on each other, travel alongside, simultaneously commanding our attention and creating a different world than either represents by itself.

Since reflexivity is a term used by many people to stand for a variety of concepts, it is essential that we attempt a formulation that includes the various current usages. Let us examine the idea from a communications viewpoint using terms borrowed from Fabian (1971)—PRODUCER, PROCESS, and PRODUCT. We chose general terms applicable to a range of phenomena because the issues raised here are general ones not confined to anthropology. By producer, we mean the sender of the message, the creator of the sign. Process is the means, methods, channel, mode, code, and the like, whereby the message is shaped, encoded, and sent. The product is, of course, the text—what the receiver or consumer gets. To be reflexive is to conceive of the production of communicative statements as interconnecting the three components thusly:

PRODUCER   PROCESS   PRODUCT

and to suggest that knowledge of all three is essential for a critical and sophisticated understanding.

Furthermore, we argue that a reflexive producer must be aware that the conditions of consumption predispose audiences / readers to infer particular meanings from a product (Sekula 1975; Ruby 1977). It therefore becomes incumbent upon producers to control the conditions and contexts in which the product appears if a specific meaning or signification is to be implied.

Significant distinctions exist between reflexiveness and related attitudes such as self-regard, self-absorption, solipsism, self-reference, self-consciousness, and autobiography. Reflexiveness does not leave the subject lost in its own concerns; it pulls one toward the Other and away from isolated attentiveness toward oneself. Reflexiveness requires subject and object, breaking the thrall of self-concern by its very drive toward self-knowledge that inevitably takes into account a surrounding world of events, people, and places.

In an autobiography the producer—the self—is the center of the work. Obviously the author has had to be self-conscious in the process of making the product, but it is possible to keep that knowledge private and to simply follow the established conventions of the genre. In fact, few autobiographies are truly reflexive. To be reflexive is to be self-conscious and also aware of the aspects of self necessary to reveal to an audience so that it can understand both the process employed and the resultant product and know that the revelation itself is purposive, intentional, and not merely narcissistic or accidentally revealing.

Self-reference, on the other hand, is neither autobiographical nor reflexive. It is the allegorical or metaphorical use of self as in Woody Allen's *Stardust Memories* or Janis Ian's song "Stars." The maker's life in these works becomes symbolic of some sort of collective Everyman—all filmmakers, all pop stars, for example. It is popularly assumed that self-reference occurs in virtually all art forms; an artist uses personal experience as the basis of his or her art. The devotees of a particular artist try to ferret out biographical tidbits in order to discover the hidden meaning in the artist's work. Again, there is the cultural fact that we believe it is quite common for producers to be self-referential. What we wish to stress is that self-reference is distinct from reflexivity; one does not necessarily lead to the other.

Being self-conscious has become a full-time occupation among many Americans. However, it is possible, and indeed common, for this kind of awareness to remain the producer's private knowledge, or at least to be so detached from the product that all but the most devoted are discouraged from exploring the relationship between the maker and the work. Only if a producer makes awareness of self a public matter and conveys that knowledge to an audience is it possible to regard the product as reflexive. Otherwise, audiences will not know whether they are reading into the product more or other than what was meant (Worth and Gross 1974).

Being reflexive is structuring communicative products so that the audience assumes the producer, process, and product are a coherent whole. To be more formal, we would argue that being reflexive means the producer deliberately, intentionally reveals to an audience the underlying epistemological assumptions that caused the formulation of a set of questions in a particular way, the seeking of answers to those questions in a particular way, and finally the presentation of the findings in a particular way.

Until recently it was thought inappropriate, tasteless, unscientific, overly personal, and trivial to include information about process and producer in a product. Moreover, it confused the audience and kept it off balance by destroying illusion and rupturing the suspension of disbelief assumed to be vital. Of late, we have grown to recognize our science, and indeed, ourselves, as imaginative works and have become less threatened by the dissolution of barriers between works of imagination and reality. Disbelief is not so often suspended, and backstage (to use Erving Goffman's term) proves to be considerably more alive and full of possibilities than the domains of well-engineered, cosmetic front regions to which we were previously confined.

Reflexivity as a Cultural Phenomenon

In contemporary America, the public examination of the self and its relationship to the ways in which meaning is constructed is becoming so commonplace as to be modish, ironically conventional. To many this is cause for concern. The distinction between true reflexiveness and self-centeredness is not always maintained by social critics who sometimes decry the "Me Generation"—a degenerate society wallowing narcissistically in empty self-preoccupation (Lasch 1978). Mark Sennett locates the demise of public responsibility in this turning inward toward private realms of personal experience. Other social critics remark that we have become a hedonistic, indulgent, and solipsistic lot, escaping self-consciousness by turning to gurus, authoritarian religious cults, and the simplifications of extreme right- or left-wing politics. There is perhaps an area where reflexivity and self-centeredness touch, possibly the point from which they both originated: the restoration of subjectivity as a serious attitude, a basis for gaining knowledge and evaluating it, a ground for making decisions and taking action.

When Thomas Kuhn published *The Structure of Scientific Revolutions* in 1962, he recognized scientific knowledge as the product of a particular paradigm and argued that science changes through the process of discovery of the inadequacy of previous paradigms and the subsequent construction of a new one. Kuhn's argument detached science from reality. Like Berger and Luckmann's *Social Construction of Reality* (1966), it drew attention to the sociological and cultural bases of *all* knowledge. Science was no longer privileged or pure. This recognition has deeply penetrated everyday consciousness (though not as a direct result of public interest in the writings of the likes of Kuhn, Berger, and Luckmann). The secularization of science has been evident for some time. The collapse of yet another authoritative ideology seemed to encourage the turning away from an idealized realm of facts and objectivity toward the recognition that the individual was in it alone. Personal experience seemed to be all that was left to throw into the breach where fixed ideological structures had once been. As we have shown, alienation and self-knowledge are tightly linked, if not causally connected, and reflection, introspection, hedonism, anomie, reflexiveness are all likely to occur under these conditions. A Kuhnian-like change in paradigm has occurred in the popular taste and has appeared in general cultural products, going far beyond the scope of a scientific revolution.

It is now a commonplace to recognize the relativity of experience. Students have heard of "cultural relativity" before they take anthropology courses! That positivism in science buckled close in time to the collapse of confidence in the authority of government augmented the sense that the world was not what it seemed to be. Added to this was the slow democratization of access to the engines of truth: citizens could afford tape recorders, still and movie cameras, then videotape equipment. Reality could be fooled with: speeded up, played backward, stopped, excised, and rearranged. The truth values once imparted to these aloof and utterly neutral records, "the really out-there," were shown to be mere imaginative products. Slowly, then, it became apparent that we do not dwell in a world that continues without our attention or active participation. As a socially made arrangement, it is a story in which citizens find themselves to be among the chief actors. Inevitably subjectivity in such circumstances must return to favor.

Examples of reflexivity abound in all of the arts, sciences, and humanities. Often they are associated with what Clifford Geertz calls "blurred genres" (1983), a confusion about what were once discrete categories for making statements. As examples of blurred genres, he cites "Harry Houdini and Richard Nixon turning up as characters in novels, . . . documentaries that read like true confessions (Mailer), parables posing as ethnographies (Castaneda), theoretical treatises set out as travelogues (Lévi-Strauss); . . . one waits only for quantum theory in verse or biography in algebra. We cannot tell literature from criticism, treatise from apologetic. . . . Something is happening to the way we think about the way we think." This, he points out, is a redrawing of the cultural map, wherein we see fewer fixed types divided by sharp boundaries. "We more and more see ourselves as surrounded by a vast almost continuous field of variously intended and diversely constructed works we can order only practically, relationally, and as our purposes prompt us" (1983). Social science turns out to be built on models taken more from aesthetics, gaming, theater, literature, play, and the like than the earlier principles, laws, and facts of science (Schechner 1982).

Geertz sees the major branches of social science as falling into three groups: those which see social life as a game (Erving Goffman); as social drama (Victor Turner); and as "texts" (Geertz and others). All have in common an emphasis on interpretation, a view of the world as basically constructed and symbolic. Reality is not discovered by scientific tools and methods but is understood and deciphered through a hermeneutic method. A profoundly different world view is implied, "a refiguration of social thought."

In the arts reflexiveness and its relatives may describe the literary characteristic that is apparent in the *Odyssey,* in figures such as Cervantes and Wordsworth, and in modern writers such as Gide, Joyce, Proust, Mailer, Updike, Barth, and Borges. Autobiography has been perhaps the strongest mode for postwar minority expression in the United States (*The Autobiography of Malcolm X, Coming of Age in Mississippi*). Increasingly writers have turned to autobiography as an avenue for self-expression (Margaret Mead's *Blackberry Winter),* as a technique for inquiry, and as material for study (the popular books by Oscar Lewis,

Erik Erikson's study of Ingmar Bergman's *Wild Strawberries*); and psychiatrists report that narcissism has become a familiar presenting symptom. We find recurring films about filmmakers, prints of printmakers making prints, photographs of photographers and their equipment, plays about playwrights.

Scientists, philosophers, and social scientists have also been engaged in reflexive activities. Psychoanalysts have been concerned with the ways in which the act of observation affects the results of the doctor-patient relationship, philosophers with the necessity of thinking about thinking, sociologists with the ways in which the investigator's culture alters the methodological process itself. Historians have applied the techniques of historical analysis to examine and revise the historical method, and scientists continuously test their own assumptions and procedures. Computers are used to check computers, and systems analysis is applied to systems analysis.

The phenomenon of the process of creation as the subject of creation, the mode and meaning of research as the subject of research, thought as the subject of thinking—in short, the inalienability of the self in cognitive and creative acts—may become, in turn, the subject of study.

To chronicle and describe these manifestations—modern and historical—would require a book-length treatment. We have merely cited a few examples in order to suggest that anthropological reflexivity is not unique nor is the interest in it merely the newest fad.

Music

Self-consciousness, self-reference, autobiography, and reflexiveness appear in the lyrics of popular songs and in performances, recorded and live. (The remarks that follow reflect personal interest in and knowledge about popular music and jazz. Similar examples undoubtedly exist in other musical forms.)

Lyrics

It is popularly assumed that composers and performers, like most Western artists, write and sing about their own personal experiences and convictions. Hence most popular song lyrics are thought to be by definition autobiographical or at least self-referential. The lyrics are regarded as a symbolic system, and young people spend much time trying to ferret out the true meaning of a song's lyrics: was "Mr. Tambourine Man" Bob

Dylan's connection? Who was Carly Simon singing about in "You're So Vain"? Some of the personal references in lyrics are so arcane and obtuse (such as Bob Dylan's "Sad-Eyed Lady of the Lowlands") they resemble South American myths and require a Lévi-Strauss to untangle them. Others are self-referential, like Janis Ian's "Stars," and still others overtly autobiographical, such as Dylan's "Sara."

The balladeer tradition of telling stories through song is an old Anglo-American musical form. At least since the emergence of rock music in the sixties, audiences have held composer/singers personally responsible for the content of their lyrics. Audiences expect these artists to believe in the personal, social, and political implications of their songs. It's very much like the song gospel singer Mahalia Jackson used to sing: "I'm Going to Live the Life I Sing About in My Songs." The personal lives of artists are critically examined by their fans to see to what degree they match the sentiments expressed in their work.

While autobiographical and self-referential statements abound, lyrics which are truly reflexive are rare. One clear exception is to be found in Carole King's song "So Far Away" (*Tapestry*): "One more song about moving along the highway / Can't say much of anything that's new. . . ." These lines clearly acknowledge that the song is an example of a song type (actually the reference is much more complicated, but for our purposes we can leave it there).

Performances and Records
If any act that deliberately attempts to test an audience's assumptions about the parameters of an art form is a reflexive act, all of John Cage's performances are reflexive. Most recordings are from a realist tradition that seeks to provide audiences with the illusion of firsthand experience. However, backstage moments, when the performer reminds the audience it is listening to a recording and not participating in a live performance, are reflexive. For example, Dylan, in the *John Wesley Harding* album, begins one song by asking the engineer/producer Bob Johnson if he is ready to record: "Are you rolling, Bob?" This type of patter exists on the heads and tails of all studio tapes. It wasn't planned. The only explanation for the inclusion being intentional is the assumption that Dylan or someone connected with the release of the record (the problem of authorship with records is a complex one) decided to include that which is normally excluded. In the album *We're Only in It for the Money,* one hears Frank Zappa musing about the engineer and his activities in

the sound booth. These musings are not part of the normal backstage of recording. They constitute a deliberate attempt by Zappa to remind audiences they are listening to a recording.

Zappa's reflexive concerns are also found in the liner notes of his albums. "This is an album of greasy love songs and cretin simplicity. We made it because we really like this kind of music (just a bunch of old men with rock and roll clothes on sitting around a studio, mumbling about the good old days). Ten years from now you'll be sitting around with your friends someplace doing the same thing if there's anything left to sit on" (*Ruben and the Jets,* Bizarre Records, V6 5055-X, 1971).

And, "Note: All the music heard on this album was composed, arranged, and scientifically mutilated by Frank Zappa (with the exception of a little bit of surf music). None of the sounds are generated electronically . . . they are all the product of electronically altering the sounds of NORMAL instruments. The orchestral segments were conducted by SID SHARPE under the supervision of the composer" (*We're Only in It for the Money,* Bizarre Records, V/V6 5045X, 1967).

And, "The music on this album was recorded over a period of about five months from October 1967 to February 1968. Things that sound like a full orchestra were carefully assembled track by track through a procedure known as overdubbing . . ." (*Uncle Meat,* Reprise Records, 2024, 1968).

Art

Self-portraits and self-reference in painting make their appearance by at least the fifteenth century. Jan Van Eyck's *Giovanni Arnolfini and His Bride* (1434) may be one of the earliest paintings to carry these ideas into a reflexive stance. In the middle of the canvas Van Eyck painted a mirror with the reflections of three people peering into the room—one of them being Van Eyck. Lest anyone not know his face, he wrote "Van Eyck was here" over the mirror.

One can easily characterize the entire Modernist movement as having a reflexive concern. The Dadaists, Surrealists, Pop, Funk, Conceptual, and Minimal artists, as well as those involved in Happenings and Performance art, all ask their audience/viewers to become self-aware about their definitions and expectations about art. (The Photorealists belong in this category and indeed the entire recent return to realism in painting, but that argument is too long and tangential to be useful here.) Among the more obvious artists who works abound in reflexivity are Duchamp, Magritte, and Warhol.

Leo Steinberg, in his brilliant introductory essay to a catalog on *Art about Art* (1978), has examined the concepts of borrowing, citing, referencing, commenting, and other means whereby one artist will explore another's work. As Steinberg points out, the primary message of these paintings and indeed of many paintings is a comment about art, that is, a reflexive communication.

In attempting to explain his Neon art, Annson Kenny, a Philadelphia artist, said, "Let me make an analogy. If I were an architect, I guess I would insist on exposed beams, and maybe I carry this sensibility too far. For if there were no beams I would insist they be installed. And if that were impossible then I would insist we construct artificial beams so that we have something to expose."

Journalism

"New Journalism," according to one of its chief practitioners, Tom Wolfe, is the writing of "accurate non-fiction with techniques usually associated with novels and short stories" (Wolfe and Johnson 1973:15). Wolfe suggests that new journalism is the direct descendant of the realist novel and the chief proponent of literary realism in the sixties and seventies.

While Wolfe looks to reporting and novel writing as the major sources of new journalism, there are two he overlooked—movies and social science, particularly anthropology and sociology. Scene by scene construction and realistic dialogue, as Wolfe points out, are found more frequently in films than in novels, particularly in the last twenty-five years. Secondly, it is possible to argue that the recognition of the need for detailed descriptions of the cultural settings and artifacts comes as much from anthropology and sociology as it does from the novel. The new journalism can be viewed as a popular manifestation of the same set of ideas that spawned the work of Erving Goffman (1956), the ethnomethodologists, and the phenomenologists, that is, a concern with accurate, realistic descriptions of the everyday life of ordinary people. Viewed from this perspective, new journalism is perhaps the widest spread of the concept of culture as a means of understanding human existence. In addition, new journalists, like ethnographers, are more concerned with "common" folk than with superstars. This interest clearly separates new journalists from their more traditional brethren.

While the new journalists have been influenced by social science, the reverse is less true. Few anthropologists have experimented by attempting to incorporate stylistic features borrowed from journalists or novelists. Oscar Lewis is a rare exception. Compare his book, *Five Families* (1959), with chapter one of Albert Goldman's *Ladies and Gentlemen, Lenny Bruce!* (1974). Both employ the composite "day-in-the-life" construction.

Without doing violence to the connotation of the term, it is possible to see new journalists as "folk" or naive ethnographers. We call them this (although it is hard to imagine Tom Wolfe in his ice cream suits belonging to any folk) for several related reasons: they seem to lack a self-awareness of the implicit epistemological basis for their activities; they do not appear to understand the folk models of description and explanation they employ in their writings; they have no desire or ability to go beyond their intuition and become rigorous, that is, social scientific. Wolfe and others like him are behaving *like* ethnographers and producing writings that clearly *resemble* ethnography, but we are not suggesting that they are ethnographers doing ethnography.

Their need to understand the scenes, dialogues, characters, artifacts, and settings of human activities forces them to become participant-observers and, like the ethnographer, to actually hang out with the people they are writing about. "They developed the habit of staying with the people they were writing about for days at a time, weeks in some cases" (Wolfe and Johnson 1973:21). The new journalists' methods are quite unlike the "literary gentlemen with a seat in the grandstand" school of journalism and the "wham-bam-thank-you-Ma'am" approach to interviews by reporters.

So-called "investigative" reporting, made popular by Woodward and Bernstein of the *Washington Post,* is obviously related to new journalism in the sense that both employed participant-observation as part of their methodology and fiction devices in their presentational styles. Wolfe would like to disassociate new journalism from investigative reporting on the basis that investigative reporting comes from the tradition of politically motivated advocate reporting, and new journalism has no such overt political tradition (1973:42–43).

Regardless of how these two are related historically, it is clear that a large number of people who call themselves journalists, nonfiction writers, and reporters have discovered the need for participant-observation and employ styles of presentation that make their writing resemble ethnographies.

Pop sociology and anthropology have come of age. Unfortunately when one examines new journalism more closely, one discovers a naive concept of realism. Wolfe describes new journalism as an amalgam of several devices: "The result is a form that is not merely *like a novel*. It consumes devices that happen to have originated with the novel and mixes them with every other device known to prose. And all the while, beyond matters of technique, it enjoys an advantage so obvious, so built-in, one almost forgets what a power it has: the simple fact that a reader knows all *this actually happened*. The disclaimers have been erased. The screen is gone. The writer is one step closer to the absolute involvement of the reader that Henry James and James Joyce dreamed of and never achieved" (1973:34).

Wolfe seems to be saying that the literary conventions of social realism, originated by nineteenth-century novelists such as Dickens, Balzac, and Zola and now employed by the new journalists to deal with "real-life" situations (as opposed to their original intended use, which was to create a fiction of verisimilitude), are not merely conventions with socially agreed upon significance and meaning but devices that provide readers with "what actually happened."

> Novelists have made a disastrous miscalculation over the past twenty years about the nature of realism. Their view of the matter is pretty well summed up by the editor of the *Partisan Review,* William Phillips: "In fact, realism is just another formal device, not a permanent method for dealing with experience." I suspect that precisely the opposite is true. If our friends the cognitive psychologists ever reach the point of knowing for sure, I think they will tell us something on this order: the introduction of realism into literature by people like Richardson, Fielding and Smollett was like the introduction of electricity into machine technology. It was *not* just another device. It raised the state of the art to a new magnitude. (1973:34)

This naive belief in realism serves to perpetuate several unfortunate folk beliefs that must be destroyed or at least discredited in order for any social science purporting to be reflexive to achieve general acceptance or even comprehension. Wolfe's simple faith in realism has to be based on the discredited idea that "the world is as it appears to be" (called phenomenal absolutism by Segall, Campbell, and Herskovitz 1966:45).

The logical corollary of this idea is that it is possible to make bias-free, value-free descriptions of the world that are accurate and realistic.

If one shares Wolfe's view, it is logical to posit a particular role for the new journalist. If the world is objectively describable, the journalist's ethical and professional responsibility is to become as transparent as possible, that is, allow the reality of the situation to predominate. From this point of view (one shared by many social scientists and filmmakers), opinions, characterizations, views of the world are never the property of the author. The author is merely the vehicle for the people he or she writes about.

In some respects new journalism is antithetical to a reflexive social science. However, its popularity helps to create a useful tension and ambivalence among readers—to confuse and confound audiences in ways similar to the confusion experienced with all blurred genres. The neat and simplistic division into fiction and nonfiction or reality and fantasy clearly cannot be used to evaluate these works.

This creative confusion is obviously not confined to the printed word. There is a similar tradition in documentary film. Jim McBride's *David Holzman's Diary* and Mitchell Block's *No Lies* follow the conventions of documentary realism. They are in fact fiction films. There is a major difference between these films and the writings of new journalists. Once the credits appear, members of the audience know they have seen a fiction film that merely fooled them into thinking it was a documentary. With new journalism one can never know which is which. The fiction film disguised as a documentary makes one aware of the conventions of documentary realism and therefore establishes the possibility of one being "fooled" by films that are not what they purport to be. This filmic confusion has reached an apex with the so-called docudramas, which follow the conventions of fiction yet apparently cause some people to believe they are documentaries because they deal with recent history.

New journalism can make one aware that the entire system dividing mediated messages into nonfiction or documentary or real versus fiction or fantasy is misleading and not particularly useful. To read something that is concerned with real people engaged in actual behavior and discover that it reads like a novel can cause readers to question their assumptions about narrativity, fiction, documentary, and even the conceptual basis of their version of reality. It can also lead them to ponder the role and responsibility of the authors/creators of mediated messages.

Some contemporary fiction writers, as we have already suggested, are expressing reflexiveness in their works. We think it is significant that such different sorts of writers as John Updike, Kurt Vonnegut, Bernard Malamud, Philip Roth, and John Irving have been writing fiction in which the writer confronts himself in the act of writing or in his role as an author. If in some ways this can be seen as a throwback to the eighteenth-century, self-conscious narrator of Fielding, it is also a very modern reaction against the well-known dehumanization of art in this century.

The novel has had an interesting history, which in many respects parallels the development of ethnography (Edgerton and Langness 1974; Rabinow 1982; Marcus 1982; Parssinen 1982). It is therefore not surprising to discover that novelists and anthropologists are both concerned with the implications of reflexiveness. To further complicate the relationship between these two forms, one can find novelists such as Vonnegut and Saul Bellow trained in anthropology.

One formal feature separating the novel from the ethnography is the fact that realistic novels, at least, employ a narrative form, while ethnographies are seldom, if ever, written as narratives. Narratives, particularly in the first person, are considered by most anthropologists and social science writers to be too personal and too subjective to be vehicles for scientific communication. It is ironic and also symptomatic of the set of problems raised by this essay that first-person narrative is perhaps the most natural way of describing experience—including the experience of doing fieldwork (Jay 1969). It is difficult to express your self-awareness and reflexiveness to others without employing some first-person narrative. Once the need to be reflexive is more widely recognized, narrative form will become more acceptable as the rhetorical form most logical for the communication of anthropology.

We have only touched on the range of examples of reflexive consciousness in our culture. Its faddishness may pass, but the consequences of being reflexive are permanent. Once you enter into the process, it is not possible to return to the naive assumptions of the past.

Reflexivity as Anthropological Praxis

Reflexivity is used in anthropology in a number of different ways. It can be a means of examining a field problem, that is, to refer to the study of the "Natives'" reflexive acts, those events wherein, as Victor Turner puts it, "[t]he community . . . seeks to understand, portray, and then act on itself, in thought, word and deed . . . public reflexivity takes on the shape of a performance." This is what happens when a group formally steps out of itself, so to speak, to see itself, and is aware of so doing. Clifford Geertz's explication of a Balinese cockfight is a classic case, in which we clearly see the Balinese playing with their most serious conceptions (1973:412–53). They are performing a story about their society intentionally and, it might be said, literally, rather than metaphorically, since they enact rather than merely refer to the interpretation involved.

Reflexivity is also a means of examining anthropology itself. Anthropology, as a branch of science, is required to be explicit about its methods. Science is reflexive insofar as its findings refer back to the system in which they are explained, making clear the means by which they were assembled. Labrot (1977) put it this way:

> Science is not static. Its development is determined to a great extent by the body of science as it stands at any given moment. This determination is not one of a natural progression to a greater and greater number of known facts built on those previously discovered. It is rather one in which the fundamental principles, the structures in a broad sense, determine the nature of the search for the facts and finally to some extent, the facts themselves. So science, which describes the world, also determined the world which it described.

This interpretation is becoming, as we indicated, widespread in all branches of knowledge. The radical objective / subjective dichotomization of experience disturbed many scientists long before reflexivity became popular. Gunnar Myrdal warned against the trap of believing in a "disinterested social science," which he insisted for logical reasons could never exist. It could only confuse and leave the researcher unaware of the operations of his or her biases.

All social sciences deal with human beings as subjects of study, but in anthropology special problems arise because of the complex relationship between the ethnographer and the subject of study. It is through the understanding of self-to-other that the investigator comes to examine culture. Often the collective, impersonal portrait of a culture is penetrated. Key informants may jump out, however briefly, standing apart from the generalized picture of the group—truly idiosyncratic people—ones who demand to be reckoned with on their own terms. Because the ethnographer is enjoined to use immediate experience to "verstehen" (borrowing Weber's term), that is, intuitively understand and empathize, he or she must project and identify. These are invaluable but not universally shared abilities that can only be employed by an individual with a finely honed sense of self. It was not mere partisan ideology that caused the early theorists in Freudian anthropology to recommend that ethnographers' studies would be improved if they undertook to be psychoanalyzed. These days we are more ecumenical; we would recommend not five years on the analyst's couch but any personal study that develops the anthropologist's self-awareness of his or her own culture. With increased self-awareness, studies can be not only more penetrating but also more reliable.

The anthropologist, as a data-generating instrument who must also make explicit the process by which he or she gathers data, is an integral part of the final product: the ethnography. The anthropologist must take his or her behavior into account as data. To quote Lévi-Strauss (1976), participant-observation, the basis of fieldwork methodology, makes this essential.

> To Rousseau we owe the discovery of this principle, the only one on which to base the sciences of man. . . . In ethnographic experience, the observer apprehends himself as his own instrument of observation. Clearly he must learn to know himself, to obtain from a *self* who reveals himself as *another* to the *I* who uses him, an evaluation which will become an integral part of the observation of other selves.

Thus the public examination of the anthropologist's response to the field situation, the inclusion of methodology, and participation in constructing the final report is reflexive in anthropology. The examination of the *form* in which ethnographic data are reported also becomes a reflexive act, that is, creating an ethnography of anthropology.

To refer to our earlier paradigm, producer, process, and product may be fully included. The process or methodology is made overt, the investigator portrayed. But in anthropology another layer may be entered into this equation: the effect of the anthropologist looking at the native looking at the anthropologist (cf. Michaels 1982). We enter the hall of mirrors, the infinite regress, yet it is undeniably necessary. The subject changes by being observed, and we must observe our impact on him or her and the resultant impact on ourselves and. . . . To refer again to the

Balinese cockfight, we first see the anthropologists looking at the Balinese, and the Balinese looking back at them; then a change occurs as
the Balinese alter their attitudes toward the anthropologists, who in turn
begin to see the Balinese differently.

Ethnographer-filmmaker Jean Rouche has some thought-provoking
comments on this matter. Borrowing Vertov's term "cinema-eye" (used
to describe a way of seeing with the camera eye that is different from
seeing with the human eye), it can be said that the ethnographer also
alters his ordinary modes of perception in the field.

> In the field the observer modifies himself; in doing his work he is
> no longer simply someone who greets the elders at the edge of the
> village, but—to go back to Vertovian terminology—he "ethno-
> looks," "ethno-observes," "ethno-thinks." And those he deals with
> are similarly modified in giving their confidence to this habitual
> foreign visitor they "ethno-show," "ethno-speak," "ethno-think."
>
> It is this permanent ethno-dialogue which appears to me to be
> one of the most interesting angles in the current progress of eth-
> nography. Knowledge is no longer a stolen secret, devoured in the
> Western temples of knowledge; it is the result of an endless quest
> where ethnographers and those they study meet on a path which
> some of us now call "shared anthropology." (1978:8)

Rouche does not go to the extreme of calling his subject an ethno-
person, but it would not be unreasonable to do so. The anthropologist
and the subject of study together construct an interpretation of a cultural
feature, an understanding of the interpreter, that would not have come
into existence naturally. The study is an artifice and resembles nothing
but itself, a collusion of two viewpoints meeting in a middle terrain,
created by the artificial circumstances of the foreigner's visit and project,
disappearing when the foreigner departs. Both the portrait of self at
work in the field (if it includes the impact of the natives' vision of self)
and, equally, the impact of the native on the ethnographer are constructions arising out of the ethnographic enterprise, studies of ethno-persons.

> The human scientist has had to learn how to relate self-knowledge
> of him- or herself as a multisensory being with a unique personal
> history as a member of a specific culture at a specific period to
> ongoing experience and how to *include* as far as possible this

disciplined self-awareness in observation on other lives and in other cultures. (Mead 1976:907)

We now wish to explore an apparent paradox within anthropology, which both reveals the need for a reflexive anthropology and explains its absence. It can be expressed as follows: Why do most anthropologists identify themselves as scientists and their work as scientific yet often fail to describe adequately the methods employed in their research and to account for the possible effects of the researcher on the research? Why is Malinowski's fifty-year-old admonition so seldom followed (1922:2–3)?

The results of scientific research in any branch of learning ought to be presented in a manner absolutely candid and above board. No one would dream of making an experimental contribution to physical or chemical science, without giving a detailed account of all the arrangements of the experiments; an exact description of the apparatus used; of their number; of the length of time devoted to them; and of the degree of approximation with which each measurement was made . . . in Ethnography, where a candid account of such data is perhaps even more necessary, it has unfortunately in the past not always been supplied with sufficient generosity, and many writers do not ply the full searchlight of methodic sincerity, as they move among their facts, but produce them before us out of complete obscurity.

A general examination of ethnographic literature reveals a fairly consistent lack of systematic, rigorous statements on method and discussions of the relationship between research and the researcher. Recently this trend has shifted with the publication of works like Berreman's *Behind Many Masks* (1962). While this and other books may signal a change, Bellah is unfortunately still accurate when he states that, "Rarely have anthropologists regarded fieldwork as a serious object of study, it is tacitly accepted as their major activity" (Rabinow 1977:ix).

In an unpublished study of reflexive elements in written ethnography, Miller (1977) has suggested two places where they are most likely to be found outside of the work, one of them being in introductory remarks or prefaces or postscripts. The tradition appears to have begun with Malinowski (1922). Yet in spite of his admonition to others, Malinowski's own methodological statements were rather perfunctory. As Young (1979:11) points out:

> Despite his incorrigible self-dramatisation and his claim that "the facts of anthropology attract me mainly as the best means of knowing myself" (Malinowski 1932:xxv), Malinowski did not propose any theory which included the observer in its frame of reference. . . . He mentions the "personal equation" of the investigator only to caution against selectivity in observation and recording, and he counsels the keeping of an "ethnographic diary" of events as a corrective measure (1922:20–21). Paradoxically, however, the field diaries which Malinowski himself kept (1967) constitute an entirely different form of document—one which, in laying bare his prejudices, gives the lie to his public image and puts his sincerity severely to the test.

Other examples of "reflexive" instructions in ethnographies include Bateson's *Naven* (1936), in which the work is bracketed with reflexive statements in the preface and postscript (cf. Marcus 1982).

The other location of reflexive elements Miller found was in travelogue-like, popularized or anthropological accounts of fieldwork. For example, Maybury-Lewis in his introduction to *The Savage and the Innocent* states that,

> *This book is an account of our experiences, it is not an essay in anthropology* (emphasis ours). Indeed I have tried to put down many of those things which never get told in technical anthropological writings—our impressions of Central Brazil, our personal reactions to the various situations in which we found ourselves, and above all, our feelings about the day-to-day business which is mysteriously known as "doing fieldwork." (1965:9)

Other examples of this form of reflexivity would include Lévi-Strauss's memoir, *Tristes Tropiques* (1955), Alex Alland's account of his fieldwork in Africa (1975), and Hortense Powdermaker's professional autobiography, *Stranger and Friend* (1966).

Perhaps the most extreme form of separation of reflexive elements from the ethnography is to be found in the writing of a novel about fieldwork under a pseudonym (Bowen 1954). While we have not systematically examined the question, it is our impression that more anthropologists than any other social scientists write novels, plays, poems, and science fiction. We believe they do so because of the strictures imposed by traditional science on the reporting of experience. They cannot do it in their ethnographies so they seek other outlets.

Further, anthropologists who want to be reflexive and still report on their fieldwork in a "scientific" manner have found it difficult to locate an acceptable form. "*The Jungle People* has a plot because the life of the Kaingang has one. Yet, since behavioral science views life as plotless, *The Jungle People* violates an underlying premise. Moreover, in behavioral science, to state that life not only has a plot but must be described as if it did is like spitting in Church" (Henry 1964:xvii). Hymes states the conflict between the reporting of experience in ethnography and the scientifically acceptable communicative forms quite well (cf. Parssinen 1982): "There is an inescapable tension in ethnography between the forms, the rhetorical and literary forms, considered necessary for presentation (and persuasion of colleagues), and the narrative form natural to the experience of the work, and natural to the meaningful report of it in other than monographic contexts. I would even suggest that the scientific styles often imposed on ethnographic writing may produce, not objectivity, but distortion" (1973:199–200).

In addition to an anti-narrative tradition within the canons of scientific communication, there are two additional strictures that further conflict with reflexivity. Scientists are supposed to use the passive voice and the third person—for example, to say, "The Bushman makes bows and arrows," not, "I saw some Bushmen make a few bows and arrows." Both literary devices cause statements to appear to be authorless, authoritarian, objective, and hence in keeping with the prevailing positivist/empiricist philosophies of science.

As Marcus (1982) argues, ethnography is virtually an unanalyzed literary genre. The art and craft of producing an acceptable ethnography is learned indirectly and accidentally. The question of the relationship between ethnography and other literary forms is seldom discussed. Langness (in Honigman 1976:254) points out that " . . . the whole question of the relationship of ethnography to poetry and playwrighting, as well as to the short story and the novel, has never been carefully examined. What, for example, are the similarities and differences between ethnography and literary 'realism'? What is the relation of the novelist's quest for verisimilitude and the task of the ethnographer? Could an ethnography be both anthropologically acceptable and at the same time a work of art?"

The following statements constitute the paradox we have been discussing:

1. Most anthropologists consider themselves social scientists and their work as being scientific;
2. To be scientific means the scientist is obligated to systematically reveal research methods and any other factors which might affect the outcome of the investigation;
3. Most ethnographies lack an adequate and integrated methodological statement; and
4. Those methodological statements that do exist are most frequently attached to the ethnography.

Some social scientists do not see the situation as being paradoxical. They feel that being reflexive is actually counterproductive to their goals. Honigman, while advocating the acceptance of a "personal" approach in anthropological research, states that

[c]ritics demanding a high degree of self-awareness of investigators using the personal approach are unrealistic. It is chimerical to expect that a person will be able to report the details of how he learned manifold types of information through various sensory channels and processed it through a brain that can typically bind many more associations far more rapidly than the most advanced, well-stocked computer. . . . Some of the individual factors operating in description can be brought into awareness and controlled, but a high degree of self-conscious attention to the process of description can only be maintained by scaling down the number and range of events that are to be studied, thereby possibly impoverishing the results while gaining a comparatively explicit account of how information was collected. (1976:243–46)

We would agree that excessive concern with either the producer or the process will obviously cause the focus of the product to turn inward; total attention to the producers creates autobiography, not ethnography. However, anthropologists have largely denied the need for reflexivity and ignored the scientific necessity for revealing their methods. As a consequence, perhaps we need a brief period of overcompensation. We need several extensive attempts to explore the implications of doing reflexive anthropology before we can establish conventions for "how much is enough." Questions of narcissism, of turning oneself into an object of contemplation, of becoming a character in your own ethnography are very fundamental and complex. Until we have a tradition, albeit a minor one, of the ethnography of anthropology (Scholte 1972), we think that a concern over excesses is a bit premature.

What anthropology has to offer is primarily a systematic way of understanding humanity—ours as well as everyone else's. Therefore, the processes we evolve to accomplish that task may be our most significant contribution, that is, teaching others to see human beings from an anthropological perspective. Geertz has said it well (1973:16):

> Anthropologists have not always been as aware as they might be of this fact: that although culture exists in the trading post, the hill fort, or the sheep run, anthropology exists in the book, the article, the lecture, the museum display, or sometimes nowadays, the film. To become aware of it is to realize that the line between mode of representation and substantive content is undrawable in cultural analysis as it is in painting; and that fact in turn seems to threaten the objective status of anthropological knowledge by suggesting that its source is not social reality but scholarly artifice.
>
> It does threaten us, but the threat is hollow. The claim to attention of an ethnographic account does not rest on its author's ability to capture primitive facts in faraway places and carry them home like a mask or a carving, but on the degree to which he is able to clarify what goes on in such places, to reduce the puzzlement— what manner of men are these?—to which unfamiliar acts emerging out of unknown backgrounds naturally give rise. This raises some serious problems of verification, all right—or if "verification" is too strong a word for so soft a science (I, myself, would prefer "appraisal"), of how you can tell a better account from a worse one. But that is precisely the virtue of it. If ethnography is thick description and ethnographers those who are doing the describing, then the determining question for any given example of it, whether a field journal squib or a Malinowski-sized monograph, is whether it sorts winks from twitches and real winks from mimicked ones. It is not against a body of uninterpreted data, radically thinned

descriptions, that we must measure the cogency of our explications, but against the power of the scientific imagination to bring us into touch with the lives of strangers. It is not worth it, as Thoreau said, to go round the world to count the cats in Zanzibar.

Anthropology has too long suffered from the popular assumption that it is "the study of oddments by eccentrics." As such we are, at best, sources of trivial information and cocktail-party conversations like, "Do the Eskimos really live in igloos?" The concept of culture as a means of understanding our humanness is a powerful idea. Too bad we haven't conveyed it to more people in a form that they can apply to their own lives. To hide our personas and our procedures from the public clearly lessens our impact.

Regardless of whether or not one is convinced by arguments pro or con for a full reflexive statement in every ethnography, there can be little argument that anthropologists tend to be remiss in fulfilling their scientific obligation to specify their methods. We believe the reasons for this apparent self-contradictory behavior are to be found in the implicit, taken-for-granted philosophical position of many American anthropologists, which we would characterize as naive empiricism and/or positivism/pragmatism. By naive empiricism we simply mean someone who "tends to believe that the world 'out there' is isomorphic in every respect with the image the detached observer will form of it" (Nash and Wintrob 1972:529). By positivism, we mean the idea "that, since experience is the sole source of knowledge, the methods of empirical science are the only means by which the world can be understood" (Stent 1975:1052).

Joined together into a philosophy of science, one that dominated the development of social science, they produce the major cause of the paradox. This point of view causes the social scientist to strive to be detached, neutral, unbiased, and objective toward the object of study; to withhold value judgments; to disavow political, economic, and even moral positions. In other words, the social scientist must attempt to negate or lose all traces of his or her culture so that someone else's culture can be studied. As Nash and Wintrob put it, "to turn the field worker into a self-effacing creature without any reactions other than those of a recording machine" (1972:527).

The procedures developed to insure the neutrality of the observer and the control necessary for this type of research were evolved in a science of subject/object relations and not an anthropological science of subject/

subject relations. Setting aside any political or ethical considerations, one cannot make another human being into an object of study in the same way that one can control animals or inanimate objects.

This conceptualization of science may be possible if one assumes that researchers exclusively use quantitative methods in controlled experimental settings. While anthropologists do employ quantitative methods (although seldom in labs), our chief claim to methodological fame and the primary method for doing ethnography is the most involved, nonstandardized, personal version of qualitative methods: participant-observation. We recognized quite early that "[t]he first means to the proper knowledge of the savages is to become after a fashion like one of them . . . " (Degerando 1800:70). While anthropologists seldom talk about it publicly, all fieldworkers know that "[i]n the field the researcher becomes trapped in the role of power broker, economic agent, status symbol, healer, voyeur, advocate of special interest, manipulator, critic, secret agent, friend or foe" (Konrad 1977:920).

Anthropologists who subscribe to a naive empiricist/positivist view of science and practice participant-observation in their fieldwork find themselves in a bind. "Since participant observation causes the researcher to become the primary instrument of data generation, his own behavior, his basic assumptions, the interactional settings where research is conducted, etc., all now become data to be analyzed and reported upon" (Honigman 1976:259). One is almost forced to conclude that " . . . an ethnography is the reflective product of an individual's extended experience in (usually) an exotic society mediated by other experiences, beliefs, theories, techniques (including objective procedures when they are used), personal ideology, and the historical moment in which the work was done" (1976:259).

The more the ethnographer attempts to fulfill a scientific obligation to report on methods, the more he or she must acknowledge that his or her own behavior and persona in the field are data. Statements on method then begin to appear to be more personal, subjective, biased, involved, and culture bound; in other words, *the more scientific anthropologists try to be by revealing their methods, the less scientific they appear to be.*

Given that dilemma, it is not too difficult to see why most anthropologists have been less than candid about their methods. They are justifiably concerned that their audience will realize that, as Sue-Ellen Jacobs has said, "[p]erhaps the best thing we learn from anthropological writings is how people who call themselves anthropologists see the world of others (whoever the others may be)" (in Chilungu 1976:469). It is asking anthropologists to reverse their traditional assumption about the ultimate goals of anthropology, and to suggest instead that what anthropology has to offer is a chance to see the native through the eyes of the anthropologist. Hence, most anthropologists would rather live with the dilemma than explore the implications of being reflexive.

Some anthropologists retreat behind slogans like, "Anthropology is a soft science," or "Anthropology is actually a humanities with scientific pretensions." Kurt Vonnegut, Jr., has summed up the position nicely in a recollection of his own graduate student days at the University of Chicago (1974:176):

> I began with physical anthropology. I was taught how to measure the size of a brain of a human being who had been dead a long time, who was all dried out. I bored a hole in his skull, and I filled it with grains of polished rice. Then I emptied the rice into a graduated cylinder. I found this tedious. I switched to archaeology, and I learned something I already knew; that man had been a maker and smasher of crockery since the dawn of time. And I went to my faculty adviser, and I confessed that science did not charm me, that I longed for poetry instead. I was depressed. I knew my wife and father would want to kill me, if I went into poetry. My adviser smiled. "How would you like to study poetry which pretends to be scientific?" he asked me. "Is such a thing possible?" I said. He shook my hand. "Welcome to the field of social or cultural anthropology," he said. He told me that Ruth Benedict and Margaret Mead were already in it—and some sensitive gentlemen as well.

Some anthropologists, particularly in the last fifteen years, have begun to seek a solution to the problem (e.g., Honigman 1976, and Nash and Wintrob 1972, represent two recent attempts to survey the literature). The reasons for this renewed interest (renewed in the sense that Mead and others actually started in the 1930s, but the interest died out) are complex and probably have their origins outside of anthropology in the culture at large. Nash and Wintrob list four factors for the emergence of what they call "self-consciousness" in anthropology: 1) An increasing personal involvement of ethnographers with their subjects; 2) the democratization of anthropology (a polite way of saying that in the sixties some lower-middle-class students who didn't share some of the "gentle-manly" assumptions of the older anthropologists got Ph.D.s); 3) multiple field studies of the same culture; and 4) assertions of independence by native peoples (1972:529). To that we would like to add: 1) The influence of other disciplines, particularly the effect of phenomenological and sym-bolic interactional sociology, ethnomethodology, and structural linguis-tics; 2) the development of Marxist criticism of anthropology in the United States—a criticism aimed at an examination of anthropology as an ideology; and 3) the rise of an urban anthropology concerned with doing ethnography in the United States, the complexity of the subject matter having caused some researchers to question such fundamental ideas as culture.

We have articulated a view of reflexivity as it pertains to anthropo-logical praxis. To summarize what should be obvious now, we have argued that anthropologists behave like scientists to the degree that they publicly acknowledge the role of the producer and the process in the construction of the product, or, simply, that being reflexive is virtually synonymous with being scientific. Moreover, we have suggested that the lack of reflexive statements on methods is a consequence of a particular view of science espoused by many anthropologists.

In some ways we have said nothing novel. Social scientists have been discussing these problems and ideas for a long time. Because of the domination of participant-observation field methods, anthropologists have been particularly occupied with creating a science that allows for both quantitative and qualitative methods that can justify qualitative procedures as being scientific.

For a variety of reasons discussed earlier, the elements are now present for the emergence of a new paradigm for anthropology and perhaps for science in general. Margaret Mead in her 1976 presidential address to the American Association for the Advancement of Science noted this development (1976:905):

> Both the methods of science and the conflict of views about their more general applicability were developed within Euro-American culture, and it is never easy to break out of such deeply felt but culturally bound conceptions. Because of the clarity which has been achieved I believe we can move from conflict toward a new kind of integration. As a first step in this direction I suggest that it is necessary to recognize that our knowledge of ourselves and of the

universe within which we live comes not from a single source but, instead from two sources—from our capacity to explore human responses to events in which we and others participate through introspection and empathy, as well as from our capacity to make objective observations on physical and animate nature.

The problem stated in its simplest form is to find a way to be scientific, reflexive, and do anthropology—to resolve the conflict between what anthropologists say and what they do.

Authors' Confessions

To be consistent with the position espoused in this essay, we should reveal ourselves as producers and discuss the process employed in the construction of this work, that is, be reflexive about our ideas of reflexivity. What follows is a brief confessional aside.

Jay Ruby

My interest in these ideas stems from what began as an elitist fascination with "backstage" (Goffman 1956). I was convinced that if I could understand how someone made something and I knew who they were, that that knowledge would make me an "insider." In time the interest broadened and became more sophisticated. It caused me to admire the novels of Kurt Vonnegut, Jr., and Tom Robbins, the music of Frank Zappa, the photography of Lee Friedlander and Duane Michaels, the films of Jean-Luc Godard and Woody Allen, the paintings of René Magritte, and the comedy of the Firesign Theatre and Monty Python. Whatever else these people were doing, they were trying to raise the critical consciousness of their audiences by being publicly, explicitly, and openly self-aware or reflexive. "I have become an enthusiast for the printed word again. I have to be that, I now understand, because I want to be a character in all my works. I can do that in print. In a movie, somehow, the author always vanishes. Everything of mine which has been filmed so far has been one character short, and the character is me" (Vonnegut 1972:xv).

Two other factors figured in the development of my interest. For the past fourteen years I have been engaged in exploring the theoretical possibility of an anthropological cinema (Ruby 1982). In this process I discovered an apparent conflict between the scientific necessity for the anthropologist to reveal his or her methodology and the conventions of documentary film, which until recently have virtually prohibited such a revelation. In seeking a solution to this dilemma, I was drawn to the literature on reflexivity. In 1974 during the Conference on Visual Anthropology at Temple University in Philadelphia, I organized a series of film screenings and discussions on autobiographical, personal, and self-referential films. In doing so, I began in a more formal and systematic way to explore the relationship between what I am now calling reflexive film and reflexive anthropology.

Finally, like many anthropologists, I have felt a progressively widening ethical, political, and conceptual gap between the anthropology I learned in graduate school and the world as I have come to know it. Among the wedges, I would note the publication of Malinowski's diary (1967) and the public disclosure of the clandestine use of social scientists in Latin America and Southeast Asia. These revelations produced a crisis of conscience and loss of innocence for many of us and gave our personal dilemmas about the role of the researcher a moral and political perspective (Hymes 1969). It should be difficult if not impossible for us now to continue to defend our naive assumptions about our responsibilities toward the people we study and toward the intended audiences for our work. We should stop being "shamans of objectivity." After the involvement of anthropologists in Viet Nam, it is an obscene and dishonest position.

It should be obvious by now that I am partisan. I strongly believe that anthropologists have ethical, aesthetic, and scientific obligations to be reflexive and self-critical about their work. I would, in fact, expand that mandate to include anyone who uses a symbolic system for any reason.

In 1977 I became aware that reflexivity was being used to explore the social construction of self and those social rituals designed for people to be reflective and reflexive. Through the works of Barbara Myerhoff, Victor Turner, Richard Schechner, Barbara Babcock, and others, I saw how social dramas, ceremonies, rituals, and fieldwork could be reflexive moments in an individual's life.

One of the functions of these performances is to give definition to self by seeing the self alongside or in opposition to "the other." Then the act of doing anthropology provides our collective self—culture—with a chance to examine itself through the other that exotic cultures represent. We are able to see ourselves anew when we experience others vicariously through the experience of being an ethnographer. The ethnographer becomes audience for a performance so that he or she can be a performer for us, the audience. Furthermore, fieldwork can be a reflexive experience, because ethnographers are trying to acquire social identities not their own. In one sense the success of ethnographers is measured by how well they can become not themselves while at the same time retaining their original identity.

Barbara Myerhoff

My interests in reflexivity go far back into my childhood, though, of course, I had no such term to apply to them. The fascinating play with alternate realities came naturally out of an unhappy childhood in which books were a great consolation, providing an alternative world, more real and better in every way than the one in which most mortals spent their time. But even before reading, I recall some of my earliest moments of private play occurred as I lay in bed during a long illness and stared at the ceiling, which I found I could make into the floor. I then entered a realm of space and privacy all my own, where strange appurtenances that others called lamps jutted abruptly into the air, asking to be used in surprising ways, as tables, chairs. I looked pityingly at the upside down mortals (all adults) living mindlessly in an unreal world below me, a Platonic shadow of the true world that I inhabited.

The play with the notion of the "real" versus the "pretend" shadow world, one actual, the other an upside-down reflection, was a theme that continued to haunt me. Many years later, I understood that this fascination was more than an idiosyncrasy, that it had religious counterparts. Working among the Huichol Indians, I participated in their experience of visiting their sacred land, a kind of Paradise, in which everything was reversed. Sacredness was the obverse of the normal or mundane, and as many actions as possible were done backwards. The suggestion of an alternative opposite realm that somehow exchanges attributes with its counterpart, blurring the clear lines between actual and imagined, was a source of continuing fascination, which I fully understood during a camping trip in 1977 when I witnessed a perfect reflection of the scene I inhabited in a still mountain lake that lay before me. So clear was the reflection that the two images were indistinguishable save that one was upside down. It was not necessary to choose between them. The image and reflection were fused, completing a reality between them, a totality that achieved a unification and state of perfection. Dream and the waking life, unconscious and conscious, the above and the below, the hidden sacred domain and the palpable ordinary one were the same. The mending of those splits was a numinous experience that told me clearly, for the first time, why I had always been so attracted to and disturbed by the problem of reflected realities.

When I grew into the world of words, my life was dominated by a storytelling grandmother, an illiterate woman of European origin, whose passion for storytelling transformed my life. Each day she told me a different story about one of the houses on the hill behind our house. We imaginatively entered each in turn, making their stories into a commentary on our own lives. One day I wept because the kitchen window was covered with frost. I thought there would be no story since we could not see out. My grandmother laughed, warmed a penny in her palm, pressed it against the glass to make a peephole in the frost, then informed me that I had all I needed there. An opening big enough to glimpse the street outside, transformed by this frame, this tiny aperture, providing the sharpest possible focus; the ordinary scene without became a spectacle, separated from the ebb and flow of mundane life around it. It was the first time I clearly understood that something magic happened when a piece of nature was isolated and framed. It was the beginning of some comprehension of the seriousness of paying attention to a selected aspect of one's life or surroundings.

Alienation came naturally to an unhappy, not too healthy child, who happened, as well, to be raised in a neighborhood and time when children of immigrants were not fully human beings. Alienation is one precondition for a reflexive attitude, but is not reflexivity itself. This private sense of separateness was transformed into a useful sensibility when I began to study the social sciences. I recall being immensely amused and reassured by encountering a Feiffer cartoon. A small boy was not allowed to play baseball with his friends. He stood on the sidelines, excluded, and, for lack of anything better to do, began to observe the rules of the game. He discovered "baseball" as a code, and in the last square was shown somewhat smugly commenting, "It's a good thing the other kids wouldn't let me play. Otherwise I never would have noticed (the rules of the game)."

An extended period of travel also paved the way for my interest in reflexivity. I recall being confused and fascinated by the sense of somehow being a totally different person as I traveled from country to country.

Something about how people saw me clearly altered the way I saw myself.

These vague interests and proclivities came into sharp focus during my first fieldwork, when I had an extreme sense of being a stranger. It was clear that I was more a nonperson to the Indians than they were to me. This was brought home to me painfully and dramatically when my key informant visited my home. With pride I showed him the things he and others from his group had given me, displayed in my home. Then I showed him pictures of my family, assuming he would be as interested in my mother's brother's son as I was in his. Nothing of the kind. The relationship between us, though strong and deep, was not symmetrical. It was not friendship, therefore, what was it? Neither of our cultures provided a suitable category. Enforced thought about how we saw each other ensued, though a term to call what we meant to each other never did appear.

Another significant experience that encouraged reflexive thinking occurred when I began to turn my dissertation into a book. I had the good fortune of working with an excellent editor who required that I specify at every point how I knew what I was reporting. She deleted all the impersonal forms, the third person, the passive voice, the editorial "we," and insisted on responsibility. "How did you know this?" "Who saw that?" "What was seen?" "Who is 'one'?" Her insistence on an active and personal voice was extremely difficult but eventually invaluable. By requiring me to insert myself and my verified observations *into* the manuscript, the editor was requiring the methodological rigor that we are simultaneously trained to value and avoid. After this bout with the editor, I found I had written a book I trusted more, that was clearer and more reliable (and, I think, more readable as well), and I had received a lesson in anthropological methods better than many I had been offered in the course of my formal training.

The last, clearest experience of reflexivity occurred in my more recent fieldwork among my own people. Required by political and personal circumstances to work at home, and among my own people (Eastern European Jews who were also very old), I found myself doing a complex enterprise that involved ceaseless evaluation of the effects of membership on my conclusions. I have written about this at some length elsewhere (1980) and will only adumbrate the high points here. It was soon evident that I knew more than I needed to, or sometimes wanted to, about the people I was studying, that at every juncture, I was looking at my own grandmother, which was to say a variation of myself-as-her, and as I would be in the future. We even looked alike. I responded with embarrassing fullness to my subjects' uses of personal mechanisms of control and interpersonal manipulation, such as guilt and tacit obligatedness, spontaneously (even involuntarily) acknowledging over and over that indeed we were one. In time I began to realize that identification and projection were enormously rich sources of information but often painful and often misleading, requiring my constant monitoring.

Another push toward reflexivity occurred when I made a film about this group. I began to understand the impact on them of being seen and saw eventually how my view of them, and my production of this view in the form of a film, affected them, and in turn affected the world in which they lived, that is, how they were seen by others (who, by the way, had previously largely ignored them). The group, it must be added, was a naturally performative one, always enacting an interpretation of themselves on which the outside world did not agree. They persisted and ultimately succeeded in convincing themselves—and anyone they managed to corral as an audience—that this was a true picture. It became that by virtue of being performed. As Geertz put it in another context, their self-interpretation came into being as it was formulated. It did not exist clearly or in a coherent fashion until it had been publicly demonstrated. "Subjectivity does not properly exist until it is thus organized, art forms generate and regenerate the very subjectivity they pretend only to display" (Geertz 1973). A consummately self-commenting and self-conscious people (as pariah people often are), the group I studied completed my conversion to reflexivity as one of the most interesting and generative attitudes possible.

The Journal as Activity and Genre

Barbara Myerhoff and Deena Metzger

Prescript

Durkheim was certainly correct in saying of modern societies that the domain of religion has contracted. Along with this, there has been a fragmentation of the sacred rituals and symbols that were once assured to us simply by virtue of our membership in an integrated society. Increasingly we find ourselves, individually and collectively, inventing our own symbols and rituals, for if the opportunities for understanding the human condition through myth and ritual have diminished, the necessity and desire for them have not lessened. Now, however, we are on our own, and we must provide meanings how and when we can—a task so significant, yet so often thorny and confusing, that it is not an overstatement to call it a heroic undertaking. Joseph Campbell (1965) describes the quest for meaning as the contemporary hero-deed, now coterminous with the confrontation with one's own unconscious. Previously, he tells us, in stabler times and places, all meaning was provided by the group in great anonymous forms. Today, to paraphrase him, all meaning is in the individual. "One does not know toward which one moves. One does not know by what one is propelled." The lines of communication, he continues, between the conscious and the unconscious zones of the psyche have been split in two.

> The hero-deed to be wrought is not today what it was in the Century of Galileo. Where then there was darkness, now there is light; but also, where light was, there is now darkness. The modern hero-deed must be that of questing to bring to light again the lost Atlantis of the co-ordinated soul. (1965:388)

Rites of passage, in the course of which individuals move between statuses or stages of self-definition, were among the most regular occasions for the development of self-understanding as well as social definition. Victor Turner (1969), building on the work of Van Gennep (1908), has explored the subject of these rites and focused our attention on the passages between stages, as well as arrivals and departures, developing a rich and useful set of concepts concerning liminality, thresholds, margins, and the in-between moments and individuals that are neither one thing nor another, but in the process of becoming. To these rites, chaos and ambiguity are endemic, but they are also possibilities for discovery, confrontation, and questioning of the deepest kind. In the very openness of liminal experiences and forms, there is danger, vulnerability, isolation, and darkness, and the possibility of creativity, discovery, and change as well. Rites of passages, then, are moments in which we are provided with cultural mirrors and possibly also with windows, or more aptly cellar doors, from which we may emerge as different creatures, rewarded for our courage and curiosity with an enlarged sense of our own possibilities.

This is a fundamentally religious and spiritual quest, so well expressed by St. Augustine in his simple, essential prayer: "O God, I beseech you, show my whole self to my self." The urge of the soul for a vision of its self, in its entirety, remains a strong human motivation. Fulfilling this impulse, however, is very difficult and the individual setting out on this adventure—the "High Adventure of the Soul"—is on an arduous and lonely journey. In this paper, we explore one of the means, used more and more often today, for seeking that whole self. Here we examine one way in which that work is done—through the journal—which can be used as an opportunity for reflection and reflexiveness. As such, it is at once a journey and a record, an activity and a genre.

In what follows, it will be clear that our process of writing and thinking is revealed, presented to the reader—in the act, so to speak—despite the discomfort and uncertainty inevitably aroused by such liminal undertakings. We hope it rewards the reader for his/her patience; revelation and discovery may occur when conventions are violated and hermetic forms opened, and here we have tried to provide for that possibility.

The Journal as Activity

Friday: Deena and Barbara start on the journal pages for the anthropology meeting. We work very hard. Good work but difficult. We can't resolve the issue of the relation of form to content, in this case antagonistic. How frustrating to try to talk about the mercurial process of the journal, without letting it harden into a closed form. The necessity for analytic, critical presentation required by an academic convention destroys the message. Even the words freeze the contents. How to transcend the specific words which trap us: "form" keeps reappearing, connotations and denotations jumbled, the old, fascinating questions about order and disorder. The morphology of the journal replicates its work, using form to embody formlessness, like ritual, the message presented by its medium. Ritual, too, suspends the critical processes, provides safety by offering railings, sufficient predictability for daring forays.

Saturday: We meet and talk more about journals and rituals. We are irritable, unsatisfied with the approach. How can we bring forth the work of journals as we see it? The journal is antistructure, yet we try to present it and it becomes structure in the course of our talk. How can we convey this unconventional, indeed, anticonventional activity in prose, much less at a convention? The inner critic voice pounds away at us. "Fools," he shouts, "how indiscreet, how inappropriate, a convention is a requirement, a law. No one does rituals in symposia on rituals. Anthropologists talk about their natives. No one brings them in person to do rain dances at national meetings. Raw materials have no place here."

We write, argue, discard. The ideas freeze at the moment of appearance. We vacillate and pace, drink too much wine, then too much coffee, but at last we hit on the idea of keeping notes on the *process* of writing the paper, a paper-writing journal. Reflexivity again: here we are, writing about the writing.

Monday: We look over some notes, reread the symposium description and the other papers. Narcissus—the key image. What really happened to him? We turn him over and over, looking at him this way and that. Deena remembers that he tried to touch his own image, finding it wet, knew that it was not he, since he had no immediate experience of being wet. Barbara remembers that he tried to kiss his beauteous image and drowned. Did he try to pass into his reflection, to become one with it, to take it into himself by reaching through the surface of the water to the being who lived beneath the surface reflection? We talk about Cooley's notions of the development of self as reflected in the eyes of others, "The

Looking-Glass Self." But how dangerous if the self is to be known only through the eyes of others. This must be originally mother and infant. And what if she hates her child, can he transcend this? Faulty reflections, though, are not the real danger. Rather it is that all single reflections are distortions. True reflections can only come from many images, a selection offered among which one chooses, discards, makes corrections. Only in maturity, with multiple images, is greater accuracy possible. Only then can one identify not only the false reflections of others, but the distortions one provides oneself. Only then can reflection be distinguished from the wishes of others—the danger of projection.

Poor Narcissus—he was not held there at the edge of the pool in a frenzy of self-adoration. He was lonely. He wanted to become whole, to fuse his experience with his vision. Perhaps when he walked away from the pool he set out to find his Beloved, the other who would be that reflected face to him. No sooner released from one enchantment than he is caught in another, a spell-bound creature who reaches for completion in romantic passion, losing himself in the other instead of accepting his solitude and seeking his completion from within.

Monday afternoon: Barbara remembers that she read about the rise of autobiography as a genre being associated with the perfecting of Venetian glass in the sixteenth century which first made accurate mirrors generally available. How silly if it is true: people thinking that the single reflection is ever accurate, that it is ever found by looking at precise surfaces. Or worse, the old Western conceit suggesting that self-scrutiny began with a technological invention, the authority of accurate measurement being equated with reality and used as the model for inner experience. Are we to believe that "benighted savages" without accurate mirrors did not look for signs of themselves? Did their myths and rituals not serve the same purposes as accurate mirrors? Yes, but the difference then was that the images were collectively provided for the individual. Those collective, eternal themes served as the individual unconscious, bringing coherence and design to private lives.

Monday after dinner: Form and procedures battle against myths, Narcissus, then Proteus, the journal being a Protean "form" (there's that deadly word again where we don't want it). The thoughts must be organized into sentences, then into paragraphs, marching precisely and inexorably across the pages toward resolution. Proteus changed from leopard to water to wind. How shall we hold the wind? Academic papers are designed to capture other prey, not to hold the wind. Maybe that is why they are so often airless.

We are getting silly, so we take a walk. It rained heavily all day. Now there is a moon and the sky is clear. It is almost autumn, and the wet leaves stick to our feet. Deena continues to talk about Narcissus with his single surface. Who can show him the back of his head? We need an image of a double mirror, reflecting in an endless regression, into eternity, bounding back and forth from surface to surface. Barbara Babcock will love all this talk of mirrors. Jim Fernandez's paper describes an African initiation ritual in which a mirror holds the timeless face of the ancestors. It is overlaid upon the initiate's reflection, an image of continuity, perpetuity, the individual depicted as one link in the eternal chain of the lineage. What a fruitful image! Why don't we have such wonderful rituals given to us?

There are puddles on the sidewalk. We stop and look into one. The wind has died and we see ourselves by moonlight, enraptured by our smiling faces, made very self-conscious by all this talk of consciousness of self. A breath of air and the reflection breaks up.

Late Monday night: We are dopey with fatigue but excited still. Barbara talks about mirrors and our lack of them as metaphors in our culture. There is one wonderful mirror story—she reminds Deena of the Snow Queen. (Deena can never remember it.) The important part is that the demons, flying over the city, carry a mirror made by Satan. They lose hold of it. It falls and shatters. The Satanic mirror reverses its images; in it everything is its own opposite—beauty reflected as ugliness, good as evil. Kay, the boy-hero, was also the opposite of his peers, the other older, rougher boys. He preferred to stay home with Little Gerda, admiring the rose they have grown together, sitting at the kitchen door listening to Gerda's grandmother's stories. When the mirror breaks, two splinters pierce him—one fragment enters his heart and another his eye. He forgets Little Gerda, and blinded to her beauty, instead follows the Snow Queen, and lives as an amnesiac, freed from time and change in her eternal, frozen, perfect crystal palace. Eventually he is rescued by Little Gerda, whose tears thaw his heart and cause his own tears to flow, dislodging the distorting fragments in his eye. He leaves the palace; his thrall is ended and, we must assume, he returns to Gerda's kitchen and garden, to family and community, to the mundane, repetitious world of flux and trivia. First he was a boy with this vision of perfection, then he is a man, laboring in the flawed mortal order. A rite of passage. As a man, does he remember the Snow Queen? What is the story telling us? Is perfection the distortion one must give up when one matures, the child closer to the original innocence and perfection of the Garden forever left behind? Or is the daily life, with its multiplicity, its fragments, flux, exaggerations, and triviality the true vision? If Kay remembers having lived with the Snow Queen, this recollection must change how he views his mortal, adult life. Does the story tell us about his memories, about his achievement of greater consciousness? We are tempted to rush to Grimm or Andersen just as the day before, we wanted to rush to Ovid, then to Freud to find out the truth about Narcissus. No, sources do not tell us these things. *We* remember what Kay saw. That is the point.

Wednesday evening: Barbara brings Deena a photograph taken during the previous summer, a perfect reflection of mountains and trees in a still lake, a mysterious image; it is a vision of completion, perfection, the world mended and made whole again, not in fantasy or dream but before one's very eyes. No need for metaphors and parables and mnemonics. There is the top and bottom with the seam fused, the water and earth, the underworld of dreams and wishes touching its other half— but only for the merest instant. That's essential, isn't it? The configuration changes as the old images are destroyed by the most minor movement. We cannot live in that place or even behold it except for mere glimpses. The fragments continually shatter, distort, realign. Perfection is unnatural.

We talk more about the double mirror image for Narcissus. Though multiple in its surfaces, it is still too rigid; mirrors never change, and we know this is a lie. The journal is not a mirror, for it is a fluid form. Within it images tremble on the water, just barely staving off the chaos they invite in so audaciously. We need a new image. We rifle through our favorite books unsystematically. We jump up and down and shriek with glee when we find just the one, which Deena had known many years before but had not remembered until now.

It is Steppenwolf's Magic Theatre. "In the end, Harry Haller, confronted by all possibility and appalled by his image as one, sees himself as an 'old weary loon,' kicks the mirror in the magic theatre to splinters. Picking up the fragments, he knew that all the hundred thousand pieces of life's game were in his pocket. A glimpse of its meaning had stirred his reason and he was determined to begin the game afresh."

Ovid, Freud, Grimm, now Hesse—what a bacchanal of sources. How messy. But even these give us no final truth, only hints. How shall we clean this up? It is no longer fun. Sweating hands slide off typewriter keys. Why is this frightening? We know why, of course. It is the liminal moment at the edge of the forest. What else will come in? This is now more than merely stage fright at being unorthodox on a professional occasion. We are the heroes in the journey. It is proper to be afraid. Here in the Magic Theatre one cannot remain oriented. Why won't Harry Haller, Narcissus, the Snow Queen, Kay fit together? They struggle toward coherence but fall short. There are so many echoes here, shrouded and haunting. Kay a boy, Haller a man. Kay is freed with tears, Haller with laughter, in the end by listening to the Silent Laughter of Mozart. But Narcissus was never freed at all. Water/mirrors; one below, one above; perfection and change; stasis and flow; childhood/adulthood. Is this some terrible Lévi-Straussian nightmare where everything is upside down and that means it is all the same? We are not heroes. Leave off! Let us write a proper paper.

Saturday: Deena tells Barbara her dream of the previous night. Narcissus, in the thrall of his image, tries to pass his fingers through the surface to reclaim his image. A wind comes up and the vision vanishes. He turns, startled, alone, bereft. He runs through the woods, falling into the wet grass. He finds himself looking into a small puddle, a rain puddle, mossy green at the edges. "What are you doing here?" he demands. "Who was that other one, whom I loved, so much more beautiful than you?" As he rises, the light strikes his ring. He gazes at the stone and finds himself there, round as a newt's eye. Laughter fills him. He looks for himself in other surfaces—glass, silver, oil, raindrops. Then Deena is he, running through the woods, shouting "Where are you?" as the invisible laughter of Narcissus bounces off the trees and pursues her. Bodiless Echo, too, laughed sardonically at Narcissus in the myth.

Saturday evening: Resignation. Compromise. Very well, allow the disorder, if you must, in the beginning. Then balance. After a while, leave off. Present a proper paper, genuflect to the occasion. The audience here is truly the other, not the self. It is suitable that it be addressed in an orderly fashion.

The Journal as Genre

The journal, as we construe it, is an activity as much as a form—a process, in the course of which a self may be constructed. Here is the difference between journals and other autobiographical forms: the latter may be primarily self-documentation, a record of what has occurred, not what is in the act-of-becoming in the course of the writing. The journal, as understood here, is a reflective and, potentially, a reflexive moment. It is reflective insofar as the subject contemplates the self, sees it, shapes it, acquires self-knowledge by beholding the self at a little distance, differentiated from the phenomenological experience of being. Nearly always, serving thus as subject and object, observer and audience, self and other at the same time, the self becomes conscious of the nature of this knowledge, and seeing itself being itself, develops consciousness about the nature of consciousness. Then the journal is reflexive as well as reflective.

The process almost inevitably leads the writer into new regions of awareness. The journal is a means for *acquiring,* not merely recording, knowledge. In this view, the journal is necessarily a protean, radically open form, unbounded by considerations of chronology, transcending past-present-future demarcations, unlimited by considerations of accuracy and verifiable truth. Its authenticity comes from the honesty of the writer and the writer's willingness to embark on an uncharted course, with courage to allow the unknown to enter. As such, the very word "form" to describe it is misleading, for the journal exists on the very edge of nonform. Paradoxically, many writers use journals to fend off chaos, to find regularity and design in life, thus staunching the metaphysical anxiety that comes from a life without clear and sustained coherence. But it requires that the writer exercise restraint and forbear from imposing form and purpose prematurely. Its success depends on abiding the anxiety attendant upon letting the unknown appear within its pages. The form of a journal replicates its function, then. It is liminal as activity and genre.

As we have noted, ritual is very often the means by which subjects make themselves known to themselves. The issue of reflexivity is especially sharply focused in rites of passage, where individuals pass from one social condition to another, and have at least the theoretical opportunity of becoming convinced themselves that a transformation of self has occurred during or as a result of the ritual.

This is most interesting, for if we consider the process of reflexivity in journal work, it becomes clear that the resemblance between that and rites of passage is striking, and probably not accidental. As Van Gennep (1908) first asserted, rites of passage consist of a three-step sequence: the subject moves first into a differentiated condition (separation), then to a threshold state "betwixt and between" what went before and what is to come (*limen*), and finally reabsorption (reaggregation) into the collectivity, as a different person, always socially and publicly transformed, and often subjectively as well. This is precisely the sequence of transformation that occurs in the journal. The self is beheld in the writing. This is the mirroring moment, when the self, as audience—differentiated—becomes separate, an object. Then the foray into liminality, the voyage to the edge of the forest, when new materials are encountered; in the public domain, this is when the ancestors present the neophyte with arcane knowledge, or privately, it is the moment when unconscious material may become conscious. Finally, there is Incorporation, the experience of integration, as the transformed self assimilates the uncovered knowledge, and a temporary clarification occurs; temporary, for none of this is permanent. It is a continual making and unmaking and remaking, and here the journal work differs from a formal rite of passage that achieves its transformations somewhat more lastingly. Here the individual copes with the dialectic between flux and fixity of the inner life. The same observations made of order and chaos in social life apply here. As Moore and Myerhoff put it:

> Since social life has some order, yet moves continuously—on the grand scale through historical time—on the micro-scale through each hour, its movement requires a great deal of subtle meshing between the regular and the improvised, the rigid and the flexible, the repetitive and the varying. Social life proceeds somewhere between the imaginary extremes of absolute order, and absolute chaotic conflict and anarchic improvisation. Neither the one nor the other ever takes over completely. (1977:3)

Through ritual, as through this journal work, "a declaration is made against indeterminacy" (Moore and Myerhoff 1977:16). In providing some order and uncovering some design, journals name, regulate, and explain. The indeterminate is never banished, it is only to some degree managed. Whether one is setting forth publicly in a ritual, or privately in a journal, some principles of order occur, and allow a pause for reflection.

Victor Turner's (1969) fecund conception of liminality applies well to the liminal dimensions of journal work. Discovery and innovation happen here. If it is frightening and dangerous, it is also antic, a kind of high play. Creation is recreation. Most anthropological studies of ritual have slighted their private aspect. What do initiates experience in the hut, in the tunnel, in the fruitful darkness? We know that the imagery describing them and providing ritual metaphors clusters around darkness, secrecy, vulnerability, nakedness, and that which is invisible, hidden, and secluded. It is no accident that journals are essentially secret and private, hidden against prying eyes. There are simple reasons for this, to be sure. The emerging self must be its own witness first. It must be kept from contact with already established, known stories during its indeterminacy, when it is becoming and has not yet hardened into being. Like all interstitial ventures, as Mary Douglas (1966) reminds us, problems of contamination appear. The public world reading the journal may destroy it, literally pollute it with external standards. Conversely, the journal is threatening to that which is already structured. All boundary phenomena trouble our categories and we hasten to put them in their place, or some place. They are messy, dirty, unpredictable, troublesome. And so journals are locked in drawers. They, the fruitful darkness, are kept in darkness. Neophytes too are secluded, protected from public view by darkness which respects their nakedness, their tender beginnings. And as Prell-Foldes (1980) tells us, even in private prayer, protection against the crush of the external forms may be offered. The observant Jew amidst his community prays, enveloped and set apart by his prayer shawl.

Journals, then, are secluded for deep reasons, not only for simple privacy or to prevent embarrassing revelations from coming to light, but also to admit the beasts and monsters, imaginings, and wishes, and to preserve for them the possibility of radical openness, of deception, and to allow fullness to occur, to forestall the premature hardening of the self into a fixed, agreed-upon image. Journals allow us to see "what ought not to be there." Thus they are kept apart, like neophytes, bounded and separated so that dissolution and decomposition of prior constructions of self may begin. In this confrontation with the dark, parturition, transformation, and reformulation of new images is undertaken.

Liminality is not only reflexive, it is also reflectiveness. Here, we think about things previously not pondered, not even raised to the level of questions. For this reason, liminality is the great moment of teachability when the tribe may impress on the neophyte its deepest wisdom. Monsters appear, not only to frighten but to raise questions. The man with the lion mask covering his head, Turner (1974) reminds us, causes us to wonder about the nature of man as well as the nature of lions, and Lévi-Strauss would add, raises all sorts of questions about the nature of the relationship of the human to the animal kingdom. So too with the deities and demons that may appear. On the individual plane, these are moments when the journalist admits to light the previously disowned, disgraced, or simply unacceptable contents of the unconscious. The events which occur, then, also have a cognitive dimension, and an opportunity is provided not only for psychic and emotional reorganization but for theoretical, philosophical enlightenment as well.

As reflexive and reflecting, as activity and genre, the journal does for us now what ritual and myth once did for others. It is a liminal genre, without conventions, limits, or boundaries, used to travel into liminality where the unknown parts of self and the environment are glimpsed. Journals allow one to construct a self, with a cogent design, a set of symbols, a history.

Having dwelled thus on the necessity for privacy, what are we to make of the fact that journal-keeping is becoming something of a national fad, an activity not pursued in solitude but in large groups, indeed presently occupying a central role in two large social movements?

Let us examine journals briefly in these contexts to see if indeed the same work of reflection and reflexiveness takes place there as well as in the solitary settings we have just described.

Journals and the Women's Movement

It is possibly no coincidence that the revival of the women's movement in the sixties coincides with the publication of two important autobiographical works by Doris Lessing and Anaïs Nin. *The Golden Notebook* by Lessing (1973), a novel in journal form, is thematically concerned with journal-keeping as a means to personal and political consciousness and the achievement of dynamic wholeness and sanity through transcending fragmentation and division. Says Lessing in the book:

> There is a skeleton, or frame, called Free Women which is a conventional short novel, about 60,000 words long and which could

stand by itself. But it is divided into five sections and separated by stages of the four Notebooks, Black, Red, Yellow and Blue. The Notebooks are kept by Anna Wulf, a central character of Free Women. She keeps four and not one because, as she recognizes, she has to separate things off from each other, out of chaos, of formlessness—of breakdown. Pressures, inner and outer, end the Notebooks; a heavy black line is drawn across the page of one after another. But now that they are finished from their fragments can come something new, The Golden Notebook. . . . In the inner Golden Notebook, things have come together, the divisions have broken down, there is formlessness with the end of fragmentation— the triumph of the second theme, which is that of unity. (1973:vii)

Volume I of the *Diary of Anaïs Nin* (1966) was the first publication of work in 200 original volumes exploring woman's experience and sensibility. The influence of these two books is incalculable. They are both standard textbooks in women's literature and studies classes, but additionally have become the self-assigned texts which serve as guides to those seeking female identity. By example they validate the simple act of personal journal-keeping as a serious activity.

"The personal is political," are by-words of the new women's movement which these two works exemplify. They were followed by the sudden publication of new and old women's autobiographical works—by, to name just a few, Kate Millet, Judy Chicago, Simone de Beauvoir, Colette, Emma Goldman, Virginia Woolf, and Elizabeth Gurley Flynn—as well as collections of works by so-called anonymous women. The cumulative impact of these publications was to create in women the habit of journal-keeping as a political and personal act in pursuit of self-exploration, self-documentation, and responsibility for one's own life. Gradually the development of individual consciousness came to be seen as the most important fundamental step toward the transformation of women as a class and society as a whole, a completely new idea for women who in the past utilized the journal because it was an appropriate form in which often disdained individuals could clarify and observe their lonely neglected concerns.

The journal is by no means an exclusively female form, nevertheless historically it has long been and is still a singularly fitting expression for women, because it allows the writer a measure of that freedom and responsibility in the personal domain which is lacking in the public sphere. Because the journal imposes no strict literary standards, it has always been used by those deprived of formal education and skills necessary to engage in more public forms of autobiographical *belles lettres.*

Even since the publication in the sixteenth century of the *Book of Margery Kempe,* women have kept secret journals, commonplace books and diaries locked in hope chests among the linens—books to which they turned to unburden the heart and to gain some precarious hold upon an existence which was otherwise consumed in duties of a most transitory and banal nature. For many women there was no other verification of an authentic existence apart from obedience to familial and social roles. For women whose traditional poignant question has so long been not "Who am I?" but "Am I?," and whose answers have been stark and uncertain, the journal has remained intensely private. While men were encouraged or expected to transform their journals into published documents, women's little collections of notes were often lost, destroyed, or discarded. Contemporary feminist interest in life histories, particularly those of anonymous women, is a response to the experience of historic alienation occasioned by the near loss of women's history, not regarded by society as worth attending to or saving. The contrast between the paucity of existing documents of women's lives and their strong habits of documentation is sad and eloquent testimony of their historical condition.

Though the major work of discovering and examining the few extant journals is yet to be done, critical speculation assumes that the journal served women in the past in the same way it served other marginal peoples—the mad, prisoners, and slaves—as a means for holding onto some core of self, holding at bay anonymity, triviality, and madness. Experience which bombards the fragile self and threatens to lead to the abyss can be transformed and integrated by a writer through the process of self-contemplation.

From Margery Kempe through Emily Dickinson, Virginia Woolf, Sylvia Plath, Anne Sexton, a common theme in the history of women's deeply autobiographical works is that of the struggle with madness. According to analyst June Singer (1974) (and many before her) the visions which appear to poets and the mad are basically the same, but "the poet is not afraid to look into the face of the emptiness of midnight [while] perhaps the madman puts his hands up over his face and screams." The journal serves the writer as a poem serves the poet—as a frame surrounding internal chaos. What is "the difference between the one whose visions overwhelm until he is burnt up in the furnace of madness and the one whose visions feed the fires of creative transformation? Surely it is not a matter of will . . . it is not the willing of the 'I,' the ego as he functions out in the world that 'does' it. Rather, it is the 'eye' turned inward upon itself the third eye to whom it appears" (1974:56). The act of contemplation, then, of examining the multiplicity of experience, the encounter with the *prima materia,* may serve as a basic healing activity. The healing process for the poet is not involved in the cultural accomplishment of the poem. It is in the reflexive aspect of art that self is constructed. And so it is, too, for the madman and for women, in their journal work.

Until recently there have been few if any adequate mirrors for women to refer to in viewing themselves. Those mirrors which existed were predominantly alien and distorted images created for women by men. The hermetic nature of the journal permits the expulsion of public images, in this case images that are often unsympathetic, provided as they are by social superordinates with vested interests in women's acceptance of these images as their own. Personally provided images replace public ones as women work on seeing themselves in fresher, fairer ways. Only non-authoritarian forms can allow for the creation of authentic selves within a historic perspective, creating a necessary bulwark between the self and a society which has in the past attempted to legislate all conditions of self as a function of social role.

Because so long isolated from each other in our society, women have been doubly deprived of their own reflection and their reflection in each other's eyes. Organized journal activities, workshops, consciousness-raising groups, women's studies programs, and various forms of feminist education efforts have combined in an increasingly popular tendency to transform journals into literature and art (*Flying, Cross Country, Confessions from the Malaga Madhouse, Primagravida, Diaries of Anaïs Nin* among them). Thus there are activities presently taking place and productions appearing which may go far in remedying the isolation between women, offering opportunities and information on the shared dimensions of women's lives and experience.

As women's journals are printed in increasing numbers or shared in formal and informal ways, women as a group move through the liminal stage toward integration, learning to see themselves simultaneously as individuals and as members of a group, with common experience, values, and goals. Essential to this process is the acceptance of formerly disowned and disdained aspects of self. Today in journal-writing workshops women write of their private lives, working in a supportive setting where the "confession" of prostitution, abortion, maternal rage, sexual fear, rape, and similar taboo experiences and emotions are not greeted with derision or shame, but received by the group as a "gift" of sharing.

Most interesting of all, perhaps, we note that in its form as well as its function, the journal is an organic expression of women's consciousness. Says Moffat in *Revelations: Diaries of Women:*

> The form has been an important outlet for women partly because it is an analogue to their lives: emotional, fragmentary, interrupted, modest, not to be taken seriously, private, restricted, daily, trivial, formless, concerned with self, as endless as their tasks. (1974:5)

Thus even the fragmentary nature of women's experience, so frequently considered a limitation, is now regarded as a potential strength. Says Painter on this,

> There is no need, however, to abandon certain habits we have lived with. Habits do not like to be abandoned, and besides they have the virtue of being tools. One in particular is the habit women have of fragmenting their activity. In the *Subjection of Women* John Stuart Mill, aside from expressing doubts that men and women have any essential differences, spoke of the capacity women apparently have of "passing promptly from one subject of consideration to another," as far more valuable than the "male capacity for absorption in a single subject . . ." the mind does more by frequently returning to a difficult problem than by sticking to it without interruption! . . . Since the diary allows for that fragmentation (even) thrives on it, there may be less need to alter our style than there is to accept and recreate what we have not yet used of ourselves. (Moffat and Painter 1974:403)

The dynamic in the journal corresponds to the dialectic which Lessing identified between fragmentation and unity. And Nin put it thus: "I used to have a garden and plant seeds. And then I would dig the earth from the plant and look at the roots because I wanted to watch them grow. Of course I ruined the plants! But there was an obsession with the desire to see how things grew and of course the next thing I realized was what

I could watch grow was myself" (1966). And the place where this growth took place, she observed, was in her diaries.

The journal is the earth, so to speak, in which the root of self expands, growing downward and upward simultaneously. The boundaries between self and journal, root and earth, are tenuous, for it is in their relation to each other that life takes place.

Uses of Journals in Psychotherapeutic Contexts

Journals are receiving more and more attention as therapeutic tools in another social setting, that of contemporary psychotherapies. Here there is time only to mention their usages. As in the women's movement, journals are used collectively as well as privately. What is of particular interest in this context is that journals are often brought in for reflexive and reflecting purposes, to hold up the self to the self, to develop insight and to construct and imaginatively rehearse changes. Significantly, the journal is used in therapies with many different theoretical approaches, cross-cutting the topology of self on which a particular treatment is based or the specific therapeutic goals. Few therapies with any theoretical base fail to differentiate some components of the self as a multidimensional construct. To the extent that a therapy takes cognizance of the individual in a social and cultural setting, the relation of the subject to the other is significant. Concerns with the issues of projection and transference, and the use of the therapist as a reflecting audience, are fundamental variables, manipulated in the course of many treatments. Insight-based therapies concentrate on clarification of the relationship between the subject and the introjected voices of society. The therapist reflects the self to the subject, formally and informally, providing a corrective lens, and sometimes realigning components of the self. Freudians may strive to alter relations between the ego, superego and id; Sullivanians and interactionists may identify the "Bad Me versus the Good Me." Transactional therapists clarify the relations between the "Inner Child" and the "Adult." Kleinians examine and rearrange the internalized configurations of the "Good Mother" and the "Bad Mother," while Jungians attend the "Animus/Anima," archetypal constellations, "Persona," and "Shadow," among others. Therapies which postulate a more unitary concept of the self work toward the emergence of a "real" or "true person." Depth and analytic therapies seek to bring out the "unconscious," "preconscious," or "repressed" contents of the psyche, while other approaches aim at discovering the mythic, archetypal, or transpersonal dimensions of the private, individual subject.

In all these forms, it can be seen that journals are suitable for re-alignments of components of the psyche, for the same reasons that curing rites have so often used various means of objectifying and mirroring the subject. The Gestaltists often objectify dreams and images in written form, including journals, as well as in dramatic enactments. Psycho- and sociodrama are premised on the same reach for objectification and reflection of components of self, while in psychosynthesis the subjectively provided images of the client are plumbed by means of written and other imaginative expressions.

Such uses of the journal or journal-like expressions not only allow for the realignment of components of self, but by enlarging the subject's immediate, private experience, by equating it with eternal and universal themes, suggest a greater meaning of the individual's personal history, approaching the curing work done by myth and religion. All these methods facilitate a "conversation" between the conscious mind and the unconscious, and postulate some "otherness" operating within the person; nearly always this leads to a re-evaluation of the role of will, reason, intellect, and intent. By means of this dialogue internal voices are personified, named, objectified, and, presumably, incorporated.

It is with interest we note that journals are presently enjoying quite a vogue, often practiced in quasi-public, and even institutionalized, settings. "Intensive journal workshops," invented by Ira Progoff (1975), have been conducted all over the country for several years. In this method, people work on journals, sometimes for a weekend, sometimes for a semester, in large groups. The work is private, though undertaken collectively. No special use is made of the public setting, in contrast to much work with journals in women's workshops and in therapy groups. Progoff has transformed the journal from a liminal into a codified and somewhat rigid form, where individuals record their materials in a structured, segmented fashion. The popularity of the approach is noteworthy—it was estimated last year that at least 15,000 people had participated in Progoff's workshops, and this figure does not take into account the sale of his books and spinoffs by disciples and imitators.

Journals appear to be gaining a general popularity in classroom settings also, where teachers in secondary schools and universities often employ them to encourage their students to develop self-consciousness about the nature of their own learning. Where the students' responses to new or unstructured situations are pertinent, part of the lesson, as it were, journals may be assigned as a means for formalizing attention to this feature.

Conclusion

In that naked darkness, in the journal, like neophytes, we may emerge from the tyranny of public interpretation, sometimes for the first time. The relinquishing of the external view of self, and substitution of an internal view of self, may lead to a dramatic and startling freedom. What is gained from this experience is the acceptance of multiple views of self, rather than a single, hard, authentic version. And there is the possibility of maturation, when the self may relinquish the romantic illusion that completion may be found by joining with one's other half, the beloved.

The self, yearning for its wholeness, considering multiplicity where before there was singleness, recognizes its fullness. With solitude as a companion in the journey through the tunnel, one may be freed from exaggerated dependence on others, from problems of the distortions reflected back to one from external sources (the problem of sympathy discussed in Marilyn DiSalvo's interpretation of the Narcissus story). The journey allows the self to be alone, exploring what is, what has been, what might yet be, what will never be, except in the imagination.

It is no accident that so many and such profound journals have been kept by the category of people Victor Turner calls liminal—by prisoners, isolates, and wanderers, all questers for their own souls. It has been said that the great journal-keepers are women and soldiers. Isolation, being shut away and confined, with one's external information limited or closed off, permits the inner quiet required for approaching the edge. Then, is it not the wish for fullness—stronger even than self-love—that held Narcissus there, in thrall, at the edge of the water?

The materials encountered in the journal process are dealt with first in their raw, highly individual, utterly subjective state. But once interpreted and assimilated, they are transformed, to some degree. Once examined, they are no longer utterly unique; they begin to reveal familiar and even universal configurations. One's own story is thus seen to contain elements of the stories of others, common to humanity. The transformation that may occur with examination of a journal's contents has the capacity to present the journalist with a picture of a life reconceptualized. Consciousness is then raised to a higher level, for the self can be seen now as the microcosm for the macrocosm of human experience.

Bibliography

Adler, Rachel. 1973. "The Jew Who Wasn't There: Halacha and the Jewish Woman." *Response: A Contemporary Jewish Review* 8 (18): 77–83.

Alland, Alexander. 1975. *When the Spider Danced: Notes from an African Village.* New York: Doubleday.

Anderson, B. 1964. "Stress and Psychopathology Among Aged Americans." *Southwestern Journal of Anthropology* 20:190–217.

Arensberg, C. M. 1937. *The Irish Countryman: An Anthropological Study.* New York: Macmillan.

Ariès, P. 1962. *Centuries of Childhood: A Social History of Family Life.* New York: Alfred A. Knopf.

Arnhoff, F. N., H. V. Leon, and I. Lorge. 1964. "Cross-cultural Acceptance of Stereotypes Toward Aging." *Journal of Social Psychology* 63:41–58.

Babcock, Barbara. 1980. "Reflexivity: Definitions and Discriminations." *Semiotica* 30 (1–2): 1–14.

Bakan, David. 1966. "The Quality of Human Existence: Isolation and Communication in Western Man." In *Women, Culture, and Society,* edited by M. Z. Rosaldo and L. Lamphere. Stanford: Stanford University Press.

Bateson, Gregory. 1936. *Naven: A Survey of the Problems Suggested by a Composite Picture of the Culture of a New Guinea Tribe Drawn from Three Points of View.* Cambridge: Cambridge University Press.

Baum, Charlotte. 1973. "What Made Yetta Work? The Economic Role of Eastern European Jewish Women in the Family." *Response: A Contemporary Jewish Review* 8 (18): 32–38.

Baum, Charlotte, Paula Hyman, and Sonya Michel. 1975. *The Jewish Woman in America.* New York: Dial.

Beattie, J. 1964. *Other Cultures.* New York: Free Press.

de Beauvoir, Simone. 1953. *The Second Sex.* New York: Alfred A. Knopf.

———. 1962. *The Prime of Life.* New York: World Publishing.

Benedict, Ruth. 1948. "Anthropology and the Abnormal." In *Personal Character and Cultural Milieu,* edited by D. G. Haring. Syracuse: Syracuse University Press.

———. 1953. "Continuities and Discontinuities in Cultural Conditioning." In *Personality in Nature, Society and Culture,* edited by C. Kluckhohn and H. A. Murray. New York: Alfred A. Knopf.

Bengston, V. 1967. "Occupational and National Differences in Patterns of Role Activity and Life-Satisfaction: A Cross-Cultural Pilot Study." Paper presented at the twentieth annual meeting of the Gerontological Society, November, in St. Petersburg, Florida.

Berger, Peter L., and Thomas Luckmann. 1966. *The Social Construction of Reality*. New York: Doubleday.

Berreman, Gerald D. 1962. *Behind Many Masks. Society for Applied Anthropology*. Monograph no. 4.

Blythe, Ronald. 1979. *The View in Winter: Reflections on Old Age*. New York: Penguin Books.

Bohannan, P. 1951. *Justice and Judgement Among the Tiv*. London: Oxford University Press.

Bowen, Eleanor. 1954. *Return to Laughter*. New York: Doubleday.

Bradbury, R. E. 1963. "Fathers, Elders and Ghosts in Edo Religion." In *Anthropological Approaches to the Study of Religion,* edited by M. Banton. New York: Praeger.

Buber, Martin. 1947. *Tales of the Hasidim: The Early Masters*. New York: Schocken Books.

Buettner-Janusch, J. 1966. *Origins of Man*. New York: Wiley.

Burke, Kenneth. 1957. *The Philosophy of Literary Form: Studies in Symbolic Action*. New York: Vintage Books.

Butler, Robert N. 1963. "The Life Review: An Interpretation of Reminiscence in the Aged." *Psychiatry* 26:65–76. Reprint in *Middle Age and Aging,* edited by B. L. Neugarten. Chicago: University of Chicago Press, 1968.

Campbell, J. K. 1964. *Honor, Family and Patronage*. Oxford: Clarendon.

Campbell, Joseph. 1965. *Hero with a Thousand Faces*. Cleveland and New York: Meridian.

Chicago, Judy. 1975. *Through the Flower*. Garden City: Doubleday.

Chilungu, Simeon W. 1976. "Issues in the Ethics of Research Methods: An Interpretation of the Anglo-American Perspective." *Current Anthropology* 17 (3): 457–67.

Chodorow, Nancy. 1974. "Family Structure and Feminine Personality." In *Women, Culture, and Society,* edited by M. Z. Rosaldo and L. Lamphere. Stanford: Stanford University Press.

Clark, Margaret. 1967. "The Anthropology of Aging, A New Area for Studies of Culture and Personality." *Gerontologist* 7:55–64.

Clark, Margaret, and B. Anderson. 1961. *Culture and Aging: An Anthropological Study of Older Americans*. Springfield: Charles C Thomas.

Cohen, Abner. 1974. *Two Dimensional Man: An Essay on the Anthropology of Power and Symbolism in Complex Society*. Berkeley and Los Angeles: University of California Press.

Colette. 1966. *Earthly Paradise*. New York: Farrar, Straus and Giroux.

Cooley, Charles H. 1956. *Human Nature and the Social Order*. Glencoe: The Free Press.

Crapanzano, Vincent. 1980. *Tuhami: Portrait of a Moroccan*. Chicago: University of Chicago Press.

Dawidowicz, Lucy. 1967. *The Golden Tradition: Jewish Life and Thought in Eastern Europe*. Boston: Beacon Press.

Degerando, Joseph-Marie. 1800. *The Observation of Savage People.* Reprint, translated by F. C. T. Moore. Berkeley and Los Angeles: University of California Press, 1969.

Dilthey, Wilhelm. 1961. *Pattern and Meaning in History.* Edited by H. P. Hickman. New York: Harper Torchbooks.

Douglas, Mary. 1966. *Purity and Danger: An Analysis of Concepts of Pollution and Taboo.* London: Penguin.

Dresner, Samuel H., trans. 1974. "The Deaths of the Hasidic Masters." In *Jewish Reflections on Death,* edited by J. Riemer. New York: Schocken Books.

Dubnow, Semen Marhovich. 1916–20. *History of the Jews in Russia and Poland.* Translated from the Russian by I. Friedlaender. Philadelphia: Jewish Publication Society of America.

Durkheim, Emile. 1915. *The Elementary Forms of the Religious Life.* Reprint, translated by J. W. Swain. New York: Collier Books, 1961.

———. 1952. *Suicide.* Translated by John A. Spaulding and George Simpson. London: Routledge and Kegan Paul.

Edgerton, Robert, and Louis Langness. 1974. *Methods and Styles in the Study of Culture.* Corte Madera: Chandler and Sharp.

Eisenstadt, S. N. 1956. *From Generation to Generation.* New York: Free Press.

Eliade, Mircea. 1964. *Shamanism.* New York: Bollingen.

———. 1969. *The Two and the One.* Translated by J. M. Cohen. New York and Evanston: Harper Torchbooks.

Erikson, Erik. 1959. "Identity and the Life Cycle." *Psychological Issues* 1:1–116.

———, ed. 1978. *Adulthood.* New York: W. W. Norton.

Evans-Pritchard, E. E. 1937. *Witchcraft, Oracles and Magic Among the Azande.* Oxford: Clarendon.

Fabian, Johannes. 1971. "Language, History and Anthropology." *Journal of the Philosophy of the Social Sciences* 1:19–47.

Feifel, H. 1959. *The Meaning of Death.* New York: McGraw-Hill.

Fernandez, James W. 1971. "Persuasions and Performances: of the beast in everybody . . . and the metaphors of Everyman." In *Myth, Symbol and Culture,* edited by C. Geertz. New York: W. W. Norton.

———. 1974. "The Mission of the Metaphor in Expressive Culture." *Current Anthropology* 15 (2): 119–33.

Flynn, Elizabeth Gurley. 1963. *My Life as a Political Prisoner.* New York: New World Publishers.

Forde, D. 1961. "Death and Succession: An Analysis of Yoko Mortuary Ritual." In *Essays on the Ritual of Social Relations,* edited by M. Gluckman. Manchester: University of Manchester.

Fortes, Meyer. 1945. *The Dynamics of Clanship Among the Tallensi.* New York: Oxford University Press.

———. 1961. "Pietas in Ancestor Worship." *Journal of the Royal Anthropological Institute* 2.

———. 1965. "Some Reflections on Ancestor Worship in Africa." In *African Systems of Thought,* edited by M. Fortes and G. Dieterien. London: Oxford University Press.

Foster, G. 1965. "Peasant Society and the Image of Limited Good." *American Anthropologist* 61:239–315.

Frazer, J. G. 1922. *The Golden Bough.* New York: Macmillan.

Freuchen, P. 1961. *Book of the Eskimos.* Cleveland: World Press.

Freud, Sigmund. 1913. *Totem and Taboo.* London: Routledge and Kegan Paul. Reprint. New York: New Republic, 1921.

———. 1965. *Death, Grief and Mourning.* New York: Doubleday.

Fried, Martha N., and Morton H. 1980. *Transitions: Four Rituals in Eight Cultures.* New York: W. W. Norton.

Garn, S. M. 1963. "Culture and the Direction of Human Evolution." *Human Biology* 35:221.

Geertz, Clifford. 1973. *The Interpretation of Cultures.* New York: Basic Books.

———. 1983. *Local Knowledge: Further Essays in Interpretive Anthropology.* New York: Basic Books.

Gluckman, M. 1965. *Politics, Law and Ritual in Tribal Society.* Chicago: Aldine Press.

Goffman, Erving. 1956. *Presentation of Self in Everyday Life.* Edinburgh: University of Edinburgh. Reprint. New York: Doubleday, 1959.

Goldin, Hyman E. 1939. *Hamadrikh, The Rabbi's Guide: A Manual of Jewish Religious Rituals, Ceremonials and Customs.* New York: Hebrew Publishing Company.

Goldman, Albert. 1974. *Ladies and Gentlemen, Lenny Bruce!* New York: Ballantine Books.

Goldman, Emma. 1931. *Living My Life.* Vol. 1. Reprint. New York: Dover, 1970.

Gould, Roger L. 1978. *Transformation: Growth and Change in Adult Life.* Louisville: Touchstone.

Goulianos, Joan, ed. 1973. *By a Woman Writ. . . .* Indianapolis and New York: Bobbs-Merrill.

Guffy, Ossie. 1971. *The Autobiography of a Black Woman as told to Caryl Ledner.* New York: W. W. Norton.

Hampl, Patricia. 1974. "A Book with a Lock and Key." *Lamp in the Spine* 9 (Summer / Fall): 49–54.

Hareven, Tamara K. 1978. "The Search for Generational Memory: Tribal Rites in Industrial Society." *Daedalus* 107 (4): 137–49.

Henry, Jules. 1964. *The Jungle People.* New York: Vintage Books.

Herberg, Will. 1955. *Protestant-Catholic-Jew: An Essay in American Religious Sociology.* New York: Anchor.

Hertz, R. 1960. *Death and the Right Hand.* Glencoe: The Free Press.

Heschel, Abraham Joshua. 1972. "The East European Era in Jewish History." In *Voices from the Yiddish,* edited by Irving Howe and Eliezer Greenberg. Ann Arbor: University of Michigan Press.

Hesse, Hermann. 1929. *Steppenwolf.* New York: Henry Hart.

Hodges, H. A. 1952. *The Philosophy of Wilhelm Dilthey.* London: Routledge and Kegan Paul.

Honigman, John J. 1976. "The Personal Approach in Cultural Anthropological Research." *Current Anthropology* 17 (2): 243–61.

Howe, Irving. 1976. *World of Our Fathers*. New York: Simon and Schuster.

Huntington, Richard, and Peter Metcalf. 1979. *Celebrations of Death: The Anthropology of Mortuary Ritual*. Cambridge: Cambridge University Press.

Hyman, Paula. 1973. "The Other Half: Women in Jewish Tradition." *Response: A Contemporary Jewish Review* 8 (18): 67–76.

Hymes, Dell, ed. 1969. *Reinventing Anthropology*. New York: Random House.

———. 1973. "An Ethnographic Perspective." *New Literary History* 5 (1): 197–201.

James, D. G. 1937. *Skepticism and Poetry*. London: G. Allen and Unwin.

Jay, Robert. 1969. "Personal and Extrapersonal Vision in Anthropology." In *Reinventing Anthropology*. See Hymes 1969.

Jung, C. G. 1959. *The Archetypes of the Collective Unconscious*. Vol. 9. *The Collected Works of C. G. Jung*. Princeton: Princeton University Press.

———. 1961. *Memories, Dreams, and Reflections*. Edited by Aniela Jaffe, translated by Richard and Clara Winston. New York: Vintage Books.

Jung, Leo. 1974. "The Meaning of the Kaddish." In *Jewish Reflections on Death,* edited by J. Riemer. New York: Schocken Books.

Kaminsky, Marc. 1984. "The Uses of Reminiscence." In *The Uses of Reminiscence,* edited by Marc Kaminsky. New York: Haworth Press.

Kaplan B., ed. 1961. *Studying Personality Cross-Culturally*. Evanston: Peterson-Row.

Kleemeler, R. W., ed. 1961. *Aging and Leisure*. New York: Oxford University Press.

Kluckhohn, F., and F. Strodtbeck. 1961. *Variations in Value Orientations*. Evanston: Peterson-Row.

Koltun, Elizabeth. 1976. "Preface." In *The Jewish Woman: New Perspectives*. New York: Schocken Books.

Konrad, Herman. 1977. "Review of *Ethics and Anthropology,*" by Rynkiewich and Spradley. *American Anthropologist* 79 (4): 920.

Kroeber, A. 1952. *The Nature of Culture*. Chicago: University of Chicago Press.

Kroeber, A. L., and C. Kluckhohn. 1963. *Culture: A Critical Review of Concepts and Definitions*. New York: Vintage Books.

Kuhn, Thomas S. 1962. *The Structure of Scientific Revolutions*. Chicago: University of Chicago Press.

Kuper, Hilda. 1964. *The Swazi: A South African Kingdom*. New York: Holt, Rinehart and Winston.

Labrot, Sharon. 1977. "Two Types of Self-Reflexiveness." Los Angeles: Center for Humanities. University of Southern California.

Lamm, Maurice. 1969. *The Jewish Way in Death and Mourning*. New York: Jonathan David.

Langer, Susanne K. 1957. *Philosophy in a New Key*. Cambridge, Mass.: Harvard University Press.

Langness, L. L. 1971. *The Life History in Anthropological Science: Case Studies in Anthropology*. New York: Holt, Rinehart and Winston.

Lansing, Stephen. N.d. "Reflexivity in Balinese Aesthetics." Ms. The Barbara Myerhoff Collection. University Archives: University of Southern California.

Lasch, Christopher. 1978. *The Culture of Narcissism: American Life in an Age of Diminishing Expectations.* New York: W. W. Norton.

Lessing, Doris. 1973. *The Golden Notebook.* New York: Bantam.

Lévi-Strauss, Claude. 1955. *Tristes Tropiques: An Anthropological Study of Primitive Societies in Brazil.* Reprint. Translated by John and Doreen Weightman. New York: Atheneum, 1973.

———. 1963. *Structural Anthropology.* Translated by C. Jacobson and B. Schoepf. New York: Basic Books.

———. 1966. *The Savage Mind.* Translated by G. Weidenfeld and Nicolson Ltd. Chicago: University of Chicago Press.

———. 1969. *The Elementary Structures of Kinship.* Translated by J. H. Bell and J. R. von Sturmer. Edited by Rodney Needham. Boston: Beacon Press.

———. 1976. "Jean-Jacques Rousseau, Founder of the Sciences of Man." In *Structural Anthropology.* Vol. 2. Translated by Monique Layton. New York: Basic Books.

Levitats, Isaac. 1981. *The Jewish Community in Russia, 1844–1917.* Jerusalem: Posner.

Lewis, Oscar. 1959. *Five Families: Mexican Case Studies in the Culture of Poverty.* New York: Basic Books.

Lifton, Robert Jay. 1967. *Death in Life: Survivors of Hiroshima.* New York: Simon and Schuster.

Linde, Charlotte. 1978. "The Creation of Coherence in Life Stories." *Structural Semantics.*

Malinowski, B. 1922. *Argonauts of the Western Pacific.* Reprint. New York: E. P. Dutton, 1961.

———. 1925. *Magic, Science and Religion and Other Essays.* Reprint. Beverly Hills: Glencoe Press, 1948.

———. 1932. *The Sexual Life of the Savages.* London: George Routledge.

———. 1967. *A Diary in the Strict Sense of the Term.* Translated by Norbert Guterman. New York: Harcourt, Brace and World.

Mannheim, Karl. 1969. "The Problem of Generations." In *Essays in the Sociology of Knowledge,* edited by Paul Kecskemeti. London: Routledge and Kegan Paul.

Marcus, George E. 1982. "Rhetoric and the Ethnographic Genre in Anthropological Research." In *A Crack in the Mirror: Reflexive Perspectives in Anthropology,* edited by Jay Ruby. Philadelphia: University of Pennsylvania Press.

Maugham, S. [1958] 1968. *Points of View: Five Essays.* New York: Greenwood Press.

Maybury-Lewis, David. 1965. *The Savage and the Innocent.* Boston: Beacon Press.

Mead, Margaret. 1976. "Towards a Human Science." *Science* 191:903–9.

Mendilow, Adam A. 1952. *Time and Experience.* London: Peter Nevill.

Michaels, Eric. 1982. "How to Look at Us Looking at the Yanomami Looking at Us." In *A Crack in the Mirror: Reflexive Perspectives in Anthropology,* edited by Jay Ruby. Philadelphia: University of Pennsylvania Press.

Miller, Ben. 1977. *Reflexivity in Ethnography: An Annotated Bibliography.* Philadelphia: Temple University.

Millet, Kate. 1974. *Flying.* New York: Alfred A. Knopf.

Moffat, Maryjane, and Charlotte Painter, eds. 1974. *Revelations: Diaries of Women.* New York: Random House.

Moore, Sally Falk, and Barbara G. Myerhoff, eds. 1977. *Secular Ritual: Forms and Meanings.* Assen, Holland: Royal Van Gorcum Press.

Myerhoff, Barbara. 1978. "The Older Woman as Androgyne." *Parabola* 3 (4): 74–89.

———. 1979. "The Renewal of the Word." *The Kenyon Review* 1 (1): 50–79.

———. 1980a. "Re-membered Lives." *Parabola* 5 (1): 74–77.

———. 1980b. "Telling One's Story." *The Center Magazine* (Santa Barbara: Center for the Study of Democratic Institutions) 13 (March): 22–39.

———. [1979] 1980c. *Number Our Days.* New York: Simon and Schuster.

———. 1984. "Rites and Signs of Ripening: The Intertwining of Ritual, Time, and Growing Older." In *Age and Anthropological Theory,* edited by David Kerzer and Jennie Keith-Ross. Ithaca: Cornell University Press.

Myerhoff, Barbara, and Lynne Littman (producer, director). 1976. *Number Our Days.* 16mm, 30 min. The Public Broadcasting Corporation.

Myerhoff, Barbara, and Deena Metzger. 1977. "At the Beck and Call of Life: Women's Role in a Changing Society." MS, The Barbara Myerhoff Collection. University Archives: University of Southern California.

Myerhoff, Barbara, and John Hirsch (director). 1981. *Number Our Days.* Dramatized and presented at the Los Angeles Mark Taper Forum.

Myrdal, Gunnar. 1969. *Objectivity in Social Research.* New York: Pantheon.

Nabokov, Vladimir. 1966. *Speak Memory: An Autobiography Revisited.* New York: G. P. Putnam's Sons.

Nash, Dennison, and Ronald Wintrob. 1972. "The Emergence of Self-Consciousness in Ethnography." *Current Anthropology* 13 (5): 527–42.

Neugarten, Bernice L. 1980. "Acting One's Age: New Rules for the Old." *Psychology Today* 13 (11): 66–80.

Nin, Anaïs. 1966. *The Diary of Anaïs Nin.* New York: Harcourt Brace Jovanovich.

Olney, James. 1972. *Metaphors of Self.* Princeton: Princeton University Press.

Ornstein, Robert E. 1969. *On the Experience of Time.* Middlesex, England: Penguin Books.

Ortner, Sherry B. 1974. "Is Female to Male as Nature is to Culture?" In *Women, Culture, and Society,* edited by M. Z. Rosaldo and L. Lamphere. Stanford: Stanford University Press.

Parssinen, Carol Ann. 1982. "Social Explorers and Social Scientists: The Dark Continent of Victorian Ethnography." In *A Crack in the Mirror: Reflexive Perspectives in Anthropology,* edited by Jay Ruby. Philadelphia: University of Pennsylvania Press.

Powdermaker, Hortense. 1966. *Stranger and Friend.* New York: W. W. Norton.

Prell-Foldes, Riv-Ellen. 1973. "The Unity of Oneness: Unification and Opposition in Jewish Ritual." Master's thesis, University of Chicago.
———. 1980. "The Reinvention of Reflexivity in Jewish Prayer: The Self and Community in Modernity." *Semiotica* 30 (1/2): 73–96.
Progoff, Ira. 1975. *At a Journal Workshop.* New York: Dialogue House.
Rabinow, Paul. 1977. *Reflections on Fieldwork in Morocco.* Berkeley and Los Angeles: University of California Press.
———. 1982. "Masked I Go Forward: Reflections on the Modern Subject." In *A Crack in the Mirror: Reflexive Perspectives in Anthropology,* edited by Jay Ruby. Philadelphia: University of Pennsylvania Press.
Radcliffe-Brown, A. R. 1950. "Introduction." In *African Systems of Kinship and Marriage,* edited by A. R. Radcliffe-Brown and Daryll Forde. London: Oxford University Press.
Redfield, R. 1953. *The Primitive World and Its Transformations.* Ithaca: Cornell University Press.
———. 1955. *The Little Community.* Chicago: University of Chicago Press.
Roe, A., and G. Simpson, eds. 1958. *Behavior and Evolution.* New Haven: Yale University Press.
Roskies, Diane K., and David G. Roskies. 1975. *The Shtetl Book.* New York: Ktav Publishing Company.
Rouche, Jean. 1975. "The Camera and Man." In *Principles of Visual Anthropology,* edited by Paul Hockings. The Hague: Mouton.
———. 1978. "On the Vicissitudes of the Self: The Possessed Dancer, the Magician, the Sorcerer, the Filmmaker, and the Ethnographer." *Studies in the Anthropology of Visual Communication* 5 (1): 2–8.
Ruby, Jay. 1977. "The Image Mirrored: Reflexivity and the Documentary Film." *The Journal of the University Film Association* 29 (4): 3–13.
———. 1980. "Exposing Yourself: Reflexivity, Film, and Anthropology." *Semiotica* 30 (1–2): 153–79.
———. 1982. "Ethnography as Trompe l'Oeil: Film and Anthropology." In *A Crack in the Mirror: Reflexive Perspectives in Anthropology,* edited by Jay Ruby. Philadelphia: University of Pennsylvania Press.
Sack, Leena. 1979. Untitled work presented at New York University seminar, "Performance and Anthropology."
Schechner, Richard. 1982. "Collective Reflexivity: Restoration of Behavior." In *A Crack in the Mirror: Reflexive Perspectives in Anthropology,* edited by Jay Ruby. Philadelphia: University of Pennsylvania Press.
Scholte, Bob. 1972. "On Defining Anthropological Traditions: An Exercise in the Ethnology of Ethnology." In *The Nature and Function of Anthropological Traditions,* edited by Stanley Diamond. Philadelphia: University of Pennsylvania Press.
Segall, Marshall H., Donald T. Campbell, and Melville J. Herskovitz. 1966. *The Influence of Culture on Visual Perception.* New York: Bobbs-Merrill Company.
Sekula, Alan. 1975. "On the Invention of Meaning in Photographs." *Artforum* 13 (5): 36–45.

Sheehy, Gail. 1974. *Passages: Predictable Crises of Adult Life.* New York: E. P. Dutton.

Shulman, Abraham. 1974. *The Old Country.* Foreword by I. B. Singer. New York: Scribner.

Simmons, L. 1960. "Aging in Pre-industrial Societies." In *Handbook of Social Gerontology,* edited by C. Tibbitts. Chicago: University of Chicago Press.

Singer, June. 1974. "Reflections on 'A Journal of the Unconscious.'" In *Lamp and the Spine* 9 (Summer/Fall): 49–54.

Sontag, Susan. 1975. "The Double Standard of Aging." *No Longer Young: The Older Woman in America.* Occasional Papers in Gerontology, No. 1. University of Michigan Institute of Gerontology, 31–39.

Spacks, Patricia Meyer. 1975. *The Female Imagination.* New York: Alfred A. Knopf.

Steinberg, Leo. 1978. "Introduction: The Glorious Company." In *Art about Art,* edited by Jean Lipman and Richard Marshall. New York: E. P. Dutton.

Stent, Gunthar. 1975. "Limits to the Scientific Understanding of Man." *Science* 187:1052–57.

Tawney, R. 1926. *Religion and the Rise of Capitalism, A Historical Study.* New York: Harcourt, Brace and Co.

Thomas, E. M. 1958. *The Harmless People.* New York: Alfred A. Knopf.

Trachtenberg, Joshua. 1939. *Jewish Magic and Superstition: A Study in Folk Religion.* New York: Atheneum.

Turner, Victor W. 1967. *The Forest of Symbols.* Ithaca, N.Y.: Cornell University Press.

———. 1968. *The Drums of Affliction.* Oxford: Clarendon Press.

———. 1969. *The Ritual Process: Structure and Anti-Structure.* Chicago: Aldine Publishing Company.

———. 1974. *Dramas, Fields and Metaphors: Symbolic Action in Human Society.* Ithaca: Cornell University Press.

Van Gennep, Arnold. 1908. *The Rites of Passage.* Translated by M. B. Vizedon and G. L. Caffee. Chicago: Chicago University Press.

Vonnegut, Kurt, Jr. 1972. "Preface." In *Between Time and Timbuktu or Prometheus-5.* New York: Delta Books.

———. 1974. *Wampeters, Foma and Granfalloons.* New York: Delta Books.

Washburn, S. L., ed. 1961. *Social Life of Early Man.* Chicago: Aldine Press.

Washburn, S. L., and P. C. Jay, eds. 1968. *Perspectives in Human Evolution.* New York: Holt, Rinehart and Winston.

Weaver, Rix. 1973. *The Old Wise Woman: A Study of Active Imagination.* New York: Putnam.

Weber, L. 1965. "Retrospect and Progress." *American Anthropologist* 67:623–37.

Whorf, B. L. 1964. *Language, Thought and Reality.* Cambridge: M.I.T. Press.

Wiesel, Elie. 1973. *Messengers of God: Biblical Portraits and Legends.* Translated by Marion Wiesel. New York: Vintage Books.

Wilson, M. 1951. *Good Company: A Study of Myakyusa Age-Villages.* London: Oxford University Press.

Wolfe, Tom, and E. W. Johnson. 1973. "Introduction." In *The New Journalism,* edited by Tom Wolfe. New York: Harper and Row.

Woolf, Virginia. 1973. *A Writer's Diary.* New York: Harcourt Brace Jovanovich.

Worth, Sol, and Larry Gross. 1974. "Symbolic Strategies." *Journal of Communication* 24 (4): 22–29.

Wyatt, F. 1963. "The Reconstruction of Individual and Collective Past." In *The Study of Lives,* edited by Robert W. White. New York: Atherton.

Young, Michael, ed. 1979. *The Ethnography of Malinowski.* London: Routledge and Kegan Paul.

Zborowski, Mark, and Elizabeth Herzog. 1962. *Life Is with People: The Culture of the Shtetl.* New York: Schocken Books.

Zelditch, Morris. 1955. "Role Differentiation in the Nuclear Family: A Comparative Study." In *Family, Socialization and Interpretation Process,* edited by T. Parsons and R. F. Bales. Glencoe: Free Press.

Zoshin, Joseph. 1974. "The Fraternity of Mourners." In *Jewish Reflections on Death,* edited by J. Riemer. New York: Schocken Books.

Index